Consumer Protection, Automated Shopping Platforms and EU Law

This book looks at two technological advancements in the area of e-commerce, which dramatically seem to change the way consumers shop online. In particular, they automate certain crucial tasks inherent in the 'shopping' activity, thereby relieving consumers of having to perform them. These are shopping agents (or comparison tools) and automated marketplaces. It scrutinizes their underlying processes and the way they serve the consumer, thereby highlighting risks and issues associated with their use. The ultimate aim is to ascertain whether the current EU regulatory framework relating to consumer protection, e-commerce, data protection and security adequately addresses the relevant risks and issues, thus affording a 'safe' shopping environment to the e-consumer.

Christiana N. Markou is an Assistant Professor of the School of Law, European University Cyprus and a practicing lawyer, founding partner of N.Markou & Co LLC, a Cyprus-based law firm.

Markets and the Law

Series Editor: Geraint Howells, City University of Hong Kong
Series Advisory Board:
Stefan Grundmann – Humboldt University of Berlin, Germany, and European University Institute, Italy
Hans Micklitz – Bamberg University, Germany
James P. Nehf – Indiana University, USA
Iain Ramsay – Kent Law School, UK
Charles Rickett – Auckland University of Technology, New Zealand
Reiner Schulze – Münster University, Germany
Jules Stuyck – Katholieke Universiteit Leuven, Belgium
Stephen Weatherill – University of Oxford, UK
Thomas Wilhelmsson – University of Helsinki, Finland

Markets and the Law is concerned with the way the law interacts with the market through regulation, self-regulation and the impact of private law regimes. It looks at the impact of regional and international organizations (e.g. EC and WTO) and many of the works adopt a comparative approach and/or appeal to an international audience. Examples of subjects covered include trade laws, intellectual property, sales law, insurance, consumer law, banking, financial markets, labour law, environmental law and social regulation affecting the market as well as competition law. The series includes texts covering a broad area, monographs on focused issues, and collections of essays dealing with particular themes.

Other titles in the series

Consumer Debt and Social Exclusion in Europe
Hans-W. Micklitz and Irina Domurath

Codifying Contract Law
International and Consumer Law Perspectives
Edited by Mary Keyes and Therese Wilson

The European Unfair Commercial Practices Directive
Impact, Enforcement Strategies and National Legal Systems
Edited by Willem van Boom, Amandine Garde and Orkun Akseli

The Law and Economics of Enforcing European Consumer Law
A Comparative Analysis of Package Travel and Misleading Advertising
Franziska Weber

Consumer Protection, Automated Shopping Platforms and EU Law
Christiana N. Markou

https://www.routledge.com/Markets-and-the-Law/book-series/ASHSER1252

Consumer Protection, Automated Shopping Platforms and EU Law

Christiana N. Markou

Routledge
Taylor & Francis Group
LONDON AND NEW YORK

First published 2020 by Routledge

2 Park Square, Milton Park, Abingdon, Oxon, OX14 4RN
605 Third Avenue, New York, NY 10017

Routledge is an imprint of the Taylor & Francis Group, an informa business

First issued in paperback 2020

British Library Cataloguing-in-Publication Data
A catalogue record for this book is available from the British Library

Library of Congress Cataloging-in-Publication Data
A catalog record has been requested for this book

ISBN: 978-1-4724-2427-3 (hbk)
ISBN: 978-0-367-72673-7 (pbk)

Typeset in Galliard
by Taylor & Francis Books

Contents

Preface

This book has been a long journey. Initially, the intention was to turn my PhD thesis titled "Consumer-oriented software agents in the buying process: risks, issues and the EU legal response" into a book. I earned my PhD degree from the University of Lancaster (UK) in 2011, believing that the years of very long hours of work have come to an end. I could not have been more wrong. As I had embarked on an academic career at the European University Cyprus simultaneously working as a practising lawyer, the book was added to an obviously long to-do list in 2013. It was something I really graved but at the same time, it was only natural that I could only make infant steps towards its completion. Moreover, since 2011, the EU legislator has been very active in the areas relevant to this book. The 2011 Consumer Rights Directive, which came to replace the 1997 Directive on Distance Selling and the 2016 General Data Protection Regulation (GDPR) that replaced the 1995 Data Protection Directive, are characteristic examples of how the relevant EU legal landscape has changed since I finished by PhD thesis. It soon became obvious therefore, that it would not be wise to stick to the content of the PhD thesis. Relevant literature had been adding up, too. Additionally, e-commerce (and the technology behind it) were bound to evolve even more rapidly than the law and indeed, the relevant field has recently seen major advancements (described in the first chapter of the book).

All in all, there had to be a book almost from scratch. Besides, I realised that I did not have to add anything substantial on the legal aspects of spam, which has been the focus of Chapter 2 of the PhD thesis. I also saw that cookies, online commercial profiling and behavioural advertising had gained particular attention during the recent years leading to rich literature, amongst others, by reference to the so-called 'big data' concept. In Chapter 3 of the PhD thesis, I emphasised the importance of separate opt-in consent to behavioural advertising illustrating that business practice was clearly not in accord with the relevant EU law. More recently, specifically in 2016, I studied the relevant issues again and in a book chapter titled "Behavioural Advertising and the New 'EU Cookie Law' as a Victim of Business Resistance and a Lack of Official Determination", I concluded that in general, compliance with the relevant EU law was still absent. The essence of my arguments was (and still is) the same, and I am glad that they remain pertinent in today's world of intensive commercial personal data processing. Again, however, I felt that there was not a lot to add to what I have already written on the matter or to the accumulated relevant literature.

After all, I needed space (or words) to focus on two different e-commerce advancements, which are interrelated. They both relate to *online platforms*, which have lately been the focus of the European Commission and which are particularly pertinent to today's e-commerce landscape and to the law seeking to regulate it. They are advanced online consumer shopping forums that signal a move away from traditional website contracting. They relate to a next generation of e-commerce that poses specific and/or peculiar consumer risks and issues that inevitably translate into new legal challenges. The important question thus arises regarding whether EU consumer protection law is well equipped to respond to these risks and issues, thereby affording sufficient consumer protection. This is the main question that this book seeks to answer, specifically by reference to shopping agent platforms (commonly known as price comparison tools) and automated marketplaces. The latter are shopping platforms that allow for (fully automated) contracting between traders and consumers without the personal involvement of any of the human parties in the contractual process; both of them are represented by software smart enough to be able to close contracts.

The book adopts a broader meaning for the term 'consumer protection' that includes not only traditional consumer protection issues (relating to contracting and product quality or safety, for example) but also data protection and security matters, which also affect consumers in their capacity as e-commerce actors. E-commerce is mainly fuelled by data and data protection or security gaps in e-commerce environments can lead to consumer economic detriment. I therefore believe that especially in the area of e-commerce, it is very difficult and perhaps, even, unwise to isolate consumer protection from data protection and information security, including payments security.

Accordingly, this book examines the said two online platforms against the EU legal regime in the area of consumer protection (in its above-explained expanded sense) consisting of several legislative measures listed in the first chapter of the book. These include older measures, such as the Unfair Commercial Practices Directive, and more recent ones, such as the Consumer Rights Directive, the GDPR, the Second Payment Services Directive and the Network Information Security Directive. The ultimate aim has been to draw conclusions regarding whether the existing EU legal regime adequately addresses the risks and issues associated with the relevant platforms and, in effect, what changes, if any, are needed to bring the law in line with the rapid developments that transformed consumer shopping. One very general but interesting conclusion arisen is that though the EU has not legislated by specific reference to the particular platforms or to the activity of fully automated contracting, multiple EU legislative measures applicable to the electronic environment (some without targeting it specifically) actually contain the solution (or at least, the raw material of the solution) to several of the arising issues. This alleviates the need for a wholly new legal regime and highlights the importance of legislation drafted so as to retain the flexibility necessary to enable it to respond to the continuously arising challenges of e-commerce technology.

I faced several difficulties during this endeavour. As said, the EU legislator has been particularly active in the fields relevant to this book. Thus, for example, the parts of the book discussing the Proposal for the GDPR and then, the Draft GDPR eventually had to be adjusted to the content of the (final) GDPR passed in 2016. There have also been important Proposals for new Directives, mainly in the area of consumer protection, such as the 'New Deal for the Consumers', which had to be left out of the book due to time and space limitations. The same holds true of other recent initiatives of the European Commission, such as the ones relating to online platforms, which are just briefly mentioned. The main research exercise for the book has been completed a couple of years ago, perhaps even more, and therefore, legal measures that are currently underway or not yet in force (such as the 2019 Directive on certain aspects concerning contracts for the sale of goods) are not analysed. Whether these measures affect the conclusions of this book regarding the adequacy of EU law and how or to what extent constitute very interesting questions to be addressed in future work. Moreover, many of the legal measures examined are very recent, and, accordingly, relevant literature and experience on their interpretation and application has been (and perhaps, still is) limited. This coupled with the fact that one of the two platforms, namely automated marketplaces, is not yet commercialised meant that a significant part of the book had to comprise an original application of new and technical, legal measures to an innovative and complex technological environment. I have dared this exercise knowing that there will probably be some oversights or gaps to be filled in by subsequent literature hopefully to be provoked by this book.

Shopping agents have not been without difficulties either. The book partly builds upon the results of relevant research conducted in the context of the PhD thesis. Yet, for the purposes of the book, I have undertaken fresh research exercises and/or experimental uses of the relevant consumer tools seeking to illustrate and confirm the risks and issues associated with their use. However, online content continuously changes, disappears or becomes outdated, leaving any observations or arguments built upon it without proper foundation. That necessitated frequent changes to the related content of the book and the risk existed that some could be missed.

It was difficult to let a book I have been nurturing for so long, go but I am extremely happy that I finally managed to do so. I am deeply indebted to Professor Geraint Howells for encouraging me to publish a book based on my PhD thesis and for accepting this book in his book series, thereby giving me the opportunity to widely address the legal community and express my views on a fascinating area of a very vivid personal interest. Special thanks must also go to Routledge, which accepted to add this book to its collection of quality academic works published under its respectable name. I am also deeply grateful to my editor, Alison Kirk, who has been by my side during these years, generously offering her support and invaluable advice. This book would not have been made a reality if she hadn't been so patient, understanding and ready to offer her much-needed insights on various related matters. Lastly, I wish to thank my husband and my two kids who have simply got used to me on the computer all the time, including during family holidays. I remember my 9-year-old daughter asking me once why I am not having fun! It was one evening in the summer of 2018 while they were all in the pool playing and I was working on the book on a sunbed nearby. "I do have fun", I replied smilingly.

I was telling the truth and nothing but the truth! I greatly enjoyed working towards making this book a reality. And I bet that the joy I feel now while holding it in my hands is the same with the joy experienced by my daughter while in the pool that warm summer evening.

1 Introduction

1.1 Setting the scene

Shopping will *not* remain a task to be performed solely by humans. "A computerized brain known as the autopilot can fly a 787 jet unaided" (Kelly, 2012), so computers must certainly be able to go shopping. The autopilot was invented in the 1910s, i.e., long before the birth of artificial intelligence (AI) in 1950 and has been followed by a century of dramatic technological advances, including the last and long lasting one, namely the digital revolution in the 1980s. More recently, the emphasis has been on automation enabled or greatly assisted by AI: "As AI capabilities improve, we can either treat it as a crutch that relieves us from thinking – examples include Waze and Google Maps – or as an asset that helps us use our brains more effectively and creatively" (Ritter, 2017).

Being the most noticeable 'product' of the digital revolution, e-commerce could not but follow the rapid revolution-driven steps forward. Unsurprisingly, therefore, online merchants have been investing in AI technologies designed to improve consumer experience and increase sales. Interestingly, the intended 'consumer experience' improvement mainly translates into making shopping less burdensome for consumers, which in turn boils down to easing or even delegating certain tasks inherent in shopping *to software*. Examples in the media are numerous and confirm that the consumer no longer shops unaided. More specifically, having referred to "advancements in AI like deep learning, in which software programs learn to perform sometimes complex tasks without active oversight from humans". Kelleher (2017), writes the following:

> Gilt deploys it to search for similar items of clothing with different features like a longer sleeve or a different cut. Etsy bought Blackbird Technologies last fall to apply the firm's image-recognition and natural-language processing to its search function . . . Adobe's marketing tools are also incorporating deep learning into offerings for retailers, using AI to predict customer behavior. Shoppers can choose to receive suggestions based on their shopping lists – a belt that matches a pair of pants, painting supplies to help with a can of paint, a wine paired to a dinner recipe.

More generally, the prevalent trends seem to be (a) natural language processing that enables precision in search results,[1] (b) personalized product recommendations that rely both on past browsing or purchasing activity and on the analysis of an abundance of relevant data

1 "You can search for phones or other electronics goods just like you would ask your friend for a recommendation and not like a robot that has been fed a list of terms to search by" (Choudhuri, 2017).

from across thousands of sources[2] and (c) smart shopping assistants using visual filters[3] or image recognition[4] to understand consumer preferences and return accurate product results and information as to availability in real time.

The latter seems to compose part of the so-called 'omnichannel approach',[5] which rejects the distinction between 'offline' and 'online' consumers. Based on the fact that consumers increasingly shop through *both* offline and online channels, this approach mainly advocates the use of technology effectively connecting the website of a retailer to its brick-and-mortar store, ensuring consistency and best consumer experience (Piotrowicz and Cuthbertson, 2014). Giant online retailers such as Amazon turn to the offline world opening up traditional stores (Fortune, 2017), and eBay seeks to integrate itself with offline, stores even directing to them consumers who cannot wait for delivery (Kopytoff, 2010; Rao, 2011). It seems that the omnichannel approach is bound to increase sales on or through the internet effectively encouraging resort to intelligent tools assisting consumers to navigate the vast online and offline marketplace.

Such tools include notification systems incorporating price-prediction algorithms that can notify consumers about upcoming price reductions effectively, advising them on the best time for a purchase (Master of Code Global, 2017) and e-commerce platforms that place unprecedented emphasis on assisting consumers effectively searching for and choosing the *right* product. A clothing and footwear platform, for example, prides itself for using massive amounts of connected data and machine learning to enable precise fit and size recommendations (True Fit Corporation, 2018). This seems to mark an important shift from '*product*' searches to '*suitable product*' searches enabled by the provision of very detailed purchase-related information.

Comparison tools returning to consumers a list of competing offerings relating to a specified product enabling them to locate the best prospective deal, have been around for quite some time, yet they remain a trend. Not only they have become mobile and thus, in the form of apps that are accessible anywhere and everywhere but also their use has been boosted due to the omnichannel approach mirroring consumers engaging in comparisons on their mobile devices while in store (*Research and Markets: 2015*, cited in Business Wire, 2016). Moreover, they are increasingly equipped with machine learning and natural

2 "What sets Watson Trend apart from other product recommendation resources is the variety and magnitude of the data it sources. The app pulls in product information from more than 10,000 sources, from major ecommerce sights, blogs, product reviews and social media" (Clark, 2016).

3 "Instead of typing into a search bar or checking filter boxes, the tech learns what the customer likes by analysing the products they click on. Selecting a pair of heeled boots, for instance, brings up more heeled boots. Judging by the images that attract the customer, the retailer can then determine that she might be interested in black rather than brown shoes, or shoes with laces rather than ones without, endlessly bringing up more styles that match their preferences" (Sentient, 2015)

4 "For instance, a budget-savvy customer at a brick-and-mortar store sees a pair of pants she likes but wishes to compare prices online. However, she doesn't know what those specific pants are called or where to start. Instead of wasting time manually searching for them, she can simply take a photo using her phone and upload it to a retailer's online store or mobile app. AI technology automatically searches for the item and quickly pulls it up on the customer's phone" (Angeles, 2017).

5 On the history and development of the omnichannel approach, see Frazer, M. and Stiehler, B.E., 2014, January. Omnichannel retailing: The merging of the online and off-line environment. In *Global Conference on Business & Finance Proceedings* (Vol. 9, No. 1, p. 655). Institute for Business & Finance Research and Lazaris, C. and Vrechopoulos, A., 2014, June. From multi-channel to "omnichannel" retailing: review of the literature and calls for research. In *the 2nd International Conference on Contemporary Marketing Issues* (ICCMI).

language processing capabilities, thus becoming smarter and more accurate in their output (Choudhuri, 2017). They are also able to assist consumers in finding a specific product (such as a good mobile phone with long battery life) rather than merely comparing prices. This involves the relevant tool using AI to sift through and make sense of "over 50,000 phone specifications, 5,000 phone variants, and over one million user reviews" (Raj, 2015).

One observes that most of the emphasis of the recent consumer-oriented technological developments in e-commerce has been placed on discovery, i.e., the easy and effective search for a desired product and the merchant whom to buy from. This is logical: "As the web itself does not provide for search functionality, search engines have become an essential gateway to everything that is available on the web. Without them, the web is like a library without a cataloguing system and librarians" (Kulk, 2011, p. 7). The same is true of the retailing area of the web inhibited by the abundance of e-shops. It is even true of certain e-shops themselves, as some sell an almost unnavigable wealth of products. Thus, most e-shops prominently display a search tool on their pages. Without a search aid, it is virtually impossible for consumers to find everything related to a need or interest online. It is thus only natural that technology (i.e., natural language processing, image recognition, rich-data-driven product recommendations and comparison tools) has mainly been geared towards easing the consumer search-and-discovery experience.

One also observes that despite their AI capabilities, *all* of the aforementioned e-commerce advancements still necessitate consumer involvement; the consumer remains tied to a screen having to *point and click* or *touch* throughout the process in order to find and eventually buy a product. Interestingly, such *beginning-to-end* consumer involvement (or active participation) seems to be a constant variable through the evolutionary journey of user–machine interaction; what changes is the nature of said involvement and, inherently, the effort required on the part of the human consumer. De Kare-Silver (2011, p. 18) describes the said evolutionary journey nicely:

> So we are moving away from Point and Click. We are firmly into an era of "Touch and Go!". It is only a matter of time before further voice integration takes us into "Touch and Talk". But is that the end of the journey?

He answers this question in the negative, describing upcoming technologies, amongst others, allowing machine control through effortless hand gestures (De Kare-Silver, 2011, pp. 18–19, 21). Those, however, *still* require a consumer's active involvement.

Indeed, the current e-commerce technological trends *lack* automation in the actual contract conclusion. Such automation involves the machine not only looking up and finding a product, its price and the retailer but also actually buying it, thereby concluding a contract in the name of the consumer. This is the missing piece of a puzzle picturing a buying process in which the consumer is (fully) substituted by *software*. Importantly, as illustrated later in this chapter,[6] there is strong evidence to suggest that marketplaces in which selling and buying software will conclude real automated contracts binding upon their human users will soon be the next big thing, which the media will be talking about. Relevant prototypes have existed in labs for more than two decades,[7] and it often takes much longer for a technology to be commercialized, and even longer to become widely available.[8]

6 See infra at p. 12
7 Ibid.
8 De Kare-Silver (2011, p. 17) refers to the first voice recognition technological component being developed in the 1964. The relevant technology became widely available in 2003 when Microsoft developed its own such technology and incorporated it in Office 2003.

Software designed to negotiate and contract on behalf of human users has been mentioned in seminal technical literature of the late 1990s. MIT researchers identified, amongst others, five main stages of the consumer buying process: need identification, product finding, merchant finding, negotiation and purchase (Guttman, Moukas and Maes, 1998, pp. 148–149) and pinpointed to technology, specifically *software agents*, which could assist or represent consumers during all those stages. Notification agents notify consumers when a specified product becomes available, while recommendation agents recommend products that a given consumer may be interested in. Shopping agents (or comparison tools) play a vital role during the product- and merchant-finding stages and finally, negotiation agents undertake the final stages of negotiation and purchase.

As a result, during the late 1990s and 2000s, there was a growing body of literature on the technical and legal aspects of software (or intelligent) agents.[9] Such literature has become scarce in the 2010s, yet one readily notices that the so-called notification, recommendation and shopping agents simply aimed at doing what has earlier been described to be the core of *current* e-commerce trends, namely, intelligently notifying consumers, offering product recommendations and comparing product offerings. It would seem, therefore, that *albeit by a different name*, [10] the technology described in the 1990s is now being commercialized and widely discussed. Obviously, this reinforces the view that more advanced technology capable of taking over the whole of the buying process, thereby completing a purchase (i.e., what was called a 'negotiation agent' in the 1990s), will probably be ready for a commercial roll-out in the (near) future.

It also follows that the current scarcity of literature on *software agents* does not mean that they have ceased posing legal challenges, amongst others, relating to the protection of consumer economic interests and privacy that merit (further) examination. Actually, these challenges have never stopped being discussed in relevant (legal) literature and major studies, the difference being that the relevant discussion has largely been unfolding by reference to their underlying processes rather than to a technological product label, such as 'recommendation agents'.

Thus, relying on the collection and use of detailed data,[11] notification and personalized product recommendation tools pose issues of data protection and privacy heavily discussed in literature on the so-called "big data"[12] and its legal ramifications. Yet, long before the birth of the 'big data' concept,[13] the consumer was known to be tracked and monitored on the web though the collection and analysis of data on her browsing behaviour. On the basis of these detailed consumer profiles, the consumer was served personalized advertising (often in the form of 'product recommendations'). Big data is very much about profiling-enabled

9 See for example infra p. 12–14, 176, n.10, n.33, n.34

10 It is not entirely clear why terms such as 'agent technology' or 'software agents' have ceased being widespread in the literature, yet "agent technology is not a new, single technology but consists of an integrated (and rapidly evolving) use of multiple technologies" (Bain and Subirana, 2003c, p. 203). Given also that agents were described by reference to the AI field and as possessing attributes such as autonomy and an ability of learning (Bradshaw, 1997, p. 8), it seems that agent technology is in fact the same with what lies behind the previously discussed current e-commerce trends, which are said to incorporate AI, machine learning and other related techniques.

11 See supra at p. 2

12 There is no agreed definition of 'big data', yet it seems widely acknowledged that it refers to massive data sets which cannot be processed leading to meaningful knowledge unless (advanced) AI techniques are applied to them; see among others, Press (2014).

13 It is believed that the said concept "became widespread as recently as in 2011" (Gandomi and Haider, 2015, p. 138). On the very short history of the concept, see also Kitchin (2014, p. 67).

personalization, as one readily understands from recent works on big data and advertising.[14] These issues and the arising legal ramifications in the areas of consumer protection and data protection have been discussed by the present author elsewhere, specifically in reference to notification and recommendation agents.[15] It is true that since then, the EU legal regime on data protection and e-privacy have undergone amendments mainly through the replacement of the 1995 Data Protection Directive with the 2016 General Data Protection Regulation. Yet, apart from the fact that the core of the EU legal principles and rights pertaining to data protection seems to be timeless and has remained unchanged, these issues are heavily discussed in the recent and quite rich (legal) literature, which has been accumulating in response to the 'big data' buzzword.[16] This book therefore leaves them out of its scope.

1.2 Shopping agents and automated marketplaces worthy of legal examination

This book is about the legal aspects relating primarily to consumer protection and privacy – or data protection – of shopping agents (i.e., comparison tools) and automated marketplaces in which contracts between merchants and consumers are concluded through software without the parties being actively involved in the (buying) process. Not only is legal literature on these technological advancements limited[17] but also the two trends seem to be closely connected in a way that mirrors a fascinating evolution in how consumers shop.

Shopping agents must be considered as one of the most important e-commerce trends discussed previously (though not necessarily from a technological point of view). These are not tools implemented on individual online stores. In most cases,they are intermediary platforms opening up a window to hundreds or even thousands of different merchants (including those selling their products on marketplaces such as Amazon or eBay), enabling consumers to reap the benefits of the intense competition online. Actually, shopping agents comprise the 'Google' of the commercial web, which would simply be unnavigable and largely unusable (to the detriment of consumers and merchants alike) without them. Thus, they are the *gateway* to many individual stores (and any intelligent tool or assistant stores choose to implement on their website). These tools can even prevent consumers from shopping from a particular store, specifically by listing (and thus, exposing) it as being the one offering the highest price.

14 See, for example, Couldry and Turow (2014, p. 1714): Advertising, big data and the clearance of the public realm: Marketers' new approaches to the content subsidy. *International Journal of Communication, 8*, pp. 1710–1726.

15 Markou (2011, Chapters 2 and 3).

16 See amongst many others, Cavoukian, A. and Jonas, J., 2012. Privacy by design in the age of big data (pp. 1–17). Information and Privacy Commissioner of Ontario, Canada; Tene, O. and Polonetsky, J., 2011. Privacy in the age of big data: a time for big decisions. *Stan. L. Rev.* Online, *64*, p. 63; Crawford, K. and Schultz, J., 2014. Big data and due process: Toward a framework to redress predictive privacy harms. *BCL Rev., 55*, p. 93; Tene, O. and Polonetsky, J., 2012. Big data for all: Privacy and user control in the age of analytics. *Nw. J. Tech. & Intell. Prop., 11*, p. xxvii; Kuner, C., Cate, F.H., Millard, C. and Svantesson, D.J.B., 2012. The challenge of 'big data' for data protection; Cumbley, R. and Church, P., 2013. Is "big data" creepy? *Computer Law & Security Review, 29*(5), pp. 601–609; Rubinstein, I., 2013. Big data: the end of privacy or a new beginning?; Cate, F.H. and Mayer-Schönberger, V., 2013. Notice and consent in a world of Big Data. *International Data Privacy Law, 3*(2), pp. 67–73.

17 As it will be shown, the first has only very recently been the subject of certain major legal studies. The second has not become a commercialized reality as yet, and mostly features in technical literature.

Shopping agents (and automated marketplaces, too) are 'online platforms',[18] and as such, they have recently attracted the attention of the European Commission which have recognized their benefits[19] and called for a "balanced regulatory framework" for them (European Commission, 2016a, p. 4). It is this regulatory framework (i.e., its existence and adequacy) that this book explores, and the need to do so is not purely theoretical, as existing evidence suggests that shopping agents are increasingly quite heavily being used by consumers.[20] Thus, the consumer actually utilizes the said platforms, enjoying the benefits but facing risks, too. This book aims to illustrate these risks, as it is by reference to them that the adequacy of the relevant regulatory framework can be assessed.

Shopping agents assist the consumer during the discovery phase of the buying process, easing her task of finding a product and a merchant from whom to buy. Admittedly, the human consumer remains actively involved on such platforms; he has to instruct the agent about what to search for and most importantly, he has to review the results returned by the agent. Then he has to follow a link to the individual store of his choice and actively go through all the steps necessary to submit an order. Indeed, shopping agents stop short of being real online marketplaces. However, as soon as they get to accept orders and payments,[21] rather than merely directing consumers to individual online stores, they will become the closest predecessor of automated marketplaces.

In automated marketplaces, it is software that reviews the various competing offerings, chooses the best and concludes a purchase. As is later illustrated this is far from a technological impossibility; marketplaces with software that autonomously buys and sells have been in the labs for quite some time[22] and some automation in the act of purchasing that reduces the human consumer role already exists in a commercial context, specifically on the eBay marketplace.[23] In fact, marketplaces such as Amazon and eBay also constitute close predecessors of automated marketplaces; those marketplaces already accept orders and payments but do not compare the various available offerings by allowing their sorting out by reference to price or other factors. These remarkable commercialized examples of marketplace platforms can also offer useful insights regarding the risks to be faced by the consumer on the (fully) automated marketplaces of the near future and the resulting related legal issues. Interestingly, these legal issues have alerted the European Parliament (2015, para. B), which has recently issued a resolution on the legal challenges presented by "more sophisticated robots, bots, androids and other manifestations of artificial intelligence ("AI") ", referring, amongst others, to "machines designed to choose their counterparts, negotiate contractual terms, conclude contracts and decide whether and how to implement them", doubting the suitability of relevant liability rules (European Parliament, 2015, para. AG).

18 Online platforms "cover a wide-ranging set of activities including online advertising platforms, marketplaces, search engines, social media and creative content outlets, application distribution platforms, communications services, payment systems, and platforms for the collaborative economy" (European Commission, 2016a, p. 2).

19 Online platforms facilitate efficiency gains, and act as a magnet for data-driven innovation. They increase consumer choice, thereby contributing to improved competitiveness of industry and enhancing consumer welfare (European Commission, 2016a, p. 3).

20 Infra at p. 11

21 This has featured as a significant disadvantage of similar tools in user reviews with their developers expressing their intention to work on accepting direct payments, thereby becoming a marketplace, see Potoska (2018).

22 Infra pp. 12–13

23 Infra at p. 12

1.3 Methodology

As already mentioned, this book explores the current EU regulatory framework pertaining to consumer protection and data protection (and privacy) in an attempt to see how (adequately) it responds to consumer risks and pitfalls associated with two online platforms, namely shopping agents and automated marketplaces. This exercise will inevitably offer relevant insights regarding online platforms in general.

As a first step, shopping agents and automated marketplaces are explained in some detail, the aim being to enable a deep understanding of how they are made available to consumers and how these platforms interact with them. This thorough explanation of the relevant platforms paves the way to the analysis of the risks and issues associated with such platforms. This explanation also provides evidence of the particular platforms *actually* being utilized by consumers (in the case of shopping agents) or being shopping environments to be utilized by them in the near future (in the case of automated marketplaces). This evidence illustrates the *non*-theoretical need for legal intervention and hence, the need for a careful examination of the relevant EU legal framework and its adequacy.

As a next step, this book attempts an introduction to and a categorization of the arising risks combined with a translation of them into *legal* issues, i.e., issues to which the answer has to be searched for in the law applicable to the online context. This risk categorization exercise discloses both the nature of the risks and the specific EU legislation to be examined in the context of the attempt to determine whether it entails a sufficient response to them. This is the main question addressed by this book.

This risk categorization will also serve as the yardstick by reference to which the analysis intended by this book will unfold. Thus, each 'risk' category will comprise the subject-matter of a chapter, which will first *illustrate each relevant risk category* and proceed with *assessing the legal response* to each category as entailed in relevant EU secondary legislation in the areas of consumer protection and privacy (or data protection). This latter part of each chapter inevitably also entails an interpretation and/or application of the relevant EU legislative measures to the particular context, which can be taken up by enforcers or offer policy makers useful insights regarding existing gaps or deficiencies, especially given that several of the legal measures analysed are very recent ones with a relatively short history of practical application and results.

When the risk is common to both platforms under scrutiny, the relevant risks will be illustrated first by reference to shopping agents and then to automated marketplaces. The same holds true of the relevant legal assessment, except where this can be performed for both platforms together without a relevant division being merited.

The 'risk illustration' exercise in the context of shopping agents is greatly assisted by the numerous commercialized examples of such agents, which the present author has carefully observed. In the case of automated marketplaces, it will mainly be guided by reference to their closest commercialized predecessors, namely shopping agents and Amazon-like marketplaces, as well as by the quite rich and relevant *technical* literature. This literature is very often revealing of important characteristics of such marketplaces, as well as of risks inherent in them, which designers often strive to address technologically. The particular analysis has been assisted by earlier work of the present author (Markou, 2011), which, following a similar methodology, has looked into shopping agents and automated marketplaces as part of a PhD thesis, covering other technological tools too.

The conclusions of each chapter, particularly regarding how well EU law performs in responding to each of the identified risk categories, are put together and discussed in the last chapter of the book, which should prove useful to a wide array of actors, including the EU legislator, judges, providers of relevant platforms, merchants selling through them (and their advisors) and of course, to others researchers in the field.

1.4 Explaining shopping agents and automated marketplaces

1.4.1 Explaining shopping agents

Shopping agents go by a number of different names: "shopping bots" (Kerr, 2004, p. 290, n. 16), "shopbots" (Fasli, 2009), "comparison aggregators" (Madnick and Siegel, 2002, pp. 39, 40), "comparison websites" (Laffey, 2008, sec. 1) and "comparison tools" (ECME Consortium, 2013) are common examples.

Consumers search for a product, and when they find one they are interested in buying, they can ask the agent to perform a comparison of relevant competing offerings by clicking a relevant link. Within seconds, the agent returns a list (table) of different merchants offering the product for sale, together with the price and other relevant information, such as the availability of free delivery. Next to each merchant offering, the agent displays a hyperlink to the page within the merchant website from which consumers can order the product. This is a practice known as 'deep-linking', and refers to the provision of a link *directly* to one of the inner pages of a website or an online store (as opposed to its homepage).[24] It obviously serves the consumer in that it alleviates the task of visiting the homepage and having to navigate to the specific page he is interested in.

Obviously, shopping agents enable consumers to take advantage of the intense competition occurring online and assist them in spotting a bargain.[25] As Pereira (2001, pp. 38–39, 44) explains, because consumers can apply their effort and time to evaluating alternatives rather than searching for them, shopping agents increase the chances of achieving a satisfactory purchase. Indeed, a Commission-funded study has found that the overall average savings resulting from the use of shopping agents can be 7.8 per cent of the online retail price (Civic Consulting, 2011, p. 171). Similarly, the Great Britain OFT (2007, p. 7) has referred to potential savings of 150–240 million per year arising out of an effective use of shopping agents. To the extent that they also allow comparison between competitors by reference to business practices and standard contract terms, they can prove an invaluable consumer guardian:

> The Internet also has taken comparison shopping to a level that is unimaginable in the real world. The ease with which consumers can compare business practices, including the content of standard forms, suggests that consumers do not need judicial intervention to protect themselves from business abuse.
>
> (Hillman and Rachlinski, 2002, p. 478)

The GB OFT has even referred to the use of shopping agents (or price comparison websites) as a way in which consumers can avoid inappropriate business practices such as drip pricing and bait pricing (GB OFT, 2010, Annex E, pp. 21, 87). Of course, this presupposes that

24 For more on the practice, see Chansey (1999, p. 230). Chancey, M.E., 1999. Meta-Tags and Hypertext Deep Linking: How the Essential Components of Web-Authoring and Internet Guidance are Strengthening Intellectual Property Rights on the World Wide Web. *Stetson L. Rev., 29*, p. 203.

25 Fasli (2006, pp. 69–70) writes more on their benefits.

shopping agents, being online businesses themselves, respect consumer rights and interests and refrain from employing similarly inappropriate practices. Whether this is the case or not is something examined later in this book.

Shopping agents can be classified by reference to the way in which they enable or perform comparison (Wan, Menon and Ramaprasad, 2003. For the purposes of this book, it suffices to state that there are those which search or scan merchant websites similarly to how search engines scan the whole of the web[26] and those allowing interested merchants to submit their product offerings to the agent database by providing a relevant technical facility.[27] As is later shown, this distinction has ramifications on issues relating to their impartiality as well as on their legal classification as passive intermediaries under the E-commerce Directive (ECD).

The number of the merchant websites searched by them varies; it can be a few dozen, hundreds or even thousands[28] – what is important is that the consumer should always be clearly informed of the extent of the shopping agent's search capabilities. The agent's revenue is often derived from the fees that participating merchants pay for its offerings to be accessible through the agent. This fee is often in the form of a commission for every click or lead to the merchant website.[29] A fee may additionally or alternatively go towards securing merchants a preferred listing,[30] appearing at a top position in search results or accompanied by the logo of the merchant.[31] Most shopping agent companies appear also to derive revenue from advertisements displayed on their website, and there may be cases (mostly for agents of the 'search engine' type) where such advertising is the sole revenue source, merchants being listed for free.

Shopping agents have not warmly been welcomed by merchants; intense competition and a reduction in buyer search costs notoriously result in lower prices and, thus, a reduction in profits, at least for some merchants.[32] Merchants had also seen a reduction in their advertising revenue; deep links de facto bypass the advertising on the homepage (Wan and Liu, 2008, p. 113). Shopping agent platforms have also been accused of permitting only an insufficient emphasis on the brand identity of the linked merchant, resulting in consumer confusion as to the actual source of the information provided or the product sold (Bagby, 2004, p. 11). Some (CIRSFID, NRCCL and FIDAL, 2006, p. 58) claim that deep linking

26 One such agent is AddAll.com (2018). For more on this task, see Madnick and Siegel (2002, pp. 35–36).

27 One such agent is Shopzilla (Connexity Inc., 2017a). According to certain consumer scientists, these are not in fact software agents (Fasli, 2006, p. 74). For the purposes of this book, however, the exact technology behind a consumer service is of less importance than the service itself and the interface between the provider and the consumer. The service and interface are the same in both cases.

28 AddAll claims to search more than 40 online bookstores (AddAll.com, 2018), whereas Kelkoo (2017d) claims to search "thousands of retailers".

29 For examples, see Connexity Inc. (2017c) and Kelkoo (2017c).

30 See, for example, Kelkoo (2017c).

31 Pricerunner International AB (2017a) lists all merchants without a fee but charges for logo and a link to merchant website. Experimental searches showed that all listings are accompanied by a link to the merchant website, and almost all bear a logo (Pricerunner International AB, 2017b).

32 As Bakos (1997) notes, "Information systems can serve as intermediaries between the buyers and the sellers in a market creating an 'electronic marketplace' that lowers the buyers' cost to acquire information about seller prices and product offerings. As a result, electronic marketplaces reduce the inefficiencies caused by buyer search costs, in the process reducing the ability of sellers to extract monopolistic profits while increasing the ability of markets to optimally allocate productive resources".

also results in consumers bypassing the 'website' terms and conditions. Yet, a link to the terms and conditions is commonly displayed on *every* webpage within a website, and the same is true of advertising. Furthermore, shopping agents do not generally intend (or attempt) to pass themselves as selling merchants. Given the entirely different web environment entered into by consumers, when they choose to follow a link to a merchant website, consumer can easily become confused. This is especially the case when deep links are marked by icons or have text stating 'visit store' or 'visit X merchant' or when a notice informing consumers of their transfer to the website of a given merchant is displayed as soon as the deep link is clicked. Such practices are commonly used by shopping agents (eBay Inc., 2017a; Kelkoo, 2017a). It is thus unsurprising that US and EU courts have rejected relevant 'unfair competition' claims against providers of shopping agents (*Ticketmaster Corp. v Tickets.com Inc., 2000, U.S. Dist. Lexis 12987, C.D. Cal., Aug. 10, 2000*); De Rocquigny, 2001) finding no possibility of consumer confusion.

Nevertheless, it would seem that merchants' negative reactions have resulted in the interests of businesses initially receiving more prominence than consumer-related issues. This is also reflected in the (limited) legal literature on shopping agents, which has largely been confined to issues relating to intellectual property (and other rights) of the agent-searched merchants.[33] Prior to the 2010s, *non-technical* academic research on shopping agents has explicitly been recognized to be limited (Laffey, 2008, sec. 1.1), and literature on *legal* 'consumer protection' issues has been even more so.[34]

In the UK, *financial-product* shopping agents have admittedly alerted both authorities (Great Britain [GB], Financial Services Authority, 2008), non-profit organizations (Resolution Foundation, 2007) and commentators (Laffey and Gandy, 2009). Many of the issues discussed, however, are specific to the narrow (and peculiar) domain of financial services (Laffey and Gandy, 2009, pp. 179–180) in which shopping agents may be considered as advisors or insurance brokers (Wood, 2007, p. 14; GB, Financial Services Authority, 2008, *Conclusion A*). Understandably, the legal basis and nature of the regulation of such shopping agents may be different from of that of shopping agents targeting standard consumer products.

Yet, such shopping agents, too, which are naturally greater in number than those focusing on specific product types, entail consumer risks and raise related legal issues meriting attention. Though their business relies heavily on consumers in the sense that the more widely their service is used by them, the more attractive it becomes as a "lead generator" (Madnick and Siegel, 2002, p. 40) for *paying* merchants, serving consumer needs may not be their top priority. The interests of the merchants from whom they derive direct economic benefit is most probably their *primary* concern. Regarding consumers, their endeavours are likely to be directed more towards securing service efficiency[35] than respecting consumer legally

33 Such literature is Cruquenaire (2001), Groom (2004), Boonk et al. (2005), Boonk and Lodder (2006) and Allgrove and Ganley (2007).

34 Some literature existed on how they can adversely affect consumer decision-making in *legally irrelevant* ways, such as by displaying an excessive number of 'product-offering' choices (Pereira, 2001, p. 44; Wan, Menon and Ramaprasad, 2009). Literature pertaining on consumer behaviour while using shopping agents also existed (Murray and Häubl, 2001; Smith and Brynjolfsson, 2001; Su, 2007), and, as it is shown later, it can serve to confirm the need for legal intervention.

35 This may consist of fast-loading pages, valid hyperlinks, short 'search' time and user-friendly layout. Non-legal literature recognizes this conflict of interest in relation to agents and, indeed, confines itself to such 'service efficacy' issues when discussing how agents can serve consumer interests (Smith, 2002, pp. 446–447, 451–452).

protected interests. This renders shopping agents suspicious from a 'consumer protection' angle and definitely worthy of an examination to determine whether a fair balance is struck between merchant and consumer interests.

This is true especially given that shopping agents are most probably here to stay. An EU-wide survey has recently identified 1,042 shopping agents, noting that "comparison tools are well established in the market, having grown considerably in number since the 1990s, and are frequently used by consumers" (ECME Consortium, 2013, p. xiv). The same study (ECME Consortium, 2013, p. xv) confirms that shopping agents have gained consumer acceptance and are widely being put in use, as "74% of consumers had used comparison tools – at least once – in the past 12 months" with a significant 22% using them bi-weekly. These statistics are consistent with earlier findings according to which 81% of the consumers surveyed have used a shopping agent in 2010 and a strong majority of 48% have used it at least once a month (Civic Consulting, 2011, p. 11).The latter study also indicates that the use of shopping agents is amongst the top-three strategies employed by consumers in preparation for an online purchase (Civic Consulting, 2011, p. 49). Any involved risks, therefore, are by no means theoretical and can actually result in consumer detriment, which can be prevented, or at least reduced, through legal intervention.

It should thus be welcomed that in the 2010s there has been shift of focus towards the consumer user of shopping agents and the protection of her interests. This shift is primarily evinced in major studies leading to detailed reports published during 2010–2014 by the OFT in the UK and also on behalf of the European Commission. The European Commission (2013, p. 6) has noted that "the rapid proliferation of CTs [Comparison Tools] and the influence they can have on consumers' decisions have also given rise to concerns about their trustworthiness. If the transparency and reliability of CTs is not guaranteed, they can become a source of consumer detriment and risk undermining consumers' trust in the market as a whole". These recent studies confirm the existence of consumer risks associated with the use of shopping agents and effectively, the need to inquire into whether these receive an adequate legal response at EU level.

1.4.2 Explaining automated marketplaces

Contracting software in automated marketplaces closes contracts on behalf of consumers effectively handling the whole of the buying process in substitution to them; these contracts are referred to in this book as automated contracts. For this reason, such software is also called a "trading agent" (Youll, 2001, p. 146; Vytelingum et al., 2005). Fasli (2007, p. 210) defines trading agents as follows: "A trading agent is an agent that lives, acts, and interacts in an electronic market. It represents a user, knows her preferences, respects the set budget, and acts in the market by negotiating and performing transactions on behalf of the user".

These agents are designed to perform on platforms that serve as marketplaces, which have been the subject of intensive research probably because their potential benefits are considerable. More specifically, they can (a) achieve a reduction in transaction costs; (b) save time, allowing it to be allocated to tasks more important than shopping and (c) even improve transaction quality or efficacy, thus benefiting economy and increasing consumer satisfaction. Indeed, experiments have shown that such contracting software has been able to strike better deals or maximize their profit or utility more successfully than humans (Graham-Rowe, 2001; Kephart, 2002, pp. 7208–7210; Vytelingum et al., 2005, p. 6).

While such marketplaces have not yet been commercialized, there are numerous examples in research labs, some of which have also been tested in practice.[36] Though the most characteristic examples are somewhat dated, relevant research is ongoing, leading to newer relevant methods and systems (Huang et al., 2010; Zarei, Malayeri and Mastorakis, 2012; Rosaci and Sarnè, 2014; Sukthankar and Rodriguez-Aguilar, 2017). Moreover, software bidding on auctions, thus taking over negotiation and contract conclusion,[37] has been in use for years. These "snipping [*sic*] agents" (Ockenfels and Roth, 2002, p. 80) are often offered by providers other than the auction website and are designed to monitor online auctions and submit bids according to user-specified criteria (mainly auction number and maximum bid). Commercial examples of such services are numerous (Minalto, 2017). eBay Inc. (2018a) also offers an automatic bidding system, which "makes bidding convenient so you don't have to keep coming back to re-bid every time someone places another bid". All in all, automated marketplaces are probably soon to be the next 'big' technological trend in e-commerce to be hitting the headlines.[38]

The earliest notable example of an automated marketplace is Kasbah (Chavez and Maes, 1996). Selling or buying software is instructed to conclude a contract in the name of human users, who control its activity by specifying the time frame within which a sale or purchase should be achieved, the desired price, the lowest or highest acceptable price and the desired strategy and by asking to have a transaction approved[39] (Chavez and Maes, 1996, pp. 2–5). Importantly, Kasbah software agents have been caught doing "dumb things that a human would never do, such as accept an offer when a better one was available" (Chavez and Maes, 1996, p. 11). This is probably because they would accept the *first* offer meeting the user-specified criteria. Could this mean that such a marketplace could be considered a defective service? Issues arise also in relation to the fact that Kasbah does *not* perform a regulative role to ensure safety and reliability (Chavez and Maes, 1996, pp. 6–7). However, it employs a 'trust and reputation' mechanism, allowing users to rate the behaviour of other marketplace participants (Zacharia, Moukas and Maes, 1999, p. 3); contracting software can use these ratings to avoid contracting with agents having a history of defaulting.

Another automated marketplace, MAGMA, is open to *heterogeneous* contracting software (Tsvetovatty et al., 1997, p. 501), i.e., software of different quality or capabilities from the software forming a MAGMA component. This means that those consumers who would use MAGMA-provided software may be less able to strike a good deal than those who would use different software. Consumer protection obviously dictates that the provider should disclose this particular characteristic of its service and its consequences on what consumers should expect from MAGMA-provided contracting software.

Importantly, however, unlike Kasbah, MAGMA contemplates many of the socio-legal implications of an operative automated marketplace, particularly through ensuring the *security of electronic transactions*, including "user confidentiality (usually achieved through encryption), data integrity (data sent as part of a transaction should not be modifiable), message authentication (achieved by using digital signatures or certificates) and non-repudiation (parties should not be able to deny their participation in a transaction after the fact)" (Tsvetovatty et al., 1997, p. 504).

36 Infra at p. 12–13

37 Auctions are often deemed negotiations (Fasli, 2007, p. 215). See also Kersten, Noronha and Teich (2000, p. 1) referring to multi-attribute auctions blurring the distinction between auctions and negotiations as they involve multiple purchase-related factors rather than just price.

38 See also supra at pp. 3–4

39 This is the tempo according to which agents should lower or increase the offered price as time goes by (Chavez and Maes, 1996, p. 3).

Information held by contracting software, such as strategies and user reservation price, are also secure so that they cannot be accessed by software acting for other users (Tsvetovatty et al., 1997, pp. 508–510). It follows that 'automated marketplace' security is technologically feasible, and that some marketplaces may be secure, unlike others. This again raises the question as to whether unsecure marketplaces are defective and/or their providers negligent, or whether there are legal measures in place seeking to ensure that relevant services will be secure.

Kasbah (Chavez and Maes, 1996, p. 4) and MAGMA (Tsvetovatty et al., 1997, p. 512) enable negotiations over price and ignore other factors, such as delivery time or the availability of a commercial guarantee. However, existing techniques enable software to negotiate over multiple factors (Maes and Guttman, 1998, sec. 3), and there are systems that support software engaging in multi-factor negotiations, often by iteratively formulating, exchanging and evaluating offers and counteroffers (Parsons, Sierra and Jennings, 1998; Chung and Honavar, 2000; Rahwan et al., 2003). If *good* purchase decisions cannot be taken on the basis of price *alone*, is it acceptable to make available price-only automated marketplaces and thus encourage consumers to price-shop, ignoring other purchase-related factors? Does the current regulatory regime ensure that consumers engaging in automated contracting will be given equal care and protection to that afforded to consumers using current less advanced shopping facilities?

AuctionBot is another notable automated marketplace (Wurman, Wellman and Walsh, 1998). It has been used to host a Trading Agent Competition (TAC), which had led to the development of sophisticated auction-handling software making complex bidding (purchase) decisions.[40] It has also demonstrated the possibility of software intended to act under the exact same circumstances having *different* quality and/or capabilities (Wellman et al., 2001, pp. 44–46; Greenwald and Stone, 2001, p. 58). Finally, eAuctionHouse can be used by *both* human users and software agents (Sandholm, 2002, p. 656). Also, users can write code or program the contracting software to achieve added functionality (Sandholm and Huai, 2000, p. 83). Thus, programming-literate consumers may use more sophisticated and efficient software than the average consumer user. The latter must thus certainly be informed that she does not stand equally vis-à-vis all users competing in the marketplace for the best deal. Similarly, consumers choosing to use the marketplace *personally* must be aware of the fact that other consumers may use contracting software instead.

Contracting software in automated marketplaces decides according to a negotiation strategy incorporated into it via relevant rules and techniques (Hou, 2004, pp. 128–129; Skylogiannis, 2005, pp. 22–23). It therefore decides automatically and, unless it malfunctions (or is caused to malfunction by a malicious alteration of their code, for example), it will follow its strategy and produce the results enabled by it. Automated shopping therefore evidently renders at least some of the traditional misleading or deceptive practices largely unworkable, as one cannot mislead software in the same way it can mislead human beings. Similarly, the subtle biases that are often exerted on shopping agent users towards merchants who pay the shopping agent more than others[41] would seem unworkable in an automated marketplace. Evidently, therefore, the automation realized by automated marketplaces may remedy some consumer protection problems. Simultaneously however, it raises questions regarding whether the legal rules devised to protect consumers against unfair commercial practices are capable of responding to such practices when exhibited in non-traditional ways,

40 The market game involved in the competition and the bidding decisions that had to be performed by the contestants are described by Wellman et al. (2001, pp. 44–46).

41 Infra at Chapter 2, p. 24

such as through a purposeful alteration of software code causing consumer software to accept an offer with a higher price.

Negotiation *protocols* are also vital to contracting software performance, as they specify the negotiation rules governing agent interactions (Beer et al., 1999, p. 2; Skylogiannis, 2005, pp. 22, 66). Strategies and protocols may present a challenge for designers. Because a "known optimal strategy" does not always exist (Vytelingum et al., 2005, p. 1), designers must design one enabling the contracting software to act efficiently. Likewise, standard negotiation protocols do not contain *all* of the rules of a particular market mechanism (Bartolini, Preist and Jennings, 2005, p. 214), and because of such gaps, "the designer of an agent using the protocol must be aware of these negotiation rules and design the agent taking them into account" (Bartolini et al., 2005, p. 214). Fasli (2007, p. 78) confirms that multi-agent systems such as electronic marketplaces "raise many difficult challenges with regard to their design and implementation". Clearly, therefore, design mistakes or omissions can possibly result in defective contracting software that may frustrate user expectations and even cause harm (e.g., by entering into an erroneous contract burdening its user with unintended legal obligations). Does the EU legal regime avail consumers a route to compensation under such circumstances?

As for the business model of automated marketplaces, this will probably be similar to that of shopping agents (i.e., mainly free for consumer buyers and paid for by selling merchants).[42] At least, this is the business model of eBay Inc. (2018b) and Amazon Inc. (2017), which are close predecessors of automated marketplaces. Again, therefore, as automated marketplaces' interests are mostly aligned to those of the merchants who pay, an investigative approach towards how they deal with consumers and their interests is merited. Less caution may be taken towards contracting software not forming a marketplace component but provided by independent providers. Independent providers will probably derive revenue directly from consumer users, as happens in relation to auction sniping agents (Abercrombie Online, 2001; Minalto, 2017), and are therefore bound to be more sensitive to consumer rights and interests.

1.5 Risks and legal issues: categorization

Having explained shopping agents and automated marketplaces, this book proceeds with the categorization of the risks and issues associated with these platforms and their translation into legal issues. There are in fact *five* different categories of risks and/or issues posed by the use of shopping agents and automated marketplaces; most of them are common to both, but there are a few that are peculiar to one or the other platform.

The *first category* encompasses risks or issues that are *information related*. Being innovative and perhaps even peculiar online services, the relevant platforms must accurately and comprehensively be described to the consumer so that he can take an informed decision regarding whether to use them, the extent to which to rely on them and how to use them safely and/or effectively, thus avoiding unsatisfactory outcomes. Failure to do so may result in bad purchase decisions, unintended or mistaken contracts and/or privacy violations. Therefore, before a consumer undertakes to use one such platform *and also while using it*, she must receive sufficient information about it and the way it works. As it will be shown, pre-contractual information about the service, though important, is not enough on its own in relation to advanced and innovative services such as shopping agents and automated

42 Supra p. 9

marketplaces. A closely related issue relates to the marketing or advertising of such platforms, which should avoid exaggerating statements. Though in relation to standard services, advertising exaggerations may readily be perceived by consumers as such, the same may not be true of innovative platforms. Especially because these are known to utilize artificial intelligence and/or other revolutionary computer techniques, they may be perceived as actually being capable of achieving 'super results'. In this respect, exaggerating statements may be taken as true assessments of their capabilities rather than the usual advertising puff not to be taken literally.

A different kind of information (other than the information to be given about them as services) is also crucial in their case. This is the information that is actually the *output* of their service, or, in other words, the actual competing product offerings or merchant listings returned by shopping agents and the information that the contracting software of automated marketplaces provides and considers during contract conclusion. This information is particularly significant, as it will effectively form the basis upon which a binding contract is to be concluded. If it is incomplete or erroneous, that may result in unintended contracts, which the consumer will want to seek to avoid. The issue is complex, especially in the context of automated marketplaces, where the 'party' receiving and considering any provided information is not the human consumer but software acting on her behalf. In such cases, difficult regulatory decisions have to be made in order to achieve sufficient consumer protection without stifling innovation.

A closely related issue (also having to do with the output of such platforms, specifically shopping agents in this case) regards their practice of flagging out specific merchant listings as 'best deals'. Such practices can effectively cause consumers to take a particular purchase decision he would not have taken otherwise and must thus be regulated in order to ensure that they are employed responsibly and contain true and accurate information.

These risks and/or issues and an exploration of the EU legal response towards them, mainly searched for in four EU Directives – specifically, the E-commerce Directive (ECD), the Unfair Commercial Practices Directive (UCPD), the Services Directive (SD) and the Consumer Rights Directive (CRD) – constitute the focus of Chapter 2. Though additional legal measures, such as the General Data Protection Regulation (GDPR), will also be inquired into, the aforementioned four Directives are clearly the most relevant. Indeed, they impose information duties on traders and are also concerned with the accuracy and quality of the information regarding goods, services and digital content provided to consumers. As it will be shown, EU law responds adequately to the relevant risks. Though the ECD, the CRD and the SD provide partial or 'patchy' solutions, the UCPD can serve as a complete relevant legal response. Not only does it prohibit misleading marketing representations but it also (indirectly) imposes specific information duties effectively requiring the provision of all necessary information about the platform service at the right time (i.e., while consumers are using the platform). As regards the issue relating to the completeness or accuracy of the output of the relevant platforms, the EU legal response is largely satisfactory, though not totally unproblematic. More specifically, the UCPD addresses the relevant issue in the context of shopping agents, however there may be some uncertainty regarding whether its provisions can be taken to require the inclusion of all of the necessary purchase-related factors in merchant listings. In relation to automated marketplaces, a direct solution is contained in the CRD, in particular, its pre-contractual information duties, however these require a careful interpretation to be able to apply to the relevant context and they may have to undergo drastic amendments to accommodate automated contracting, when, in the future, this becomes commonplace.

Chapter 3 discusses a different risk associated with the use of shopping agents and automated marketplaces, namely fraudulent and/or unfair or unreliable transactions. As these platforms essentially serve as consumer gateways to merchants seeking to offer their products for sale, they can lead consumers to unscrupulous or unreliable merchants who may never deliver a product or mislead them into purchasing an unintended product or violate contract terms, thereby increasing costs and hassle for consumers. This risk refers to (traditional) fraud or deception that does not involve any unauthorized interference with consumer personal data or data inherent in consumer contracting software.

The question arises regarding whether the consumer is adequately protected against these (traditional) risks on the relevant platforms and, in particular, whether platform providers are directly or indirectly imposed with a legal duty to pre-screen participating merchants, thereby keeping their platform 'clean' and safe for consumers. The answer to this question is searched for in the E-commerce Directive, specifically its provisions on intermediary liability and the Unfair Commercial Practices Directive, which seeks to prevent unfair dealings and transactions. The liability-related Directives, namely the Consumer Sales Directive and the Product Liability Directive, will also be examined in an attempt to determine whether any legal liability threat can effectively lead to an obligation to employ measures ensuring that only honest and reliable merchants are allowed on their platforms. Such obligation is very important, as it operates *ex ante*, preventing harm from arising in the first place; *ex-post* solutions that facilitate the recovery of damage are important, yet the former are much more effective in boosting consumer confidence and trust. Yet, as a result of the intermediary liability exemptions of the ECD, it is unclear whether platform providers can be burdened with one such obligation. The liability-related Directives are not equipped to impose the said obligation and therefore, its only possible source is, again, the UCPD. The relationship between the UCPD and the liability exemptions of the ECD merits examination, however. Moreover, the relevant potential of the UCPD seems not have sufficiently emphasized so far. In light of this, coupled with certain enforcement-related issues relating to the UCPD in the relevant context, the EU legal response towards the relevant risk arises as not being fully satisfactory. The Second Payment Services Directive (PSD2) does increase the security of marketplaces, but it focuses on *payment* security and can thus be of no help in the context of shopping agents nor even in all cases in the context of automated marketplaces.

Chapters 4 and 5 concern data protection (and privacy) risks and issues pertaining to transactional security respectively. These very important 'risk' categories are only applicable to automated marketplaces. These platforms enable contract conclusion and probably require the provision of detailed personal data, such as consumer names, addresses and payment details. When personal data is compromised or mishandled, the resulting harm can be extensive. It may not be the intangible harm inherent in the violation of the human rights to privacy and data protection only. Tangible harm resulting from fraud may also arise; most of the fraud committed online (naturally) results from prior personal data breaches or entails an unauthorized use of personal data (Bush, 2016). Protecting personal data, therefore, means affording protection against data-driven fraud, too. The same is true of affording sufficient extra protection to payments, which are most likely to occur on automated marketplaces and that form the very point at which an attempt to defraud a person whose personal data has been compromised proves successful or not. The adequate legal solution to these risks should, as is explained in Chapter 4, consist of six different elements, which are shown to exist in the EU data protection regime, namely the E-privacy Directive and the GDPR, if suitably be interpreted.

Contract conclusion, particularly when expensive products are involved, additionally necessitates the employment of effective 'transactional security' measures ensuring authentication, data integrity and non-repudiation. As is explained in Chapter 5, transactional security reduces fraud, contractual breaches and difficult-to-resolve disputes and is not always effectively achieved through data protection. It should thus be deemed a protection-deserving value *per se*, or regardless of whether personal data is involved or compromised triggering the EU data protection legal regime. The examination of whether EU law (adequately) boosts and protects transactional security and payments within automated marketplaces will be conducted by reference to a wide number of relevant EU measures, including the General Data Protection Legislation, the e-Privacy Directive, the eIDAS Regulation, the Network Information Security Directive and the Second Payment Services Directive. All of these measures are relevant to transactional security and though none of them fully addresses the issues involved, they can work in synergy, thereby collectively providing for a legal solution related to transactional security that is largely satisfactory.

A further category of risks (or issues) refers to the legal validity of contracts concluded in automated marketplaces and the possibility of a malfunction or a user causing software to conclude a mistaken or unintended contract. The two issues are interrelated; as it will be shown, the theory adopted to explain the legal validity of automated contracts must be consistent with the legal rules affording consumers an escape route from mistaken or unintended contracts. They are also significant issues because any legal uncertainty surrounding the validity of automated contracts will naturally hinder the successful commercialization of automated marketplaces and prevent full automation in consumer shopping. By the same token, consumers would want to know whether they will be able to avoid a mistaken contract concluded by malfunctioning software, otherwise, consumer trust and confidence will be difficult to be placed on such platforms, which would inevitably constitute particularly risky shopping environments for consumers.

These two issues are discussed in Chapter 6. This chapter explores traditional contract law theories and principles that also appear in EU model contract laws, such as the Draft Common Frame of Reference (DCFR), and additionally inquires into whether EU measures, such as the Unfair Contract Terms Directive and the Second Payment Services Directive can afford an (indirect) solution to the problem of malfunction-caused mistaken contracts. As regards consumer-caused mistaken contracts, certain information duties imposed by the E-commerce Directive are shown to be directly relevant to the issue of whether a relevant escape route exists. Importantly, the same measure seems also to guarantee the validity of electronic contracts including (automated) contracts concluded on automated marketplaces, even though it does not dictate the theory explaining validity.

Chapter 7 is devoted to a further issue, namely, the availability of a legal route to compensation in the case of consumer damage resulting from the use of a shopping agent or an automated marketplace. In this context, the exact source of the arising damage is important. Indeed, if the damage arises out of a privacy violation (or a data protection compromise) such as a 'personal data' leak, the General Data Protection Regulation is the main legislative instrument to be looked into a route to compensation. On the other hand, if the damage course is a practice qualifying as an unfair commercial practice, the relevant measure is the Unfair Commercial Practices Directive. As it will be shown, the exact type of the damage, specifically whether this is economic or some non-economic harm such as inconvenience, is also crucial to answering the question as to whether the aforementioned measures constitute a viable route compensation for aggrieved consumers. For strictly financial damage resulting from an unauthorized electronic payment, the Second Payment Services Directive is the measure that should primarily be looked into. Where, however, the damage is attributable to other causes, such as a system malfunction because of a negligent design error, for example, general tort law principles (that also exist in non-binding texts such as the *Principles of European Tort Law*) merit discussion. Finally, relevant to legal liability and, thus, to all of the aforementioned cases of damage, is notoriously the possibility of insurance. Amongst others, therefore, the application of the insurance-related provisions of the Services Directive to automated marketplaces are also examined.

Chapter 8 summarizes the book in terms of the main risks identified, the EU legal measures, which have been examined in search for how EU law responds to those risks and the afforded legal solutions, together with an assessment as to their adequacy. It also pinpoints some general conclusions, amongst others, relating to the platform that poses more risks, the legal measures that do most of the work in responding to consumer risks in this context and the overall adequacy of EU law in accommodating the needs of consumers in innovative (and technologically advanced) online shopping environments. At a more general level, the reader is informed of the puzzle of EU legal measures essentially composing the answer of EU law to the so-called digital economy (to the extent, it affects consumers) and of how well the said laws adjust to the relevant challenges. Can appropriate modifications and suitable interpretations do the job or is the EU in need of a new digital consumer protection law? This book provides evidence that it is the former that holds true.

Evidently, this book focuses on EU consumer protection law in an expanded sense that also encompasses data protection and information and payment security laws. This is a logical choice given that consumers are e-commerce actors and e-commerce is fuelled by data. Though criminal law may also have an (indirect) impact on the level of protection afforded to the consumer in the relevant context, criminal law is outside the scope of this book. More relevant to this book will be a future inquiry into whether very recent measures or draft measures in the areas covered by this book, such as the 'New Deal for Consumers' and the EU Cybersecurity Act significantly improve the EU legal response toward the consumer risks and issues associated with shopping agents and automated marketplaces. Due to being very recent, such measures have escaped an in-depth analysis, yet they are briefly mentioned to illustrate that their impact should not be expected to be great.

2 Information-related risks

Bad purchase decisions and frustration of consumer expectations

2.1 General

This chapter looks into the risks and issues relating to information, information that refers both to the relevant platforms as services and the information that comprises those services' output, such as the shopping agents' search results or their 'fuel', namely the purchase-related factors that software on automated marketplaces utilizes to conclude contracts. Each of the relevant risks or issues (or risk categories) is illustrated together with the need for appropriate legal intervention. This illustration is followed by an assessment of the current EU legal response.

The *first* risk to be discussed refers to exaggerating marketing representations regarding the relevant platform services and the closely related (broader) issue of their many limitations and other peculiar characteristics, about which adequate information should be provided to consumers to enable them to take informed decisions and avoid harm arising out of their use. The *second* risk relates to the information that shopping agents provide to consumers when being utilized and more specifically, the information relating to purchase-related factors, such as price and delivery, contained in the product offerings displayed as search results. In the context of automated marketplaces, the relevant issue concerns the purchase-related information that selling and buying software considers while concluding contracts in the name of merchants and consumers respectively. Consumer harm can arise either from an uninformed use of such platforms (and software) or as a result of the latter providing or considering incomplete purchase-related information and ignoring vital purchase-related factors, which should be taken into account if reliable purchase decisions are to be formed. Such harm consists of bad or unintended purchase decisions that would frustrate the consumer expectations, ultimately causing economic damage and distress.

2.2 Marketing representations and information on limitations and characteristics: illustrating the risks

2.2.1 Marketing representations

Though software, or more generally, technological tools, can be empowering, they are never perfect. Thus, though shopping agents can assist consumers in finding a bargain, they do not search *all* of the existing online stores, and offline stores are often ignored. Accordingly, as experimental uses have illustrated (Wildstrom, 1998), a merchant *not* searched by the shopping agent may offer a better deal than the best available on the shopping agent platform. If consumers are told (or are left to believe) otherwise, they will be able to make only an uninformed decision about, amongst others, the extent of their reliance on the agent and most certainly, they will be unable to avoid forming unrealistic relevant expectations. As Howells (2005, p. 355) explains, "Harm will be reduced by ensuring goods and services are more likely to be in line with realistic consumer expectations based on reliable information".

Thus, highly promising statements such as "Find the Lowest Price on the Net" or "Get the Best Deal", especially when *not* accompanied by relevant clarifications, should not be used by shopping agent platforms. "Find the lowest price – Compare 145 book stores, 60,000 sellers, in a click" (Cygnus Software Ltd, 2017) seems an acceptable representation because it discloses the number of participating merchants and, thus, the relevant capability of the agent.[1] The possibility of misleading statements in the course of the marketing of relevant platforms cannot be excluded and the issue is of course pertinent in the context of automated marketplaces, too. A statement reading "Strike the Best Available Deal", for example, would be misleading in the case of the Kasbah marketplace where the buying software agents *cannot*, as said, choose *the best* amongst *various offers* meeting user-specified criteria.[2] The issue is much broader, of course, as there may be misleading representations regarding several attributes of the platform that can influence consumer decision-making regarding the relevant service and its use. More specifically, such representations may relate to (a) the impartiality of shopping agents, (b) whether (more advanced) customizable or heterogeneous contracting software is allowed in the automated marketplace and (c) whether providers screen participating merchants against criteria of reliability or apply technical measures of protection.

Especially, where the services at stake embody significant technological innovation and quite impressive capabilities that enable them to perform processes or tasks traditionally reserved to humans, misleading representations are very likely to result, particularly from zealous providers aiming to ensure that the consumer will actually realize and appreciate those capabilities. By the same token, consumers are more likely to take exaggerating representations literally, when these refer to such 'intelligent' services, than when those representations accompany a less remarkable product, such as beer or furniture.[3] The relevant risk is thus acute in this context.

2.2.2 *Information on limitations and other characteristics*

A closely related issue pertains to the need for information that enables consumers to understand, evaluate and/or *correctly* use the platform. This need is important, as illustrated by reference first to shopping agents and then to automated marketplaces. The principal source of the said need is the numerous limitations that relevant platforms suffer from. The existence of such limitations in general, as well as each one of them individually, is explained in the following section, together with the need for appropriate legal intervention, by reference to each of the relevant platforms.

2.2.2.1 *Shopping agents*

2.2.2.1.1 LIMITATIONS IN GENERAL AND INACCURATE INFORMATION

Information errors cannot be eliminated (Fasli, 2006, p. 71; Fasli, 2009, p. 25) and, indeed, experimental uses of agents showed that products marked as being in stock were, in fact, not

1 This is so assuming that the relevant statement is true and accurate, of course.
2 Supra p. 12
3 On the capabilities of these services, see supra Chapter 1, pp. 2–4, 8, 11–13.

(Rothman, 2007). Baye, Morgan and Scholten (2004, p. 475) additionally refer to the "bait and switch strategy – listing a low price with no intention of honoring it" to attract leads. The accuracy of the agent-provided information has been pinpointed as an issue also in relation to shopping agents focusing on financial products (Great Britain, Financial Services Authority, 2008, Conclusion B). Users also report that the price stated on the platform often greatly differs from the price offered on the website of the financial institution to which they are directed (BBC, 2009). Along similar lines, a web trawl on ten (10) shopping agent platforms conducted by the (Great Britain OFT, 2010, Annex K, p. 2) found that "there were still cases where a product was not available, prices were not the same on click through or were only 'base prices' with additional charges added on click through".

Other studies confirm that 65% of consumers have faced at least one problem while using a shopping agent:

> The most commonly reported problem was the unavailability of a product at the seller's website (32%). Incorrect prices and incorrect product information were reported by, respectively, 21% and 18% of consumers, while 14% of consumers were faced with incorrect information about the delivery time. Other issues reported included: incorrect links on the site (14%), misleading reviews (12%) and misleading ranking (10%)
>
> (ECME Consortium, 2013, p. 232)

One observes that inaccurate information regarding the product and other core purchased-related factors, such as availability, price and delivery time, is the most common problem faced by consumers. The fact that no problem was reported by 35% of consumers should *not* be interpreted as meaning that no problem existed in their case; at least part of that percentage must be attributed to the inability of consumers to spot (or realize) a problem, a view reinforced by evidence that the relevant percentage dropped when frequency of use (and thus consumer experience) increased.[4] The limitation regarding the accuracy (or quality) of the agent-provided information, therefore, is both real and significant and is certainly exasperated by the fact that, as ECME Consortium (2013, pp. 233, 243) concluded, platform providers do not always identify themselves on their websites and often offer no information on complaint-handling procedures. Strikingly, even shopping agents bearing a quality mark (or a certification seal) were found to not provide information on their identity (ECME Consortium, 2013, p. 243).

Perhaps unsurprisingly, shopping agent providers do *not* guarantee the accuracy of the agent-provided information. Though it is true that given the high speeds of automation and data handling, the relevant problem cannot be eliminated; consumers must be alerted to the relevant possibility so as to make informed decisions and take self-protective measures. A shopping agent displays the following statement on its 'search result' pages:

> Stores are responsible for providing Shopzilla with correct and current prices. Sales taxes and shipping costs are estimates; please check store for exact amounts. Product specifications are obtained from merchants or third parties. Although we make every effort to present accurate information, Shopzilla is not responsible for inaccuracies. We encourage you to notify us of any discrepancies by clicking here.
>
> (Connexity Inc., 2017b)

4 This is stated by ECME (2013, p. 232).

Evidently, consumers are informed of the possibility of imperfect information and are encouraged to review the information on the online store. Yet, shopping agents may not always display such warnings on their list of results. Though some may refer to the said limitation in their terms of use, such reference does not really qualify as a warning or more generally, as an acceptable way of providing crucial information to consumers.[5] Moreover, even when displayed in the 'results' list, relevant statements may be in very small, light-coloured letters at the very bottom of the 'search result' pages and below numerous sponsored links and other advertisements. Thus, they can easily be missed.

Price and perhaps other information errors on shopping agent platforms can prove particularly dangerous to consumers when occurring in combination with a practice sometimes employed on such platforms, namely the practice of 'smart buy' seals or other similar seals or marks. These seals are attached by shopping agent providers to merchant offerings with the lowest price that also meet certain criteria as to, *inter alia*, trustworthiness and cannot be purchased by merchants, unlike premium listings, which, as explained later, can. Apart from bearing the seal, the relevant listings may also be highlighted or otherwise flagged so they cannot easily be missed. Provided that this practice is used responsibly, it can assist consumers in spotting the objectively best deal, thus avoiding biases exhibited through the use of other flagged listings such as premium listings, which are simply bought by the merchants featured therein. Conversely, however, if such 'sealed and highlighted' offerings contain inaccurate information, the practice can obviously direct and perhaps even lure consumers towards a bad or erroneous purchase decision and, thus, exasperate the risk relating to the accuracy of the information provided on shopping agent platforms.

2.2.2.1.2 INCOMPLETE INFORMATION

Important pieces of information are often ignored by shopping agents: "A user . . . has no way of knowing if a product is in stock and when it will arrive" (Punj and Rapp, 2003, p. 9). Surveys performed in the context of major studies have also confirmed "a lack of adequate information on aspects like delivery costs, delivery time, taxes, and availability of products" (Civic Consulting, 2011, p. 6). Another study specifically refers to the comprehensiveness of the agent-provided information and recommends that "terms of purchase should be specified in detail, including delivery time, main contract terms and special clauses, etc." (ECME Consortium, 2013, pp. 294, 300).

A particularly important piece of information sometimes omitted is the time within which products are dispatched and, in effect, *when* a product will be received.[6] The importance of

5 Evidence suggests that consumers do *not* read and/or consider standard terms *even* when they have to click a button explicitly signifying their acceptance to those terms (Hillman, 2006, pp. 840–842). Comparably to what applies in relation to most other websites, shopping agent platforms display their standard terms and conditions on a webpage that can simply be browsed without requiring any positive action on the part of the consumer signifying his or her acceptance of the said terms. What is more, even consumers who would access those terms will probably face difficulties in getting sufficiently informed given that relevant texts are notoriously too long and technical for non-legal minds.

6 It should be noted that the research conducted by the present author has revealed that more and more shopping agents now provide this piece of information, when available, so the relevant problem is not as serious as it used to be. See, for example, Kelkoo Inc. (2017b) and Pricerunner International AB (2017b).

order-processing/delivery time is indisputable.[7] A consumer may be willing to pay a 'good' price for a product to be received in days, whereas he may be unwilling to pay anything for a product to reach him several weeks later. Indeed, delivery time may have economic and other implications. A consumer who orders a particular auto spare part may have to use a rental car in the meantime, while another who orders a book may need it for a paper presentation at a conference to take place at a particular date. Thus, failing to take the delivery factor into account could result in the consumer making a bad purchase decision and suffering damage.

This limitation regarding important missing information becomes more serious in light of the fact that shopping agents tend to provide *too much other* information, such as merchant average ratings and detailed product descriptions or reviews, as well as information on applicable discount codes, other special offers and/or product availability.[8]

The provision of all of this (admittedly) useful information may operate as a double sword. While it renders shopping agents more efficient assistants, it may simultaneously induce consumers to fully rely on their output, feeling that they get all the information they need, thus making a purchase decision without carefully reviewing the relevant offering on the merchant website to which they are directed. Put another way, it may create a dangerous *sense of* certainty; research on consumer behaviour confirms that the more certain consumers are or feel, the less the likelihood of further information seeking (Sternthal and Craig, 1992; cited in Su, 2007, p. 137).

Research further suggests that, owing to cognitive limitations regarding information search and processing, consumers rely *heavily* on the information *as displayed by the agent* (Murray and Häubl, 2001, p. 164). Experiments also show that a purchase-related factor on which information is provided by the agent has a dominant role in decision-making, whereas omitted factors are less influential (Murray and Häubl, 2001, p. 168). Shopping agents can thus adversely influence consumer decision-making if they omit information on vital purchase-related factors.

Shopping agents often make no attempt to reduce this possibility, as they fail to display warnings or otherwise alert the consumer to the fact that important information such as order-processing/delivery time is missing. This factor is sometimes not mentioned at all in their list of results, and consumers are not notified about its absence or the need to search for the relevant information on merchant websites. Yet, it is not impossible to do so. Some shopping agents effectively alert consumers to the absence of the said piece of information by including in their search results a column referring to delivery or order-processing time. Where that information is unavailable, the agent displays a 'check site' or 'refer to shop' message (Pricerunner International AB, 2017b). The same shopping agent also displays a prominent warning about the possibility of inaccuracies in the information it provides for delivery costs, urging consumers to verify costs with the merchant website. The use of such warnings has also been recommended by the UK Financial Services Authority to financial-product agent providers (2008, Conclusion B).

2.2.2.1.3 MERCHANT ACCESS TO PLATFORM NOT SCREENED

As discussed in more detail in the following,[9] shopping agent providers often do not vet the merchants appearing in the results they return to consumers and in any event, they do not

7 Kerr (2004, p. 312) writes that "other than shipping charges and delivery time, it really doesn't matter who the merchant happens to be".

8 See, for example, the returned results of Kelkoo, though this agent does provide information on delivery time (Kelkoo, 2017b).

9 Infra Chapter 3 p. 77

guarantee their reliability. This is another serious limitation that the consumer should be alerted to, as it may affect its decision as to whether to use the agent or not and most importantly, as to how she is to deal with its output or results; if she is aware of the limitation, she may take care to investigate the reliability of the merchant from whom she considers buying. One shopping agent explicitly warns consumers of the particular limitation and urges them to check the reliability of merchants before proceeding with a purchase. Yet, it places the said information and warning behind links, which are themselves placed behind the 'about us' link on its website (Pricerunner International AB, 2017a), which is likely not to be read by consumers. Information, particularly in the form of warnings such as 'this site does not vet merchants', displayed close to the 'search results' table and, thus, exactly at the time consumers need it, would obviously be much more effective.

2.2.2.1.4 LACK OF IMPARTIALITY

Another common limitation of shopping agents is their lack of impartiality. Most of those that do not work like search engines[10] are typically limited to merchants who *pay* to participate. Relevant providers often invite merchants to register with their platform, thereby depositing an initial amount of money against which consumer clicks to their website will be debited (Connexity Inc., 2017c). Moreover, the higher that fee, the heavier the promotion the merchant will receive on the platform through premium or top listings, as is illustrated in the following. This practice further causes them to lose impartiality, as Kerr (2004, pp. 311, 312), Fasli (2009, p. 26) and Rothman (2007) acknowledge.

Bagby (2004, pp. 4–5), nevertheless, considers such agents to be unbiased shopping tools, unlike traditional search engines; a non-negligible consumer segment, specifically 56% of the consumers surveyed, seems to agree (ECME Consortium, 2013, p. 191).[11] Remarkably, the same study suggests that consumers greatly value impartiality as a characteristic of shopping agents (ECME Consortium, 2013, p. 202). It thus seems to be confirmed that the lack of impartiality of relevant platforms (which translates into the offerings on the platform *essentially being advertisements*), is *not* self-evident. Consumers need, therefore, to be informed about it in order to avoid harm, such as a deal which is not the best possible.

Indeed, it is scientifically confirmed that top placements have a strong influence on consumer decision-making; the higher the position of the merchant in the agent search results, the higher the chance of consumers buying from that merchant (Riemer and Lehrke, 2009, p. 67, 71; ECME Consortium, 2013, p. 216). An experiment conducted by the ECME Consortium (2013, p. 219) also confirmed that at least some consumers will choose to buy from one of the merchants appearing first or on top, effectively possibly turning down an optimal deal listed in the (same) results.

Commentators (Fasli, 2009, p. 32) and researchers seem to call for impartial shopping agents, which would present no such consumer risks; amongst the list of recommendations drafted in the context of a major study on shopping agents is one reading as follows: "Comparison should be impartial and not be affected by any contractual relationship with the sellers, manufacturers or providers". Yet, impartiality cannot really be made a legal

10 Supra Chapter 1, p. 9
11 An earlier study also confirmed that shopping agents "are largely perceived by users to be doing a good, unbiased job in finding correct information about prices and delivery charges from different sellers (Civic Consulting, 2011, p. 6). Surveys show that consumers perceive traditional search engines, too, as impartial despite their similarly biased nature (Fallows, 2005, pp. 15, 23, 25; Princeton Survey Research Associates, 2002, p. 17).

requirement. Shopping agent platforms are comparable to TV stations; they offer a valuable service to consumers for free and derive revenue from advertising. The longer the duration of a TV advertising spot, the higher the fee charged by the TV station. The same is true where the spot is broadcasted during prime zones, i.e., where viewer numbers at their peak. The Audiovisual Media Services Directive[12] controls TV impartiality,[13] yet it does not prohibit the aforementioned practices. Prohibiting premium listings on shopping agent platforms would be an excessive interference with their freedom to conduct business, especially given that relevant providers are private parties providing services in a purely commercial setting.

The position may be different in the specific (and limited) cases in which shopping agents receive a boost by the law, as is the case with the Payment Accounts Directive (PAD).[14] By virtue of the said Directive, consumers must have access to at least one comparison tool with the help of which they can compare the fees and/or charges of the various payment service providers.[15] According to the PAD, comparison tools can be provided by either private or public entities that must meet certain conditions, amongst others, with regard to their impartiality and independence from payment service providers.[16] This mirrors the law creating or significantly boosting a specific market of shopping agents, and it thus makes sense to impose conditions as to impartiality. In relation to standard product shopping agents that comprise unregulated private businesses, however, a softer regulatory approach that involves the government accrediting ***impartial*** agents (Great Britain, Office of Fair Trading, 2009) sounds more suitable, and could probably encourage relevant providers to operate as impartial tools and develop revenue streams that do not affect their impartiality. In fact, the ECME Consortium (2013, pp. 114–124) identifies some accreditation systems for shopping agents in the domains of energy and electronic communications, which are administered by relevant regulators and require adherence to rules relating, amongst others, to impartiality, yet given the voluntary nature of the accreditation, participation is rather low.

However, although legally mandated impartiality is *not* a viable possibility in the majority of cases, *legally mandated transparency* about the lack of impartiality certainly is; if consumers are unaware of the lack of impartiality of shopping agents, they cannot possibly develop resistance against the aforementioned subtle influences. False or misleading representations as to impartiality in the marketing of relevant platforms should thus be considered unacceptable. Moreover, existing biases should adequately be disclosed, as they constitute information enabling consumers to understand, assess and correctly use the relevant service. As is the case with other limitations, however,[17] no adequate disclosure is always made in the particular context, as will now be illustrated by reference to the different aspects of this lack of impartiality.

12 Directive 2010/13/EU of the European Parliament and of the Council of 10 March 2010 on the coordination of certain provisions laid down by law, regulation or administrative action in Member States concerning the provision of audio/visual media services (Audiovisual Media Services Directive) OJ L 95, 15.4.2010, p. 1–24.
13 Articles 9–11.
14 Directive 2014/92/EU of the European Parliament and of the Council of 23 July 2014 on the comparability of fees related to payment accounts, payment account switching and access to payment accounts with basic features (Payment Accounts Directive), OJ L 257, 28.08.2014, pp. 214–246.
15 Article 7, PAD.
16 Article 7(3)(a) and Recitals 22–23, PAD.
17 Supra pp. 20–24

One such aspect is the omission of merchants from whom shopping agents do not receive a fee (Rothman, 2007). Consumers will not probably know unless relevant providers disclose information about their business model.[18] Yet, many shopping agents do not sufficiently disclose their business model. More specifically, prominent statements reading 'all results displayed are sponsored by merchants or affiliates', such as the one displayed by shopping.com (2017), are rare. Some agents clearly disclose their business model in their terms and conditions,[19] while others do so on pages titled "merchants" and "merchant listings" (Connexity Inc., 2017c; Kelkoo, 2017c) that are clearly not addressed to consumers. These anecdotal observations seem to be backed by the findings of mapping and mystery shopping exercises funded by the European Commission: "less than half (37%–45%) of comparison tools were willing to disclose details on their supplier relationship, description of business model" (ECME Consortium, 2013, p. xv) and "Comparison tools did not appear keen to divulge details on how they generated income; the proportion of shoppers finding information on income-generation remained below 37% across all markets" (ECME Consortium, 2013, p. xix).

Biases are also evinced in the top, preferred or premium, listings that feature merchants paying a fee or an increased fee for their listing to be placed at a top position. Consumers do not seem sufficiently to be informed of this practice, either. Research conducted in the early 2010s (Markou, 2011, pp. 193–199) indicated that several shopping agents were using 'featured store' or 'featured seller' seals attached to preferred or premium listings. In some cases, the seal was clickable and led to a pop-up window with information disclosing the payment of a fee by merchants. Those seals, however, were often very discrete and their *clickable* nature was not apparent. Unsurprisingly, the UK Advertising Standards Authority (ASA), upholding a complaint against a search engine regarding how it was identifying paid results, opined that the information placed behind a link, the purpose of which is not evident, is not sufficient (ASA, 2004).

It seems that this is no longer a preferred practice, as fresh experimental searches on various shopping agent platforms did not return any listings bearing such seals. The practice of top placement (and the inherent biases) have not, however, been abandoned. In fact, the problem may even have gotten worse. Most shopping agents' revenue is now calculated and charged on the basis of the so-called Cost-Per-Click (CPC) bidding system, which allows advertisers to bid on certain keywords (relating to their products) signifying the maximum amount they are willing to pay per each click to their website. This is the system used by Google in the context of its notorious AdWords advertising service that is responsible for the sponsored results appearing at the side of the organic results returned by the search engine. The particular system is complicated, but the higher the bid of the advertiser, the more prominent the position of its listing: "A higher bid generally helps your ad show in a higher ad position on the page" (Google Inc., 2017a).

Thus, shopping agents now often make no reference to preferred or premium listings, but this is not necessarily because the relevant biases no longer exist. Rather it is because such listings and related biases are now inherent in the very remuneration system used and need not, therefore, be offered as a separate product like when the CPC system is *not* used. As a result, the information provided by agents on their business model is bound to be obscure to consumers and perhaps even to merchants, who, however, receive a detailed explanation

18 Disclosure of business model has also been identified as a key principle for comparison tools (European Commission, 2016c, p.125).

19 These are often not read by consumers, see supra at p. 22n5

of it from the platform provider. On its pages addressed to merchants, one shopping agent does not confine itself to a mere reference to CPC and thus reveals (and effectively) confirms that preferred or premium listings on agent websites do exist: "The bidding interface allows you to give more visibility to selected products, for example top sellers or products on sales. Increasing CPC for a selection of products will result in prominent placement within our Kelkoo Group sites and network" (Kelkoo, 2017c).

Yet, shopping agents do not seem to separate such CPC-system-afforded premium listings from the rest of the listings. In fact, such an identification mechanism is probably not possible when complex algorithms automatically choose the position of listings when they are about to appear on the consumer's screen[20] and when no merchant actually pays what could clearly be distinguished as an *extra* fee.

The way in which results are displayed by agents can shed further light on how this modern type of preferred listings seems to work. Some agents offer consumers the option of manually ranking results in accordance with price or store rating, yet they do not clearly explain the *default* order, i.e., how they are originally returned to the consumer is decided.[21] The default ranking in other cases refers to the criterion of 'relevancy',[22] yet it is not entirely clear how this can be a valid criterion when the consumer searches for one very specific product, such as an iPhone 5s Black. The present author has also observed that, in some cases, agents may originally only display a *sole* merchant listing and offer the possibility to compare prices as between all participating merchants behind a relevant link that consumers are called to follow if they wish to have a comparison. The table list of results, then, contains two merchants only, with the consumer having to click yet another link if he wants a full comparison table. These one or two offerings appearing at first are likely to be of merchants who have placed a higher bid in the context of the CPC remuneration system.

It follows that ways in which merchants paying *more* could be rewarded with prominence do exist, yet there may often be nothing that sufficiently explains this to consumers. Perhaps the clearest attempt to offer some relevant explanation is made by Kelkoo, through a link reading 'About these search results' placed at the bottom of its pages and quite far away from the results to which it refers. What is more is that the content of the pop-up window behind that link seems to confirm that the CPC algorithmic bidding system allows for very *general* explanations that do not really enable the consumer to understand what exactly lies behind the appearance of a particular offering:

> Kelkoo's Shopping Popularity algorithm ranks search results (product offers) according to their popularity throughout the site, as determined by Kelkoo users. The majority of retailers listed on Kelkoo don't pay to be there, but some retailers do. The algorithm takes keyword relevance, 'freshness' and availability into account. This allows Kelkoo Product Search to display extremely relevant results for all kind of products and services in just thousandths of a second.
>
> (Kelkoo, 2017b)

20 "Every time an AdWords ad appears, it goes through what we call the ad auction, a process that decides which ads will appear and in which order" (Google Inc., 2017b).

21 One example is Connexity (2017d).

22 One example is Kelkoo (2017b).

Thus, the 2012 findings and recommendations of the (GB) OFT remain pertinent, especially given the introduction of the CPC bidding system in the shopping agent context, which apparently allows for *clandestine algorithmic biases*: "PCWs are not always transparent about how search results are presented. In particular, it is not always clear how results are ranked and the effect that any commercial relationships may have on the ranking" (Great Britain, OFT, 2012, p. 13).

Recent studies (ECME Consortium, 2013, p. xix) recommend that "comparison tools should be transparent about their business and financing models, including owners, shareholders and relationship with manufacturers, sellers or providers of the goods and services featured" and that "criteria used for the rankings should be clearly and prominently indicated, as well as, where relevant, any specific methodology used" (ECME Consortium, 2013, p. xxi).

Indeed, the only way in which the relevant issue could be addressed[23] is through the provision of clear and readily available information on how fees affect the presentation of results. The OFT (2012, p. 20) suggests the placement of a link reading "Why am I being shown this offer? Click here for details". Examples of the particular practice existed since quite a few years ago (Markou, 2011, p. 197) and still exist,[24] though the relevant link is often tiny and in light-grey fonts. Moreover, it is placed at the very bottom of the results and is thus effectively hidden on a page full of flashy offerings and other ads.

Shopping agents commonly also display ads referring to merchants, products and other shopping forums, mainly as part of their participation in Google AdSense, a scheme administered by Google that pays other platforms for displaying advertisements of its customers (Google Inc., 2017d). These are invariably placed below the 'search result' table returned by the agent and occupy a totally different section, which, in some cases, bears the headline 'sponsored links'. The acceptability of the use of the relevant term in the agent context is questionable, however. It can certainly sufficiently distinguish paid and non-paid listings on traditional search engines, yet shopping agents may not display *any non-paid* results at all. When *all* of the listings or results displayed are sponsored, the selective use of the term 'sponsored' for the purpose of identifying only certain listings or links may cause confusion as to the nature of the rest of the agent-displayed results and wrongly suggest that those not labelled as sponsored are non-paid, organic or *neutral* ones. A similar argument could be made in relation to the use of the alternative term 'ads' utilized by some shopping agents.[25] The practice favoured by others that use the heading 'ads by Google' (or similar) instead[26] is obviously more appropriate, because the nature and source of the said links, as well as their relationship with the rest of the results (links), is not revealed.

23 A similar issue arose in relation to traditional search engines which in earlier days were not sufficiently distinguishing sponsored (or paid) results from organic ones. The practice provoked objection in the US resulting in the Federal Trade Commission issuing guidelines that mainly had to do with sponsored results having to be placed at clearly separate sections on the search result pages and clearly identified as sponsored (United States of America, FTC, 2002; Wouters, 2004, 2005). This solution cannot be applied in the context of shopping agents, where *all* of their results are sponsored. It could be used in relation to shopping agents following the earlier 'featured seller seal' approach which could be asked to separate featured sellers paying a higher than the standard fee but not where all merchants paying a varying fee in the context of the CPC bidding approach that allows for unlimited variations in the fee paid.

24 An example of the practice can be found on the website of DealTime run by eBay Inc. (2017b).

25 An example is Connexity Inc. (2017d).

26 An example is eBay Inc. (2017b).

Finally, earlier research (Markou, 2011, p. 199) found yet another practice entailing bias, namely the display by some shopping agents of specific products or brands in sections headlined as 'top products', 'featured brands' or 'daily picks', often without an explanation regarding the criteria used to choose those products and, effectively, a disclosure as to whether they were paid or not. Around the same time, the GB OFT (2012, p. 20) also referred to such practices, providing a hypothetical example referring to the "Offer of the Week!". The same issue, specifically in relation to "features such as best buys and editor's picks" has also been raised in regard to shopping agents comparing financial products (Resolution Foundation, 2007, p. 3). The anecdotal research of the present author suggests that the practice is no longer widespread on shopping agent platforms, but it is not extinct either.[27] As shopping agents often act as intermediaries *not* selling any products themselves, any commercial intent behind such practices is not apparent, unless clearly disclosed. Without relevant disclosure, consumers may perceive them as objective recommendations of a third party, namely the shopping agent, possessing extensive knowledge of the market.

2.2.2.1.5 OTHER CHARACTERISTICS ON WHICH DISCLOSURE IS WARRANTED

Important information that needs to be provided to consumers, thereby enabling them to assess the shopping agent and decide whether to use it and how, is not confined to limitations of the service but extends to the number and, perhaps, the names of participating merchants as well as to instructions of use and an explanation of important features, such as the availability of the option to sort results by price, average rating or alphabetically.[28]

Market coverage is officially acknowledged as important (Great Britain OFT, 2012, pp. 14–15, 20) and indeed, the smaller it is, the more the consumer may want to extend its research to other websites. Moreover, research suggests that the number of merchants searched by the shopping agent has implications on the average price offered by them on the agent platform (Iyer and Pazgal, 2003, pp. 92–97, 100). This information is often omitted by relevant platform providers (ECME Consortium, 2013, p. 229). The names of participating merchants are also important, as the information can enable consumers to check whether particular stores are covered and, more generally, to evaluate the quality of the agent service. Unsurprisingly, Iyer and Pazgal (2003, p. 90) confirm that the reputation of the participating merchants has implications on the popularity of the agent service. Some agents provide this information through making available a 'store directory',[29] something that can also substantiate common representations about the agent searching hundreds or thousands of merchants.

A proper explanation of features, such as the sorting of results by reference to various criteria like price and merchant rating, is also important.[30] Not only does it enable the

27 Mona, a shopping assistant, offers the 'Daily Top 20', which "brings you 20 of the best promotions daily that match your personal style" (Apple Store, 2017).

28 Without information on how the agent works or how it should be used, consumers may not use it properly and, therefore, fail to reach the best possible purchase decision through it. For example, a consumer aware of the option to sort search results alphabetically, and therefore objectively, will certainly be in a better position to avoid any biases.

29 An example is Connexity (2017e).

30 This has been recognized as one of the 'key principles for comparison tools' developed by a multi-stakeholder tool on comparison tools for the European Commission (2016c, p.125).

consumer to make correct and effective use of the agent service[31] but also it allows the consumer an 'escape route' from the biased default rankings discussed previously.[32] Therefore, those agents especially, which do not offer the possibility of re-sorting results and do not use a ranking-by-price default either acutely need to clearly reveal their possible lack of impartiality to consumers or clearly, explain their business model. The present author (Markou, 2011, p. 185) has elsewhere noted shortcomings in the information practices utilized by agent providers who *do* provide the option of manually re-sorting results. These could explain earlier research findings according to which "most customers did not use this option, whether from lack of ability or time" (Riemer and Lehrke, 2009, p. 73). The least satisfactory practice identified, then, involved the clickable word 'price' placed at the top of the search results' table; a click on it was sorting results by price, yet there was nothing indicating this purpose of the 'price' word or even its clickable form. Fortunately, the said practice is not currently widespread, and many shopping agents use the phrase 'sort by' before the various sorting options, thus making the relevant possibility apparent.

More generally, as it arises from the preceding discussion, the material information regarding the shopping agent service, its limitations and characteristics must not just *exist* on the platform but must effectively be communicated to consumers. Hiding it behind hidden links or links addressed to merchants or advertisers should not qualify as sufficient provision of the said information.[33] Moreover, because shopping agents are forums on which consumers spend time actively considering the conclusion of contracts, the information relating to their service and its characteristics is not enough to be given at the early stage at which the consumer is offered the service and contemplates using it. As has been shown, most of the said information must in fact be provided *while* the consumer is actually using the platform and therefore, *after* she has already taken the decision to do so. This has important ramifications on the appropriateness of a possible legal response that is *exhausted* to *pre-contractual* information duties, as is explained in more detail in the following section.[34]

2.2.2.2 Automated marketplaces

The lack of sufficient information regarding the platform service poses an even more serious risk in the context of automated marketplaces, which go beyond merely influencing the decision of the consumer and actually form that decision on her behalf, thereby altering her legal status. Unsurprisingly, therefore, it has troubled commentators not only in the specific context of automated marketplaces (Brazier et al., 2003a, p. 24; CIRSFID, NRCCL and FIDAL, 2006, p. 112; Heckman and Wobbrock, 1999, p. 101) but also in relation to digital products in general. Europe Economics (2011, p. 57), for example, identifies the lack of information as one of the main sources of consumer detriment arising from the use of digital content or services.

31 Experiments have shown that significantly more consumers have chosen the best deal when the results have been ranked by reference to price or store rating than when they were ranked randomly (ECME Consortium, 2013, pp. 214, 216).

32 See supra at pp. 26–27

33 It is widely accepted that the prevailing practice of signalling the presence of crucial information behind microscopic links at the very bottom of websites should not be considered acceptable (Gautrais, 2003–2004, p. 196; CIRSFID, NRCCL and FIDAL, 2006, p. 58).

34 Infra at pp. 36–37, 51

The pieces of information necessary to be communicated to consumers for the purposes of evaluating and effectively and/or correctly using an automated marketplace are largely the same with those discussed in the context of shopping agents. Instructions and guidance regarding platform use and features, including features enhancing security and privacy, are necessary to reduce the risk of consumer omissions or mistakes possibly leading to software agent failures – namely, contracts with unreliable merchants, mistaken or unintended contracts and privacy violations. Thus, though security and privacy can be seen as a separate source of consumer detriment (European Economics, 2011, p. iv), it is not entirely distinct from the failure to provide vital information about the platform service. Information on the business model of the automated marketplace is also important, as it has ramifications on its impartiality and, in effect, on the number and quality of merchants that are accessible through it, as earlier illustrated by reference to shopping agents.[35]

Information on service limitations, such as incomplete information considered and the non-vetting of merchant participants, is crucial, too. One additional limitation specific to automated marketplaces is the discrimination that may exist against certain consumer users. Recall that a marketplace may be open to heterogeneous agents possessing increased capabilities[36] or to *both* human consumers and speedier (and more efficient) (Graham-Rowe, 2001; Kephart, 2002, pp. 7208–7210; Vytelingum et al., 2005, p. 6) consumer software agents.[37] It may also allow for the option to customize marketplace-provided agents using programming, thus giving them an extra advantage.[38] When consumers decide to use a marketplace, they may ignore these possibilities and, in effect, the possibility of other users managing to take up the 'best' offers owing to them using software with increased capabilities. Consumers should be enabled to make an informed choice regarding whether they wish to participate in a given marketplace and/or the type of software agent to use. Similarly, consumers should know that a marketplace is open to both humans and (more efficient) agents.

The examination of (commercialized) shopping agents against this need for 'information' provision revealed that important information is often omitted and/or provided in a piecemeal fashion across various and often 'hidden' or unsuitable sections of the platform.[39] The situation may not be different in relation to (future) commercialized automated marketplaces.

2.3 Marketing representations and information on limitations and characteristics: the EU legal response

2.3.1 General

EU law is notorious for the significance it attaches to the provision of information to consumers (Howells, 2005, p. 351) and, indeed, several Directives impose information duties on traders. The E-Commerce Directive (ECD) and the Consumer Rights Directive (CRD), amongst others, require that certain information be provided to consumers before contract conclusion. The Unfair Commercial Practices Directive (UCPD) imposes further information duties and, more generally, controls the quality of any representations made not only before contract

35 Supra p. 29
36 Supra p. 12
37 Supra p. 13
38 Ibid.
39 Supra Chapter 2.2.2.1

conclusion but also during product promotion and even supply. The latter is of particular importance given that as already emphasized, information may mostly be needed while the consumer utilizes the platform service. The Services Directive (SD) also contains certain information duties. The main question is twofold: are these Directives applicable to the relevant platforms and, if yes, do they afford the necessary solutions in the particular context? This question is answered in the following section by reference to each of the aforementioned Directives. It should be noted that the Proposed Directive on better enforcement and modernisation of EU consumer protection rules, Article 2(4) (European Commission, 2018a) seeks to impose further information duties, specifically on online marketplace providers, yet those are only partially relevant to the issues under discussion and moreover, they are not intended to apply to platforms, such as shopping agents, which do not host contract conclusion.[40]

2.3.2 E-Commerce Directive (ECD)

Being provided at a distance, through electronic means and at the request of service recipients, shopping agents and automated marketplaces clearly qualify as 'information society services',[41] and are, thus, subject to the E-Commerce Directive.[42] The particular measure does not however concern itself with the accuracy or fairness of online marketing representations. The only relevant provision to this issue is Article 6, which refers to commercial communications constituting or forming part of an information society service. As it arises from its wording, however,[43] this provision does not purport to tackle the issue of misleading exaggerations in such communications.

40 See the definition of the term 'online marketplace' in Article 2(1) of the Proposed Directive.

41 The relevant definition was contained in Article 1(2), Directive 98/34/EC of the European Parliament and of the Council laying down a procedure for the provision of information in the field of technical standards and regulations and of rules on Information Society services as amended by Directive 98/48/EC (the Technical Standards Directive) and now in Article 1(1)(b) of the Directive (EU) 2015/1535 of the European Parliament and of the Council of 9 September 2015 laying down a procedure for the provision of information in the field of technical regulations and of rules on Information Society services, which has replaced Directive 98/34/EC. The relevant provision provides as follows: a 'service' is "an information society service, that is to say, any service normally provided for remuneration, at a distance, by electronic means and at the individual request of a recipient of services. For the purposes of this definition: – 'at a distance' means that the service is provided without the parties being simultaneously present, – 'by electronic means' means that the service is sent initially and received at its destination by means of electronic equipment for the processing (including digital compression) and storage of data, and entirely transmitted, conveyed and received by wire, by radio, by optical means or by other electromagnetic means, – 'at the individual request of a recipient of services' means that the service is provided through the transmission of data on individual request".

42 Article 1, ECD.

43 Article 6, ECD reads as follows: "In addition to other information requirements established by Community law, Member States shall ensure that commercial communications which are part of, or constitute, an information society service comply at least with the following conditions: (a) the commercial communication shall be clearly identifiable as such; (b) the natural or legal person on whose behalf the commercial communication is made shall be clearly identifiable; (c) promotional offers, such as discounts, premiums and gifts, where permitted in the Member State where the service provider is established, shall be clearly identifiable as such, and the conditions which are to be met to qualify for them shall be easily accessible and be presented clearly and unambiguously; (d) promotional competitions or games, where permitted in the Member State where the service provider is established, shall be clearly identifiable as such, and the conditions for participation shall be easily accessible and be presented clearly and unambiguously".

Neither is the issue regarding the lack of information on limitations and other characteristics of the relevant platform services fully tackled by the ECD. The measure contains significant information duties, specifically in Article 5[44] and Article 10,[45] yet these do not require (all) the pieces of information regarding the relevant platform services, which have earlier been illustrated as vital. Thus, the possible assistance of the Directive in relation to this issue is confined to the effect of Article 6(a)[46] regarding a duty to disclose the 'shopping agent' business model, particularly through the sufficient identification of paid listings as such,[47] as is later illustrated.[48]

Indeed, Article 5 mandates the provision of information as to the identity, whereabouts and other details of the provider,[49] which cannot assist consumers in understanding its service and deciding whether and how to use it. Article 10(1)[50] is similarly unsuitable for the particular purpose. Article 10(1)(a) requires instructions on how to conclude a contract with the provider, (in this context the shopping agent and automated marketplace provider) rather than on how its service should be used. It is true, however, that in the context of automated marketplaces, the provider burdened with the relevant information duty will also be the merchant using the marketplace to sell his products.[51] Article 10(1)(a) therefore effectively requires the provision of guidance on how the marketplace should be used to conclude a contract, and the same may be true of Article 10(1)(c) that requires information on how errors can be identified and corrected before contract conclusion. In this respect, Cevenini, Contissa and Laukyte (2007, p. 228) are correct to observe that Article 10 "contributes to the use of SAs [software agents] in contract-making because it makes it mandatory to specify the functioning of SAs".[52] Clearly, however, in this particular context,

44 "1. Member States shall ensure that the service provider shall render easily, directly and permanently accessible to the recipients of the service and competent authorities, at least the following information: a) the name of the service provider; b) the geographical address at which the service provider is established; c) the details of the service provider, including his electronic mail address, which allow him to be contacted rapidly and communicated with in a direct and effective manner; d) where the service provider is registered in a trade or similar public register, the trade register in which the service provider is entered and his registration number, or equivalent means of identification in that register; e) where the activity is subject to an authorisation scheme, the particulars of the relevant supervisory authority; f) as concerns the regulated professions: . . . g) where the service provider undertakes an activity that is subject to VAT, the identification number referred to in Article 22(1) of the sixth Council Directive 77/388/EEC of 17 May 1977".

45 "1. Member States shall ensure, except when otherwise agreed by parties who are not consumers, that at least the following information is given by the service provider clearly, comprehensibly and unambiguously and prior to the order being placed by the recipient of the service: (a) the different technical steps to follow to conclude the contract; (b) whether or not the concluded contract will be filed by the service provider and whether it will be accessible; (c) the technical means for identifying and correcting input errors prior to the placing of the order; (d) the languages offered for the conclusion of the contract. 2. Member States shall ensure that, except when otherwise agreed by parties who are not consumers, the service provider indicates any relevant codes of conduct to which he subscribes and information on how those codes can be consulted electronically. 3. Contract terms and general conditions provided to the recipient must be made available in a way that allows him to store and reproduce them".

46 Supra n. 43

47 On this issue, see supra at pp. 26–28

48 Infra at pp. 34–36

49 Supra n. 44

50 Supra n. 45

51 This is explained in more detail later, see infra Chapter 6 p. 189

52 'SAs' stands for software agents.

it effectively mandates the said information *after* the consumer has decided to use the platform and while she is using it. Thus, it can serve the purpose of ensuring correct use but not also the purpose of enabling consumers to assess the service and decide whether to use it. Moreover, Articles 10(1)(a) and (c) are confined to information on how to conclude a contract and could not therefore also be taken to require information on the use of additional features such a reputation mechanism or any privacy-enhancing tools. They are therefore too narrow for the information needs of consumers using automated marketplaces and totally unsuitable in relation to shopping agents which do *not* allow for contract conclusion at all.

Article 10(2) refers to codes of conduct to which the provider subscribes,[53] which again concerns the quality of the provider, and only indirectly and very generally that of its service. Likewise, the duty in Article 10(3)[54] regarding the format of the general terms and conditions does not obviously serve the aforementioned "understanding, assessing and deciding" purpose because it does not touch upon the *content* of those conditions. Thus, Article 10 of the ECD has clearly not been devised to respond to the 'information' need existing in relation to the relevant platforms and, as such, tackles the issue only subtly and indirectly.

However, the ECD – specifically through Article 6(a), requiring that commercial communications that are part of, or constitute, an information society service are clearly identifiable as such – specifically addresses part of the relevant information need, particularly its part referring to the need to identify *paid* merchant listings as such.

A 'commercial communication' is defined broadly by Article 2(f):

> "commercial communication": any form of communication designed to promote, directly or indirectly, the goods, services or image of a company, organisation or person pursuing a commercial, industrial or craft activity or exercising a regulated profession. The following do not in themselves constitute commercial communications: . . . communications relating to the goods, services or image of the company . . . compiled in an independent manner, particularly when this is without financial consideration.

Preferred (top) listings and sponsored links have been explained to be *by nature* biased (as opposed to independently compiled) and also offered in exchange for consideration.[55] They are not, therefore, exempted from the definition of 'commercial communications' and, as they clearly promote the goods or services of the merchants featured therein, they clearly qualify as such. Top (or featured) products, shopping picks and product recommendations[56] similarly constitute 'commercial communications' (unless, of course, they are compiled in accordance with objective criteria such as popularity). Do the rest of the listings, namely standard listings qualify as 'commercial communications' too?

The term 'communication' is not defined in the ECD, yet even if it is restrictively taken to mean "information exchanged or conveyed between a finite number of parties",[57] *any* listings, links and picks on shopping agent platforms, being essentially web content in most cases, will qualify as 'communications. Indeed, though web content is ultimately accessible to the indefinite number of visitors, it is actually conveyed to each consumer user who has

53 Supra n. 45.
54 Ibid.
55 Supra pp. 24, 26
56 Supra p. 29
57 This is how the term 'communication' is defined by Article 2(d) of the E-Privacy Directive.

requested it, specifically by clicking the 'search' button causing the server hosting the website to return relevant search results. This is, in fact, because of the HTTP protocol which enables and governs communication on the WWW.[58] Web content thus comprises information conveyed between a finite number of parties, namely the website owner (in this context, the 'shopping agent' provider) and each consumer who conducts searches on the relevant platform, thus requesting the 'search results' content, including any preferred listings.

Moreover, as shopping agents are clearly 'information society services',[59] these commercial communications, being displayed on said platforms, are part of an information society service and are therefore subject to the 'identification' requirement of Article 6(a). Accordingly, they must clearly be identified as being *paid* (as opposed to organic and neutral) listings.

It follows from the previous analysis of the relevant definition that *even standard listings* qualify as 'commercial communications' subject to Article 6(a), ECD, where the 'shopping agent' provider receives a fee from the merchants featured therein. Consequently, standard listings must also be identified as being 'commercial communications' so that consumers are prevented from perceiving them as neutral results provided by an independent (and impartial) third-party intermediary. In this respect, Article 6(a) indirectly addresses the related issue concerning the possibly misleading nature of the term '*sponsored*' on shopping agent platforms, where *all* links or results are sponsored (or paid for).[60] The identification of standard listings as paid would obviously prevent any confusion possibly caused by the *selective* use of the term 'sponsored' (only) by reference to certain other links displayed on the relevant platform.

One could envisage compliance with the relevant legal obligation through the display of a clear statement saying that *all* listings are paid for. Accordingly, Article 6(a) seems to respond well to the earlier illustrated information need on shopping agent platforms, specifically its part concerning the disclosure of information regarding the agent business model.[61] Moreover, being specifically drafted as an '*identification*' (as opposed to a more general '*information*') duty, Article 6(a) effectively also addresses the question of the timing that the relevant information must be provided; it is indeed difficult for the said duty to be accepted as being complied with by the provision of the information at any place other than the 'search results' page on which the merchant listings are displayed. As previously stated, it is important that such information is provided while consumers utilize the platform having previously decided to do so rather than at some pre-contractual stage (or while contemplating using it).

Importantly, however, as a result of the fact that *all* listings on shopping agent platforms (preferred and standard) qualify as 'commercial communications', there is one aspect of the issue of bias that cannot be addressed by the 'identification' duty of Article 6(a). More specifically, as the said provision effectively requires disclosure of the commercial nature of communications *in general*, it does not obviously provide for any differentiation between *various kinds* of commercial communications and, effectively, for the separation of preferred listings from standard ones. It is of course true that when merchants are charged by the platform provider in accordance with the CPC bidding system, it may not be possible to separate listings of merchants who pay more from those of merchants who pay a lower fee or

58 For more on HTTP (and what happens behind the scenes) when users interact with the web, see Lifewire.com (2019).

59 See supra p. 32

60 Supra p. 28

61 Supra pp. 27–28

otherwise, identify the former as 'preferred' by attaching to them a relevant seal.[62] The particular purpose could be equally achieved by providing a statement explaining the top or higher position of certain listings in search results by reference to the payment of a higher fee by the merchant featured therein. For the reason just explained, however, Article 6(a) is not detailed enough to give rise to such specific and detailed 'identification' duties, and in this respect, its response to the issue of shopping agent biases cannot be considered as complete.

Finally, it may be useful to note that Article 6(a), ECD is not explicitly worded in the form of an obligation burdening the provider of the 'information society service' consisting of or containing commercial communications.[63] Thus, it is easy to consider the Article 6(a) obligation to be enforceable both against, the said provider, namely the provider of the shopping agent who receives payment and the merchant featured in listings appearing on the relevant platform, who pays for them. It should also be noted that the fact that the service of the shopping agent is not paid for by consumer users is totally irrelevant, as it arises from Recital 18, ECD and relevant CJEU case law.[64]

2.3.3 Consumer Rights Directive (CRD) and Services Directive (SD)

The CRD regulates, amongst others, distance (including online) contracts, and, as such, it focuses on pre-contractual and contractual practices employed by traders. Accordingly, the focus of the said measure is *not* on consumer protection *post-contractually* and certainly, not on information provision *during the utilization* of a service. It does impose rich *pre-contractual* information duties, which certainly strengthen the position of the consumer, but these are inapplicable to shopping agents and are too narrow to address the previously discussed information needs of consumers on automated marketplaces. Though it contains some obligations referring to the point in time that the consumer is actually using or interacting with an online store,[65] those obligations are not relevant to platforms that do not allow for contract conclusion, such as shopping agents, or do not involve the consumer's personal participation, such as automated marketplaces. The issues of accuracy and quality of marketing representations are dealt with by the Consumer Rights Directive (CRD), albeit indirectly.

The main information duty provision of the Distance Selling Directive (DSD), the predecessor of the CRD, was Article 4(1).[66] However, it did not specifically require the provision of information on limitations and risks or guidance on correct use.[67] Though it expressly acknowledged that consumers contracting from distance are unable "actually to . . . ascertain *the nature of the*

62 This has been explained earlier, see supra p. 27
63 The wording of the said provision targets the commercial communications as such rather than the relevant 'information society service' provider; see Article 6(a), ECD, supra n. 43
64 *C-291/13, Sotiris Papasavvas v O Fileleftheros Dimosia Etaireia Ltd and Others, 11 September 2014.*
65 These are Articles 8(2), 8(3) and 22, CRD.
66 "In good time prior to the conclusion of any distant contract, the consumer shall be provided with the following information: (a) the identity of the supplier and, in the case of contracts requiring payment in advance, his address; (b) the main characteristics of the goods or services; (c) the price of the goods or services including all taxes; (d) delivery costs, where appropriate; (e) the arrangements for payment, delivery or performance; (f) the existence of a right of withdrawal, except in the cases referred to in Article 6 (3); (g) the cost of using the means of distance communication, where it is calculated other than at the basic rate; (h) the period for which the offer or the price remains valid; (i) where appropriate, the minimum duration of the contract in the case of contracts for the supply of products or services to be performed permanently or recurrently".
67 Ibid.

service provided before concluding the contract",[68] it was clear from the nature of the mandated information that the principal concern was that the consumer was made aware of the price in full and that there would be no surprises regarding costs and contract performance. Apart from the identity and other details of the supplier mandated in Article 4(1)(a), the only exception was the information on the right of withdrawal mandated by Article 4(1)(f) and on the main product or service characteristics required by Article 4(1)(b). As regards the former, the 'withdrawal' right[69] may be of limited use to the consumer of *free* online services,[70] such as the relevant platforms, where no price is paid. Moreover, the first exception to the right contained in Article 6(3) would in most cases be applicable to the relevant platform services anyway.[71] Article 4(1)(b) is the only provision coming close to addressing the earlier-mentioned information needed in the relevant platforms. Yet, it was a very general provision; by merely requiring information on the 'main service characteristics', it did not specifically require information on risks, limitations and correct use, thus leaving too much to individual interpretation.

In any event, Article 4(1), DSD was a pre-contractual duty, i.e., the relevant information was required to be given *before* contract conclusion. It could not thus respond to the information needs of consumers on shopping agent platforms, which, as illustrated, necessitate pertinent information to be provided *while* the platform service is being used. Importantly, the same holds true of the enhanced pre-contractual duties of the CRD, which has replaced the DSD and is currently applicable to automated marketplaces. Similarly, Article 22(1)(j) of the Services Directive (SD), requires that service providers (including information society service providers) make available to service recipients the information on "the main features of the service, if not already apparent from the context". It clearly arises from Article 22(4), however, that Article 22 (1) is a mere *pre-contractual* information duty, too; the required information must be provided amongst others "in good time before conclusion of the contract or, where there is no written contract, before the service is provided".

Article 5(1), DSD[72] which required that certain information be provided in *durable form* at the latest *after* contract conclusion was an 'information format', rather than an 'information content' obligation. Thus, it mainly sought to ensure that the consumer would receive the information of Article 4(1), DSD in durable form (such as in an e-mail) so that he could readily access it, if needed, after contract conclusion. Obviously, even if the said provision was requiring information on risks, limitations and correct use, it would still not meet the

68 Recital 14, emphasis added.

69 It is discussed in more detail later, infra at pp. 69 and Chapter 6 pp. 183–184

70 Note that it may be of some importance however, when the consumer paid no price but provided personal data instead.

71 Provision of online cases normally begins instantly, and Article 6(3) first ident exempted contracts of services when service provision began with consumer consent prior to the lapse of the seven-day period within which the withdrawal right had to be exercised. See also Subirana and Bain (2005, pp. 168–169).

72 "The consumer must receive written confirmation or confirmation in another durable medium available and accessible to him of the information referred to in Article 4(1)(a) to (f), in good time during the performance of the contract, and at the latest at the time of delivery where goods not for delivery to third parties are concerned, unless the information has already been given to the consumer prior to conclusion of the contract in writing or on another durable medium available and accessible to him. In any event the following must be provided: - written information on the conditions and procedures for exercising the right of withdrawal, within the meaning of Article 6, including the cases referred to in the first indent of Article 6(3), - the geographical address of the place of business of the supplier to which the consumer may address any complaints, - information on after-sales services and guarantees which exist, - the conditions for cancelling the contract, where it is of unspecified duration or a duration exceeding one year".

information need relating to the relevant platforms. As explained, that need entails the provision of information to consumers not so much in durable form or any other format but at an appropriate time, this being the time during which consumers actually utilize the service.

Perhaps most importantly, the DSD as a whole was probably inapplicable to the shopping agent platforms. This is more clearly so in relation to web-based shopping agents. It applied to distance *contracts*, specifically "contracts concerning goods or services"[73], whereas shopping agents, unlike automated marketplaces which will normally require registration, are *not* normally provided under a click-wrap agreement requiring a positive action (such as clicking an "I agree" button) for the acceptance of the terms of use. Rather, they are offered in the same way as traditional search engines such as Google are offered. This view seems to be reinforced by the European Commission (2014a, p. 64), albeit by reference to the new CRD:

> Since the Directive applies to 'contracts concluded between consumers and traders' . . . it should not apply to online digital content provided by means of broadcasting of information on the internet without the express conclusion of a contract. In itself, access to a website or a download from a website should not be considered a 'contract' for the purposes of the purposes of the Directive.

The position may be different when the shopping agent is app based, mainly because of the consumer having to actively download the relevant app to her device and, probably, being asked to signify agreement with certain terms and conditions. In this case, there would certainly be a contract, yet the applicability of the DSD to shopping agents would remain questionable, and the same holds true of automated marketplaces, too. Indeed, as already explained, both platform services are likely to be provided to consumers for free. Though "contracts concerning goods or services"[74] to which the DSD was applicable did not seem limited to a remunerated service, its provisions revolved very much around 'price'.[75] Moreover, the relevant Directive contained no direct or even indirect indication (or acknowledgement) of its applicability to free services, as the E-Commerce Directive does, for example. The latter measure, which is explicitly applicable to both paid *and* free services,[76] does not include 'price' in the information mandated by its Article 5(1).[77] Instead, its Article 5(2) deals separately with the cases in which a price is involved.

The CRD, which has replaced the DSD, remedies some but not all of these applicability problems in the context of shopping agents and automated marketplaces. It has brought important changes in the way distance contracts are regulated, yet it is applicable to *contracts*[78] meaning that its information duties can be of no use to web-based (as opposed to app-based) shopping agents. This seems to be an illogical result; there seems to be no valid reason behind the consumer being owed certain information when she contemplates using an app-based service but *not* when she contemplates using the same service on the web. Its applicability to *free services* and, thus, to app-based shopping agents and automated marketplaces is less of an issue, yet the matter remains somewhat unclear, as is illustrated in the following. The content of the information duties has been enriched, yet information on risks, limitations and correct use is still

73 Articles 1 and 2(1), DSD.
74 Article 2(1), DSD.
75 With the exception of Articles 9 and 10, all of the substantive provisions of the Directive, i.e., Articles 4–8, contain a reference to price.
76 Recital 18, ECD.
77 Supra n. 44.
78 Article 1, CRD.

not expressly mandated. Relevant Commission guidance, however, facilitates a demanding interpretation of relevant information duties, which is an important step forward. Of course, the information duties of the CRD built upon those existing in the DSD. Accordingly, they remain pre-contractual, and the 'durable medium' information duty that affects the post-contractual stage does not respond to the need to provide information during utilization of the platform service.

The CRD clearly speaks the language of the WWW, thus specifically regulating pre-checked boxes,[79] charges imposed for the use of payment means such as credit cards,[80] 'order submission' buttons[81], digital content[82] and restrictions to acceptable payment means or delivery locations.[83] Most importantly, pre-contractual information duties have become richer and the 'withdrawal' period longer.[84] More specifically, the *nine* pieces of information required by Article 4(1), DSD have now increased to *20* in Article 6(1), CRD. Admittedly, ten of them are expanded versions of the pre-existing ones and most of the additional ones, including, amongst others, the information on the obligation of the consumer to pay for the return of the goods in cases of withdrawal[85] and a reminder of the existence of the legal guarantee[86] do not serve the purpose of enabling consumers to understand the platform services, their risks and limitations and correctly use them, should they decide to do so. However, two newly introduced required pieces of information in conjunction with related guidance issued by the Commission relating to them and the information required by Article 6(1)(a), CRD, namely on "the main characteristics of the goods and services" significantly improve the position of the users of the relevant platform services.

The newly introduced mandated information relates to digital content; the trader must inform consumers about "the functionality, including applicable technical protection measures, of digital content"[87] and "any relevant interoperability of digital content with hardware and software that the trader is aware of or can reasonably be expected to have been aware of".[88] 'Digital content' contracts, as opposed to 'sales contracts'[89] and 'service contracts',[90] are an innovation of the CRD, probably in response to their recent popularity. If the digital content is not supplied on a tangible medium, 'digital content' contracts are neither sales nor service contracts,[91] yet they are nowhere defined in the Directive. 'Digital content' is defined

79 Article 22, CRD. It prohibits securing consumer consent to additional payments through pre-checked boxes.
80 Article 19, CRD. It prohibits charging consumers, fees for the use of 'payment' means higher than those borne by the merchant and charged by the payment service provider.
81 Article 8(2). The consumer should clearly be informed that his order entails an obligation to pay through for example an 'order placement' button labelled with the words 'order with obligation to pay', otherwise, the consumer will not be bound by the contract.
82 Infra pp. 39–40
83 Article 8(3). They must do so "at the latest at the beginning of the ordering process".
84 For the 'withdrawal' right, see infra pp. 69 and Chapter 6 pp. 183–184
85 Article 6(1)(i).
86 Article 6(1)(l).
87 Article 6(1)(r).
88 Article 6(1)(s).
89 Article 2(5): "'sales contract' means any contract under which the trader transfers or undertakes to transfer the ownership of goods to the consumer and the consumer pays or undertakes to pay the price thereof, including any contract having as its object both goods and services".
90 Article 2(6): "'service contract' means any contract other than a sales contract under which the trader supplies or undertakes to supply a service to the consumer and the consumer pays or undertakes to pay the price thereof".
91 Recital 19.

as "data which are produced and supplied in digital form"[92] and includes "computer programs, applications, games, music, videos or texts, irrespective of whether they are accessed through downloading or streaming".[93] Being software, automated marketplaces would seem to qualify as digital content when downloaded (probably, in the form of apps) to consumer devices. The same is true of app-based shopping agents to which the CRD would also apply, as explained previously.[94] Yet, when are to be accessed on the web perhaps comprising SaaS, that is, 'software as a service' defined by Europe Economics (2011, p. 9) as "software where applications are hosted by a vendor or service provider and made available to customers over a network, typically the internet", the answer to the relevant question is not entirely clear.

Online (or information society) services *in general* are not expressly included in the examples of digital content provided in the CRD. At the same time, such services are not excluded from the definition of 'service contracts' either. Moreover, the recent guidance of the European Commission appears contradictory on whether the provision of information society services (including automated marketplaces) should be considered as coming under a 'service' or a 'digital content' contract. On the one hand, it would seem to suggest that a contract for access to a website would be a 'digital content', rather than a service contract (European Commission, 2014a, p. 64). Europe Economics (2011, p. 9), in a Commission-funded study, defines 'digital content' as every service received by consumers online, which reinforces the view that digital content encompasses online services. The Proposed Regulation on a European Sales Law takes a similar stance by defining digital content as excluding online services, such as banking and electronic communication services, *but not* other online services.[95]

On the other hand, however, the European Commission (2014a, p. 51) refers to *paid* subscriptions to social networks, online weather services or online newsletters as "services that are provided by electronic means", i.e., as 'information society services' and discusses them in reference to the right of withdrawal in the context of service contracts. It would seem, therefore, that the answer *cannot* lie with the type of the product (or content) involved,[96] and, indeed, the difference between digital content made available online and online services is blurred; it is perhaps not a coincidence that the combined term "digital content services" (Loos and Mak, 2012, p. 16; Europe Economics, 2011) is often used.

The relevant answer seems to lie instead with whether the contract involves a remunerated (or paid) product or not. Indeed, Recital 19, CRD states that a 'digital content' contract is one that cannot be classified as a service or a sales contract. 'Digital content' contracts, unlike service (and sales ones),[97] do *not* involve a 'price' element, as they are nowhere in the Directive defined by reference to the payment of a price; the European Commission (2014a, p. 64) also confirms that the Directive applies to *free* online digital content. It must follow that contracts for *free* online services (including contracts for the use of automated marketplaces) do not qualify as 'service contracts' and are therefore bound to be classified as 'digital content' contracts.

92 Article 2(11).
93 Recital 19.
94 Supra p. 38
95 Proposed Regulation on a European Sales Law, Article 2(j).
96 See however Markou (2017a, p. 188) and Recital 21 of 2019 Directive on certain aspects concerning contracts for the supply of digital content and digital services (drawing a distinction between digital content and digital services based on the continuity of the involvement of the provider in the supply).
97 See supra n. 89 and n. 90.

Provided that this reasoning is correct,[98] being applicable to app-based shopping agents and automated marketplaces, the information duties specifically referring to digital content require the provision of information on functionality and interoperability with hardware and software.[99] The European Commission (2014a, p. 69) acknowledges a link between these two newly introduced pieces of information and the piece of information required by Article 6(1)(a), CRD, which refers to "the main characteristics of the goods or services, to the extent appropriate to the medium and to the goods or services".[100] The latter applies to digital content, too, and importantly, according to the European Commission (2014a, p. 22), the "detail of the information to be provided depends on the complexity of the product".

Automated marketplaces (and app-based shopping agents, too) are indisputably of (even) greater complexity than other (standard) digital content, which (Loos et al., 2012, p. 12) recognize as complex due to the involvement of inherently complex technology. Their complexity is exasperated by the fact that they are also 'experience products', the characteristics of which can only be ascertained after they are consumed or fully utilized (Laine, 2012 p. 34). Indeed, it seems difficult for consumers fully to understand what exactly it means for software to roam an online (marketplace) system, find merchants, close deals with them and do so satisfactorily. No matter how clearly this is explained beforehand, consumers would probably have to repeatedly use the said software in order fully to understand its capabilities. As Rayna (2008, pp. 28–29) writes "the value of digital goods in [*sic*] not necessarily fully revealed after the initial episode of consumption, and some digital goods, such as music, software or video games, generally need to be experienced several times before their true value becomes known to the consumer". In the specific context of automated marketplaces, the average, programming-illiterate consumer has no (technical) knowledge on how relevant software works (or could work) and/or how their quality and level of performance can be affected by factors such as the possibility of software-customization available to other users. He would probably have difficulty in assessing whether the it performs satisfactorily even after repeated use. A similar argument can be made in relation to app-based shopping agents and their own peculiar characteristics, such as their lack of impartiality. Doubtless, the relevant platforms comprise digital content of high and peculiar complexity.

The fact therefore that the nature or extent of the information required on the main characteristics of the service under Article 6(1)(a), CRD depends on the complexity of the

98 The 2019 Directive on certain aspects concerning contracts for the supply of digital content and digital services retains the 'digital content' definition of the CRD but introduces the notion of a 'digital service'. The latter seems to cover web-accessible automated marketplaces (see definition in Article 2(2) of said Directive and infra Chapter 7, pp. 200), something that inevitably makes it somewhat difficult for the particular platform services to be regarded as 'digital content' for the purposes of the CRD. Of course, the 2019 Directive explicitly applies to free services meaning that a digital service contract under said Directive cannot be regarded as a 'service contract' under the CRD. Though another draft measure, namely the Proposed Directive on better enforcement and modernisation of EU consumer protection rules (Article 2) seeks to expand the definition of 'service contracts' under the CRD to include 'digital service contracts', this will not bring automated marketplaces within the definition of 'service contracts' in all cases, as the provider may not use consumer-provided personal data for purposes other than simply to provide the services.

99 Supra p. 39

100 This effectively means that even if due the upcoming developments described above (supra n. 96 and n 98.), platforms are to be regarded as 'services' rather than 'digital content', there will be no problem deriving the required detailed information duties in their case. Their source will however only be Article 6(1)(a), CRD.

service[101] is a desirable clarification offered by the CRD (and the relevant Commission guidance). This is because it obviously allows for a ***demanding interpretation*** of the relevant information duty that takes into account the peculiarity and high complexity of app-based shopping agents and automated marketplaces. It can thus be taken to require information on risks, limitations and correct use, thereby adequately responding to the earlier-illustrated information need in the particular context, at least during the pre-contractual (pre-use) stage.

This purpose could further be assisted by the CRD, specifically by the aforementioned newly introduced duties referring to the functionality and interoperability of digital content. While the latter will mostly be relevant in the case of downloadable (app-based) platforms,[102] the former (on functionality) is much broader and thus, relevant in all cases, including where the platforms are offered and accessed on the web. In its guidance, the European Commission (2014a, pp. 67–68) offers a long list of information items that could come under the term 'functionality', including the language of the content, whether the trader will maintain or update the product, the need for an internet connection and also limitations of use such as any limits on private copies, whether there are any restrictions depending on the location of the consumer and any additional functionalities that have to be paid for. Several of them could evidently assist the consumer also in the case of app-based shopping agents and automated marketplaces but what is more important is that the list is not exhaustive and the trader should decide upon what information he should provide to comply with his relevant duty "according to a particular product's characteristics" (European Commission, 2014a, p. 67). Similarly to Article 6(1)(a), the duty of Article 6(1)(r) on 'digital content' functionality is perfectly eligible to an interpretation requiring app-based shopping agents and automated marketplace providers to assist consumers in understanding and correctly use their product, specifically, by offering information on any safety or 'search result sorting' features available and/or on any limitations regarding its capabilities owing to its design and/or any existing possibilities of customization or participation of heterogeneous contracting software. Importantly, according to CJEU case law, if the provided information is wrong or misleading, the information will be deemed as omitted in breach of the relevant information duties.[103] Thus, albeit indirectly, the CRD also tackles the issue of misleading marketing representations regarding app-based shopping agents and automated marketplaces.

It follows that the CRD brings about a significant improvement in the way EU law responds to the information needs of consumers in automated marketplaces and app-based shopping agents. Recall, however, that the relevant legal response only covers the pre-contractual phase and is therefore not complete given that, as earlier illustrated, the relevant need entails information provision not only pre-contractually but also ***during consumers actually making use*** of the platform.

The relevant 'gap' is not filled in by Article 8(7)(a), CRD. Similarly to the pre-existing Article 5, DSD, discussed previously,[104] the said provision requires traders to provide consumers with confirmation of the information required by Article 6(1) on a 'durable medium' "at the latest . . . before the performance of the service begins" and though not referring to

101 Supra p. 41

102 "Interoperability can be described by giving information on devices that the content can be used with; where applicable this should include information about the necessary operating system and additional software, including the version number, and hardware, such as processor speed and graphics card features" (European Commission, 2014, p. 68).

103 *C-412/06, Annelore Hamilton v Volksbank Filder eG, 10/4/2008, para. 35.*

104 Supra at pp. 37, 69

digital content, it is applicable to digital content, too (European Commission, 2014a, p. 36). Since a 'durable medium' is any medium enabling "the consumer to store the information for as long as it is necessary for him to protect his interests stemming from his relationship with the trader",[105] this obligation inevitably ensures that consumers will have access to the information assisting them to understand and correctly use the agent *after* contract conclusion.[106] Yet, the platform provider will be able to comply with the obligation either by sending the consumer an e-mail, as is most likely to be the case in relation to digital content, or by uploading the information to the consumers' private account on the platform (European Commission, 2014a, p. 36). Evidently, therefore, this obligation does not go as far as to require that the information be provided in real time, i.e. while the consumer is interacting with the platform and at the place she actually needs it.

2.3.4 Unfair Commercial Practices Directive (UCPD)

The Unfair Commercial Practices Directive constitutes a significant addition to the consumer *acquis* relating to the information provided to consumers. Most importantly, it controls the content, quality, format and even timing of that information, as is demonstrated in the following. Thus, it directly addresses both misleading marketing representations regarding shopping agents and automated marketplaces *and* the earlier-illustrated consumer information need on such platforms. Despite the (possible) absence of a contract under which shopping agents are made available to consumers, the UCPD is applicable to their case, nevertheless. What is more is that the particular measure will be shown to require the provision of information not only pre-contractually *but also* while the platform is being used so that the consumer will effectively receive it exactly when she needs it. Thus, it goes a long way towards filling in the gaps left by the ECD and CRD. Though, in relation to certain information such as on security and privacy features, it may have to be complemented by the data protection regime, it can safely be argued that because of the UCPD, EU law responds adequately to the risks associated with shopping agents and automated marketplaces currently under discussion.

The UCPD prohibits unfair commercial practices, specifically through establishing three tools for controlling their quality and more generally, fairness:

> First, there is a general clause designed to catch all practices that are not in accord with honest commercial practices (good faith) and which are likely to distort consumer economic behaviour. Secondly, the Directive specifically prohibits misleading actions, that is, the provision of false or inaccurate information on various elements of a transaction such as the product price. It also prohibits misleading omissions, that is, the failure to provide information that consumers need to take an informed decision as well as aggressive practices entailing undue influence, coercion or harassment. A third tool of fairness control is a black list of commercial practices which the Directive renders automatically unfair.
>
> (Markou, 2014, p. 554)

105 Recital 23. It also offers the examples, amongst others, of paper, e-mails and CDs.

106 The primary purpose is to enable consumers to pursue their rights against the trader, hence, amongst others, the emphasis placed by the European Commission (2104a, p. 36) on the need to provide the relevant confirmation before the expiry of the right of withdrawal period.

A 'commercial practice' is defined very broadly as "any act, omission, course of conduct or representation, commercial communication including advertising and marketing, by a trader, directly connected with the promotion, sale or supply of a product to consumers".[107] It arises that the subject matter of the UCPD is not confined to pre-contractual practices but extends to all practices directly connected with *the supply* of a product to consumers. Accordingly, information provided during the supply and hence, the utilization of the relevant platforms by consumers are covered. Moreover, the relevant platforms are gateways to products offered by other traders, namely participating merchants. Thus, any information given or omitted by the platform provider *while* the consumer utilizes the platform, thereby considering a purchase, is bound to be 'directly connected' with the promotion or sale of a product to consumers, thus constituting a 'commercial practice'. The term 'product' is also widely defined as "any goods or service including immovable property, rights and obligations",[108] thereby encompassing both the platform service as such and the standard consumer goods offered by other traders through it.

The UCPD prohibits unfair commercial practices including misleading and aggressive practices.[109]Apart from the specific examples of misleading commercial practices listed in the Annex to the Directive, a misleading commercial practice is also any practice that contains false information or in any another way is likely to deceive consumers in relation to a long list of elements mainly referring to the product (such its existence or risks), the trader (such as his commitments or sponsorships) or the terms of the transaction (such as price or delivery arrangements). This is so according to Article 6(1), UCPD which also states that such practice is misleading for the purposes of the UCPD only if it causes or is likely to cause consumers to take a 'transactional decision' they would not have reached *but for* the false (or inaccurate) information.

The list of factors in Article 6(1), UCPD contains more than 40 elements grouped under seven broad categories (a)–(g) and thus effectively "sets out the ways in which actions by traders could deceive consumers" (European Commission, 2003a, p. 14). Being so detailed, it allows enforcers enough room to assess a commercial practice and decide upon its misleading nature by taking into account the product type and all the circumstances. Thus, where false (or inaccurate) information is provided regarding the capabilities, security features, limitations and business model of shopping agents and automated marketplaces, that could result to a finding of a misleading commercial practice. There is indeed in Article 6(1) specific reference to false or deceptive information relating to "the . . . nature of the product",[110] "its benefits, risks, execution . . . usage . . . or the results to be expected from its use"[111] and "the motives for the commercial practice".[112] As already seen, the ECD and the CRD do not make explicit reference to such elements. The European Commission (2003a, p. 14) states that "it will be misleading to deceive consumers about the results to be expected from the product, such as weight loss . . . or enhanced performance", yet the 'expected results' element would obviously also cover representations that software agents can strike the best deal in an automated marketplace or that a shopping agent searches all online stores. Similarly, the 'commercial practice motives' element is broad enough to cover not only information on why a sale is made, such as stock clearance, closing down or

107 Article 2(d), UCPD.
108 Article 2(c), UCPD.
109 Article 5(1), UCPD.
110 Article 6(1)(a), UCPD.
111 Article 6(1)(b), UCPD.
112 Article 6(1)(c), UCPD.

damaged stock due to a flood (Ryder et al., 2008, p. 368) but also representations relating to the business model of a promoted shopping agent or automated marketplace. These would clearly cover statements to the effect that the platform provider does not receive a commission or other benefit from merchants participating on the platform. Doubtless, therefore, because of Article 6(1), UCPD, the UCPD successfully tackles the issue of misleading marketing representations relating to the relevant platforms.

What about the broader issue regarding the earlier-illustrated information need of consumers when using the relevant platforms, however? Article 6 addresses false representations and does not impose an information duty. Article 7(1), UCPD, however, expressly deals with 'misleading omissions' deeming as misleading a practice that "omits material information that the average consumer needs, according to the context, to take an informed transactional decision and thereby causes or is likely to cause the average consumer to take a transactional decision that he would not have taken otherwise". The provision does not comprise "a positive duty to disclose" (European Commission, 2003a, p. 8) or "a comprehensive list of information to be positively disclosed in all circumstances" (European Commission, 2003a, p. 14), as that would probably be very onerous for traders (European Commission, 2003a, p. 8).

Still, Article 7(1) implicitly requires that traders disclose material information needed for the formation of a transactional decision. As the term 'material' is not defined, the duty is essentially one to provide *any* information that enforcers may consider fit in a given case. Indeed, as the European Commission (2009a, p. 48) has stated that "national authorities and courts will need to use their judgement in assessing whether key items of information have been omitted, taking into account all features and circumstances of a commercial practice and the limitations of the communication medium". Apparently, traders will need to exercise similar judgement in complying with the relevant duty.

Article 7(1), UCPD, therefore, allows enforcement authorities and courts to derive sufficiently detailed and suitable information duties on a case-by-case basis, thus filling in any gaps of protection. Accordingly, the peculiar characteristics and complexity of shopping agents and automated marketplaces could be taken into account effectively resulting in the imposition of *specific* (and suitable) information duties through the *general* Article 7(1). Notably, the list of information elements in Article 6(1) can help with the application of Article 7(1) (Collins, 2005, p. 435). Thus, any of the numerous information elements listed in Article 6(1), UCPD could be considered as 'material', since their inclusion in that list entails an acknowledgement of their potential relevance to a transactional decision. As the said list explicitly covers all of the information earlier identified as vital in the context of shopping agents and automated marketplaces,[113] the potential role of Article 7(1), UCPD in addressing the information need of consumers on the relevant platforms is reinforced. This is true given also that information such as on risks, limitations and correct use has already been explained as having repercussions on consumer understanding of the platform service and hence, on consumer decision-making regarding whether to use it and how.[114]

This important potential of Article 7(1) seems to find support in the literature, too. Referring to the UCPD, Twigg-Flesner et al. (2005, p. 35) suggest that traders may be under a duty to advice (as opposed to merely inform) consumers in situations where there is "special sector specific information that the seller [is] more likely to know". It may thus be filling in the gap that Coteanu (2017, p. 173) has described as the absence of "an obligation

113 Supra Chapters 2.2.2.1 and 2.2.2.2
114 Ibid.

to advise on the existence of specific risks or limitations in the use of products and/or services". It is worth mentioning that such obligation to inform on existing risks exists in the Product Safety Directive (PSD): "Producers shall provide consumers with the relevant information to enable them to assess the risks inherent in a product throughout the normal or reasonably foreseeable period of its use, where such risks are not immediately obvious without adequate warnings, and to take precautions against those risks".[115] Yet, even if PSD were to be considered applicable to digital (or non-tangible) products, such as the relevant platforms, the relevant risks are ones to consumer health and safety and not the economic risks (such as bad purchases or fraud) associated with such platforms. Similarly, the Product Liability Directive contains an implicit obligation to inform on the risks involved in the use of products,[116] yet it only concerns with risks relating to death, personal injury and damage to property; pure economic loss is excluded from the relevant right to compensation.[117]

Doubtless, therefore, the role of the UCPD in meeting consumer information needs on platforms is important, even more so because it also addresses the issue regarding where and when the necessary information should be provided.[118] Indeed, according to Article 7(2), the *hiding* of material information or its provision "in an unclear, unintelligible, ambiguous or *untimely manner*"[119] will not prevent the practice from being deemed a misleading omission and hence, an unfair commercial practice. Thus, the UCPD, in particular Articles 6 and 7, entail a *thorough* response to the problem of misleading marketing representations on the relevant platforms and to the specific information needs of platform users.

It would therefore be particularly unfortunate if the UCPD were inapplicable to the relevant platforms. This is fortunately *not* the case, yet relevant analysis is warranted particularly because of the 'transactional decision' ingredient of Articles 6(1)[120] and 7(1).[121] The relevant provisions only prohibit an information act or omission *if* it "causes or is likely to cause the average consumer to take a transactional decision that he would not have taken otherwise". As Twigg-Flesner et al. (2005, p. iii) put it, "The notion of a 'transactional decision' acts as a limitation in that unfair behaviour which does not, and is unlikely to, bring about a transactional decision is not covered by the UCPD".

A 'transactional decision' is defined by Article 2(k) as

> any decision taken by a consumer concerning whether, how and on what terms to *purchase, make payment* in whole or in part for, *retain or dispose of a product* or *to exercise a contractual right* in relation to the product, whether the consumer decides to act or to refrain from acting.[122]

At first glance, the definition seems confined to action (or inaction) in relation to a product to be purchased or that has been purchased, or at least one which, though free, has some

115 Article 5(1), PSD.

116 This is by virtue of Article 6(1) of the Directive which defines a defective product as one which does not provide the safety that one is entitled to expect and explicitly refers to "the presentation of the product" as one of the factors to be taken into account in determining the level of safety one is entitled to expect.

117 For more on the Product Liability Directive and its potential role in the context of shopping agents and automated marketplaces, see infra at pp. 93, 202

118 On this aspect of the relevant information need, see supra at p. 30

119 Emphasis added.

120 Supra p. 44

121 Supra p. 45

122 Emphasis added.

monetary value and can therefore have some economic implications.[123] Thus, the act or omission of a platform provider can cause a consumer to decide not to use the *paid* version of the platform service, if any, or to purchase any available add-on features, thus making a transactional decision. Yet, as said, *all* shopping agents and most probably, all automated marketplaces are or will be provided to consumers for free without a paid version of the service being available at the same time. When *all* of the alternatives are free, the resulting consumer decision *with regard to the platform service* cannot be a decision relating to a purchase or a payment.

The Directive expressly aims to regulate practices that "directly harm consumers' economic interests"[124] and economic interests could not be harmed *directly* when the *only* subject matter is a totally free service accessible online. Its retention or disposal cannot have any direct economic implications in the absence of paid alternatives either. Furthermore, when the platform service is not provided under a contract at all, as is the case with shopping agents,[125] there is no contractual right to be exercised, and, as Twigg-Flesner et al. (2005, p. 39) write, "Where the consumer has no 'contractual rights' to exercise, there will be no transactional decision, and the Directive will not be applicable".

Thus, there seems to be some difficulty in locating a 'transactional decision' when traders promote and/or supply a *free* service. However, the term 'economic' "has to be understood very broadly" (Wilhelmsson, 2006, p. 58) and the same is true of the notion of 'transactional decision' itself (European Commission, 2016c, p. 33). The European Commission (2016c, pp. 34, 36) clarifies that a 'transactional decision' can be the decision to "enter a shop", "agree to a sales presentation by a trader" and "spend more time on the Internet engaged in a booking process". Obviously, these examples of decisions mirror the consumer deciding to get involved in situations whereby the possibility of taking a classical transactional decision, i.e., a purchase is real and increased. Indeed, when the consumer is made to enter a shop, the consumer is clearly placed closer to a transactional decision. Such decisions are thus clearly ones "directly related to the decision whether or not to purchase a product", and as such, qualify as 'transactional decisions' themselves, according to the CJEU, too.[126]

Of course, the 'transactional decision' definition in the UCPD remains tied to purchases and payments so that the *more distant* a classical transactional decision is from the free service subject to the commercial practice, the less likely the Directive will be applicable. Indeed, Robertson (2010) does not see "how that can be interpreted to include a decision to view a website, especially if the site isn't selling anything". Fortunately, the free service of shopping agents and automated marketplaces (and the decision to use it) is so close and connected to a purchase, i.e., a classical transactional decision, that there should not be any issue with the applicability of the UCPD to these platforms. Indeed, the decision of a consumer to use one such platform is very similar to the aforementioned decision to enter a shop, which qualifies as a 'transactional decision', as already discussed. Shopping agents – effectively a type of online shopping mall – exactly aim at assisting consumers in making a purchase from a participating merchant. This is even more clearly so in the case of automated marketplaces, which can even form such transactional decision on behalf of consumer users.

123 Twigg-Flesner et al. (2005, pp. 13–14) offer examples of transactional decisions.
124 Recital 6.
125 Supra p. 38
126 *Case C-281/12, Trento Sviluppo srl, Centrale Adriatica Soc. coop. arl v Autorità Garante della Concorrenza e del Mercato, OJ C 235, 4.8.2012, para. 38.*

As a result of this *very close proximity between a platform and a purchase*, any information affecting consumer decision-making regarding whether and/or how to use the platform essentially affects whether a transactional decision such as a contract with a participating merchant will subsequently be formed and/or the terms of such a contract. This is indisputable in relation to omitted information, which, though about the free platform service, is directly relevant to participating merchants (and their product offerings). Thus, omitting to disclose risks and limitations such as that the shopping agent will *not* necessarily close the best deal is likely to cause consumers to decide to use the agent and, in effect, buy from a participating merchant (instead of another non-participating one). The same is true of omitted information on the privacy risks inherent the platform, the absence of relevant privacy or security features and the fact that access is limited to merchants from which the platform provider derives a benefit. All can effectively cause the consumer to buy from a merchant that participates in the platform rather than from a non-participating one. Similarly, omitted information regarding how to use the platform – such as how to sort search results, utilize a reputation mechanism or set the parameters of the activity of the buying software agent – can clearly affect a transactional decision as to which merchant to buy from or on what terms.[127]

The answer appears to be somewhat less clear regarding omissions of information on *how* to use certain privacy-enhancing features of the automated marketplace, such as an option to negotiate or buy anonymously or other available security-enhancing tools. Is such information sufficiently connected to the transactional decision (purchase) to be taken through the relevant platform? Certainly, it does not relate to the merchant whom to buy from or to any purchase terms and in this respect, an affirmative answer to this question could mean stretching the 'transactional decision' definition to its most extreme limits.

In any event, this would not greatly affect the overall performance score of the response of EU law to the issues currently under discussion. Indeed, it may be that any gap relating to the existence of an obligation to provide user instructions on anonymity (or other privacy or security-related) features is in fact filled in by EU data protection legislation. More specifically, the principle of data minimization in Article 5(1)(c), GDPR,[128] effectively means that personal data shall only be processed if the purpose could not readily be fulfilled by the processing of anonymized (or non-personal) data. Additionally, Article 5(1)(f), GDPR effectively requires controllers[129] to process personal data "in a manner that ensures appropriate security of the personal data, including protection against unauthorised or unlawful processing and against accidental loss, destruction or damage, using appropriate technical or organisational measures".[130] Article 32, GDPR specifically obliges controllers to employ technical measures achieving such protection. Moreover, Article 6(1)(a), GDPR legitimizes 'personal data' processing if the data subject (in this context, the consumer) has provided her consent, which, amongst others, needs to be *informed.* [131]

127 See supra p. 24 about how the ordering of search results can affect consumer decision-making.

128 "Personal data shall be adequate, relevant and limited to what is necessary in relation to the purposes for which they are processed ('data minimisation')", Article 5(1)(c), GDPR.

129 This concept covers providers of automated marketplace providers, see infra at pp. 119–120

130 A direct relevant obligation exists in Article 32, GDPR. For more on these security obligations, see infra at pp. 127–129

131 "'Consent' of the data subject means any freely given, specific, informed and unambiguous indication of the data subject's wishes by which he or she, by a statement or by a clear affirmative action, signifies agreement to the processing of personal data relating to him or her", Article 4 (11), GDPR.

An anonymization feature certainly minimizes the personal data processed in the marketplace, when used. Also, anonymity and other security features obviously qualify as security measures protecting the confidentiality and integrity of personal data and the obligation to employ such measures may not be discharged if their use by consumers is not explained. Similarly, it is questionable that the 'personal data' processing will be one to which the consumer has sufficiently consented if the consumer has not been given enough information enabling her to limit the extent of that processing or the risks involved. It follows that a duty to provide consumers with information and/or instructions on the use of available privacy-enhancing and/or security-related features of the platform may be derived from the aforementioned GDPR provisions.

Of course, an *explicit* relevant information duty would constitute a far more adequate and/or effective response to the relevant issue. Article 21(4) of the Universal Service Directive,[132] represents one such duty; it requires that 'electronic communications service providers' inform recipients as to "the means of protection against risks to personal security, privacy and personal data when using electronic communication services". Yet, as is later illustrated,[133] automated marketplace providers would not, in most cases, qualify as electronic communications service providers. The GDPR, which does apply to them, contains a rich information duty in Article 13, which specifies the pieces of information that need to be provided to the data subject when personal data is collected from her.[134] Article 13, GDPR does not, however, require the relevant piece of information to be provided to data subjects. Another relevant legal measure, namely the Network and Information Security (NIS) Directive, which addresses the security of networks and information systems and is, as is later illustrated,[135] applicable to at least some automated marketplaces too, contains no such information duty either. Given all of the emphasis that EU law places on information duties in the area of consumer protection as well as on data protection and security,[136] it is rather unfortunate that an *explicit duty* to inform consumers on how they can protect themselves against security and privacy risks inherent in goods and services is absent.

The question next arises regarding whether the UCPD also addresses the issue peculiar to shopping agents referring to their lack of impartiality inherent in preferred/top listings and product picks or recommendations when the latter are paid (as opposed to objectively compiled). Doubtless, all such content on shopping agent platforms compose a 'commercial practice' defined very broadly in Article 2(d), UCPD.[137] Article 7(2) renders an omission "to identify the commercial intent of the commercial practice if not already apparent from the context" a misleading omission and, therefore, a prohibited unfair commercial practice. Obviously, the relevant indirect 'identification' duty is similar to that of Article 6(a), ECD which does *not* go so far as to require an identification of *highly paid listings* as such.[138] Thus, though the commercial intent behind product offerings listed on platforms of

132 This Directive is now part of the Directive (EU) 2018/1972 of the European Parliament and of the Council of 11 December 2018 establishing the European Electronic Communications Code.

133 Infra at pp. 134–135

134 In the context of automated marketplaces, that would be the point where the consumer registers with the marketplace so that he can proceed with instructing a buying software agent to conclude a contract.

135 Infra at pp. 160–161

136 As is shown in Chapters 4 and 5, there is a wealth of measures at EU level concerned with data protection, privacy and security of networks, services and systems.

137 See the relevant definition supra at p. 44

138 Supra at pp. 35–36

third-party intermediaries (who do not themselves sell any goods or services) is *not* apparent from the context, Article 7(2), UCPD would most likely be complied with by a clear statement disclosing the paid nature of *all* listings. Such provisions do not seem to contemplate situations in which identification is necessary to distinguish *not only between paid and not paid listings*, a matter arising on traditional search engines,[139] *but also between different kinds of paid ones*, a matter pertinent to shopping agent platforms.

A different provision of the UCPD, namely Article 6(1)(c), provides that a commercial practice is misleading if, in any way, including its overall presentation is likely to mislead the consumer, amongst others, in relation to "the motives for the commercial practice". This is obviously more demanding than Article 7(2), as, unlike the latter, it does not merely require disclosure of *commercial intent.* Commercial intent seems confined to the existence of payment or some benefit behind the practice, whereas the text 'the motives for the commercial practice' seems broad enough to be eligible to an interpretation covering the fact that *increased* payment lies behind the *top placement* of a given product offering. Displaying *all* product offerings indiscriminately in a 'search results' list without explaining what lies behind the position of certain such offerings in the said list seems capable of misleading consumers in relation to the motives behind the top-placed offerings. However, it remains to be seen whether courts (and enforcement authorities) will interpret Article 6(1)(c), UCPD as entailing the stated detailed identification requirement warranted in the context of shopping agent platforms.

Regarding picks and recommendations, there also seems to be a direct (or specific) response in the UCPD where these are made to look like (objective) editorial content offered by the third-party platform provider (with experience in the market of consumer goods and services).[140] Paragraph 11 of the Annex to the UCPD (in conjunction with Article 5(5), UCPD which refers to the said Annex) renders the practice of "using editorial content in the media to promote a product where a trader has paid for the promotion without making that clear in the content (advertorial)" as automatically unfair and prohibited under all circumstances. It is worth mentioning that Article 1(6) of the Proposed Directive on better enforcement and modernisation of EU consumer protection rules seeks to replace this provision with another one, which explicitly refers to 'secret' or unclear paid placement or inclusion too (European Commission, 2018a). Moreover, the European Commission (2016c, p.125) confirms that the aforementioned and additional provisions of the UCPD effectively require that paid inclusion is made sufficiently clear to consumers by shopping agents.[141]

It is important to note that, similarly to what has been said in relation to the similar duties of the ECD,[142] the prohibitions (and duties) of the UCPD pertaining to the proper identification of merchant listings as paid, are enforceable in most cases both against the platform provider and the merchants featured in the relevant listings, as they all qualify as 'traders' for the purpose of the said measure.[143]

139 In France, Google-sponsored links have judicially been considered as misleading for not clearly arising as advertisements or not being sufficiently separated from *non-paid* search results (Leroux and Lagache, 2008, para. 29). See also supra p. 28n23.

140 Earlier research (Markou, 2011, p. 224) illustrates that product picks can indeed take such form, particularly when they are drafted as personal stories or life events.

141 "As discussed in Section 5.2.1.5 on search engines, the UCPD requires all traders to clearly distinguish a natural search result from advertising. This also applies to operators of comparison tools. The relevant provisions in this respect are Article 6(1)(c) and (f), 7(2) and points No 11 and No 22 of Annex I UCPD".

142 Supra p. 36

143 For more on this matter, see infra p. 56

2.3.5 Legal response to the issues pertinent to marketing representations and information on limitations and other characteristics: concluding remarks

The preceding discussion has shown that five different EU legal measures can be used to tackle the problems of misleading marketing representations relating to the relevant platform services and the broader issue referring to the need for disclosure of information on risks, limitations and other important characteristics of the said services. The relevant legal response is found mainly in the ECD, the CRD and the UCPD and is complemented by relevant provisions in the SD and the GDPR. The ECD only addresses a specific aspect of the issue, namely the one referring to the lack of impartiality of shopping agent providers and thus, to the provision of information on the business model of the platform and the proper identification of merchant listings thereon. The relevant response towards the said issue is not complete, as Article 6(a), ECD does not seem to account for the need to separate between different kinds of *paid* listings. It may, however, be complemented by an appropriate interpretation of Article 6(1)(c), UCPD.

A broader response to the relevant issues is contained in the CRD and its detailed information duties, which can be interpreted to require the provision of information on risks, limitations and other important characteristics of the platform services. The relevant response is again not complete; the measure only imposes *pre-contractual* information duties, which do *not* therefore take into account the fact that platform consumers need most of the relevant information while they actually use the service, i.e., post-contractually and at appropriate places on the platform. The same is true of the SD, which contains similar pre-contractual information duties. Moreover, the CRD may not be applicable to web-based (as opposed to app-based) shopping agents at all given that these may not be provided under a contract and its applicability to app-based shopping agents and automated marketplaces as free digital content or a service could have been clearer.

Nevertheless, EU law scores highly regarding how effectively it responds to the relevant issues, and this is largely because of the UCPD, which has been shown to be filling in the 'gaps' left by the ECD and the CRD. This is due to it being capable of giving rise to quite specific information duties that directly respond to the particularities of the consumer information actually needed on the relevant platforms. Though, the UCPD requires the involvement of a 'transactional decision', something that may cause questions regarding its applicability in the relevant context, the said measure has nevertheless been shown actually to be applicable both to shopping agents and automated marketplaces.

Perhaps the only aspect of the issues in relation to which the UCPD does not *clearly* afford a *direct* solution relates to the provision of information and guidance on privacy- (and security-) enhancing features of automated marketplaces. This role has however been shown to be performed by the GDPR, specifically through a suitable interpretation of certain of its provisions, mainly the data protection principles contained in Article 5, GDPR. Overall, therefore, though EU law should have probably contained an explicit information duty (referring to existing security and privacy features) applicable to online services including the relevant platforms, it contains particularly relevant (and useful) provisions which can be interpreted and/or applied so as to adequately and comprehensively address the issues regarding misleading marketing representations and the provision of information on risks, limitations and other characteristics.

2.4 Purchase-related information provided and considered on the relevant platforms: illustrating the risks

The relevant platforms comprise peculiar services in the sense that apart from being services themselves (about which sufficient information must be offered as discussed in the preceding part of this chapter), they are intended to assist consumers in purchasing (or deciding to use) *other* services or goods. Automated marketplaces even make such decisions and purchases themselves, binding their (consumer) users. Therefore, the question of whether they provide or consider all of the information that is vital to a purchase decision is an issue that merits specific attention.

EU law and, in particular, the CRD and the UCPD discussed previously, exactly aims at ensuring that consumers receive sufficient information on all of the vital purchase-related information, thereby being able to avoid bad or unintended purchase decisions. The imposition of the relevant information duties entails a recognition that without certain information being considered, there is an increased risk of a bad or unintended purchase decisions. Thus, platform services designed to place themselves between merchants and consumers during the (pre)-contractual process should not hinder the provision of that information, thereby weakening the position of the consumer. The law should therefore make sure that this is not allowed to be the case.

It is not difficult to illustrate that the non-provision of information on *all* of the factors that are vital to the taking of a purchase decision on shopping agent platforms is actually a problem that merits legal intervention. The omission *as such* of information on key purchase-related factors such as order processing and in effect, delivery time has earlier been shown to be an important reason why the use of shopping agents may be risky.[144] A similar problem labelled as "completeness of information provided" has been identified also in relation to some financial-product agents (Resolution Foundation, 2007, p. 6). Research shows that shipping or delivery time is considered highly significant by some consumer users of shopping agents (Smith and Brynjolfsson, 2001, p. 556). The same and other literature (Su, 2007, pp. 138–139) suggest that those consumers who value such attributes more than price may end up buying from a well-known brand, as they derive from it an assurance of 'right' delivery time. Evidence also suggests that the provision of comprehensive information dramatically increases best-value or rational choices and decreases inappropriate choices focusing solely on brand or price (Su, 2007, pp. 149, 152). Indeed, even the simplest product purchases, such as for stationary or CDs, should, at the very least, be affected by information on delivery time, otherwise consumers risk purchasing a product to be delivered (much) later than desired. Moreover, it has been shown that factors about which information is *not* provided or emphasized by software shopping assistants tend to influence consumer decision-making less than others which are provided.[145] Doubtless, therefore, the provision or non-provision of information by shopping agents can significantly influence consumer decision-making.

Services designed to assist consumer decision-making must therefore abide to a specific obligation to provide information on all vital purchase-related factors so as not to place their consumer users at a disadvantaged position. As is explained in the following, such legal requirement is neither unreasonable nor problematic. Thus, it inevitably comprises the proper legal response to the particular issue, and if it is not contained in EU law, something that is examined later on,[146] EU law cannot be said to adequately respond to the particular issue.

144 Supra pp. 23–24
145 See supra p. 23
146 Infra Chapter 2.5

A legal requirement for the provision of information on all vital purchase-related matters *readily* arises as unproblematic in the case of shopping agents that provide a wide array of purchase-related information and do not limit their service to price comparison. Such agents obviously have the technical ability and financial resources to provide *rich* purchase-related information, and it is thus reasonable to expect them to direct their investment towards ensuring their service is safe and reliable for consumers. Obstacles, if any, to acquiring (comprehensive) information covering all vital purchase-related factors can be considered as easy to overcome. Accordingly, there seems to be no valid reason behind tolerating the omission of any vital piece of purchase-related information on their part.

Price-only shopping agents, on the other hand, usually only compare simple products such as CDs, DVDs, books and video games. Price comparison is certainly useful, and one could say that to oblige relevant providers to offer the variety of information offered by bigger shopping agents would effectively mean requiring an unstainable change in the nature of their business. Indeed, referring to 'search engine' shopping agents,[147] Fasli (2006, pp. 71–73) explained that the provision of limited information may stem from certain technological limitations (probably existing at the time).

Yet, the view that price-only shopping agents should accordingly be exempted from the suggested legal requirement would be misguided. Shopping agents indeed started off as mere price comparison tools 'suffering' from certain technical and other limitations, but this is perhaps true of every technological product while in its initial or primitive version. The aforementioned technical literature does not seem to have suggested an impossibility of progress or development. Most importantly, in looking at the risks inherent in new technological goods or services, the law should not simply adjust to their initial limitations. On the contrary, it should boost (and even force) improvement by insisting that they meet relevant consumer protection standards. In fact, as is shown later,[148] this is one area in which the law effectively did so, albeit without targeting the particular services. Interestingly, some price-comparison shopping agents already display information on availability and delivery costs (Best-dvd-price.co.uk, 2017b; 123PriceCheck, 2017). This reinforces the view that shopping agents have been developing and advancing and that legal requirements regarding the information they provide to the consumer would *not* most probably prescribe a technological impossibility.

Doubtless, the need for shopping-assisting tools or services to provide information on all vital purchase-related factors is even more acute in relation to automated marketplaces; in that context, software does not just assist consumers in deciding upon a purchase but substitutes them in the relevant decision-making. Though consumers using such software will not *personally* consider any provided information, the need for quality purchase decisions (based on all vital factors) obviously remains. Thus, complete purchase-related information must inevitably be provided to the buying software entrusted with the making of purchase decisions on behalf of consumers.

As already seen, there may be price-only software agents,[149] meaning that automated marketplaces will not necessarily allow for contract conclusion based on multi-factor information. Understandably, a legal requirement mandating the provision of certain minimum purchase-related information by merchant-representing software would indirectly prohibit the use of price-only automated marketplaces, yet this is not necessarily undesirable. The benefits of full automation in shopping should not be accepted *at all costs* and most certainly, these should

147 Supra Chapter 1 p. 9
148 Infra Chapter 2.5.1
149 Supra Chapter 1 p. 13

not come at the expense of 'purchase-decision' quality to the detriment of consumers. Thus, the law should ensure that purchases formed automatically on automated marketplaces are not based on less information than other online consumer purchases. Moreover, it again seems to be the case that a relevant requirement would not prescribe a technological impossibility; as already illustrated, there is both a willingness and an ability on the part of technology to make available multi-attribute automated marketplaces.[150]

Interestingly, such multi-attribute automated marketplaces have the potential of greatly improving consumer decision-making, eliminating hasty purchases, specifically by responding to the notorious problem of consumers actually ignoring or not adequately processing information, (even) when provided to them, due to consumers' cognitive limitations.[151] Indeed, as the consumer will have to instruct the software agent representing her, the consumer will effectively be prompted (or nudged) to direct her mind towards all vital purchase-related factors if these are mentioned in the relevant web form that she will have to fill in for the particular purpose. If a consumer does not give specific instructions by reference to delivery time, for example, it will most probably be because she really does not care about delivery time, rather than due to her accidentally missing the importance of the relevant factor. The actual processing (or consideration) of all relevant information for contracting purposes will then be left to software. The latter probably has greater information-processing capabilities than human consumers and is impossible to fail to consider information that is provided to it (unless, of course, it malfunctions). It would therefore be unfortunate for the law to fail to exploit these possibilities of enhanced consumer protection by hesitating to impose relevant information duties relating to contracts concluded on automated platforms.

Of course, information duties normally require *the provision* of information and do not, at least explicitly, touch upon its *consideration* by the party to whom it is provided. This is only natural; no law could obligate consumers actually to consider the mandatorily provided information. Given, however, that the same is not true of software substituting consumers (as the law can certainly control the technical capabilities of commercialized technological tools), the question arises as to whether any relevant information duties applicable to automated marketplaces should specifically require not only the provision of information by merchant contracting software but also its consideration by consumer software. In fact, there may not be a pressing need for a legally mandated technical capability of 'information *consideration*'. Marketplaces offering merchant software that *can* provide certain information are highly unlikely to have *consumer* software *not* technically able to *consider* it. The relevant state of the art illustrates that such marketplaces comprise uniform systems in which components are designed so as to be able to work together towards achieving contract conclusion on behalf of human contracting parties.

The issue is admittedly less straightforward in relation to buying software agents *not* offered as a marketplace component but made available by third-party providers, as is currently the case with snipping software provided for use on marketplaces administered by different providers such as eBay.[152] Though such providers will have their interests aligned to those of consumers[153] and will therefore probably ensure that their software is capable of considering all of the provided purchase-related information, the possibility cannot be excluded of software that is incapable of actually acting upon the provided information

150 Supra Chapter 2 p. 13
151 For a literature review of the general problem of information overload, see Roetzel, P.G. (2018).
152 Supra Chapter 1 p. 12
153 Supra Chapter 1 p. 14

being made available to consumers. As is explained in the following sections,[154] whether consumer software is actually (technically) capable of considering the provided information is important and cannot be isolated from the question relating to meaningful information duties in the particular context.

2.5 Purchase-related information provided and considered on the platforms: the legal response

This issue obviously concerns the information upon which *contracts between merchants and consumers* are concluded on 'shopping agent' platforms and automated marketplaces. This translates into a need for information on all vital purchase-related factors to be shown on 'shopping agent' platforms or exchanged and utilized on automated marketplaces. Thus, the relevant EU legal response will be examined by reference to each of the relevant platforms and (mainly) in the light of EU measures addressing the content and quality of the information provided to consumers pre-contractually, including at the advertising stage. These are the CRD, which is mostly relevant to automated marketplaces and the UCPD, which, for the purposes of the question currently under discussion is relevant to shopping agents, as is explained in the following section.

2.5.1 Shopping agents

Though the CRD exactly aims at ensuring that consumers will receive (comprehensive) information on all vital purchase-related factors before committing to a purchase through imposing sufficiently detailed information duties, it does not in fact address the particular issue. It applies to distance contracts between a trader and a consumer[155] and thus, to contracts that consumers conclude with the merchants they find on 'shopping agent' platforms but its information duties are not addressed to such third parties. The European Commission (2014a, p. 31) takes the opposite view in relation to online platforms allowing for contract conclusion, which it says may qualify as 'traders' acting on behalf and in the name of other 'traders', namely the merchants who sell.[156] Yet, shopping agent platforms do not allow for contract conclusion. Rather they direct consumers to the contract conclusion facilities or websites of each participating merchant.

Of course, the information duties of Article 6(1), CRD burden the merchants who participate on the shopping agent platform and enter into distant contracts with consumer users of the platform. The consequences of non-compliance may, in fact, be heavy, as not only will there be a violation of the CRD but also a violation (in the form of a misleading omission) of the UCPD.[157] Importantly, however, Article 6(1) only requires that the information be provided *before the consumer is bound by a distance contract.* It can thus fully be

154 Infra pp. 70–71
155 See supra p. 38
156 This view is critically discussed later, see infra p. 72–73
157 Article 7(5), UCPD renders information relating to commercial communications required under other EU measures as material information, the omission of which may lead to a misleading omission under Article 7(1), UCPD, discussed previously (see supra at p. 45). Thus, "with the help of unfair commercial practices law, it sanctions violations of pre-contractual and post-contractual information obligations" (Micklitz, 2010, p. 235) and thus, strengthens the incentive for compliance with the information duties of the CRD.

complied with by merchants displaying the required information on their own websites to which the shopping agent directs consumers through a relevant link as explained earlier. Accordingly, Article 6(1), CRD does not give rise to a requirement that the particular information be disclosed (or contained) in the merchant listings displayed on the 'shopping agent' platform. Indeed, the CRD does not impose information duties in relation to *all or any particular commercial communications* of a merchant, yet a requirement of exactly this type is what is needed to ensure that certain minimum information is actually included in merchant listings on shopping agents.

Nevertheless, this role is played by another EU legal measure, namely the UCPD. As they clearly promote products to consumers, 'shopping agent' listings clearly constitute 'commercial practices'[158] subject to the UCPD. Unsurprisingly, therefore, the European Commission (2009, p. 8; 2016c, p.122) has specifically referred to them, confirming that the providers of price comparison websites (or shopping agents) qualify as 'traders' bound by the provisions of the UCPD, unless of course they are run on a non-profession basis. The GB OFT (2010) even devoted a significant part of a major study to the application of the Consumer Protection from Unfair Trading Regulations 2008 (the UK measure transposing the UCPD into UK law) to shopping agents. Similarly, the UK Law Commission (2008, pp. 7, 15) explained that the said Regulations apply not only to traders in a contractual relationship with the consumer but also to third parties (including price comparison websites) who promote products or are directly connected with such product promotion to consumers.[159] Thus, the UCPD applies in this context and can be enforced both against relevant platform providers and the merchants who pay to be listed on their platform. Indeed, both of them are 'traders' for the purposes of the UCPD.[160]

In relation to shopping agents of the 'search engine' type however,[161] to the extent that they list merchants without the latter paying or even knowing of the particular fact, the platform provider is the *only* party creating, compiling and publishing the relevant commercial practices. The said provider therefore is the only person against whom the Directive may lead to sanctions. Though, in the UK, the relevant Regulations make available certain defences, those are only available in cases where enforcement of the Directive is sought through criminal proceedings[162] and do not affect civil or administrative enforcement.[163] In any event, 'search engine' shopping agents operating without merchant active involvement cannot rely on the "innocent publication of advertisement" defence, which pre-supposes no (material) involvement in the advertisement content.[164] A trader can also avoid liability if the offence has been committed owing to "the act or default of another person",[165] yet especially in the case of misleading omissions, the failure to extract and publish required information can only be attributed to the agent provider.[166]

It has been shown that the UCPD is applicable to commercial practices comprising 'shopping agent' listings and thus, regulates the conduct of both 'shopping agent' providers and participating merchants (where the latter are willingly involved). The question that now

158 See relevant definition, supra p. 44
159 See also supra p. 50
160 See the relevant definition in Article 2(b), UCPD, infra pp. 61, 73
161 See supra Chapter 1 p. 9
162 Regulations 8–18.
163 Regulations 19–27.
164 Regulation 18.
165 Regulation 17(1)(iii).
166 On these defences see also infra p. 62 and Chapter 3 p. 95

needs to be examined is whether the particular measure affords the solution to the issue regarding incomplete information on vital purchase-related factors; as already explained, such a solution should entail a rule mandating the existence of complete information on all such factors in the listings on the relevant platform. As will be shown, the provisions of the UCPD on misleading omissions do contain the 'raw material' of the said solution, yet appropriate interpretation is necessary to ensure suitability, completeness and effectiveness.

'Shopping agent' listings clearly qualify as 'invitations to purchase' defined by Article 2(i), UCPD as "a commercial communication which indicates characteristics of the product and the price in a way appropriate to the means of the commercial communication used and thereby enables the consumer to make a purchase". The relevant listings have earlier been explained invariably to include product price, and the same is true of the characteristics of the product: "the 'characteristics of the product' requirement, mentioned in Article 2(i) of the Directive is invariably present as soon as there is a verbal or visual reference to the product" (European Commission, 2016c, p. 47). The European Commission (2016c, p. 47) explained that the second part of the definition starting with the word 'thereby' does not add to the necessary ingredients of an 'invitation to purchase'. It is thus not necessary for the practice to include for example, "a phone number or a coupon" (European Commission, 2009a, p. 47), thereby enabling consumers immediately to act upon it, in order to qualify as an 'invitation to purchase'. The CJEU has also confirmed that the said part of the definition only discloses the purpose behind the ingredient referring to product characteristics and price:[167] "For a commercial communication to be capable of being categorised as an invitation to purchase, it is not necessary for it to include an actual opportunity to purchase or for it to appear in proximity to and at the same time as such an opportunity."[168]

This broad interpretation of the notion of an 'invitation to purchase' is particularly interesting in the context of shopping agents. Indeed, even advertisements such as supermarket leaflets and TV spots qualify as invitations to purchase and hence as "a direct and immediate form of product promotion, triggering a more impulsive reaction from consumers and thus exposing them to higher risks" (European Commission, 2009a, p. 49). Thus, though such advertisements usually reach consumers while the latter *are (far) away* from the point of sale (or purchase), they are nevertheless recognized as entailing higher risks to consumers. This reinforces the view expressed earlier regarding the peculiarly (or excessively) risky nature of 'shopping agent' listings,[169] which not only include product characteristics and price but also sit *very close* to an actual opportunity to purchase. Indeed, though they may not include a 'phone or coupon', they contain a link directly to the page of the online store on which the facility to submit an order is provided.[170] In fact, order placing is effectively only two clicks away, meaning that consumers have little time to 'break free' from the influence of the said listings. This highlights the acute need for such listings to contain information on all vital purchase-related factors.

The UCPD entails a conscious attempt to respond to this need, as Article 7(4) subjects 'invitations to purchase' and hence, 'shopping agent' listings to 'minimum information' requirements, which are not applicable to other commercial practices.[171] As is explained in Recital 14, UCPD, the said provision specifies "a limited number of key items of information

167 *C-122/10, Konsumentombudsmannen v Ving Sverige AB, 12 May 2011, para. 30.*
168 Ibid at para. 32.
169 Supra Chapter 2.2.2.1.2
170 Supra Chapter 1 p. 8
171 See Recital 14, UCPD.

which the consumer needs to make an informed transactional decision",[172]obviously in order to ensure that the consumer will *not* be lured to acting upon incomplete purchase-related information. The key items of information required by Article 7(4) are: (a) the name and address of the trader; (b) the main characteristics of the goods or services; (c) the price, including any charges or delivery costs (or information on how it could be calculated); (d) "the arrangements for payment, delivery, performance and the complaint handling policy, if they depart from the requirements of professional diligence"[173] and (e) the existence of a right of withdrawal, where applicable. The required information could obviously cover *all* of the vital purchase-related factors, yet there are problems with the said provision that prevent one from safely deeming it as the required solution.

The most important of these problems is that the requirement relating to 'arrangements for payment, delivery, performance' in Article 7(4)(d), UCPD is expressly qualified by reference to a condition of departure from professional diligence. Unfortunately, this qualification is inappropriate, as it may effectively permit the omission of important pieces of information such as delivery time, which happens to be the very factor that has earlier been identified as being absent from some 'shopping agent' listings.[174] According to Article 2(h), UCPD "'professional diligence' means the standard of special skill and care which a trader may reasonably be expected to exercise towards consumers, commensurate with honest market practice and/or the general principle of good faith in the trader's field of activity". Willett (2008, p. 89) explains that arrangements for payment and delivery, when *beneficial* to the consumer, are likely to be deemed in accord with professional diligence and can therefore be omitted. Along similar lines, the European Commission (2016c, p. 72) states that they must be displayed only when they are "to *the consumer's disadvantage* when compared to the good diligent market practice".[175]

Difficulties may however arise when relevant arrangements are neither *clearly* beneficial nor *clearly* disadvantageous to the consumer. In the context of online and, especially, cross-border shopping, differing delivery times (such as a nine-day delivery by one merchant and a three-day delivery by another) may *both* be in accord with professional diligence (as neither of the two could be considered as 'disadvantageous') and *yet* make an important difference to the consumer purchaser. What is more is that even a clearly beneficial (or advantageous) arrangement such as same-day delivery may, for a number of reasons, be undesirable to the consumer.[176] It would seem, therefore, that the 'professional diligence' qualification to the requirement to disclose arrangements on delivery may be wholly inappropriate, particularly in the online context. Additionally, given the previously illustrated *increased* significance of delivery time as a purchase-related factor,[177] the relevant information should have been required in *all* cases of invitations to purchase, at least in the context of distance (including online) selling. Admittedly, Article 6(1)(g), CRD requires the provision of information on delivery arrangements in all cases of distance selling (*without* subjecting the duty to a similar qualification), yet it has already been explained that the CRD is unable to respond to the need for complete information provision on shopping agent platforms.[178]

172 Recital 14.
173 Article 7(4)(d).
174 Supra pp. 22–23
175 Emphasis added.
176 For example, the consumer may not be in a position to accept delivery at the particular day or would not want another household member to receive the product.
177 Supra p. 23
178 Supra pp. 55–56

The relevant gap could be remedied by an application of Article 7(1), UCPD, which renders the omission of material information as misleading[179] and affords authorities and courts wide discretion in deciding what constitutes 'material' and, hence, required information in a given case. Though Article 7(4) is a *specific* provision, its wording only renders certain information items as 'material' for invitations to purchase and does not seek exhaustively to regulate the latter. It can thus be seen as complementing rather than superseding the *general* Article 7(1) provision and indeed, the CJEU has clarified that despite Article 7(4), invitations to purchase *remain* subject to all of the rest Article 7, UCPD including Article 7(1).[180] Clearly, therefore, Article 7(4) does not preclude a court (or an enforcement authority) from deeming information *not* listed in the said provision as material in the context of an invitation to purchase and, consequently, from finding a misleading omission under Article 7(1), UCPD. Yet, arrangements on delivery are *explicitly listed* in Article 7(4), as already seen, and are specifically rendered 'material' *only* if not in accord with professional diligence. At the very least, this express stance taken by the legislature in Article 7(4) would seem to make the adoption of a directly conflicting approach by the enforcers somewhat uncertain.

Another problem with Article 7(4), UCPD when applied to shopping agents could arise from Article 7(3), UCPD, which as the CJEU has confirmed,[181] applies to invitations to purchase too. Article 7(3) provides as follows:

> Where the medium used to communicate the commercial practice imposes limitations of space or time, these limitations and any measures taken by the trader to make the information available to consumers by other means shall be taken into account in deciding whether information has been omitted.

It arises that the UCPD does not totally prohibit the omission of information listed in Article 7(4) in an invitation to purchase; such omission may, by virtue of Article 7(3), be acceptable if two conditions are met, namely, if the information is made available to consumer by others means, and the omission is due to space or time limitations. By displaying a link directly to the selling page within the merchant website, where all of the required information may be displayed, the platform provider could be taken to have taken measures to provide the information by other means, thereby satisfying the first condition.[182] If that alone were enough to legitimize the omission of the information, the relevant provision would divest Article 7(4), UCPD of its potential to address the issue under discussion; it would effectively reduce it to a general pre-contractual information duty, such as the one in Article 6(1), CRD, and which has already been explained as being unable to respond to the issue of incomplete information on vital purchase-related factors in the 'shopping agent' listings *as such.* [183]

Fortunately, this loophole is avoided by the existence of the second condition, which effectively legitimizes omissions that are attributable to space or time limitations. This is, of

179 Supra p. 45

180 *C-122/10, Konsumentombudsmannen v Ving Sverige AB, para. 24.*

181 Ibid, *para.* 67.

182 Notably, similar provision in the CRD, namely Article 8(4), CRD is expanded upon in Recital 36, CRD by reference to the consumer being directed to "another source of information, for instance by providing a toll free telephone number or a hypertext link to a webpage of the trader where the relevant information is directly available and easily accessible".

183 See supra pp. 55–56

course, so, provided that the latter are given a strict (or literal) interpretation. Time limitations are obviously not applicable in the case of shopping agents. The notion of 'limitations of space' is not expanded upon in the UCPD, but the same concept exists in the CRD, where it is explained by reference to "*technical* constraints of certain media such as the restrictions on the number of characters on certain mobile telephone screens"[184] Though the relevant explanation does not belong to the operative provisions of the Directive, it can certainly guide enforcers towards a literal (rather than a liberal[185]) interpretation of the relevant ingredient of Article 7(3), thereby avoiding the aforementioned possible loophole in the context of shopping agents. Indeed, 'shopping agent' platforms do not obviously suffer from technical space limitations. Their user interface is most often *a website*, and websites are notoriously of *unlimited* space. The same is probably true of apps.

Nor is the inclusion of all information mandated by Article 7(4), UCPD in the 'shopping agent' listings (or on the 'shopping agent' platform) necessarily incompatible with the need to keep relevant listings concise or the platform user-friendly and useful.[186] Indeed, there are examples of relevant platforms having a column in their 'search result' table devoted to information on delivery time and their listings seem neither overloaded nor less effective than those of the platforms which omit the said information. Moreover, the linking system that is central to the internet enables 'shopping agent' providers to place some of the information required by Article 7(4), such as the address of the merchant behind links consuming negligible space placed within a listing,[187] or above the 'price comparison' table (if it is information applicable to *all* listings such as detailed product characteristics and the right of withdrawal).[188]

All in all, the escape route of Article 7(3), UCPD from the obligation of Article 7(4), UCPD is, as it should be, unavailable to shopping agents, and this view seems to have received judicial acceptance. Indeed, the German Supreme Court held that price comparison websites must provide information on shipping costs and that the fact that these can be found on the linked merchant website does not suffice (BGH, Urteil vom 16.7.2009, Az. I ZR 140/07 – Versandkostenangabe in Preisvergleichslisten). Accordingly, the UCPD, through Article 7(4), contains a direct solution to the problem under discussion, though as explained, the qualification of 'a departure from professional diligence' to Article 7(4)(d) referring, amongst others, to arrangements for delivery, merits careful interpretation in the online context, so that the provision of information on delivery time is deemed as required in all cases in the online context.

A related issue relating to shopping agents has been explained to be inherent in the practice of 'smart buy' seals. 'Smart buy' seals are basically representations that a given product offering listed on the 'shopping agent' platform meets certain specified criteria as to merchant reliability and/or (lowest) product price. These (together with the product offering to which they are attached) clearly qualify as 'commercial practices' and are thus controlled by the

184 Recital 36, CRD, emphasis added.
185 A liberal interpretation would probably bring within the notion of 'space limitations' arguments to the effect that the space consumed by shopping agent listings should be kept limited so that they can allow for quick comparisons between product offerings, thus adequately perform their purpose.
186 See supra n. 185
187 Pricerunner International AB (2017c) was in 2014 seen by the present author using tiny links right under the name or logo of each listed merchant reading 'Info on [name of merchant]'. Since 2017, however, it seems to have ceased the practice.
188 Most shopping agents display generic links such as 'Overview' and 'Product Information' at the top of the page displaying the 'price comparison' table. One could envisage another such link reading 'Your Rights', for example.

UCPD.[189] They also clearly qualify as 'invitations to purchase' within the meaning of Article 2 (i), UCPD explained previously.[190] As a result, they must not contain false or inaccurate information, amongst others, on price or on the approval of the merchant, otherwise they will constitute (prohibited) misleading actions as per Article 6(1)(c)[191] and (d),[192] UCPD respectively. In effect, EU law prohibits the attachment of such seals to product offerings which do *not* really offer the lowest price and/or do *not* come from the merchant with the highest consumer rating. Additionally, if the listing bearing the seal does *not* contain all of the information required by Article 7(4), UCPD, it will comprise a misleading omission under Article 7(1), UCPD, for the reasons already discussed in relation to 'shopping agent' listings in general,[193] and therefore (again) a prohibited unfair commercial practice.

It follows that the use of 'smart buy' seals does not raise any peculiar issues regarding the application of the main provisions of the UCPD, which seems effectively to tackle the issues involved. Yet, two relevant points merit discussion. Firstly, as in relation to merchant listings in general, *both* the featured merchant and the platform provider may qualify as a 'trader'.[194] However, as 'smart buy' seals are *not* purchased or in any way requested or affected by the merchants whom they refer to, arguably they could not be viewed as commercial practices for which they should be deemed responsible. They comprise a sole initiative of the platform provider, who effectively endorses the listing to which it attaches the seal and promotes it as the best choice. The 'smart buy' seal therefore (as attached to a given offering) may constitute a 'commercial practice' for which the platform provider *alone* may be responsible though the underlying listing or offering (in isolation from the seal) will, in most cases, be a commercial practice of the platform provider *and* the featured merchant as explained earlier.[195]

The platform provider derives no profit directly from the 'smart buy' commercial practice and may even *lose* profit in the sense that the practice may direct consumer attention to a non-paying (or a lower paying) merchant. Yet, this does not affect the capacity of the provider as a 'trader' for the purposes of the UCPD. By virtue of Article 2(b), UCPD, a trader is "any natural or legal person who, in commercial practices covered by this Directive, is acting for purposes relating to his trade, business, craft or profession and anyone acting in the name of or on behalf of a trader". Evidently, the definition is by no means dependent upon a requirement that there be a financial benefit derived *directly* from the commercial practice. Even if it is read "as excluding business activities which are not intended to make a profit" (European Research Group on Existing EC Private Law, 2009, sec. IV.1(b)), the 'trader' definition would still cover 'shopping agent' providers *vis-a-vis* smart buy seals; the latter are clearly employed by the said providers in the context of and for purposes relating to its *for-profit* business.

189 Supra p. 44

190 Supra p. 57

191 A commercial practice is misleading if, amongst others, it contains false information as to "the extent of the trader's commitments, the motives for the commercial practice and the nature of the sales process, any statement or symbol in relation to direct or indirect sponsorship or approval of the trader or the product".

192 A commercial practice is misleading if, amongst others, it contains false information as to "the price or the manner in which the price is calculated, or the existence of a specific price advantage".

193 Supra pp. 57–58

194 Supra p. 56

195 Ibid. Of course, it could be counter-argued that from the moment the merchant willingly participates in the shopping agent service, the merchant should be recognized as jointly responsible with the shopping agent provider.

Thus, 'smart buy' seals are sufficiently regulated by the UCPD, which effectively prohibits their irresponsible use by the platform provider. Though, the said provider has the same duties in relation to the underlying merchant listing (in isolation of the attached 'smart buy' seal), the nature of such seals as regulated 'commercial practices' under the UCPD and the related capacity of the platform provider as a 'trader' is significant. Indeed, first of all, the possibility exists of the listing *as such* being accurate, the misleading action *solely* being inherent in the seal falsely describing it as the cheapest or smartest option. Secondly, a *misleading seal* is likely to be considered a more serious violation of the UCPD (leading to stricter sanctions) than a non-sealed listing containing inaccurate information. As already explained,[196] such seals entail *increased* promotion of the seal-bearing listing and are likely to have an even greater impact on consumers than non-sealed invitations to purchase. Finally, where the seal has mistakenly been attached as a result of inaccurate information in the underlying listing, there will be much less room for platform providers successfully to invoke the available defences to criminal liability under the relevant UK transposition measure.[197] Indeed, it is only fair to deem the attachment of the seal as entailing the provider actively and voluntarily endorsing the content of the listing or even adopting it as his own. This greatly limits the possibility of such provider successfully invoking the act or default of some other party or the exercise of due diligence as is required by the relevant defences.[198] In fact, the attachment of a seal of approval to a misleading listing will, in most cases, probably serve as proof of an omission to exercise due diligence.

2.5.2 Automated marketplaces

Communications between merchant and consumer software agents are essentially contractual communications between the human contractors behind the relevant software. Accordingly, being applicable to distance contracts between traders and consumers,[199] the CRD is the most natural source of a direct solution to the issue regarding the completeness of the purchase-related information on the basis of which automated contracts are concluded. Indeed, Recital 20, CRD makes it clear that online platforms that allow for contract conclusion qualify as 'organized distance sales schemes', thereby leading to 'distance contracts' that are subject to the CRD; recall that by virtue of Article 2(7), CRD only distance contracts concluded under an organized distance sales scheme are governed by the CRD.[200]

As already seen, Article 6(1), CRD requires that the consumer be provided with specific information that is detailed enough to include information on *all* of the vital purchase-related factors.[201] Nevertheless, the CRD does not adequately address the relevant issue, the main reason being that its provisions, in particular, the information duties of Article 6(1), have not been devised with automated contracting in mind. As will be shown, some of the required information items would be useless to contracting software. It would more generally be

196 Supra p. 22
197 On these defences, see also supra at p. 56 and infra at p. 95
198 Infra p. 95
199 Supra n. p. 55
200 Of course, the European Commission (2014a, p. 31) further opines that the information duties of the CRD may burden not only the selling merchant but also the platform provider, something which is discussed later, see infra at pp. 72–73
201 The main such purchase-related factors are referred to in the information items in paragraphs (a), (e) and (g) of Article 6(1), CRD. For a detailed analysis of these and the rest of the information items of Article 6(1), CRD, see Markou (2017a, para. 7, 40-7.67).

useless pre-contractually and thus, even if the trader were to secure a channel of direct communication with the human consumer. This raises concerns not only regarding whether Article 6(1), CRD is capable of affording sufficient protection to consumers contracting on automated marketplaces but also in relation to legal certainty that is important to traders. Indeed, a violation of Article 6(1) has significant adverse implications for traders,[202] and it is therefore important that they know how they can comply with it on automated marketplaces.

This (un)suitability of the said information duties to wholly automated contracting environments has been the special focus of other recent research (Markou, 2017b), on which the following discussion is primarily based. As will be shown, the best way forward is for Article 6(1) to be interpreted as requiring that some of the mandated information be provided to the consumer software while the rest be provided centrally on the website through which the marketplace is made accessible to the consumer. In the future, however, a more drastic approach that removes certain software-unsuitable information items from Article 6(1) may be warranted. There are five possible approaches to the application of Article 6(1), CRD to automated contracting. Each one is discussed in order to illustrate the aforementioned two points regarding the appropriate approach for now and in the future.

Other commentators also see an issue with the application of Article 8(7), CRD, though, as it will be shown, a more pressing issue has to do with the application of the definition of the term 'trader' in the context of automated marketplaces.

2.5.2.1 The appropriate approach to the application of Article 6(1), CRD

2.5.2.1.1 THE 'SOFTWARE AS THE CONSUMER' AND THE 'DIRECT COMMUNICATION' APPROACHES

Albeit by reference to the DSD, the predecessor of the CRD, Bain and Subirana (2003a, p. 381) assert that in the context of contracting by software, the information that the law requires that it be provided to *the consumer* must be provided to the software agent acting for the consumer. This view would seem to be shared by Lodder and Voulon (2002, p. 283). It basically endorses the notion of the '*software as the consumer*' (Markou, 2017b, pp. 10–11) derived from the fact that software substitutes consumers in the contractual process, effectively acting as an extension of them. This approach simply brings said notion into the law without questioning its suitability. Its obvious advantage is simplicity; it enables the application of the legal information requirements to automated contracting without necessitating any change to them whatsoever. If the merchant software communicates the required information to the consumer software, the information duties of the CRD are complied with.

There is another equally straightforward approach, which rejects the adoption of the '*software as the consumer*' notion in the context of applying the law to fully automated (software) contracting. It is the one proposed by Cross (2007, p. 31): "The only satisfactory means for a supplier to ensure full compliance with these obligations is to communicate directly with the consumer". The consumer (buying) software is, in fact, *not* the consumer and thus the required information has to be provided to the consumer personally, for example, *via* e-mail to the e-mail address that the consumer will have to specify when registering with the

202 Apart from administrative fines or injunctions, depending on the piece of information omitted, the period of withdrawal may be extended to 12 months and 14 days as per Article 10(1), CRD or the trader may not be entitled to the payment of additional charges or taxes as per Article 6(6). See also infra at pp. 69–70

marketplace or instructing the software regarding a potential purchase. This may be referred to as the '*direct communication*' approach (Markou, 2017b, pp. 10, 12–13).

There are problems with both of these approaches. The first remains indifferent to whether the purpose of the information duties of the CRD, which is to enable consumers to take a quality purchase decision and more generally, to strengthen their position *vis-a-vis* merchants, is served. In the context of automated contracting, it is software, not consumers, which are to consider any provided information. Software operates automatically and therefore, 'thinks' and 'decides' (very) differently from humans. Accordingly, the said software will probably make *no* use of some of the required information under Article 6(1), CRD and thus some of the relevant information duties are simply superficial in the context of automated contracting. This is fairly obvious in relation to information on the right of withdrawal, a reminder of the existence of a legal guarantee for goods, codes of conducts and methods for accessing redress mechanisms.[203] To require that information that is impossible to have *any* effect on decision-making be provided would be to adopt a purely formalistic approach insisting in 'empty' legal requirements.

The alternative (second) approach of communicating *directly with the consumer* is free from the aforementioned objection but avoids it only superficially. Moreover, it does so by refusing to accept that consumers will, in fact, be substituted by software and effectively by rejecting the idea of automated contracting. Indeed, requiring a merchant who deals with consumer software to provide the required information *directly* to the (human) consumer (for example, by e-mail) again means taking a superficial approach towards information duties that insists in the provision of information that will *not* probably be utilized. Clearly, a consumer who will want to receive and review any information personally will not probably turn to automated marketplaces that entail delegating the relevant task to software.

2.5.2.1.2 THE 'FROM THE SOFTWARE TO THE CONSUMER' APPROACH

A middle approach, namely the '*from the software to the consumer*' approach (Markou, 2017b, pp. 10, 11–12), basically relying on the fact that the software will be able to communicate the information received to the human consumer, is not very different and can only provide a temporary solution. It should be recalled that it is possible for software to seek the approval of their user before finalizing a transaction.[204] In the context of seeking such approval, consumer software may in fact communicate information provided by merchant software to the (human) consumer. As others state, "If the . . . information is provided to the agent, the user of the agent will be able to obtain the information" (Lodder and Voulon, 2002, p. 283). This approach obviously still insists in communication with the human consumer treating consumer (buying) software as the standard means of communication utilized rather than substituting the consumer.

In the early days of commercialized automated marketplaces, consumers will probably want the software to seek their prior approval before entering into a binding contract. As Fasli (2007, p. 358) observes, software will initially be allowed only an advisory role, and it is as time goes by and trust builds up that it will be allowed totally to substitute human users. During these early times of automated marketplaces, therefore, Article 6(1), CRD could be

203 These are provided by Article 6(1)(d), (h), (i), (j), (k), (l), (n) and (t), CRD. For a detailed illustration of the information items of Article 6(1), CRD which can be considered as unsuitable in the context of automated contracting, see also Markou (2017b, pp. 7–10).

204 Supra Chapter 1 p. 12

interpreted as obliging merchants to choose marketplaces that incorporate a 'prior approval' option. What is more, as Article 6(1) requires that they merely *provide* that information,[205] they will comply even when consumers choose not utilize the said option, thus authorizing software to complete a transaction without securing their approval.

Clearly, however, this approach remains tied to communication with the (human) consumer and thus only achieves a solution by rejecting fully automated contracting.[206]As a result, interpreting Article 6(1), CRD as explained previously effectively amounts to insisting in the provision of information despite knowing that it will probably serve no purpose at all; it cannot be used by the software and will not probably be utilized by the human consumer. The greatest disadvantage of this approach is that it settles with a shallow compliance with legal duties, thereby preventing focus on constructing a suitable information duty that would help improve the quality of the decisions taken by software, thus ensuring sufficient consumer protection in automated contracting environments.

2.5.2.1.3 THE 'CENTRAL PROVISION OF SOFTWARE-UNSUITABLE INFORMATION' APPROACH

A fourth approach, namely the '*central provision of software-unsuitable information*' approach (Markou, 2017b, pp. 10, 13–15) would seem to provide an appropriate solution to the problem of applying the CRD pre-contractual information duties to automated marketplaces. As explained elsewhere (Markou, 2017b, p. 13), Article 6(1), CRD only requires the provision of the information items listed therein before the consumer is bound by a distant contract. This requirement is broad enough to allow for the said information to be provided at different points in time (as long as it is pre-contractually) and in different ways, as long as it is provided on the means of distant communication used for contracting. The latter arises implicitly from Article 8(4), CRD which allows the provision of certain information in other ways or on other means *only* when the means used for contracting suffer from limitations of space or time.[207] Moreover, Article 8(1), CRD confirms that the Article 6(1) information has to be provided, amongst others, "in a way appropriate to the means of distance communication used". Accordingly, some of the information items, in particular those that can exploited by contracting software, can be provided to consumer software (in the context of software-to-software contracting communications on the automated marketplace) while other information items, specifically the software-unsuitable ones, can be provided *centrally* on the automated marketplace, as explained in the following. In this way, *all* of the information listed in Article 6(1), CRD is, in fact, to be provided on the medium used for contracting, i.e., the automated marketplace, exactly as required by Articles 6 and 8, CRD. Basically, this approach comprises a combination of the '*software as the consumer*' and the '*direct communication*' approaches discussed earlier, which accepts the realities of fully automated contracting and, at the same, strives to ensure an effective, rather than shallow, application of the information duties in the particular context.

The consumer inevitably interacts *personally* with the website (or other medium) that makes accessible the automated marketplace, particularly while she instructs buying software to close a

205 On the concept of 'provide', see infra at pp. 70–71

206 For as long as consumers choose to review and approve each and every transaction, there will not be (real) automated contracting in place and hence, no problem with the information duties of the CRD.

207 For more on Article 8(4), CRD see infra at p. 68

contract for a particular product. As a result, the consumer can directly be provided with the software-unsuitable information items of Article 6(1), CRD on the said website or app:

> While the consumer fills in the Web-based instruction form ordering the software to purchase a particular model of a camera for example, a window or dialog box can appear on screen informing him or her about the existence of and procedures relating to the exercise of the right of withdrawal. Similarly, when the product that the consumer instructs the software to purchase is one of those for which there is an exemption from the right of withdrawal in accordance with Article 16 of the CRD, the appearing window or dialog box can inform him or her about the absence of a 'withdrawal' right or about the circumstances described in Article 16, under which that right will be lost. Another piece of information that has been said to be useless to automated contracting software, namely a reminder of the existence of a legal guarantee for goods as required by Article 6(1)(l) also can be provided in the way just described.
>
> (Markou, 2017b, pp. 13–14).

The same is largely true in relation to all of the information items referring to the right of withdrawal, namely the ones required by Article 6(1)(h), (i),[208] (j) and (k), CRD.

In fact, this way of communicating important information may be more effective than placing all of the information on a webpage, for example. In this respect, automated contracting, which relieves consumers from the task of reviewing certain information (leaving it to software) in conjunction with the approach that provides for the provision of specific information items through dialog boxes seems effectively to address the notorious problem of information overload relating to consumers not being cognitively able to make use of all of the provided information.[209]

Of course, not *all* information items that are software unsuitable can be provided in the particular (effective) way. Indeed, *trader-specific* information, such as the geographical address for complaints and the codes of conduct or redress mechanisms to which the trader submits required by Article 6(1)(d), (n) and (t), CRD, cannot be provided while consumers instruct the software; at that time, the trader with whom consumer (buying) software is to negotiate and contract will, in many cases, be unknown. This information, therefore, can presumably only be provided through the display of a list of participating merchants (together with their complaints address, codes and redress mechanisms) on the website hosting the marketplace.

Given that Article 6(1), CRD only requires that the information be 'provided' to the consumer as opposed to be 'received' by her, this way of providing *trader-specific* information would most likely satisfy the said requirement; according to the CJEU, information is provided to the consumer, simply when it is made available or accessible to her.[210] Though the consumer is unlikely to thoroughly review such a merchant list before setting contracting software in operation, this is not a serious problem given that such information is mostly useful post-contractually and does not refer to vital purchase-related factors. Moreover, as is explained later, this information must also be provided to consumers on a durable medium at the latest right after contract conclusion meaning that consumers will have ample opportunity to consult it.[211]

208 For Article 6(1)(i), CRD, however, see also infra at p. 67

209 On this problem, see Nordhausen (2006, pp. iii, 9).

210 Infra pp. 70–71

211 This is because of Article 8(7), CRD. For more on this provision, see infra at pp. 68–69 and Chapter 2.2.5.2

A similar issue exists regarding the information item required by Article 6(1)(i), CRD. The said provision relates to the (fortunately limited) circumstances in which the goods cannot be returned by post (due to their size, for example) and the trader is not willing to undertake the said cost himself. According to Article 6(1)(i), the trader must inform the consumer of the said cost, yet, this may be impossible pre-contractually, i.e., *before* the consumer software concludes a contract with a given trader. Indeed, even assuming that the size of the goods and the delivery address of the consumer will be known at the time the consumer finishes with instructing the software, such cost also depends on the geographical location to which the goods are to be returned, which will be that of the trader. Recital 36, CRD acknowledges that it may be difficult to calculate the said cost in advance, stating that "the trader should provide a statement that such a cost will be payable, and that this cost may be high, along with a reasonable estimation of the maximum cost, which could be based on the cost of delivery to the consumer". Yet, for the reasons just explained, 'a reasonable estimation of the maximum cost' may still be impossible to offer pre-contractually, unless perhaps the software is instructed to conclude a contract with a trader from a specific geographical area. This reinforces the view that the information duties of the CRD are not geared to work in the context of automated marketplaces. Thankfully, consumer protection can, to a significant extent, be secured by the display of a statement about the said cost and the fact that may be high as per Recital 36, CRD.

2.5.2.1.4 THE 'INFORMATION REMOVAL' APPROACH

Finally, a more drastic solution entailed in the so-called '*information removal*' approach (Markou, 2017b, pp. 10, 15–18) may be merited, especially if, in the future, wholly automated contracting becomes widespread and breaks free from the 'walls' of closed marketplace systems accessible through given websites. Under such circumstances, it will probably become necessary to introduce machine-suitable information duties that would also be free from the uncertainty inevitably surrounding the application of legal requirements to contexts which they were not devised for. This approach simply 'surrenders' to the realities of automated contracting and accepts that the (human) consumer is *not* to consider any information. Pre-contractual decision-making is delegated to software, and therefore the consumer herself is not to benefit from any information provided prior to contract conclusion. Accordingly, any attempt to provide all of the information currently required is abandoned and information items that are clearly software unsuitable are simply removed from the list to which a pre-contractual information duty refers to.

Such information removal has been considered even outside the context of wholly automated contracting as a response to the general problem of information overload, albeit with hesitation, as "information is the key element to enable a free choice for the consumer" (Nordhausen, 2006, p. 9). However, the reduction of the information required pre-contractually inevitably becomes a serious policy choice when the non-processing of such information is owed not to cognitive limitations of humans but to unavoidable (technical) restrictions. Moreover, as it will be shown, the CRD does not allow for its adoption and would also need certain adjustments in order to accommodate it. These adjustments are not drastic, however, meaning that it would not be necessary to introduce a separate (or significantly amended) consumer protection measure to govern automated contracting, nor would the level of consumer protection achieved by the CRD be greatly affected by the adoption of the said approach.

Yet, such a legislative move must be preceded by the law answering a difficult question relating to the exact information items that *must* be included in a pre-contractual information duty specifically devised for automated contracting. The answer to this question, which is central to the achievement of a sufficient level of consumer protection, will have to be determined through a synergy between law and technology. The law should take a careful look into 'automated contracting' technology in an attempt to understand its actual capabilities and/or limitations. For example, requiring software to act upon information *on the existence* of out-of-court redress mechanisms or after-sales support may be reasonable, while requiring it to utilize information on the methods, procedures or conditions of access to such mechanisms or support may be not. Based on a thorough understanding of technology, the law can then rely on the Article 6(1) list of information items (as these have already been accepted as having a useful or necessary role in consumer pre-contractual decision-making) and carefully 'trim' it down, thereby constructing a suitable information duty. Technology must then strive to release software that can comply with such carefully devised information duty, thereby avoiding legally incompliant contracting software and automated marketplaces.

The 'information removal' approach is not therefore eligible to immediate adoption, yet it is interesting to see how ready the CRD is to accommodate it for when the time comes. The CRD requires the provision of the information items listed in Article 6(1) *without* providing for any exception that would come close to the 'information removal' approach. The only provision that somewhat loosens the relevant information duty is Article 8(4), CRD, which, where the means of distance communication used for contracting is subject to limitations of space or time, permits the trader to provide on the said means a reduced amount of information, namely, "the main characteristics of the goods or services, the identity of the trader, the total price, the right of withdrawal, the duration of the contract and, if the contract is of indeterminate duration, the conditions for terminating the contract, as referred to in points (a), (b), (e), (h) and (o) of Article 6(1)". According to the same provision, "the other information referred to in Article 6(1) shall be provided by the trader to the consumer in an appropriate way in accordance with paragraph 1 of this Article" such as "by providing a toll free telephone number or a hypertext link to a webpage of the trader where the relevant information is directly available and easily accessible".[212] It arises that Article 8(4) insists in the provision of *all* of the information *pre-contractually*, just *not* on the same means of distant communication. It is thus inconsistent with the 'information removal' approach, which removes certain (software-unsuitable items) from the *pre-contractual* information duty. Additionally, Article 8(4) is explicitly tied to the existence of limitations of space and time and does not thus cover other technical constraints, namely an inability to process or act upon certain information. Finally, the minimum information required by Article 8(4) includes information such as on the right of withdrawal, which is software unsuitable and is amongst the information items that are to be removed in the context of the 'information removal' approach. This reinforces the view that the said approach cannot find support in Article 8(4), CRD.[213]

Though the CRD does not already allow for the relevant approach, it can accommodate it with minor adjustments and without lowering the afforded level of consumer. This is because Article 8(7) requires that all of the Article 6(1) information be provided to the consumer on a durable medium within reasonable time after contract conclusion and at the

212 Recital 36, CRD.
213 On this issue, see also Markou (2017b, p. 18).

latest at the time of the delivery of the goods or before the instigation of the performance of the service. Thus, human consumers, who are the ones actually capable of processing or acting upon a reminder of the existence of the legal guarantee or the procedures for the exercise of withdrawal, for example, would still receive that information on paper (with delivery of the goods or before service performance) or *via* e-mail.[214]

It is not a problem that Article 8(7) allows for the *post-contractual* provision of the relevant information; the information items to be removed through the adoption of the 'information removal' approach, are not particularly influential on pre-contractual decision-making and are mostly useful post contractually.[215] It is perhaps not a coincidence that the predecessor of the CRD, namely, the DSD did not require the provision of the trader address for complaints, the procedures relating to the withdrawal right and information on after-sales rights and guarantees pre-contractually; the said information were *only* required by Article 5, DSD, which is the corresponding provision of Article 8(7), CRD.

The adoption of the 'information removal' approach would however necessitate certain adjustments to some of the rest of the provisions of the CRD, particularly those pertaining to the right of withdrawal. First, unlike the DSD, in which the beginning of the withdrawal period began to run provided that the 'durable medium' obligation of Article 5 was met[216] and, thus, remained unaffected by compliance (or non-compliance) with the pre-contractual duty of Article 4, in CRD the opposite is true. Its provisions relating to the withdrawal periods do not refer at all to the 'durable medium' obligation of Article 8(7) and only depend on compliance or non-compliance with the pre-contractual information duty of Article 6(1).

More specifically, according to the CRD, the standard withdrawal period of 14 days begins from the day of receipt of the goods and from the day of service contract conclusion,[217] irrespective of *when* the information has been supplied on a durable medium and even if that has been supplied *after* contract conclusion. That would be problematic in the context of fully automated contracting, where consumers would *not* consider the said information item pre-contractually (if the relevant information item were to be removed from the pre-contractual Article 6(1) duty). The European Commission (2014a, p. 36) has clarified that "the requirement for the confirmation to be sent within a 'reasonable time' implies that it should be sent early enough to allow the consumer to exercise the right of withdrawal", the relevant reasonableness test having to be applied on a case-by-case basis. This however does not exclude the possibility of the consumer being provided with the said information only after some part of the withdrawal period has already passed.

Secondly, the CRD, specifically, Article 10(1), extends the withdrawal period by 12 months, *not* when Article 8(7) is not complied with, but when the trader violates the pre-contractual obligation of Article 6(1)(h) to provide information on the right of withdrawal. If the particular information item were to be removed, Article 10(1), as it now stands, would

214 For more, see infra pp. 71–72

215 The only exception relates to Article 16(m), CRD which exempts contracts for online digital content from the right of withdrawal when he has specifically consented to performance beginning prior to the expiry of the withdrawal period. In such cases, the consumer must be asked for his relevant consent and acknowledgement of the resulting loss of the withdrawal right. Unless contracting software can respond to such questions on behalf of the consumer, the relevant consent and acknowledgement provision facility must be provided while the consumer instructs the consumer. A similar issue arises in relation to Article 16(a), CRD and the exception referring to service contracts. Article 14(4), CRD is also relevant to these two cases.

216 See Article 6(1), DSD.

217 Article 9(2), CRD.

result in an 'automatically' extended withdrawal period in relation to ***all*** fully automated (or software-concluded) contracts, something that may be undesirable in principle.[218] In practice, however, this is not a major problem. Article 10(2), CRD would enable merchants to prevent any such extension of the withdrawal period; it provides that if the information is provided within 12 months from the date that the initial 14 began to run in accordance with Article 9(2), i.e., from the date of receipt of the goods or 'service contract' conclusion, "the withdrawal period shall expire 14 days after the day upon which the consumer receives that information". It follows that if the merchant complies with his Article 8(7) obligation, for example, through a paper note or e-mail, handed or sent at the time of delivery of goods or contract conclusion, the withdrawal period will effectively be kept to the standard (or minimum) duration of 14 days.

More difficult is the (third) problem arising in relation to Article 6(6), CRD, which frees the consumer from the obligation to pay the cost for the return of the goods if he withdraws from the contract where the trader has not pre-contractually informed him of this obligation in violation of Article 6(1)(i), CRD. The CRD does not provide for any exception to this rule. Accordingly, if the 'information removal' approach were to be adopted, the said provision would need to be amended so that the situation whereby the trader is 'penalized' for not providing *non*-required information is avoided. Policymakers could opt for making this cost payable by the trader at the same time relieving him from the obligation of Article 13 (1), CRD to return the initial delivery cost, thereby striking a fair balance. Similar issues that may have to be resolved arise in relation to the cases where the consumer contracts for a service or digital content not supplied on a durable medium. [219]

Another issue raised by the 'information removal' approach (as well as by the previously discussed approach entailing provision of some information to the consumer software) is whether there should be a legal duty ensuring that consumer software is *technically capable of considering* the provided information. Article 6(1), CRD *per se* does not impose (at least, expressly or directly) such requirement, as it merely requires that traders *'provide'* the relevant information. It thus opts for what the CJEU has, by reference to the DSD, described as "a neutral formulation"[220] that differs from the concepts of 'given' or 'received', which have "greater implications for business".[221] Accordingly, if the merchant software sends the information to the consumer software, merchants need not be concerned with whether that information has been received, read or acted upon. However, the CJEU did not certainly mean that the neutral 'provide' requirement would be satisfied even if it was impossible for the consumer to access or review the provided information. The provision of information should at least entail the ability of the person who is to be provided with it to use it. Thus, when the party having to discharge the relevant duty knows very well that such ability does *not* exist,[222] it is difficult to see how that party could be considered to have provided the information. Indeed, what the CJEU has said is that the requirement is satisfied even when the consumer must take some action in order to gain access to the information such as by clicking on a link provided in an e-mail and thus, when such access is not possible by him

218 It is not logical to 'penalize' the non-provision of information that is *not* required. For more on this issue, see Markou (2017b, p. 17).

219 This is mainly because of Article 14(4), CRD, which relieves the consumer from the obligation to pay for services or digital content received if he has not received certain information pre-contractually. See also supra n.217.

220 *Case C-49/11 Content Services Ltd v Bundesarbeitskammer, para. 35.*

221 Ibid at para. 35.

222 The reader should recall that acceptance of real automated contracting requires acceptance of the fact that it is only consumer software that will consider any provided information pre-contractually.

remaining passive.[223] Evidently, the underlying assumption is that the consumer is, in fact, capable of accessing and reading the information and of course, of acting upon it, too. Accordingly, if consumer software is technically incapable of making any use of the information provided by merchant software, Article 6(1), CRD should not be considered as being complied with.

A different interpretation would be void of any justification. Indeed, albeit by reference to the term 'provide' in Article 8(7) (rather than Article 6(1), CRD), the European Commission (2014a, p. 37) seems to endorse the view that the relevant term results in a less demanding requirement. Its explanation is that "the trader is not in control of the confirmation email's transmission process". Thus, traders will comply with the relevant information duty merely *by sending* the e-mail with the information. By contrast, when traders choose to direct their activities through automated marketplaces, effectively inviting consumers to use marketplace-provided software in order to shop from them, it makes perfect sense to require such traders to ensure that the systems of such marketplaces allow for *meaningful* automated contracting; the latter presupposes that consumer software is actually capable of considering information provided by merchant software. This technical capability is obviously *under the control of the marketplace provider* to be chosen by the trader. Admittedly, *open* marketplaces are accessible by heterogeneous consumer software supplied by third parties unrelated to the traders participating in one such marketplace or the marketplace provider. In such cases, a requirement inspired by Section 102(14), Uniform Computer Information Transactions Act (United States of America, 2002) deeming a term as "conspicuous" if "it is presented in a form that would enable a reasonably configured electronic agent to take it into account or react to it" can achieve an appropriate balance between the interests of consumers and traders. In the context of the 'information removal' approach, such requirement would actually play the role of Article 8(1), CRD, which requires that the information be provided "in plain and intelligible language".

2.5.2.2 Problems with Article 8(7), CRD?

Brazier et al. (2003b, p. 5) would also see a problem with the application of Article 8(7), CRD in the context of automated marketplaces: Does contracting software receiving the Article 6(1) information qualify as a *durable medium* [224] on which a confirmation of the said information must be provided as per Article 8(7)?[225] Yet, the this problem is not particularly serious. The confirmation of information required by Article 8(7) can be sent during contract performance, which is normally taken over by the human parties involved. Traders participating in automated marketplaces do not have fewer options regarding how to communicate the required confirmation than other online traders. Thus, they can deliver it with the purchased product (Bradgate, 1997, para. 9; Lodder and Voulon, 2002, p. 283) or use electronic mail, especially if the subject matter of the contract is a service or a digital product.[226] They do not *have* to do so *via* the systems of the automated marketplace. Thus, the question regarding whether contracting software qualifies as a durable medium is not a pressing one.

223 Ibid paras. 33, 35.
224 The particular concept is explained earlier, see supra p. 43
225 The said commentators refer to Article 5(1) of the DSD, the predecessor of the CRD which corresponds to Article 8(7), CRD.
226 E-mail is a durable medium defined by Article 2(10) and expanded upon in Recital 23, CRD as any instrument enabling consumers to store information in its original for future reference such as e-mail, USB sticks, paper and CDs.

Even when *electronic products* are not only sold but also *delivered* to consumer software in automated marketplaces, the required confirmation could probably be delivered to the consumer together with and in the same way as the electronic product itself. Brazier et al. (2003b, p. 5) propose technical means making this possible, but one could probably take this for granted. Indeed, if an electronic product can be delivered and be accessible to the consumer through software representing her, information in durable form must be capable of being delivered to her in the same way. Moreover, as automated marketplaces will in most cases be accessible through websites or apps[227] with which consumers will have to register, thus acquiring a private account, the said information can be uploaded to that private account. According to the European Commission (2014a, p. 35), such private accounts can qualify as durable media. Alternatively, in the context of registering with a marketplace, since the consumer will probably have to provide a valid e-mail address, the confirmation of information can be sent to that address.

Admittedly, traders in marketplaces open to *heterogeneous* consumer software will not have control over consumer buying software and its ability to receive and store information in durable form. The CRD assumes that the merchant will have control over the means of distance communication, as it imposes on him the burden of proof of compliance.[228] This may not be impossible to discharge, however. Indeed, merchants must choose to sell their products in automated marketplaces that enable them to comply with their legal duties. They may thus have to choose marketplaces that require consumer registration, thereby maintaining the possibility of compliance with Article 8(7) (through uploading the required information to a private account on the marketplace or sending a relevant e-mail, as explained previously). The latter solution would seem to comprise an example of the steps that Cross (2009, p. 28) suggests that merchants take to ensure direct communication with the consumer, albeit in relation to Article 8(7), rather than Article 6(1), CRD. As Article 8(7), CRD is a *post-contract conclusion* duty that does not affect the pre-contractual or contractual stages involved in automated contracting, the objection against the relevant suggestion in relation to Article 6(1)[229] is not valid.

2.5.2.3 The term 'trader' under the CRD in the context of automated marketplaces

Having shown how the information duties of the CRD could apply to automated marketplaces (now and in the future), thereby addressing the second of the risks or issues associated with such marketplaces, it is important to inquire into the party who could be considered bound by the relevant duties in the particular context. Is it just the merchants using an automated marketplace or are marketplace providers also bound by the relevant duties? Obviously, the latter would mean an increased effectiveness of the CRD. Moreover, it makes perfect sense for parties providing and benefiting from (technical) environments enabling business-to-consumer contracting to be required to ensure that consumers buying on their systems are to receive all of the legally mandated information. It is true that the contractual consequences of incompliance with the Article 6(1) information duties, such as the extension of the withdrawal period by twelve (12) months[230] and the relief of the consumer from

227 See also supra pp. 65–66
228 Article 6(9), CRD.
229 See supra at pp. 63–64
230 Article 10, CRD.

the obligation to pay non-disclosed taxes or charges,[231] only affect merchants closing contracts with consumers within the marketplace. This does not however necessarily mean that the said duties are not addressed to marketplace providers, too; they can be enforced against them through the administrative penalties provided for in Article 24, CRD.

For marketplace providers to be considered as addressees of the CRD information duties, however, they must qualify as 'traders' within the meaning of Article 2(2), CRD. According to the said provision, a 'trader' is "any natural person or any legal person, irrespective of whether privately or publicly owned, who is acting, ***including through any other person acting in his name or on his behalf***, for purposes relating to his trade, business, craft or profession in relation to contracts covered by this Directive".[232] The European Commission (2014a, p. 31) takes the phrase 'including through any other person acting in his name or on his behalf' in Article 2(2) to support the view that "when a trader uses an online platform to market his products and conclude contracts with consumers, the provider of that platform shares, ***in so far as he is acting in the name of or on behalf of that trader***, the responsibility for ensuring compliance with the Directive".[233] First of all, online platforms do not *de facto* act in the name or on behalf of the traders selling their products therein. If they are neutrally doing nothing more than providing the systems enabling contracting and are not involved in contract performance, they do not really qualify as 'traders'. Indeed, the (identical) concepts of 'acting in the name' and 'acting on behalf of' in the UCPD are explained by the European Commission (2016c, p. 30) by reference to the example of app-selling platforms, such as Apple App Store, which notoriously charge app sellers a commission and are involved in the collection of payment by app buyers (Mackenzie, 2012). At least some automated marketplaces will thus not qualify as 'traders' for the purposes of the CRD and, accordingly, they will not share responsibility for compliance with the relevant information duties. Others, however, particularly those involved in contract performance such as payment of collection and/or product delivery, would be considered as 'traders'.

However, as noted elsewhere (Markou, 2017a, pp. 185–186), the way Article 2(2), CRD is drafted does not really support an interpretation rendering a party acting on behalf of another trader a 'trader' himself. Unlike the 'trader' definition in Article 2(b), UCPD, according to which a 'trader' is expressly *not only* any person acting for business purposes *but also* 'anyone acting in the name of or on behalf of a trader', Article 2(2), CRD rather says that a 'trader' is any person acting for business purposes, *even when* not acting alone but through another person representing him. Accordingly, it certainly clarifies that traders selling their products on online platforms administered by third parties remain 'traders' subject to the CRD, but its letter at least, does not go so far as rendering such third parties 'traders' themselves. The resulting uncertainty is somewhat reduced by Article 6(1)(c), CRD. By requiring that the trader provide the consumer with "where applicable, the geographical address and identity of the trader on whose behalf he is acting", it actually implicitly acknowledges that the trader to whom Article 6(1) addresses the relevant information duty may very well be one *not* acting on his own account but on behalf of some other trader. Yet, to ensure certainty and the avoidance of doubt, the 'trader' definition in CRD may have to be re-drafted along the lines of the corresponding definition of the UCPD. After all, there seems to be no obvious reason behind this inconsistency concerning the 'trader' definition between the two Directives.

231 Article 6(6), CRD.
232 Emphasis added.
233 Emphasis added.

2.5.3 Legal response pertaining to purchase-related information provided and considered on the platforms: concluding remarks

Regarding the issue relating to the completeness of the information provided by shopping agents (in the merchant listings they return following a consumer search), EU law has been shown to offer an adequate solution. Though the pre-contractual duties of the CRD are not suitable mainly because they cannot be interpreted as requiring the relevant information to be provided on the shopping agent platform as such, the UCPD is eligible to one such interpretation. Merchant listings displayed on shopping agent platforms qualify as 'invitations to purchase' and as such, they are subject to specific information duties imposed by the UCPD against both the shopping agent providers and the individual merchants listed on their platform in most cases. These duties, contained in Article 7(4), UCPD, require the inclusion in invitations to purchase of all of the necessary purchase-related information and a relevant exception provided for by Article 7(3), UCPD is fortunately not applicable to shopping agents. There is a problem with Article 7(4), however, which mandates information, amongst others, on delivery time only when not in accord with professional diligence. This qualification is not appropriate in the online context and may result in uncertainty regarding whether information on delivery time is required or not. The question can be answered in the affirmative, amongst others, by reference to Article 7(1), UCPD. If this uncertainty is resolved, perhaps by a relevant CJEU ruling, the EU legal response could readily be considered adequate. The same measure also provides an adequate solution to the problem of misleading 'smart buy' seals sometimes attached to merchant listings by shopping agent providers. Those, too, qualify as commercial practices employed by the said providers and, as such, they cannot be misleading according to the UCPD.

The legal solution to this issue in the context of automated marketplaces has been found in the CRD, given that the communications exchanged between selling and buying software thereon are clearly pre-contractual communications triggering the CRD pre-contractual information duties. However, though those information duties (contained in Article 6, CRD) are detailed enough to require all of the information that needs to be considered by a consumer when contemplating a purchase, they are not fully compatible with automated contracting; some of the required information is totally unsuitable, where the information is not to be considered by a human consumer but by software substituting him. This chapter has considered a number of approaches towards the application of the CRD information duties to automated marketplaces and has shown that it can be achieved through requiring that some of the required information pieces be provided to the consumer software while others, specifically those that would be totally useless to that software, centrally on the website through which the marketplace is made accessible. The relevant exercise has been quite complex, as any solution should not be achieved simply by abandoning the idea of fully automated contracting. Thus, solutions that insist in the provision of the required information directly to the *human* consumer are not really solutions.

It has thus advocated the adoption of a more drastic approach that entails the removal of some of the information pieces required by Article 6, CRD, which has been explained as being more suitable in the context of automated contracting for when this is not to be conducted within closed marketplaces. As it has been explained, the CRD cannot currently accommodate that approach, and its adoption may, in any event, be pre-mature while automated marketplaces are still at their infancy and have not been commercialized. However, when the time comes, it can be adopted without lowering consumer protection through effecting certain amendments to some of the provisions of the CRD. All in all, though the EU legal response to the relevant issue as entailed in the CRD can be considered as adequate, the application of the relevant provisions realizing the said solution is bound to prove problematic in the context of automated marketplaces. They thus need special (and careful) interpretation to be able to produce the required effects.

Given that the confirmation of the pre-contractual information required to be provided to consumers by Article 8(7), CRD can be given *post*-contractually, i.e., when the human consumer takes over, no serious problem arises with its application in this context. A more basic but real issue arises with whether the definition of 'trader' in the CRD is drafted so as to cover the automated marketplace provider too (as opposed to the merchants selling through the marketplace only). Though the intention of the legislator has probably been to cover platforms actively involved in contract conclusion and performance, its current wording does not fully support a relevant interpretation and may result in unnecessary uncertainty.

3 Unreliable transactions and traditional fraud risks

3.1 General

The risk of fraud (or unfair or fraudulent dealings) applicable to both shopping agents and automated marketplaces mainly refers to the platform operating as a consumer gateway to fraudulent, unscrupulous or unreliable merchants mainly because it does not vet merchant participants.[1] It is mostly about traditional fraud or unfair practices, *not* involving an unauthorized interference with software code or consumer data but rather a non-delivery of products, misleading consumers towards buying a product or a violation of contract terms increasing costs and hassle. A legal obligation on platform providers to vet merchant participation on their platforms would be an ideal solution, yet as is shown in this chapter, it does not clearly arise from EU law.

3.2. Unreliable transactions and traditional fraud: illustrating the risks

An issue associated with shopping agents and even more so, with automated marketplaces relates to the creditworthiness (or reliability) of participating merchants. While these platforms may facilitate consumer access to merchants offering quality products at low prices, they can also serve as cheap (or even free) tool in the hands of fraudsters or unreliable merchants helping them to reach and defraud or more generally, harm consumers.

If such platforms are to be beneficial consumer services and comprise acceptable marketing tools for merchants, platform providers – who derive revenue by making them available – should be required to ensure their 'safety'. They should therefore be expected to examine potential merchant participants against criteria relating to their reliability and perhaps to monitor their activity on the platform in order to terminate those falling below certain standards. In other words, those serving as gateways or intermediary environments aiming at bringing merchants and consumers together can play an important role in battling online fraud. Indeed, as the online marketplace becomes difficult to navigate without aid, such intermediary platforms are likely to comprise the necessary step prior to the individual website of online merchants for nearly all consumers. Importantly, this seems to be a role that they can practically play. Indeed, Kirsner has quoted the provider of MortgageQuotes.com – a website comparing mortgage quotes from various lenders – stating that they terminated the participation of lenders who were offering unreasonably and/or suspiciously low mortgage rates (Collins, quoted in Kirsner, 1999, para. 12). Moreover, platform providers need not act as accreditors screening

1 Supra Chapter 1, p. 16 and Chapter 2.2.2.1.5

every potential merchant participant themselves, but they can exploit relevant self-regulatory measures admitting only accredited merchants for example, as it will be explained.[2]

Unfortunately, however, anti-fraud policies are not the norm on relevant platforms. Consumer watchdogs refer to the risk inherent in the inclusion of listings "without checking the source and integrity of the information" (OnlineShoppingRights, n.d.). Other anecdotal research (Markou, 2011, p. 192) showed that some shopping agent providers were evaluating merchants only for the purpose of attaching a trust mark to those meeting certain criteria rather than to exclude or terminate those who were not. Moreover, one shopping agent explicitly addresses the issue of fraudulent or unreliable merchants but effectively admits that it does not take an active role in eliminating them; it includes a guide regarding how consumers can spot and avoid suspicious or unreliable merchants (Pricerunner International AB, 2017a).

However, the burden of guarding against fraud should not be placed on consumers. Rather, it must largely be discharged by the shopping agent provider, which effectively leads consumers to merchants. The aforementioned shopping agent explains that it can only have a limited relevant role in relation to those merchants with whom it has no direct business relationship, and which are simply searched or picked up by its algorithm (Pricerunner International AB, 2017a). Yet, apart from the fact that it may be the provider who chooses (and he can check out) the merchants from whom information is scrapped,[3] this apparently confirms that platform providers can have an increased role in ensuring the reliability of merchants who submit their offerings to them and with whom they therefore have a direct business relationship.

Recent investigations or studies (ECME Consortium, 2013; OFT, 2010; OFT, 2012) focusing on the 'consumer protection' aspect of relevant platforms have not touched upon these issues. One study that did so, implicitly seems to confirm that agent providers do not undertake any fraud-preventive role: "Only one of the 99 price comparison websites contained a policy for dealing with rogue or fraudulent traders, and only two allowed customers to report suspicious activity of this sort directly to the site" (Consumer Focus, 2013, p. 9).

Admittedly, a reliable merchant rating system, if applied on shopping agent platforms, can serve as an effective anti-fraud measure. It can alert consumers to the risk and provide the means through which consumers can verify reliability, thereby avoiding low-rating (unreliable) merchants. Yet, studies find that providers often provide no explanation on the methodology behind merchant ratings and reviews and that only a minority of providers control their source and/or quality or reliability (ECME Consortium, 2013, p. 230). Such reputation systems, therefore, cannot effectively substitute a duty on providers to vet merchants and/or their listings.

The risk of fraud exists in the case of automated marketplaces, too. Electronic markets in general, "provide a fertile ground of deceitful participants to engage in old as well as new types of fraud" (Fasli, 2007, p. 359). One obvious example involves fraudsters 'hiding' behind software and posing as real businesses while having no intention to deliver any products. Accordingly, automated marketplace providers, too, should have an obligation to vet merchant participants and their activity on the marketplace. This is even more the case given that the European Commission (2016b, p. 7) accepts that "online platforms are well-placed to proactively reduce the amount of illegal content that passes through them". In fact, this need is more acute in their case than it is in relation to shopping agents, as while on

2 Infra p. 78. The idea of the exploitation of self-regulatory schemes in the context of access control is analysed by reference to privacy credentials, see Chapter 4 p. 113

3 See infra p. 86

automated marketplaces, consumers are substituted by software and cannot thus take any self-protective measures themselves (such as checking merchant websites for signs of unreliability). Moreover, as is illustrated in the following, technology exists that makes this obligation practically dischargeable, thereby rendering its imposition perfectly justifiable.

Actually, the role of e-marketplaces as regulators and even guardians of their users seems widely to be accepted, and the same is true of the relationship of such intermediaries with failures like fraud and privacy violations.

Fasli (2007, p. 359) puts it clearly:

> To minimize risk in electronic marketplaces, the issues of trust management and security need to be addressed. In particular, electronic marketplaces must address how they intend to provide trust, security, enforce contracts and establish a legal framework. The marketplace itself may provide safeguards and guarantees against fraud and breaches of the protocol, as well as impose sanctions on those who have deviated from the prescribed rules.[4]

One way in which the marketplace could discharge such duty is through consumer software that can make sense of merchant ratings (or reputation mechanisms) (Fasli, 2007, pp. 359–360), such as the 'trust and reputation' mechanism of the Kasbah marketplace (Zacharia, Moukas and Maes, 1999, p. 3).[5] As already hinted at, however, these suffer from limitations, such as collusions between merchants and some consumers leading to untruthful ratings, fear of submitting negative feedback and merchant self-rating (Fasli, 2007, pp. 369–370).[6] An access control mechanism seems therefore indispensable; comparably to what has been argued by reference to shopping agents,[7] each merchant seeking access to an automated marketplace should be required to provide information about his identity and creditability, particularly in the form of digital credentials possibly issued in the context of independent self-regulatory schemes.[8] Access control can be conducted automatically (Mont and Yearworth, 2001, pp. 2–4; Collins et al., 1997, pp.6–7) and, hence, consistently with the automation inherent in automated marketplaces.

An automated marketplace can assume an even broader regulatory role, thus also monitoring post-access behaviour, effectively acting as a "trusted intermediary" (Collins et al., 1998, p. 63).[9] The MAGNET marketplace, for example, seems to have been given such role: "By independently verifying the identities of participants, by tracking the state of the negotiations and any commitments that result and by enforcing the rules of the protocol, fraud and misrepresentation are curtailed" (Collins et al., 1998, p. 63).

Having illustrated the risk of fraud (or unreliable and/or unfair dealings) associated with shopping agents and automated marketplaces, as well as the need for a legal obligation on such platforms to monitor merchant access to (and perhaps even activity) on their systems,

4 See also Bailey and Bakos (1997, pp. 2, 3) and Verhagen, Meents and Tan (2006, p. 544).
5 Supra Chapter 1 pp. 0
6 On the limitations of reputation systems and a relevant literature review, see Riefa (2015, pp. 153–156).
7 Supra p. 77
8 Supra n. 2
9 For example, a marketplace can ensure that "the seller gets paid and the buyer gets the goods" by dividing an exchange into pieces so that "each party is motivated to follow the exchange at every step in anticipation of the profit from the rest of the exchange instead of vanishing with what the other party has delivered so far" (Sandholm, 2002, p. 670).

the important question arises as to whether one such obligation can be derived from EU law. If this question can be answered in the affirmative, at least as far as access control is concerned, the response of EU law towards the relevant risk could be regarded as satisfactory.

3.3. Unreliable transactions and traditional fraud risks: the EU legal response

3.3.1 Introductory remarks

Explicit references to the risk of fraud are found in EU Directives regulating the telecommunications and electronic communications sector, but these Directives are not applicable to shopping agents and automated marketplaces. More generally, EU law does not contain a direct and/or explicit obligation on online service providers to prevent fraud.

More specifically, the Universal Service Directive (USD)[10] had been amended by the Citizens' Rights Directive, amongst others, to include Article 28(2) providing as follows:

> Member States shall ensure that the relevant authorities are able to require undertakings providing public communications networks and/or publicly available electronic communications services to block, on a case-by-case basis, access to numbers or services where this is justified by reasons of fraud or misuse.

The objective of this provision is to "progressively minimise the role of the 'relevant authorities' regarding the fighting against fraud or misuse" (BEREC, 2012, p. 6) leaving it up to the providers of public communications networks and/or publicly available electronic communications services to monitor the use of their services and block access to fraudulent numbers or associated services. However, shopping agents and automated marketplaces providers do not qualify as public communication networks or electronic communications services.[11]

Another Directive, namely the Radio Equipment Directive (RED), subjects the entry into the market of radio equipment to certain essential requirements, including, amongst others, a requirement that such equipment "supports certain features ensuring protection from fraud".[12] Again, however, the concept of 'radio equipment' covers electrical or electronic products emitting or receiving radio waves for the purpose of communication.[13] These would include mobile phones but not shopping agents and/or automated marketplaces; these do not emit or receive radio waves.

Despite the fact that operating on the internet, information society services are notoriously a breeding ground for fraud (mainly attributable to the anonymity they usually allow for), EU law does not subject their providers to a similarly explicit obligation to prevent fraud. The E-Commerce Directive, which regulates information society services, is not underpinned by a concern to guard users against the risk of fraud. Right on the contrary, it seeks to shield certain online intermediaries from liability for the unlawful (or fraudulent) use of their services. Its provisions on intermediaries will, in fact, be shown to risk blocking the imposition of the suggested fraud-preventive obligation on the relevant platform providers. It is thus important to examine whether such an obligation could be derived from any

10 Supra n. 132.
11 Infra pp. 134–135, where this is illustrated by reference to automated marketplaces. It can readily arise from the said analysis that this is true of shopping agents too.
12 Article 3(3)(f), RED.
13 Article 2(1)(1), RED.

other EU legal measure as well as the relationship of any such measure with the ECD provisions on intermediaries.

It will be shown that a fraud-preventive obligation cannot be derived from the liability-related Directives, while one such obligation existing implicitly in the Unfair Commercial Practices Directive is at least uncertain and may not be powerful enough. In both cases, the said obligation may be prevented by the ECD, if the latter is *not* interpreted so that this result is avoided. The Second Payment Services Directive seeks to protect users against fraud in a different way; it provides, as it will be shown, an *ex-post* solution, which is however only partial and *ex-ante* protection, which is admittedly important, yet its applicability to automated marketplaces poses interesting questions that need to be answered.

A Communication by the European Commission (2016a) on online platforms followed by a 2018 Proposal for a Regulation on promoting fairness and transparency for business users of online intermediation services (European Commission, 2018b) are also relevant but being very recent, inevitably escaped the scope of this book. In any event, the Proposed Regulation (which, just before this book was sent to print, has become a Regulation) focuses on the protection of business users and thus inevitably stops short of significantly strengthening the EU legal response towards the risk of consumer fraud and filling in any relevant gaps. This is so despite the fact that amongst the guiding principles of the Communication were "responsible behaviour of online platforms to protect core values" and "transparency and fairness for maintaining user trust" (European Commission, 2016b, p. 5).

3.3.2 The E-Commerce Directive (ECD)

3.3.2.1 General

Articles 12, 13 and 14 of the E-Commerce Directive exclude the liability of certain intermediaries for unlawful conduct exhibited by recipients of their services if the former have not contributed in or had knowledge of the said conduct. Moreover, Article 15(1) prohibits subjecting those intermediaries to a "general obligation to monitor the information which they transmit or store" or to "a general obligation actively to seek facts or circumstances indicating illegal activity". Understandably, whether these provisions cover shopping agents and automated marketplaces is extremely relevant to the question regarding whether EU law contains an adequate solution to the relevant risk of fraud.

Facilitating communication and/or contracting between merchants and consumers, 'shopping agent' and 'automated marketplace' providers are certainly intermediaries. Yet, the aforementioned liability limitations do not cover *all* intermediary activities but only those specified in Articles 12, 13 and 14: "The limitations on liability in the Directive apply to certain clearly delimited activities carried out by internet intermediaries, rather than to categories of service providers or types of information" (European Commission, 2003b, p. 12). The idea is that those activities, which include internet access and web hosting services, are vital to the operation and development of the WWW Accordingly, by reducing the risk of liability, the law facilitates the development of the Internet and that of the services and opportunities it enables.

As the relevant liability exemptions cover "liability, both civil and criminal, for all types of illegal activity" (European Commission, 2003b, secs. 4.6, p. 12),[14] if shopping agent and automated marketplace services fall within Articles 12, 13 or 14, the question arises as to

14 This has been confirmed by Attorney-General Szpunar in his Opinion in the Case *C-484/14, Tobias Mc Fadden v Sony Music Entertainment Germany GmbH, 16/3/2016, para. 64.*

whether one could derive a fraud-preventive obligation vested on them in the form of an access control mechanism (or otherwise). Fraud certainly qualifies as 'illegal activity', and indeed, the European Commission (2017a, para. 28) has recently referred to "illegal commercial practices online" as qualifying as such activity for the purposes of the ECD. It may be difficult to derive an indirect relevant obligation (resulting from a liability threat created by any of the liability-related Directives) if the ECD liability limitations actually remove the risk for liability of platform providers for any fraudulent activity on their platforms. The boundaries of Article 15 also merit examination; is it intended to preclude legal obligations involving vetting users? If the answer to this question is affirmative, then EU law even precludes Member States to impose one such obligation (through national law).

Admittedly, there may be important reasons for shielding such platforms from liability. CDT (2010, p. 5) emphasizes that "online marketplaces like Amazon or eBay . . . drive down transaction costs, create new distribution channels, increase competition, lower prices, and help connect global markets" whereas "intermediary liability tends to create barriers to information exchange and inhibit many of these market benefits". Yet, CDT also clarifies that "the reasons in favor of protecting intermediaries from liability are premised on the notion that the intermediaries themselves did not create the illegal content" (CTD, 2010, p. 4).

Though shopping agents and automated marketplaces may not entirely create the content themselves, they are often heavily involved both in its creation and in its promotion, as the whole of their business model relies on that content. In any event, shielding them from liability for the fraud of their (trader) users, does not necessarily mean that they should not be obligated to check the credibility of those users, thereby *ex-ante* reducing the risk of unlawful activity. Liability could then accrue not for the unlawful activity *per se* or even for aiding or abetting it but for their failure to put in place measures limiting the relevant risk, where they could have done so, both technically and economically.[15] Such liability could be such as to result to lighter consequences and these could also only be administrative (as opposed to civil and/or criminal) but there will at least be some liability.

Given that Article 13 refers to caching mainly performed by ISPs, when transmitting content to internet users (Article 29 DPWP, 2000, pp. 42, 81, 98), only Articles 12 and 14 are relevant in this context. Article 12(1) provides that

> Where an information society service is provided that consists of the transmission in a communication network of information provided by a recipient of the service . . . the service provider is not liable for the information transmitted, on condition that the provider: (a) does not initiate the transmission; (b) does not select the receiver of the transmission; and (c) does not select or modify the information contained in the transmission.

15 Mann and Belzley (2005, pp. 266–268) favour a liability regime concentrating on whether intermediaries *can* detect and prevent unlawful behaviour on their systems, given the various technologies facilitating this task. Indeed, if the cost of preventing unlawful behaviour is technically possible and economically reasonable meaning that no unreasonable burden will be placed on intermediaries, the argument in favour of giving them "gatekeeping roles" (CDT, 2010, p. 12) becomes strong. This view seems to be shared by the European Commission (2017a, para. 28): "Online platforms are entitled to prevent that their infrastructure and business is used to commit crimes, have a responsibility to protect their users and prevent illegal content on their platform, and are typically in possession of technical means to identify and remove such content".

Article 12(2) clarifies that any storage of the transmitted information must occur "for the sole purpose of carrying out the transmission in the communication network, and provided that the information is not stored for any period longer than is reasonably necessary for the transmission".

According to Article 14(1),

> Where an information society service is provided that consists of the storage of information provided by a recipient of the service . . . the service provider is not liable for the information stored at the request of a recipient of the service, on condition that: (a) the provider does not have actual knowledge of illegal activity or information and, as regards claims for damages, is not aware of facts or circumstances from which the illegal activity or information is apparent; or (b) the provider, upon obtaining such knowledge or awareness, acts expeditiously to remove or to disable access to the information.

Article 14(2) excludes the application of Article 14(1) "when the recipient of the service is acting under the authority or the control of the provider".

The main arising question is whether the relevant platform providers could successfully invoke the ECD liability limitations, in which case they will be able to escape liability and as a result, they will have little (legal) incentive to monitor access to their systems. Importantly, if they could do so, no direct obligation (to prevent fraud) could be imposed on them either (by operation of Article 15, ECD). The relevant examination will be conducted first by reference to automated marketplaces and then, in relation to shopping agents.

3.3.2.2 *The case of automated marketplaces*

The information exchanged during negotiations between merchant and consumer software within a marketplace system is "information transmitted in a communications network", thus triggering the aforementioned Article 12(1). However, given their tasks of actively supporting negotiations and contracting, automated marketplaces would probably store the software-exchanged contractual information, and that storage would probably not be temporary storage strictly for the purpose of transmission as required by the aforementioned Article 12(2). It would most likely be permanent storage for the purpose of the information being accessible to human users for review especially should a dispute arise. Accordingly, most automated marketplaces are unlikely to qualify as Article 12(1) services.

Indeed, even some e-mail services (which are obviously mainly information transmission ones) may escape Article 12(1) on the ground that they involve storage beyond what is necessary for transmission (Collins, 2005, paras. 17.07–17.08; cited in *Bunt v Tilley [2006] EWHC 407 (QB), [2006] 3 ALL ER 336 (QB), para. 49*; Smith, 2007a, p. 374). Moreover, the Article 12 liability exemption has recently been recognized to a provider of an anonymous access to a wireless local area network, such as the one provided by many cafeterias, restaurants and stores in collaboration with a telecommunication company (*Case C-484/14, Tobias Mc Fadden v Sony Music Entertainment Germany GmbH, 15/9/2016)*. Obviously, automated marketplaces differ enormously from Wi-Fi networks, which are confined to passively enabling access to the internet.

As for the Article 14 exemption, the European Commission (2003a, p. 12) clarified that it is not confined to the passive storage involved in standard web hosting services but extends to services offering *added* functionality, such as bulletin boards and chat rooms. This obviously opens up the possibility of automated marketplaces falling within Article 14(1), ECD, yet the question is not that simple.

Spindler et al. (2007, p. 36) refers to a French case in which the court found that the intermediary did not qualify as a host within the meaning of Article 14 because it was providing its clients with templates which they could use to generate the content hosted by the intermediary. It seems that absent *passiveness* on the part of the provider, it is likely that its service will not qualify as a hosting service under Article 14. Such interpretation is supported by the ECD, stating that the activity must be "of a mere *technical, automatic and passive nature*"[16] and also by CJEU case law. More specifically, the CJEU has confirmed that Article 14 "must be interpreted as applying to the operator of an online marketplace where that operator *has not played an active role* allowing it to have knowledge or control of the data stored".[17] It further explained that "the operator plays such a role when it provides assistance which entails, in particular, optimising the presentation of the offers for sale in question or promoting them".[18] In an earlier case involving Google AdWords, the CJEU clarified that the fact that Google is paid for its keyword advertising service or sets the payment terms or gives its users general information do not evince an active role on its part.[19] Yet, it added that its role in the creation of the advertising content stored on its systems and in the selection of the keywords triggering the display of the ads of its customers may point to the opposite direction.[20] This came to be referred to as the so-called 'neutrality test'.

More recently, the CJEU seems to have accepted that a social networking platform, which "stores information provided by the users of that platform, relating to their profile, on its servers" comes within the Article 14 exemption. However, the judgement did not involve an application of the 'neutrality test', as the passiveness of the service was not "in dispute" (*C-360/10, Belgische Vereniging van Auteurs, Componisten en Uitgevers CVBA (SABAM) v Netlog NV, para. 27, 16/2/2012*). Thus, a social networking platform may be considered as active enough to be deprived of the exemption. Indeed, Woods (2017) refers to services that Facebook provides, specifically the "News Feed algorithm and content recommendation algorithm as well as Ad March services", stating they should prompt an investigation into the neutrality and/or passivity of the provider.

It arises from the aforementioned CJEU case law that the type of involvement (or active role), which excluded Articles 12 and 14, ECD is one relating *to the generation, optimization or promotion of the third-party content.* It seems highly unlikely that automated marketplaces (and also shopping agents) will have no such involvement in the content generated by merchants and consumers using their service. Yet, one could not safely conclude that the relevant liability exemptions are irrelevant to such providers. This is because relevant national case law has not been consistent on the application of these provisions.

Thus, in France, commission-accruing sale facilitation offered by the marketplace in cases against eBay involving the sale of counterfeit products (Riefa, 2008, p. 13) has deprived providers of the Article 14 exemption. Other French courts have taken a similar stance, which has been upheld by the French Court of Cessation (Fernández-Díez, 2014, p. 29). The relevant exemption was also considered unavailable due to relatively minor added

16 Recital 42, ECD, emphasis added.

17 *C-324/09, L'Oréal SA and Others v eBay International AG and Others, 12 July 2011*, emphasis added.

18 Ibid.

19 Cases *C-236, 237 & 238/08 Google France SARL and Google Inc. v Louis Vuitton Malletier SA; Google France SARL v Viaticum SA and Luteciel SARL; Google France SARL v Centre national de recherche en relations humaines (CNRRH) SARL; Pierre-Alexis Thonet, Bruno Raboin and Tiger SARL [2010] All ER (D) 23 (Apr), para. 116.*

20 Ibid at para. 118.

functionality, such as placing user-generated content under specific categories in cases against social networking websites (Vatis and Retchless, 2008, pp. 6–7). In other French cases, however, eBay has been found to be sufficiently passive and neutral to be eligible to the exemption (Riefa and Markou, 2015, p. 10).

In Italy, a video exchange platform was denied the benefit of Article 14 because it was providing a keyword-based video search engine, video recommendations to users and a reporting system for infringing videos (Fernández-Díez, 2014, p. 44). Other Italian and German case law, however, have been prepared to allow the exemption unless the intermediary adopted the third-party content as its own so that the latter was not sufficiently distinguished as content coming *not* from the intermediary but from third parties (DLA Piper,2009, p. 16). Understandably, this approach allows for the neutrality of providers to be established more easily and if it were to be followed, both shopping agents and automated marketplaces would be eligible to the Article 14 exemption.

In other Member States, too, courts have taken a lenient stance towards the availability of the exemptions. Accordingly, Peguera (2009, pp. 486, 508) reports that a Belgian court has held that eBay qualifies as a 'host' under Article 14 and, relying on Article 15, it has refused Lancôme an injunction prohibiting eBay from allowing the advertising or sale of counterfeit Lancôme products. Similarly, a social networking website has also been found to qualify as an Article 14 host (Fernández-Díez, 2014, p. 13). In the UK, the exemptions, in particular Article 12, have mainly been applied to internet access providers, such as the telecommunications company BT, in relation to copyright infringements committed and/or assisted by third parties using their services.[21] More recently, however, the English High Court accepted Facebook to be a host and, therefore, was found as being eligible to the relevant limitation (*J20 v Facebook Ireland [2016] NIQB 98, para. 48*), meaning that in the UK, too, providers who are *not* totally passive and/or neutral are afforded the protection of the Article 14 liability shield.

DLA Piper (2009, p. 25) is thus right to observe that "online service providers, users and third parties face *considerable legal uncertainty* in the European Community, in particular when it concerns services that do not qualify as the 'traditional' internet access, caching or web hosting services envisaged by the eCommerce Directive".[22] Along similar lines, Spindler (2017, p. 308) notes that "it seems difficult to develop one-size-fits-all criteria for the qualification of an active role of a provider". Accordingly, comparably to eBay, automated marketplaces may promote merchant offerings and make available advanced search facilities (especially if the marketplace is usable both by human users and contracting software). They may also offer guidance on how to instruct contracting software or draft commercial offers and even operate a reporting or dispute resolution centre. Such functions would seem to give them an active role excluding them from Article 14, yet as already seen e-Bay and eBay-like services have not consistently been denied the exemption. Given the important repercussions that the matter has on their obligation (direct and indirect) to take measures to keep their system clean from fraud and other unlawful activity, this uncertainty is definitely undesirable and inevitably leads to the conclusion that the EU legal response to the risk of fraud in this context is inadequate.

21 *Dramatico Entertainment Ltd v British Sky Broadcasting Ltd [2012] EWHC 1152 (Ch)* and *Twentieth Century Fox Film Corp v British Telecommunications plc [2011] EWHC 1981 (Ch).*

22 Emphasis added.

3.3.2.3 The case of shopping agents

Whereas the application of the CJEU 'neutrality test' to shopping agents would seem clearly to exclude them from the Article 14 (and Article 12) exemptions, it is not entirely clear that this will in fact be the case.

The European Commission (2003a, p. 13) has stated that none of the provisions on intermediaries contemplates search engines and (presumably) other information location tools, though some Member States, not including the UK (Great Britain, Department of Trade and Industry, 2006, paras. 3.11–3.15; Pinsent Masons LLP, 2007), have extended their ambit to include them. According to Spindler, Riccio and der Perre (2007, pp. 86–99), in some Member States information location tools are deemed as 'mere conduits' or 'hosts', thus coming within Article 12 or Article 14, ECD, whereas elsewhere either specific rules have been developed or general rules of law are applied. Notably, however, none of the cases reviewed in the said study featured a shopping agent. Moreover, where content aggregators or 'specific content' search engines were involved (which are very similar to shopping agents),[23] the unlawful activity at stake was often copyright infringement (not fraud), inevitably resulting in the application of specific rules relating to copyright liability.

Yet, no matter what legal approach is chosen to address intermediary liability in relation to information location tools including shopping agents of the 'search engine' type,[24] it is difficult to envisage one not depending on the activeness of the role of the intermediary in the creation and transmission of third-party content. Indeed, Spindler et al. (2007, p. 18) state, "Liability exemptions should take into account the different levels of control and of awareness that a provider of information location tools has concerning the content to which the tool directs the user". If one examines shopping agents against these factors, it immediately surfaces that no general liability exemption should be available to them. This is so even if traditional search engines would in fact benefit from such exemption. Indeed, important differences between shopping agents of the 'search engine' type and traditional search engines render the former more akin to content *creators* than passive and neutral intermediaries.

More specifically, Google, a traditional search engine, usually displays the owner-specified title of each listed website and a totally unchanged part of the website content accompanied by three dots (...), signalling that there is more on the relevant page. Furthermore, what is displayed by Google in its search results is of little value without resource to the listed website. Finally, traditional search engines are expected to search the web at large and do so as part of an automatic and indiscriminate process (Google Inc., 2019). By contrast, shopping agents communicate to consumers *modified* 'third-party' content; they isolate certain pieces of information, which they arrange into a table, and often attach to them seals or representations.[25] Additionally, the content of their search results is perfectly usable without resource to the website from which they have been extracted, as they comprise product offerings (or invitations to purchase), as earlier explained.[26] Additionally, shopping agents

23 Information location tools mainly include search engines, hyperlinking, i.e., the setting of links to other websites and content aggregators that amass specific content from various other websites to which they link. Given that shopping agents and specifically, those of the 'search engine' type, search and locate commercial offerings on the internet and provide a link to the merchant website following relevant consumer searches, they would seem to qualify as information location tools.

24 On the two types of shopping agents, see supra Chapter 1 p. 9

25 Supra Chapter 2 pp. 22, 26

26 Supra Chapter 2 pp. 57

do not indiscriminately search the web; they aim at online stores and, importantly, they may *choose* those that they search and list. The directory of the searched merchants displayed on some shopping agent platforms[27] proves this choice made by the provider. Other commentators (Gulli, 2005, p. 880; Cruquenaire, 2001, p. 328) confirm the existence of such choice and control in the hands of similar services, news search engines. Spindler (2017, p. 310) also regards the act of setting a hyperlink to a webpage (which, as seen, is one that is central to the performance of shopping agents),[28] as evidence of additional control, involvement or knowledge on the part of providers: "Unlike search engine operators that conduct automatic searches without taking notice of the search results at all, the placing of a hyperlink is a deliberate action by the person setting the hyperlink".

Apart from confirming the justifiability of the imposition of a fraud-preventive obligation on relevant shopping agent providers, the aforementioned factors would seem to exclude them from the ambit of Articles 12 and 14. Article 12 requires that the transmitted information is *not* modified or selected by the provider,[29] while Article 14 is limited to information stored at the request of service recipients,[30] which is not what happens in the case of shopping agents; the initial selection of the stored content is made by the provider. Indeed, a French court has, on the basis of similar factors, denied the Article 14 exemption to a content aggregator (Peguera, 2009, p. 505). The same approach has been adopted in relation to the news search engine of Google by a Belgian appellate court on the ground that Google was creating summaries of the news articles, thereby modifying third-party content (Fernadez-Diez, 2014, p. 14). Unfortunately, however, most shopping agents are not of the 'search engine' type, so their uncontroversial exclusion from the ECD liability limitations is of little practical significance.

Many shopping agents provide the tools enabling merchants to submit their product offerings to their database,[31] and their function is closer to the advertising service of traditional search engines than to their main 'search' task. In France, Google, in its capacity as an advertising services provider, has been denied the Article 14 exemption on grounds relating to its involvement in the content and management of the advertisements submitted into its database, amongst others "by editing advertisements, then by taking decisions on their presentation and their location, and by making available to the advertisers computer tools for changing the wordings of these advertisements" (*CA Paris, 4e ch., A, 28 June 2006, Google France v. Louis Vuitton Malletier*; cited in Prouteau, 2008, pp. 2–3). However, that was before the 2010 CJEU 'neutrality test',[32] which has been followed by French decisions adopting the opposite view, thereby highlighting the existence of great legal uncertainty.

As already mentioned,[33] the CJEU has opined that the interference of Google in the drafting of advertisements generated through its platform is relevant to whether Google qualifies as a host under Article 14, ECD. Applying this guidance, however, a French court has deemed Google as a neutral 'host' whereas four other French decisions in which the liability exemption has been refused have been overturned by the Court of Cassation on the ground that they did not apply the 'neutrality' test laid down by the CJEU (Fernadez-Diez, 2014, p. 31). This is so despite the fact that in his Opinion, Advocate-General Maduro

27 Supra Chapter 2 p. 29
28 Supra Chapter 1 p. 8
29 Supra p. 81
30 Supra p. 82
31 Supra Chapter 1 p. 9
32 Supra p. 83
33 Supra n. 19 at paras. 114–120.

(paras. 141, 144) expressly stated that unlike the *search* service of Google, its *advertising* service should not qualify as a 'host' for the purposes of Article 14, ECD. On the other hand, the European Commission (2016c, p.114) reports that in another case, the French Supreme Court has refused the liability exemption to a comparison tool (i.e. a shopping agent) on the ground that "by top ranking products against remuneration by third party traders, was indirectly promoting these products and thus acting as an active provider of a commercial service for these traders".

Shopping agents *also* interfere with the content of the listings they display by deciding on their presentation, location and the type of information to be included. Indeed, while Google leaves the content of the advertisements totally up to the third-party advertiser, shopping agents actually dictate what type of information merchants should submit; recall that all merchant offerings are displayed in a comparison table and therefore there has to be some consistency in their content. Accordingly, shopping agents effect a wider interference with third-party content on their platform than Google. To the extent that they may also attach to such content various seals such as 'featured offer' and 'smart buy', the said interference becomes even more substantial.

It follows that the Article 14 exemption should not be considered available to shopping agents, something that would leave the possibility open for the imposition of liability for fraud (and thus, an indirect fraud-preventive obligation). Unfortunately, however, unless courts accept the role (or involvement) of shopping agent providers in third-party content as more substantial than that of Google, it is not certain that shopping agents will be denied the relevant exemption.

3.3.2.4 Searching for a solution

Given the risk of automated marketplaces and shopping agents being allowed the benefit of the liability exemptions of the ECD and also shielded against the imposition of a direct obligation to limit fraud on or through their systems, it is important to examine whether and/or how the provisions of the ECD may limit the relevant adverse consequences. As it will be explained, these allow for the issuing of injunctions against qualifying intermediaries, yet the permitted injunctions cannot effectively replace the previously suggested fraud-preventive obligation. A solution does probably exist but seems 'hidden' in those provisions themselves, the problem lying with their interpretation which so far keeps it under the surface.

The issuing of injunctions is not affected by the liability exemptions; Articles 12(3), 13(2) and 14(3), ECD expressly provide that service providers falling within the exemptions can still be ordered to terminate or prevent an infringement. Recital 47 further clarifies that the Article 15 prohibition of general monitoring obligation does *not* affect monitoring obligations in "a specific case" and in particular, the issuing of relevant injunctions.

The injunction approach seems to have been the prevailing approach in Germany. Thus, without denying eBay the status of a 'host' under Article 14, the German Federal Court of Justice (*GE13. – BGH, 19.4.2007, I ZR 35/04, MMR 2007, 507 – Internetversteigerung II*; cited in Spindler, Riccio and der Perre 2007, pp. 48–49, 84) has concluded that "eBay must take reasonable measures to prevent recurrence once it is informed of clearly identified infringement" (eBay Inc., 2007, p. 38). Similar rulings have been issued by a French court in a case concerning the unauthorized posting of a copyrighted video on a video-sharing website (Spitz, 2007) and by a German court in a case involving identity theft (Smith, 2007b, para. 2; Viefhues and Schumacher, 2009, p. 63). The same holds true of another German case against eBay concerning the distribution of harmful (i.e., violent or pornographic) material to minors

(*GE14. – BGH, 12.7.2007, I ZR 18/04*; cited in Spindler, Riccio and der Perre 2007, p. 85). As Smith (2007b, para. 2) reports, according to that decision,

> in the event of the defendant becoming aware of a specific instance of a listing(s) harmful to young people the defendant was hence obliged not only to block the listing (s) in question but also "to take care to prevent to the best of his/her/its ability any comparable breach of the law from happening in future".

The review of 2004–2012 case law conducted by Fernández-Díez (2014, pp. 35–37) concerning auction houses, video exchange platforms and other Web 2.0 intermediary services indicates a steady approach of recognizing them as 'hosts' but targeting them with an injunction obliging them actively to search, detect and prevent material that has *already* been identified as infringing or unlawful (through proper notification) from reappearing on their systems in the future. They should do so through technically feasible and economically reasonable measures, such as automatic or manual searches or keyword-based filtering.

Though the possibility of injunctions requiring not only the termination of specific unlawful activity *but also its future prevention* comes close to a general monitoring obligation, such injunctions are in fact prohibited by Article 15 and indeed, in some cases, the German approach has been criticized as being in contravention of Article 15, ECD (Smith, 2007a, p. 579). For this reason, such (general) injunctions are not a real (or reliable) possibility or solution. Indeed, it clearly arises from the several German injunction cases that the obligation to prevent future infringements refers to the *specific* already-identified as infringed trademark or copyrighted material, and not to future such infringements in general. The UK High Court also acknowledged that any monitoring obligation imposed through an injunction must be specific, *not* general, to be permitted by Article 15, ECD (*Twentieth Century Fox Film Corp v British Telecommunications plc [2011] EWHC 1981 (Ch), para. 162*).

Moreover, whereas the CJEU has expressly left the possibility open for injunctions concerning the prevention of *future* infringements (*C-324/09, L'Oréal SA and Others v eBay International AG and Others, 12 July 2011, paras. 141, 144*), it also expressly stated that such measures "cannot consist in an active monitoring of all the data of each of its customers in order to prevent any future infringement of intellectual property rights via that provider's website" (para. 139). Accordingly, the CJEU has later ruled that injunctions ordering the adoption of a filtering system affecting all content and all users of a social networking platform for an unlimited period for the purpose of identifying files infringing the IP rights of a given party or prevent future IP infringements were *not* permissible (*C-70/10 Scarlet Extended [2011] ECR I-11959, paras. 36, 39–40; C-360/10, Netlog, para. 38)*.

The injunction approach therefore, not only creates safety-related obligations *after the fact*, i.e., after the provider has become aware of specific illegal or unlawful activity but also only protects the *specific* person who has been affected, i.e., a particular trademark holder or a wider group (such as minors) but only against a sufficiently delimited risk, i.e., a specific harmful video (as opposed to harmful videos in general). Thus, it stops short of *generally* and *proactively* improving the security and reliability of online environments similarly to how the suggested fraud-preventive obligation would.

Furthermore, it is worth noting that the various literature, studies and case law on intermediary liability are not concerned with consumer fraud but with "obscenity, defamation, hate speech, intellectual property infringement" (CDT, 2010, p. 3), which are "the most significant examples of violations in the process of information dissemination on the internet" (Miskevich, 2012, p. 7). Unlike these illegal activities, consumer fraud does *not* have *a well-defined subject matter* (such as *named* harmful videos or a *specific* trademark). Thus, a relevant injunction could at best require the monitoring of content coming from a specific previously identified fraudulent or unreliable merchant. DLA Piper (2009, p. 22) and Fernández-Díez (2014, p. 36) report case law in which the intermediary has been ordered to monitor the content coming from a specific previously identified infringer.

Yet, again, online fraudsters can have many different 'identities' or many available ways to conceal their true identity and, therefore, it is unlikely for an injunction of the aforementioned type to be effective in all cases. Additionally, unlike IP-infringing material, for example, fraudulent contractual communications (or offerings) may not have any external signs of illegality. One such sign may be an unreasonably low price but, in general, offers coming from fraudsters may very well look just like any other (real) offering. In one of the very few cases concerning advertising-related violations (that are somewhat closer to fraud), the Austrian Supreme Court of Justice has, according to Spindler, Riccio and der Perre (2007, p. 38), confirmed that "legal considerations referring to advertising and general terms and conditions" are far from readily identifiable as illegal activity. Thus, even a general ('all content') monitoring obligation would not be suitable in the case of fraud; this reinforces the necessity of a fraud-preventive obligation in the form of an 'access control' mechanism as suggested previously.

The searched-for solution therefore must lie with whether an obligation of this type in fact falls within the prohibition of Article 15, ECD or whether the said provision could be interpreted as not covering it.[34] This is even more so the case given that other solutions, particularly, in the form of liability based on a 'take-down notice' approach, for example, already exist in the ECD and are again unsuitable for the case of fraud.

Indeed, Mann and Belzley (2005, pp. 277–279, 285, 296–298, 300–301) conclude that 'take-down' or 'hot-list' approaches[35] may be appropriate because they shift the burden of monitoring away from intermediaries towards other parties. Those other parties are, in relation to the sale of counterfeit products, the (often powerful) brand owner, who can identify counterfeited products and serve 'take-down' notices on marketplace providers (Mann and Belzley, 2005, pp. 277–279). In relation to illegal gambling websites, in reference to which a hot-list requirement is said to be the most appropriate, the parties burdened with the monitoring are the law enforcement authorities, which "are likely better placed than ISPs to identify illicit gambling sites" (Mann and Belzley, 2005, p. 285).

By contrast, online fraudsters or fraudulent commercial practices have neither a specific subject matter nor a sufficiently specified target. Also, those who will have to serve such take-down notices are *the consumers*; it is unfair (and also ineffective) to place the burden of the safety of online platforms on consumers, who often have limited resources and are the ones in need for protection. Additionally, such notices, especially when sent by the (inexperienced) consumer, will not necessarily result in the removal of fraudulent material. Even if the provider is specifically notified, knowledge on the part of the intermediary is only found if the notifying party is sufficiently credible and authoritative (Spindler et al., 2007, pp. 36–41). Indeed, the CJEU (*Case C-324/09, L'Oréal SA and others v eBay International AG and others, para. 122, 12/7/2011*), has noted the possibility of such notifications being

34 Infra at pp. 91–92

35 'Take down' allows for intermediary liability only after a take-down notice of the illegal activity has been served on the intermediary, whereas 'hot list' refers to service providers being required to exclude service recipients who are specified in a hot list drafted by enforcement authorities (Mann and Belzley, 2005, pp. 270–272).

"insufficiently precise or inadequately substantiated" and opined that a notification should not automatically deprive the provider from the Article 14 liability exemption. In any event, given the probably enormous number of consumers on relevant platforms, coupled with the fact that it may take a consumer some time before managing to serve a relevant notice (and even realizing that he has been defrauded), 'fraudulent content' removals may not take place *before* a considerable number of additional consumers have been defrauded. The said approach appears to be even more unsuitable in the context of automated marketplaces, where consumers do not personally deal with merchants and could not therefore look for external 'unreliability' signs, such as website appearance.[36]

All in all, (successful) *liability-triggering* consumer-oriented take-down notices are likely to be limited and, therefore, the relevant liability threat is likely to be too weak to operate as an indirect obligation proactively to keep platforms clean from fraud. Mann and Belzley would probably argue that market incentives already 'push' marketplace intermediaries towards employing relevant technological measures of protection (2005, pp. 304–305). However, though relevant market incentives do exist (Calliess, 2008, p. 20), market-driven safety-related measures are prone to be shallow and confined to what is enough to make users feel safe and use the service. Indeed, commentators convincingly argue that the eBay reputation system of eBay only affords an often-false sense of security and is incapable of actually protecting consumers against fraud (Calkins, 2001, paras. 74, 89–92; Rietjens, 2006). The fact, therefore, that, as the European Commission (2016b, p. 7) observes that "many platforms have already voluntarily put in place some proactive measures which go beyond their legal obligations" including "ex-ante control of suppliers' credentials" should not be accepted as an answer to the problem rendering a legal fraud-preventive obligation unnecessary.

An obvious solution would be to ensure that Articles 12–15 are strictly confined to purely technical and automatic activities entailing the intermediary as a passive and neutral provider. The Commission (2016a, pp. 7–8) has recently recognized that the intermediary liability system of the ECD "was designed at a time when online platforms did not have the characteristics and scale they have today", and a Commission guidance on the relevant provisions explaining their *limited* scope may be merited. The CJEU could also help with the materialization of this solution through issuing judgements that clearly emphasize this limited scope.

Another solution focuses on Article 15, ECD and the type or extent of the prohibition it imposes. Thus, though it may be unreasonable to pre-screen all persons *seeking to access the internet* (as it would be the case in relation to an ISP), it does not sound similarly unreasonable to pre-screen merchants seeking access to a shopping agent or an automated marketplace. Moreover, the prohibition on a general monitoring obligation is almost invariably justified by reference to the millions of pages, posts or listings that an intermediary will have to review. By contrast, the suggested fraud-preventive only entails a screening, not of the vast content originating from third parties, but of the smaller and probably manageable number of the third parties using the relevant platform services. Given that in 2013, eBay UK (one of the largest online marketplaces) had 60 million active listings but only 190,000 registered businesses, it follows that a general monitoring obligation in the form of an access control mechanism is not excessively burdensome. This is true especially in the case of shopping agents, which often only have dozens, hundreds or a few thousands of merchant

36 There are various external factors that the ECC-NET (2017, pp. 15–18) advises consumers to look for in assessing merchant reliability.

participants.[37] Moreover, at least when implemented in the form of an 'access control' mechanism requiring the certain reliability-related credentials before access is allowed (and provided that such credentials are readily accessible to all), a relevant obligation would not unduly restrict fair competition or freedom of speech, as those some commentators suggest (Julià-Barceló, 1999, pp. 19–21; Julià-Barceló and Koelman, 2000, pp. 233–234; CDT, 2012, pp. 20–21).

Article 15, ECD proscribes an obligation "to monitor *the information* which they transmit or store" and "a general obligation actively to seek facts or circumstances indicating illegal activity".[38] A literal reading of the first limb of the provision suggests that the proscribed obligation is one of information (or content) monitoring, not of service recipients (merchants) monitoring. So, the said part of Article 15, ECD does not seem to prohibit the imposition of the suggested fraud-preventive obligation in the form of an access control mechanism but clearly prohibits, an additional information to monitor behaviour on the platform. The second limb is more general, as it is not confined to the information (or content) stored. Accordingly, 'facts or circumstances indicating illegal activity' may *liberally* be taken to include the lack of reliability credentials resulting in an obligation to apply an 'access control' mechanism requiring merchants to submit certain credentials being considered a general monitoring obligation falling afoul of Article 15. As already explained, however, the justification of the Article 15 prohibition is absent in the case of the relevant platforms, at least. Thus, an interpretation of Article 15 in line with its spirit on a case-by-case basis could leave outside its scope a fraud-preventive obligation of the particular type in the case of the relevant platforms at least.

The CJEU has reviewed injunction-flowing obligations relating to filtering systems applied to all data (or content) transmitted or stored finding them as prohibited by operation of the (uncontroversial) first limb of Article 15.[39] There seems however to be no judicial opinion on the aforementioned second limb of the provision, at least at EU level, that effectively clarifies its ambit. Recital 48, ECD, which clarifies that the Directive does not preclude Member States from requiring intermediaries to apply duties of care, *"which can reasonably be expected from them"*, in order to detect and prevent certain types of illegal activities would seem to assist such interpretation; it seems to confirm that Article 15 is not intended to impose an all-sweeping prohibition on the obligation of all intermediaries falling within Articles 12–14 to take care to reduce risks from illegal activities.

The Commission does not explicitly touch upon the proper interpretation of Article 15, ECD in its recent Communication (European Commission, 2017a) and subsequent Recommendation (European Commission, 2018c). Yet, it strongly encourages the voluntary adoption of measures of protection, dispelling voices suggesting that such behaviour effectively furnishes intermediaries with an active role and thus deprives them of the benefit of the liability provisions of the ECD[40] (European Commission, 2017a, sec. 10; European Commission, 2018c; Recital 26 and para. 18). This is very important; if EU law were not only to omit imposing a relevant legal obligation but also to discourage intermediaries from assuming a protective role voluntarily, that would be a major legal oversight. That this is not the case seems implicitly to be confirmed by Recital 40, ECD, stating that "the provisions of this Directive relating to liability should not preclude the development and *effective*

37 Supra Chapter 1, p. 9
38 Emphasis added.
39 Supra p. 88
40 For an example of such voices, see Spindler (2017, p. 307).

operation, by the different interested parties, *of technical systems of protection and identification and of technical surveillance instruments made possible by digital technology*".[41] Unfortunately, however, through Recital 20 of the Proposal for a Directive on better enforcement and modernisation of EU consumer protection rules, the European Commission (2018a) seems to take for granted that Article 15 does not permit the imposition of an obligation on online marketplaces "to verify the legal status of third party suppliers". Prior to that, the European Commission (2016c, p.114) again suggested that online platforms cannot, because of Article 15, be imposed with "a general obligation to monitor or carry out fact-finding" and referred to certain consumer protection duties that such platforms may have which are nowhere near an obligation to vet merchants promoted or selling on their platforms.

3.3.3 Liability and safety-related Directives

As already explained, legal liability (or sanction) threats may effectively result in an indirect obligation on the relevant platforms to apply measures designed to limit or eliminate the risk of consumer harm arising as a result of fraud committed on or through their systems. The EU Directives on contractual or product liability and on product safety are classical examples of measures that do create such liability threats, yet, as is shown in the following, their applicability to shopping agents and automated marketplaces is at least doubtful, meaning that the suggested fraud-preventive obligation could not safely be derived from them. Moreover, their relationship with the ECD as discussed previously is not specifically spelled out. Accordingly, being a measure *specifically* governing intermediary liability, the ECD is likely to prevail over *general* measures, such as the Directives discussed herein in the following. As a result, even if they were applicable to the relevant context, the successful reading in them of an indirect fraud-preventive obligation would depend on how Articles 12, 14 and 15, ECD are to apply to the case of the relevant platforms.

Automated marketplaces and shopping agents are software running on the websites of the providers enabling them to offer their service to consumers (and merchants). There is no physical medium such as a CD involved, and, as a result, such software, including software agents, have often been categorized as 'services' rather than 'goods' (Feliu, 2001, p. 240; Lloyd, 2000, pp. 500, 502; Bainbridge, 2000, p. 168). Though the question of whether software comprises goods or services may be more complex than the 'physical medium involvement' criterion suggests, the absence of a physical medium inevitably renders software *intangible* and thus clearly outside the scope of the Consumer Sales Directive (CSD). The latter obliges sellers to provide *goods* that are in conformity with the contract, the term 'goods' being defined in the said measure as "*tangible* movable items".[42] Moreover, when the seller fails to provide goods in conformity with the contract and the goods are proved to be of unsatisfactory quality,[43] for example, the CSD entitles consumers, *inter alia*, to product repair or contract rescission. It does not provide for a remedy of damages, let alone for the recovery of consequential losses (Gomez, 2002, pp. 70–71), which is what a platform user is most likely to suffer as a result of fraud on the platform. Accordingly, even if the lack of adequate fraud-preventive measures were accepted as rendering the platform of unsatisfactory quality, the available remedies are wholly unsuitable for the specific context.

41 Emphasis added.
42 Article 1(2)(b), CSD, emphasis added.
43 Article 3, CSD.

It is not similarly clear that software is excluded from the scope of the Product Safety Directive (PSD) and the Product Liability Directive (PLD). These impose 'product safety' obligations on producers and create the risk of sanctions in case of their violation and (civil) strict liability for damage caused by a defect in their products respectively. The PLD applies to products as movable items,[44] rather than *intangible* movable items, something that resulted in a lack of consensus on whether the definition was intended to cover incorporeal products like software or not (Howells, Twigg-Flesner and Willett, 2017, pp. 189–190.). The European Commission (1988) has in the past expressed the opinion that software is actually covered by the PLD, but the question seems to remain open. Indeed, the European Commission (2016d) has very recently announced an evaluation of the PLD, asking in particular whether software not supplied on a physical medium and not embedded in any tangible product is covered by the said measure. Some convincingly argue that it should be covered, at least when software acts as a product, as opposed to merely providing information such as a GPS (Howells et al., 2017, pp. 191, 192). The results of the evaluation of the European Commission (2018d, pp.2,6) suggest that the question has been left open.

Though software in this context is more akin to a product used in the context of the supply of a service, namely the platform service (rather than one directly supplied to the consumer), it would still fall within the scope of the Directive, which could then be enforced against the platform provider in his capacity as a 'producer' within the meaning of Article 3, PLD. If the platform provider disclosed a different party as the developer/producer of the platform software, the Directive could be enforced against that other party. These points arise clearly from Article 3, PLD[45] combined with CJEU case law, specifically, *Case C-495/10, Centre hospitalier universitaire de Besançon v Thomas Dutrueux and Caisse primaire d'assurance maladie du Jura, 21 December 2011.* [46]

Yet, again, the remedies made available by the PLD are not suitable in the context of automated marketplaces and shopping agents and the risk of fraud existing thereon. Fraud is *de facto* associated with economic damage, whereas the PLD only allows for compensation for death, personal injury and damage to property.[47]

The PSD excludes services from its scope[48] but defines 'product' as "*any* product – *including in the context of providing a service*".[49] Obviously, the definition is broad enough to cover software used in the context of supplying a service. Again, however, the said Directive focuses on consumer health and safety.[50] More specifically, it does not define an unsafe product by any reference to the risk for economic losses, which, as said, constitute the type of damage that may be suffered by consumers as a result of a platform lacking sufficient fraud-preventive properties.

44 Article 2, PLD.

45 The provision defines the term 'producer', amongst others, as "the manufacturer of a finished product, the producer of any raw material or the manufacturer of a component part *and any person who, by putting his name, trade mark or other distinguishing feature on the product presents himself as its producer*", Article 3(1), PLD (emphasis added). Moreover, Article 3(3) states that the supplier (in this case, the marketplace provider) shall be deemed a producer and thus, subject to liability under the PLD, if the producer is unknown or cannot be identified.

46 For more on the application of the PLD to the context of shopping agents and automated marketplaces, see infra Chapter 7, p. 202

47 Article 9, PLD.

48 Recital 9, PSD.

49 Article 2(a), PSD, emphasis added.

50 Article 2(b), PSD.

Of course, the Directives do not negate the general contractual or non-contractual regimes of the Member States, yet, in general, liability regimes could not really serve as an (indirect) source of a powerful obligation on platform providers to employ fraud-preventive technologies. Consumer goods or services are generally considered to be of satisfactory quality and in compliance with the contract, if they can perform *similarly* to other goods or services of the same category. This approach is also codified in the CSD, according to which, consumer goods are presumed to be in conformity with the contract if, *inter alia*, they "*show the quality and performance which are normal in goods of the same type* which the consumer can reasonably expect".[51] In tort, too: "If use of technical aids is not commonplace, then a failure on the part of a particular defendant is unlikely to constitute negligence" (Lloyd, 2000, p. 533). Thus, unless the marketplace provider specifically presents a limited risk of fraud as an existing characteristic of its service, it is only if the use of adequate or effective fraud-preventive technologies becomes *commonplace or the norm* (possibly as a result of market pressure) that a *real* liability threat will exist against those not using such technologies. Understandably, if effective fraud prevention somehow becomes the norm, the need for the relevant liability threat as a source of an indirect obligation to employ relevant measures will become less acute (if not obsolete).

Moreover, given the limited resources of individual consumers and the small amounts often at stake, relevant contractual or tortious lawsuits would unlikely become commonplace enough to create a real pressure to adopt anti-fraud measures. This applies even more so, given the existence of Article 73, PSD2,[52] which renders resort to liability-related regimes unnecessary, at least, in some cases of fraud.

3.3.4 Unfair Commercial Practices Directive (UCPD)

As fraud in the context of shopping agents and automated marketplaces will naturally consist of false (or deceptive) product offerings or contractual information addressed to consumers or consumer software, the suggested fraud-preventive obligation seems indirectly to arise from the UCPD. The 'trader' definition of the UCPD clearly covers the relevant platform providers,[53] who profit from bringing merchants and consumers together enabling the former to address commercial practices to the latter. Being traders, such providers are subject to the UCPD-imposed prohibition on unfair commercial practices.[54] Importantly, such practices cover not only false, deceptive or misleadingly incomplete commercial information[55] but also any act, omission, representation or behaviour[56] that is contrary to professional diligence (i.e., good faith or honesty) and can result in consumers taking a transactional decision they would not have otherwise taken.[57] Accordingly, the UCPD is also capable of addressing the risk of non-traditional fraud, such as malicious alterations of

51 Article 2(2), Consumer Sales Directive, emphasis added.
52 Supra Chapter 3.3.5.1, Chapter 6 pp. 187–188 and Chapter 7.2.2
53 See the relevant definition supra Chapter 2 p. 61; as it arises from the definition, the 'trader', who is the addressee of the prohibitions and obligations of the UCPD, a trader need not be the one featured or promoted in the commercial practice at stake. Thus, magazines or websites containing or displaying a commercial practice and thus the relevant platform providers, too, qualify as traders for the purposes of the UCPD.
54 Article 5(1), UCPD.
55 Article 6 and 7, UCPD.
56 See definition of 'commercial practice' in Article 2(d), UCPD, supra Chapter 2 p. 44
57 This is the general clause of the UCPD in Article 5(2), UCPD.

consumer software code causing such software to buy more products or at higher prices than instructed. In fact, such fraud possibly to be committed on automated marketplaces[58] comprises an example of cases in which the general clause of the UCPD,[59] which currently seems to be of limited application, can prove useful. Understandably, more traditional fraud (in the form of false information as to price for example) can be tackled by the UCPD provisions on misleading actions, namely Article 6, if the communications originating from merchant software are imputed to the merchant.[60]

To avoid proceedings and sanctions under the UCPD, which, in some Member States such as the UK, are not confined to civil or administrative ones but include criminal sanctions too,[61] the relevant platform providers must take measures to limit unfair commercial practices (and thus, fraudulent listings or contractual communications) on their systems. In fact, the UK Consumer Protection from Unfair Trading Regulations 2008 imposes a fraud-limiting obligation almost explicitly by availing the 'due diligence' defence to criminal liability to parties who have taken "all reasonable precautions and exercised all due diligence to avoid the commission of . . . an offence",[62] where the offence was attributable to "(i) a mistake; (ii) *reliance on information supplied to him by another person*; (iii) *the act or default of another person*; (iv) an accident; or (v) another cause beyond his control".[63] Thus, to avoid criminal liability for an unfair commercial practice, a platform provider will have to show that the practice has been employed by a (merchant) user of its service and thus, by 'another person' and that the provider took measures to avoid the employment of the practice, for example, by vetting merchant users and admitting only those in possession of certain reliability credentials (or by screening the content they store on its systems). This obviously equates with the suggested fraud-preventive obligation.

Of course, not all national implementations of the UCPD criminalize a violation of their provisions or lay down a related 'due diligence' defence. Yet, by addressing its obligations and/or prohibitions to 'traders' without excluding from the relevant definition third parties hosting or disseminating commercial practices featuring other traders (such as selling merchants), the UCPD could be said indirectly to impose on those third parties a duty to detect and prevent unfair practices (in order to avoid the consequences of liability). One could even see an express obligation of this kind arising from their qualification as 'traders' combined with Article 5(2), which effectively requires that traders do not act contrary to professional diligence; professional diligence is defined by Article 2(h), UCPD as "the standard of special skill and care which a trader may reasonably be expected to exercise towards consumers, commensurate with honest market practice and/or the general principle of good faith in the trader's field of activity.

Importantly, the extent to which the suggested fraud-preventive obligation could be derived from the UCPD in the way just explained would depend on enforcement and the quality of the measures that platform providers would be required to employ in order to avoid liability under the UCPD. It is certainly uncertain whether it will in fact be interpreted as entailing the obligation of merchant vetting. Moreover, a relevant weakness is that the

58 On this (technical) possibility, see Fasli (2007, p. 353).
59 Ibid.
60 This imputation would perhaps require the adoption of a legal fiction similar to the one discussed by the reference to automated contract validity and the doctrine of unilateral mistake, infra Chapter 7 pp. 176–178
61 The Consumer Protection from Unfair Trading Regulations 2008 No. 1277, Part 3.
62 Regulation 17(1)(a), Consumer Protection from Unfair Trading Regulations 2008 No. 1277.
63 Ibid. Emphasis added.

burden of uncovering unfair commercial practices 'hiding' in 'closed' automated marketplaces or within 'shopping agent' listings primarily lies with the consumer. Platform providers may therefore face relevant proceedings infrequently or, at least, not frequently enough to have a strong incentive to employ preventive measures. By contrast, an express obligation to vet merchants would enable enforcement authorities to target platform providers directly and screen their relevant fraud-preventive measures or practices without having either to wait for a consumer to complain or resort to costly and time-consuming relevant platform sweeps in search of fraudulent practices.

Regardless of the previous, the relationship between the UCPD and the provisions on intermediaries of the ECD is interesting, as a conflict may arise between the former, which may indirectly impose a monitoring obligation and the latter which prohibits the imposition of such obligation on qualifying intermediaries. According to Article 3(4), UCPD if there is a conflict between the provisions of the UCPD and other Community rules "regulating specific aspects of commercial practices", these other Community rules "shall prevail and apply to those specific aspects". The ECD regulates 'specific aspects of commercial practices', specifically through its Articles 6–8, which impose relevant transparency requirements and regulate unsolicited electronic communications as well as electronic communications by regulated professionals. Most likely, it is these rules *only* that are covered by Article 3(4), UCPD and *not* the provisions of the ECD on intermediaries. Being drafted as general and broad intermediary liability limitations, they do not really qualify as provisions 'regulating specific aspects of commercial practices' subject to Article 3(4), ECD.

That does not however exhaustively answer the question whether the obligation to prevent fraud on their systems indirectly arising from the UCPD contradicts Article 15, ECD. To an important extent, this shall depend on whether the said provision is interpreted to cover and prohibit an obligation to pre-screen merchant participants. Moreover, it should be recalled that Recital 48, ECD, clarifies that the ECD does not preclude Member States from imposing on intermediaries, duties of care to detect and prevent certain illegal activities. Such duties of care have been shown to exist in the UK implementation of the UCPD (in the form of defences to criminal liability)[64] (as well as in all national implementations of Article 5(2), UCPD[65]) and they seem not to be "blocked" by the ECD. Moreover, the UCPD is a more recent measure than the ECD and also *specifically* governs fraud (in the form of intentional unfair commercial practices) and, therefore, it should probably prevail in case of an inconsistency. Accordingly, the suggested fraud-preventive obligation derived from the UCPD would seem to remain unaffected by the liability provisions of the ECD. This view seems to be shared by the European Commission (2016c, pp.114–115) which bases it on Article 1(3), ECD providing that the ECD does not prejudice other Community rules protecting consumer interests. Unfortunately, however, the European Commission also suggests that though certain platform providers may be recognized with some duties such as to require "relevant third party traders to clearly indicate that they act, vis-à-vis the platform users, as traders", Article 15, ECD precludes a monitoring or fact-finding obligation on such intermediaries. This makes the suggested fraud-preventive obligation difficult to be allowed to derive from the UCPD.[66] This is unfortunate given that the UCPD is the only EU measure from which such obligation applicable to all cases could be derived.

64 Supra p. 95
65 Ibid. p. 95
66 See also supra p. 92

3.3.5 Second Payment Services Directive (PSD2)

In the case of automated marketplaces (on which payments will probably be made), the UCPD response is complimented by the PSD2. It affords consumer protection against fraud both *ex-post* in the form of refund rights and *ex-ante* in the form of strict and detailed security obligations going beyond the security obligations of other measures, such as the General Data Protection Regulation (GDPR). These solutions are mostly relevant in the case of electronic fraud (resulting from a misappropriation of consumer payment details, which qualify as 'personal data'). For this reason, the PSD2 could belong in Chapter 4 and it is true that it assists in tackling data protection risks. It is however examined in this Chapter, as it can (indirectly) push towards the adoption of an access control mechanism, thereby compensating, to some extent, for the absence of a positive fraud-preventive obligation vested on marketplace providers.

3.3.5.1 Refund rights

Some of the fraud on automated marketplaces is bound to consist of unauthorized charges to consumer payment accounts resulting from a misappropriation of personal data, i.e. consumer financial details, namely personalized security credentials (held by the consumer contracting software). Article 73, PSD2 obliges payment service providers to refund any amounts charged due to an *unauthorized* 'payment transaction', i.e., "an act, initiated by the payer or by the payee, of placing, transferring or withdrawing funds".[67] This provision obviously places the relevant risk of loss on payment service providers, i.e., on powerful parties who profit from the use of their payment services by consumers and are also able to spread the risk to all of their customers through a suitable adjustment of the price of their services.

This right to a refund is discussed in more detail in Chapter 7, as it is directly relevant to the issue of the recoverability of damage arising in connection with the use of automated marketplaces.[68] However, it is worth noting that the term 'funds' is broadly defined to include 'electronic money',[69] i.e., "electronically . . . stored monetary value"[70] and, therefore, unlike the no longer existing Article 8 of the Distance Selling Directive (DSD),[71] which allowed for refunds by reference to 'payment cards',[72] Article 73, PSD2 can be useful in cases of fraud affecting not only payment cards but also digital (or electronic) money, which is likely to become the norm, especially on automated marketplaces.

Of course, the said 'refund' right only constitutes a partial solution that cannot substitute the suggested fraud-preventive obligation in the form of a requirement to employ technologies of protection at the point of access to the marketplace. First of all, it only operates *after the fact*, seeking to correct resulting harm, whereas the said obligation strikes at the root of the problem curtailing its occurrence in the first place, thus preventing consumer harm and contributing in trustworthy online shopping environments. Secondly, not all fraud on automated marketplaces will consist of a misappropriation of security credentials and

67 Article 4(5), PSD2.
68 Infra Chapter 7.2.2
69 Article 4(25), PSD2.
70 Article 2(2), E-Money Directive.
71 It has been deleted by Article 89, First Payment Services Directive (PSD1).
72 Subirana and Bain (2005, p. 179) had rightly observed that Article 8, DSD could be of no use in the large number of transactions performed with digital money.

consequent unauthorized payment transactions covered by the relevant refund right. Instead, the fraud may consist of an alteration of consumer software code or some other "malfunction" causing ***an authorized, yet unintended*** transaction, to which the application of the said right may pose questions, as is later explained.[73] Thirdly, the payment transaction may be perfectly authorized, the fraud involving a fictitious merchant or an undelivered product.

3.3.5.2 Payment security obligations

3.3.5.2.1 CONTENT, RELEVANCE AND IMPORTANCE

The PSD2 is not exhausted to 'refund' rights and *ex-post* protection. It puts major emphasis on *ex-ante* protection, too. Though such protection is confined to ***the payment part of a transaction***, it is greatly relevant to automated marketplaces hosting not only contract conclusion but also payments. Payments can be seen as the part of a transaction that is highly prone to fraud and therefore increased payment security can go a long way towards addressing the risk of fraud on automated marketplaces.[74] Thus, the security provisions of the PSD2 merit examination, as does the question regarding whether automated marketplace providers qualify as 'payment service providers' and are, thus, directly subject to those provisions.

The PSD2 imposes security obligations specifically targeting payment transactions and aiming at increasing the security of payments (Haataja, 2015, p. 16; Valcke, Vandezande and De Velde, 2015, p. 19; Donnelly, 2016).[75] Recital 95, PSD2 highlights this aim with specific reference to e-commerce and the risk of fraud:

> Security of electronic payments is fundamental for ensuring the protection of users and the development of a sound environment for e-commerce. All payment services offered electronically should be carried out in a secure manner, adopting technologies able to guarantee the safe authentication of the user and to reduce, to the maximum extent possible, the risk of fraud.

The PSD2 subjects payment service providers to the EU data protection legal regime,[76] and its security-related obligations discussed in Chapter 4. [77] Additionally, a whole section of the PSD2, namely its Chapter 5, is devoted to security. More specifically, it obliges payment service providers to adopt measures managing security risks, detect major security incidents and report to a competent authority on any risks and the adequacy of the adopted measures. Moreover, payment service providers are imposed with duties analogous to the 'security breach' notification duties of the GDPR[78] and must thus inform the competent authority and (if there is an impact on the financial interests of users) those users, too, of any major

73 Infra Chapter 7.2.2
74 This is reinforced by commentators who go as far as to suggest that identity verification or authentication in e-commerce is not particularly necessary because payment systems and methods take care of identification (Lentner and Parycek, 2016, p. 11).
75 Doubtless, the emphasis on security is much stronger than it was in the PSD1. It is worth mentioning that the term 'security' appeared in the PSD1 a total of ten (10) times while 'security' is mentioned sixty-eight (68) in the PSD2.
76 Article 94, PSD2.
77 Infra Chapter 4.3.4
78 Article 95, PSD2.

security incident.[79] These obligations, however, do not go much further than the security obligations of other EU legal measures discussed later, such as the GDPR and the NISD.

Remarkably, this is not true in relation to other security obligations of the PSD2, especially the one referring to strong authentication in Article 97, PSD2. When applied before access to (or payment from) a payment account is allowed, strong authentication will *de facto* be placed *between* the automated marketplace hosting the negotiation and contracting processes *and* the payment account of the consumer. It could thus operate as a shield additional to any other security measures applied by the marketplace.

However, the important question arises as to whether the strong customer authentication requirements of the PSD2 are actually compatible with automated marketplaces. An equally important question pertains to whether 'automated marketplace' providers would qualify as 'payment service providers'. It is only if they qualify as such that the relevant platform providers will be subject to the (extra) security obligations of the PSD2 described in the following sections. Moreover, as it arises from the following sections, how the said provisions can apply to automated marketplaces depends on *the type* of payment service provider that automated marketplaces may be.

3.3.5.2.2 STRONG CUSTOMER AUTHENTICATION AND AUTOMATED MARKETPLACES

Subject to specified exceptions (European Commission, 2018e, Chapter III), the application of strong customer authentication is an obligation imposed on payment service providers by the PSD2, where "the payer (a) accesses its payment account online; (b) initiates an electronic payment transaction; (c) carries out any action through a remote channel which may imply a risk of payment fraud or other abuses".[80] On most automated marketplaces, consumer software representing the payer cannot but perform one of the three aforementioned actions; at the very least, it will initiate an electronic payment transaction, otherwise it will be unable to pay for a purchased product.[81] Thus, payment transactions initiated on or through automated marketplaces will be subject to the 'strong customer authentication' obligation, unless such transactions fall within one of the narrow exemptions allowed by Article 98(1)(b) and (3), PSD2.[82]

Yet, can the concept of strong customer authentication work in practice when payment transactions are initiated on or through automated marketplaces? According to Article 4 (30), PSD2 "'strong customer authentication' means an authentication based on the use of two or more elements categorised as ***knowledge*** (something only the user knows), ***possession*** (something only the user possesses) and ***inherence*** (something the user is) ***that are independent, in that the breach of one does not compromise the reliability of the others***".[83] Where the user initiates an *electronic* payment transaction, the applied strong customer authentication must also include "elements which dynamically link the transaction to a specific amount and a specific payee".[84]

79 Article 96, PSD2.
80 Article 97(1), PSD2.
81 As the European Banking Authority (2015, p. 12) clarifies "the initiation of electronic payment transactions would cover all payment transactions within the scope of PSD2 (such as card payments, credit transfers, e-money transactions, direct debits), except where the payment instruction is not electronic".
82 Supra.
83 Emphasis added.
84 Article 97(2), PSD2.

The European Banking Authority (EBA), which is entrusted with the important role of preparing draft regulatory technical standards specifying the requirements relating to the authentication (and security) obligations of Article 97, PSD2,[85] has given guidance on key terms pertaining to the said obligations. Thus, in relation to the aforementioned three elements of strong customer authentication, the EBA (2015, p. 12) clarifies that ***knowledge*** refers to "static passwords, codes or a personal identification number known only by the user", while ***possession*** covers "possession of a physical object or potentially data controlled only by the PSU [payment service user]".[86] Physical objects can be mobile devices or smart cards. Finally, ***inherence*** refers to "biometric characteristics of the PSU such as a fingerprint or an iris scan". These can be stored in or read from something possessed or controlled by the user. Obviously, this involves the intermingling of two authentication elements, specifically that of possession and inherence, nevertheless according to the EBA (2016, p. 12), this is permissible provided that technical solutions are applied mitigating any risks.

If the consumer payer acted personally, these requirements would mean that the consumer would have to use a password (provided by the account servicing payment service provider)[87] and also a physical device through which to generate a transaction authentication number (TAN).[88] The said TAN must work for the specific transaction he purported to pay at the particular time (specific amount and payee) and not for any payment transaction from his account.[89] He would then type the generated TAN on the relevant payment webpage (form) and conclude the transaction. On automated marketplaces however, the consumer payer does not act personally; he is represented by software.

Thus, if the 'possession' element was confined to physical possession of (tangible) devices, strong customer authentication involving possession would readily arise as unworkable in the context of automated marketplaces; software is incapable of possessing a mobile phone for example. Even though the EBA explicitly states that the said element can alternatively involve data, such as an app or software (as opposed to a tangible device), still any such data must be controlled *only* by the user.[90] Stakeholders propose the adoption of "measures regarding the software installation, the user impossibility to modify the software, and other restrictions related to the devices where the software is installed to prevent misuse and unwanted modifications" (Banking Stakeholder Group, 2016, p. 3). This requirement of *sole* user control obviously becomes problematic when the data must be held and utilized by consumer contracting software controlled by the (third party) marketplace provider .

A similar point can be made in relation to the first authentication element. Thus, if any password or identification number is passed to consumer software administered by the marketplace provider, it ceases being something known *only* by the user. In effect, if two out of the three possible authentication elements are unworkable, then strong customer authentication, necessitating the use of *at least two* authentication elements,[91] cannot work in practice in this context.

Yet, marketplace providers can be (and are in fact) imposed with heavy security obligations, resulting in those credentials actually being secure. More specifically, there is nothing to suggest that such providers will be unable to keep the different authentication elements

85 See Article 98, PSD2.
86 'PSU' stands for payment service user.
87 This would be the 'knowledge' element of strong customer authentication.
88 This would be the 'possession' element of strong customer authentication.
89 This would satisfy the additional requirement of a dynamic link between the transaction and a specific amount and payee.
90 See Article 4(30), PSD2, supra p. 99
91 Ibid. p. 99

independent from each other or in "separated trusted execution environments", consistently with EBA draft regulatory standards (EBA, 2016, p. 32).

Thus, if security is *not* threatened, the compatibility problem relating to strong customer authentication in the context of automated marketplaces caused by the requirement of *sole user control* should be overcome. Inspiration could be drawn from the eIDAs Regulation discussed in Chapter 5 and the way it addressed a similar problem existing regarding the security requirements of 'digital signatures' under the (previous) Electronic Signatures Directive; in fact, there is more generally plenty of room for synergy between the PSD2 and the eIDAs Regulation, which can be particularly fruitful regarding enhancing security on automated marketplaces.[92] Keeping consumers *personally* involved in payment transactions amounts to resisting automation and technological innovation and hindering the development and commercialization of (fully automated) automated marketplaces.

Importantly, the relevant compatibility problem may also result in adverse consequences regarding the legal position of consumer payers (effectively operating towards keeping them away from automated marketplaces). According to Articles 69(1)(a) and 69(2), PSD2, the payment service user must comply with the terms of use of his or payment instrument and "as soon as in receipt of a payment instrument, take all reasonable steps to keep its personalised security credentials safe". If a consumer furnishes contracting software with any of the personalized security credentials[93] of his payment instrument, will such a consumer be deemed to have failed to comply with his or her obligations under Article 69? This question is important, especially given that users who breach their Article 69 obligations "with intent or gross negligence" are *not* entitled to the previously discussed 'refund' right of Article 73. According to Article 74(1), PSD2, they "shall bear all of the losses relating to any unauthorised payment transactions". Unfortunately, given the requirement of sole user control inherent in strong customer authentication,[94] the terms of payment service providers issuing personalized security credentials are most likely to require that the user does *not* share them with any other party. Accordingly, the utilization of automated marketplaces and the disclosure to them of consumer personalized security credentials would *de facto* be considered as amounting to an intentional violation of the Article 69 obligations of the consumer user.

Fortunately, the problem is not irreparable, but the solution depends on a rather difficult question regarding whether automated marketplace providers qualify as 'payment service providers' themselves.

3.3.5.2.3 AUTOMATED MARKETPLACE PROVIDERS AS PAYMENT SERVICE PROVIDERS

The PSD2 explicitly disallows payment service providers to subject the use of payment instruments to terms effectively prohibiting or hindering the use of the services of *other regulated payment service providers such as payment institutions or payment initiation service providers.*[95] Moreover, the PSD2 essentially obliges credit institutions and other account

92 Infra p. 107
93 "Authentication elements include the Personalised Security Credentials (PSCs), i.e. the personalised features provided by the payment service provider to the PSU for the purposes of authentication, as well as devices and software used to generate or receive authentication codes that may either be provided by the payment service provider to the payment service user or possessed by the payment service user without being provided by the payment service provider" (EBA, 2016, p. 10). PSU stands for payment service user.
94 See supra pp. 99–100
95 Recital 69, PSD2.

servicing payment service providers to co-operate with other payment service providers, such as payment institutions and payment initiation service providers, thereby allowing them access to user payment accounts and authentication procedures so that they can provide their services.[96] Payment service providers expressed concern regarding this 'green light' given by the PSD2 for the disclosure of security credentials to other payment service providers often referred to as third-party payment service providers (Swift, 2015, p. 20). The European Payments Council (2015) expressed the view that consumers must *not* share their security credentials with *any* third party other than the payment service provider providing them and that a liability model must be established on the basis of that principle. These concerns reinforce the view that account servicing payment service providers would most probably subject payment instruments to terms prohibiting disclosure of security credentials to automated marketplaces, if the latter do *not* qualify as 'payment service providers' themselves.

The critical question thus arises as to whether automated marketplace providers qualify as 'payment service providers', since if the answer is affirmative, payment service providers who provide and service payment accounts will be disallowed from prohibiting the disclosure of user-personalized security credentials to marketplace providers. Moreover, an affirmative answer would mean that automated marketplace providers would be subject to the additional security obligations of the PSD2, something that will further enhance security in such environments. They may also be encouraged to use strong customer authentication themselves. Put otherwise, if automated marketplace providers do qualify as payment service providers, that should be considered as good news *both* for them (and their viability as e-commerce actors) *and* for consumer protection.

In addressing this question, the starting point should be the exceptions from the scope of the PSD2. The exception that is mostly relevant to automated marketplaces is the one contained in Article 3(b), PSD2 referring to "payment transactions from the payer to the payee through a commercial agent authorised via an agreement to negotiate or conclude the sale or purchase of goods or services on behalf of only the payer or only the payee". The application of this exemption in the PSD1 has not been consistent across Member States;[97] in Germany, for example, electronic marketplaces have been unsuccessful in invoking it and have thus been deemed as payment service providers having to obtain permission for their services, specifically as 'payment institutions'[98] (Osborne Clark, 2015; Egertz, 2015; EmoneyAdvice.com, 2015). The PSD2 explicitly acknowledges the uncertainty surrounding the particular exemption in the PSD1 and endeavours to offer relevant clarifications. Thus, referring to "e-commerce platforms that act as an intermediary on behalf of both individual buyers and sellers without a real margin to negotiate or conclude the sale or purchase of goods or services", Recital 11 effectively discloses that the exception is *not* intended to cover such parties. Recital 11, PSD2 further states that "the exclusion should . . . apply when agents act only on behalf of the payer or only on

96 See Recital 30, Article 36, Article 97(5) and most importantly, Article 66(1), (2) and (4), which specifically refer to a right of users to use a payment initiation service and an obligation of account servicing payment service providers to co-operate with the provider of that service.

97 Recital 11, PSD2.

98 Being defined by Article 4(4), PSD2 as "a legal person that has been granted authorisation in accordance with Article 11 to provide and execute payment services throughout the Union" and with the concept of 'payment services' being defined by Article 4(3), PSD2 as all the services listed in Annex I of the PSD2, the concept of the 'payment institution' obviously comprises the broadest category of payment service providers eligible to accommodate all services that are in one way or another involved in the handling or processing of payments.

behalf of the payee, regardless of whether or not they are in possession of client funds". It also adds that "where agents act on behalf of both the payer and the payee (such as certain e-commerce platforms), they should be excluded *only if they do not, at any time enter into possession or control of client funds*".[99]

The concept of a 'commercial agent' is implicitly defined in Article 3(b), PSD2 by reference to the corresponding definition in the Commercial Agents Directive, where it is stated that a "'commercial agent' shall mean a self-employed intermediary who has continuing authority to negotiate the sale or the purchase of goods on behalf of another person, hereinafter called the 'principal', or to negotiate and conclude such transactions on behalf of and in the name of that principal".[100] Though marketplaces are certainly *not* amongst the most obvious cases of commercial agents, the argument that they do qualify as such is strong. eBay Inc. (2017c), for example, does not deny the capacity of a commercial agent (unlike that of a "traditional auctioneer"). The argument becomes even stronger when marketplaces charge a commission on the sales achieved on their platforms payable by the seller.

Consumers will most probably not pay any remuneration to the marketplace provider, yet that does not necessarily result in the said provider being considered as acting solely on behalf of the merchants. Indeed, commercial agents who are not paid by their principal are excluded from the Commercial Agents Directive *but* they are *not* denied the label of a 'commercial agent' by the said measure.[101] Automated marketplaces, therefore, will, in most cases, act *both* for the merchant (seller or payee) *and* the consumer (buyer and payer), as their systems and platforms, which essentially take over negotiation and contracting, are made available to both and assist both in finding a party with whom to conclude a contract. Egertz (2015) takes this for granted, albeit by reference to traditional online marketplaces such as eBay.[102]

If automated marketplaces are accepted to act for and on behalf of *both* parties, Recital 11 is categorical that they would fall within the 'commercial agent' exception of the PSD2 *only if they never come in possession or control of client funds.* Automated marketplaces, which would handle payments themselves, thereby receiving consumer funds in a payment account of their own,[103] would clearly qualify as 'payment service providers', specifically, payment institutions. These payment service providers provide more limited services than credit institutions, but they are entitled to hold client funds.[104] PayPal, for example, holds client funds (paid to a PayPal account holder by his friends or clients or taken from his credit card or bank account) in the so-called PayPal Balance (PayPal Inc., 2017).

An alternative for electronic marketplaces (which would prefer to fall within the exception, thereby avoiding having to apply for a license as a payment institution under the PSD2) would be to distance themselves from the task of payment handling and establish a co-operation with a payment institution instead (Osborne Clark, 2015). Exactly for this

99 Emphasis added.

100 Article 1(2), Council Directive 86/653/EEC of 18 December 1986 on the coordination of the laws of the Member States relating to self-employed commercial agents.

101 Article 2(1), Commercial Agents Directive.

102 Of course, the possibility cannot be excluded of automated marketplaces arranging their business structure so as to act solely for merchants, a possibility further explained, by reference to non-automated marketplaces by Osborne Clark (2015).

103 This can be for the purpose of crediting the 'wallet' of consumer software agents on their marketplace or otherwise, using consumer funds to effect appropriate payments to merchants, having first taken the former in their possession.

104 See Recital 34, PSD2.

purpose, several payment solution providers, who are authorized 'payment service providers', have been offering marketplace providers PSD2-compliant payment solutions entailing a total outsourcing of the payment processing.[105] This alternative may not, however, be available to *automated* marketplace providers. Indeed, as the whole idea behind the latter is the full automation unleashed by software substituting human contracting parties during the whole of the buying process, a co-operation with a different entity (a payment service provider) to which users will be redirected so that they can personally effect payment runs counter to their very nature and forces a step back to less advanced *non*-automated marketplaces. Unless therefore this re-direction can occur automatically (without the consumer having to get involved), the said solution will be unavailable in the context of real automated marketplaces.

On the other hand, applying for authorization as a *'payment institution'* sounds like entailing a dramatic extension in the business model of automated marketplaces, and not all them could be expected to go down that route. Most of them may therefore choose to operate as payment initiation service providers (PISPs). These are the new breed of payment service providers who must also secure authorization under the PSD2.[106] According to Article 4(15), PSD2, "'payment initiation service' means a service to initiate a payment order at the request of the payment service user with respect to a payment account held at another payment service provider". Recital 27, PSD2 explains that they establish "a software bridge between the website of the merchant and the online banking platform of the payer's account servicing payment service provider in order to initiate internet payments on the basis of a credit transfer".[107] The Swedish 'Trustly', the German 'SOFORT' and the Dutch 'iDEAL' constitute the most common examples of payment initiation services (Valcke et al., 2015, p. 6; Reijers, 2016, pp. 31–32).

Taking the example of SOFORT, when, while on the website of a merchant, a consumer chooses SOFORT as her preferred payment method, she is redirected to and accesses the SOFORT platform to which she has to input her personalized security credentials provided by the provider of her payment account (most commonly, her bank), thereby initiating a payment to that merchant from the said payment account (SOFORT GmbH, 2017). Automated marketplaces cannot work in the same way because the consumer will *not* be involved personally in the process. Presumably, the relevant providers will use as part of their marketplace system, a SOFORT-like software system, the only difference being that contracting (consumer) software (i.e. the marketplace provider) would hold consumer personalized security credentials and utilize the SOFORT-like software of the marketplace, thereby initiating payment.

105 One such payment service provider states the following: "The new Ingenico Payment Solution for Marketplaces is a scalable, secure and fully PSD2-compliant solution that helps online marketplaces grow beyond their borders and simplify the transaction process for both sellers and buyers. Ingenico's Full Service model means the company collects all funds on behalf of the marketplace operator. In this model, the marketplace operator becomes an agent of Ingenico, a licensed payment service provider, which removes the need for the marketplace operator to upgrade its company structure to become a licensed payment service provider itself" (Ingenico Group, 2017).

106 The capital and other requirements for such authorization however are significantly less stringent than those applying to payment institutions, see Recitals 34–35, PSD2.

107 Though the said Recital makes reference to banking, the definition of 'payment initiation service providers', referring to payment accounts in general would seem to cover services that facilitate the initiation of payment not only from a bank payment account but also from a payment account held by a 'payment institution' instead such as PayPal.

A condition precedent to being a 'payment initiation service provider' is that the provider never holds user funds,[108] which automated marketplaces working as described previously would obviously meet. It is worth clarifying that the fact that they will not hold user funds does not bring them within the 'commercial agent' exception. As already stated, online platforms acting on behalf of both buyers and sellers only fall within the exception if 'they do not, at any time enter into possession or control of client funds'. Evidently, the concept of 'control' is broader than that of 'possession'. Thus, though automated marketplace providers operating as described previously will never acquire possession of consumer funds, they cannot be regarded as *not* in control of such funds. Indeed, from the moment the security credentials enabling payments from consumer payment accounts will be submitted to their systems, they will certainly get in control of the funds existing in those payment accounts (in the sense that they will be able to initiate payments using those funds). Importantly, this finding also clarifies that such automated marketplaces will not fall within the so-called 'technical services' exception of Article 3(j), PSD2 either,[109] as the said provision explicitly excludes from its ambit payment initiation service providers.

3.3.5.2.4 THE SIGNIFICANCE OF THE QUALIFICATION OF AUTOMATED MARKETPLACES AS PISP

The qualification of automated marketplaces as 'payment service providers' is of great importance in several respects. It effectively means that at least in relation to software-held personal data in the form of payment details (or personalized security credentials), there is an extra layer of legally mandated security applied by the PSD2 co-existing with that of other measures such as the previously-discussed GDPR and the NISD discussed in Chapter 5. At least for the kind of fraud involving compromise of consumer payment details, this additional protection is particularly important and to some extent compensates for the absence of an explicit and powerful legal obligation to apply marketplace access control mechanisms proactively, ensuring that the marketplace remains 'clean' from unreliable or fraudulent merchants.

Indeed, apart from the general security-related obligations mentioned previously,[110] PISPs are subject to Article 97(3), PSD2 requiring that they "have in place adequate security measures to protect the confidentiality and integrity of payment service users' personalised security credentials". Additionally, Article 66(3)(b), PSD2 requires that payment initiation service providers "ensure that the personalised security credentials of the payment service user are not . . . accessible to other parties and that they are transmitted by the payment initiation service provider through safe and efficient channels". Admittedly, though they expressly refer to personalized security credentials, these obligations do not add much to the security-related obligations derived from GDPR and the NISD. This is so mainly because personalized security credentials clearly qualify as personal data triggering the demanding data protection obligations of the GDPR.

108 Article 66(3)(a), PSD2 and Recital 35, PSD2.

109 Article 3(j), PSD2 excludes from the scope of the PSD2 "services provided by technical service providers, which support the provision of payment services, without them entering at any time into possession of the funds to be transferred, including processing and storage of data, trust and privacy protection services, data and entity authentication, information technology (IT) and communication network provision, provision and maintenance of terminals and devices used for payment services, *with the exclusion of payment initiation services* and account information services", emphasis added.

110 Supra pp. 98–99

Importantly, however, the PSD2 goes much further. As is explained in the following, if automated marketplaces qualify as payment service providers, they may indirectly be obliged to use strong customer authentication, too. This means that such authentication will have to be applied at the point of access to their own service, resulting in two 'authentication walls' and thus, to increased security.

Albeit incidentally, it may effectively also result in the earlier-suggested marketplace access control mechanism. Indeed, if consumer access to the marketplace will be subject to strong customer authentication, it may be unlikely that merchant access will just be free and easy. The strong authentication procedures to be established for consumer payers in response to the relevant obligation of the PSD2 may extend to merchant payees, too, especially given that automated marketplaces form uniform systems operated by one and the same provider.[111] In such a case, the possibility of fraudsters or unreliable merchants accessing the marketplace will be reduced.

More specifically, Article 92(1), PSD2 creates a strong incentive for third-party payment service providers such as PISPs to take adequate security-enhancing measures and to use strong customer authentication, thereby avoiding being the culprit behind a security breach and an unauthorized transaction. The particular provision does so by conferring a right of recourse to the benefit of the payment service provider who suffers damage, amongst others, as a result of complying with his refund obligations discussed previously.[112] When the damage is attributable to "another payment service provider or to an intermediary",[113] the aggrieved payment service provider can turn against the responsible payment service provider or intermediary for compensation. Moreover, Article 92(1), PSD2 explicitly states that compensation may be recoverable *where a payment service provider does not use strong customer authentication*. This right to compensation can certainly operate as an indirect, yet powerful, force towards the adoption of strong customer authentication and, more generally, of adequate security measures by *all* payment service providers involved, including the automated marketplace provider

The PSD2 can potentially indirectly improve the security of automated marketplaces in additional ways. According to Article 97(2), PSD2, in the case of remote electronic payment transactions (such as those to be initiated by automated marketplace providers),[114] strong customer identification must also enable a dynamic link between the transaction and a

111 Another incentive for marketplace providers to employ strong customer authentication may derive from the fact that the payment service provider servicing the payment account of the consumer may choose to exempt payment initiation service providers applying strong customer authentication themselves from the requirement to go through strong customer authentication procedures for accessing consumer payment accounts on its system. For this possibility of exemption, see EBA (2018, paras 38–39). This may greatly simplify the tasks and duties of automated marketplace providers relating to having to store and use the consumer security credentials provided by the payment service provider servicing the payment account of the consumer.

112 Article 92(1), PSD2 reads as follows: "Where the liability of a payment service provider under Articles 73 and 89 is attributable to another payment service provider or to an intermediary, that payment service provider or intermediary shall compensate the first payment service provider for any losses incurred or sums paid under Articles 73 and 89. That shall include compensation where any of the payment service providers fail to use strong customer authentication".

113 Article 92(1), PSD2. It is worth noting that the term 'intermediary' is unwisely not defined in the PSD2, it seems to arise from Recital 87, PSD2, however, that it intends to cover intermediaries of payment service providers such as processors of such providers (i.e., technical parties which process data on their behalf or otherwise assist them in providing their services) rather than unrelated intermediaries such as a marketplace not a payment service provider itself.

114 Supra p. 99

specific amount and payee.[115] According to the EBA, this 'dynamic linking' can be achieved through the use of *digital signatures* operating as authentication codes, i.e., TANs.[116] Automated marketplace providers will have to follow the authentication procedures of the payment service provider servicing the payment account of the user so that if that payment service provider opts for dynamic linking through digital signatures, the marketplace provider will have to hold the digital signature of the consumer user. This would inevitably bring digital signatures, which are certainly security-enhancing tools (and the qualified services associated with their use) governed by the eIDAs Regulation discussed later in this book[117] 'closer' to providers of automated marketplaces and, possibly, encourage a wider adoption of them, thereby enhancing overall marketplace security.

Notably, the security-related requirements of the PSD2 have the important potential of 'forcing' the market to accept and utilize the trust services regulated by the eIDAs Regulation to the benefit of security. Put another way, though trust services are voluntary under the eIDAs Regulation,[118] because of the PSD2, they effectively become a way of complying with mandatory (legal) requirements, thereby becoming somewhat less voluntary. It should thus be welcomed that the EBA (2015, pp. 26–28; 2016, pp. 12, 19, 21) has seen this possibility of interaction between the eIDAs Regulation and the PSD2, though it states that the eIDAs Regulation offers solutions amongst several possible others.[119]

3.4 Unreliable transactions and traditional fraud: concluding remarks

This chapter has focused on the risk of consumer fraud associated with shopping agents and automated marketplaces. In its first part, it has illustrated the existence of the relevant risk as well as the need for legal intervention in the form of a fraud-preventive obligation imposed on the relevant platform providers. In particular, it has been shown that if this obligation is implemented in the form of an access control mechanism resulting in merchant participants being vetted against certain criteria of reliability, it is both technologically feasible and by no means overly burdensome for the particular intermediaries who significantly profit from the provision of their services and must therefore be expected to keep them safe for consumer users.

In its second part, this chapter has reinforced the justifiability of the aforementioned obligation, illustrating that it cannot really effectively be replaced by a different legal approach. It has then searched for such an obligation in various relevant EU legal measures and found that none of them imposes a direct (or explicit) relevant obligation on the relevant parties, meaning that the relevant EU legal response cannot be regarded as adequate. More specifically, it has examined the application of the provisions on intermediary liability of the ECD to the relevant platforms, concluding that the possibility cannot be excluded of both shopping agent and automated marketplace providers being accepted as qualifying as hosting providers under Article 14, ECD. As a result, not only they may be exempted from

115 Ibid.
116 Ibid.
117 Infra Chapter 5.3.3.2.3
118 Infra Chapter 5 p. 164
119 Notably, however, regarding communication between various payment service providers, Article 20 of the Draft EBA Regulatory Standard obliges such providers (including automated marketplace providers) to "rely on Qualified certificates for website authentication as per article 3(39) of Regulation (EU) No 910/2014" (EBA, 2016, p. 41). This constitutes a clear example of trust services that are voluntary under the eIDAs Regulation becoming mandatory by the PSD2.

liability for the fraud committed through their services but also Article 15, ECD may even prohibit the imposition of a legal fraud-preventive obligation on them.

It has, of course, been illustrated that the correct interpretation of the relevant ECD provisions should exclude the relevant platform providers from their scope, yet national case law has been such as to prevent a confident conclusion that this will in fact be the case. The related part of the chapter has also suggested solutions for avoiding this undesirable outcome, such as giving Article 15 a restrictive interpretation excluding the suggested fraud-preventive obligation in the form of an access control mechanism from the prohibition it imposes. It is however highly uncertain that this interpretation will be adopted by courts, even more so because the European Commission seems to think otherwise.

This chapter has proceeded with examining the application of the EU Directives relating to contractual liability for goods as well as product liability and safety in an attempt to see whether the arising liability threats can result in an *indirect* fraud-preventive obligation at least. The answer to the relevant question has been negative, as the CSD is wholly inapplicable to the relevant platform providers whereas the PLD and the PSD, which can be applicable, are not concerned with the type of damage, namely economic loss, which the consumer may suffer as a result of fraud on the relevant platforms. A fraud-preventive obligation has been shown to be possible indirectly to arise from the UCPD, which can tackle both traditional fraud in the form of deceptive merchant listings or contractual communications and less traditional fraudulent techniques, such as a malicious alteration of consumer software code. It has been explained however, that the said potential of the UCPD remains unrecognized so far and that it must also overcome the Article 15 general prohibition of the ECD, something which provokes an interesting discussion on the relationship between the UCPD and the ECD. In any event, its effectiveness will very much depend on how strict relevant enforcement will be. The fact that it is mainly up to the consumer to uncover fraudulent practices, thereby triggering enforcement has been said to constitute an important relevant weakness, particularly, in the context of automated marketplaces in which consumers have no active involvement in the contractual process and thus, insufficient knowledge of how merchants act or behave.

Finally, this chapter has examined the application of the PSD2 to automated marketplaces and has concluded that powerful protection is afforded against consumer fraud not only *ex-post* but also *ex-ante*. Its refund rights, which are triggered in cases of unauthorized transactions resulting in consumer financial harm, only provide for a partial solution, as fraud will not always be in the form of unauthorized payment transactions for the purposes of the relevant PSD2 provisions. However, its *ex-post* controls in the form of very demanding payment security obligations and the obligation for strong customer authentication in particular have a great potential of significantly enhancing the security of automated marketplaces, thereby protecting consumer payers against fraud. It has been shown that the ingredients of strong customer authentication may cause problems of compatibility in the context of automated marketplaces also resulting in payment service providers administering payment instruments and/or servicing payment accounts to 'block' consumer resort to such marketplaces.

Yet, the said problems are not impossible to overcome, mainly because such marketplaces may qualify as 'payment service providers', specifically PISPs. Accordingly, not only are payment service providers prohibited from refusing to co-operate with automated marketplace providers but also the latter are subject to the detailed security obligations of the PSD2 themselves, something that may improve the 'safety' of their service. Moreover, the application of the PSD2 to automated marketplaces provokes or at least strongly encourages the use of technical measures of increased security, such as digital signatures, which remain voluntary under the eIDAs Regulation.

Overall, the EU legal response to the risk of (traditional) fraud in this context cannot be considered as adequate; there is no positive obligation on platform providers to vet merchant participants and the relevant gap is only reduced by indirect, partial and highly uncertain solutions arising from EU legal measures.

4 Risks relating to data protection (and privacy) on automated marketplaces

4.1 General remarks (and the relationship between data protection and transactional security)

Being systems designed to support the formation of binding contracts between human contracting parties on the open and notoriously unsecure internet, automated marketplaces should apply measures ensuring transactional security. Referring to automated marketplaces in which parties are substituted by software agents, Jonkheer (1999, para. 17) has emphasized that "agents have to be secure from manipulation to ensure their effectiveness". 'Transactional security' is a broad term encompassing user confidentiality, data integrity, data authentication and non-repudiation (Tsvetovatty et al., 1997, p. 504, Fasli, 2007, pp. 18–20). Put simply, the privacy of users should be respected, and the data exchanged between the parties should not be vulnerable to unauthorized alterations. Users should also be able to know that data really originates from the party they actually negotiate with and that the said party could not just deny involvement in the transaction. Obviously, there can be no contracting without transactional security and albeit by reference to B2B marketplaces, issues of transactional security are rightly recognized as central to *trust*, without which there can be no business (Expert Group on B2B Internet Trading Platforms, 2003, pp. 28–29; Perogianni, 2003, pp. 21–22).

It follows that transactional security is closely related to data protection and privacy and is also by no means unrelated to fraud; thus, increased transactional security entails a response to the risk of data protection (or privacy) violations and to the risk of fraud. In relation to the latter, unlike in Chapter 3, fraud mainly refers to (less traditional) electronic fraud types committed not simply by providing false or deceptive information but by electronically interfering, manipulating or misappropriating data and/or software code or by exploiting the unsecure nature of the Internet to deny involvement in a transaction or faking identity, though as it clearly arises, there is inevitably some overlapping between the two categories of fraud.

This book will illustrate these risks in the context of automated marketplaces and will do so through a discussion and explanation of the aforementioned four elements of transactional security, namely user confidentiality, data integrity, data authentication and non-repudiation. The present chapter, however focuses on user confidentiality, i.e., the heated topic of privacy and data protection. Following the illustration of the relevant risks, it will be examined whether current relevant EU legal measures impose sufficient privacy-respecting obligations on providers of automated marketplaces. The next chapter, Chapter 5, will focus on data integrity, data authentication and non-repudiation, i.e., the rest of the elements of transactional security.

4.2 Data protection (and privacy): illustrating the risks and an appropriate legal response

User confidentiality entails the crucial issue of data protection and consumer privacy within automated marketplaces (Fasli, 2007, p. 18). From as early as 1999, the relationship of software acting on behalf of users in contracting (this being referred to as software agents) with privacy has been acknowledged (and emphasized) as a highly problematic one:

> We wish to raise a note of caution, however, because such agents may also pose a serious threat to the privacy of their users – intelligent agents operate by accessing a detailed personal profile of the user, which enables them to execute their user's wishes. The potential loss of control over one's profile and the prospect of having the details of one's life accessed by unauthorized third parties looms like a black cloud over any potential benefits that may accrue.
>
> (Borking, van Eck and Siepel, 1999, Preface)

Indeed, contracting software will naturally hold and deal with consumer personal information and have thus unsurprisingly been described as a serious privacy threat capable of leading to multiple privacy or data protection violations (Borking et al., 1999, pp. 23–31). The main privacy threat arises from the central task of contracting software, namely the communication with other software and the exchange of information for the purpose of contracting. As Fasli (2007, p. 382) writes, "If intercepted by a third party, such data render the user/owner of the agent identifiable, thus breaching their privacy". During such communications, there may be a leak of personal data and thus, a data breach for a myriad of known and unknown reasons. Known reasons include a system malfunction, the existence of malicious parties aiming at stealing personal information and an external system attack.

Consumer data protection (or privacy) risks can be divided into two categories, namely, those existing while software negotiates and transacts *within* the marketplace (*marketplace risks*) and those arising *after* personal data leaves the marketplaces and gets into the systems of the merchant contractor, which would normally be after contract conclusion (*merchant risks*) (Markou, 2011, p254. In both cases, the answer lies with the employment of privacy-enhancing technologies.

Regarding marketplace risks, official studies propose the use of an Identity Protector (IP) to be placed, *inter alia*, between the consumer contracting software and its environment preventing *involuntary* 'information' flows from consumer software to merchant and other consumer software participating in a marketplace (Borking et al., 1999, p. 34). Secure interaction protocols (Brazier et al., 2004b), digital signatures (Hes and Borking, 2000), digital pseudonyms (Hes and Borking, 2000), proxy components disallowing direct software-to-software interaction (Collins et al., 1998) and, more generally, encryption can serve as an agent IP protector. Encryption enables the exchange of encrypted software communications so that only the software of the parties taking part in a given transaction can read them (Hes and Borking, 2000; Song and Korba, 2001; Fasli, 2007).

Encryption can thus guard against involuntary or accidental disclosures of personal data inherent in software contractual communications. It can also protect data relating to the consumer software strategy or user-specified 'price' range (and other user parameters). As Sartor (2009, p. 286) rightly acknowledges, such data should also not be accessed by or disclosed to merchant software, because that could undermine the ability of consumer software to achieve the best possible deal for its consumer user. Presumably, encryption can also shield consumer software code from unauthorized interference leading to an involuntary change of the behaviour of the said software and, thus, to advanced fraud, as explained earlier.[1] In this respect, the technology of encryption sounds to entail a thorough response not only to plain privacy or data protection risks but also to fraud-related risks. Accordingly, legal regimes which are shown specifically to exploit encryption can be accepted as going a long way towards responding to the said risks.

Such technologies, however, are sometimes regarded as a consumer product to be purchased by privacy-sensitive consumers (Borking et al., 1999, pp. 44–45; Rasmusson, Rasmusson and Janson, 1997, sec. 2.1). This is not an approach that should be taken up by the law. Indeed, systems supporting transactions cannot exist in isolation from transactional security including user confidentiality, as in the absence of the latter, such systems or services cannot really serve their purpose.[2] Transactional security (including data protection/privacy) must therefore be a built-in feature rather than a paid add-on burdening the consumer, rather than those providing (and profiting from) automated marketplaces. This inevitably translations into a legal obligation vested on marketplace providers to utilize privacy-enhancing technologies and covering the inherent cost from their profits and probably, sharing some of it with the merchant users.

The need for *such legally mandated technological data protection* (or the approach of building privacy into system programming code, i.e., privacy by design) had been emphasized by legal and technical experts decades ago. The idea of *technological* data protection can be traced back to the 1970s. It was brought into the surface in the 1990s and in the 2000s, it came to be discussed as a necessary *legal* requirement. It is thus a well-thought-out idea that makes perfect sense especially in the context of highly technical environments.

More specifically, Burkert (1998, p. 136) referred to a German article of the 1970s on the first 'data protection' law, which "pointed to the need to accompany such legislation . . . with privacy-ensuring technical designs". Burkert observed that the focus in Europe (and elsewhere) had instead been on enacting and properly administering 'privacy' legislation and noted that privacy perceptions must in fact be considered "whenever we set to design technical systems in social environments". Around the same time, Clarke (1996) also stated that identification and anonymity are both "*a vital systems design* and public policy issue".[3] Also, studies conducted by data protection authorities in Europe and beyond (Hes and Borking, 2000) as well as European projects such as PISA (which focused on software agents acting on behalf of human users) had been offering practical guidelines of privacy-friendly system design involving the use of various existing privacy-enhancing technologies (European Commission, 2005).

Importantly, commentators such as Edwards (2003, p. 226) called for "a new effort . . . not to abandon law as unenforceable in dealing with problems such as spam and privacy, but to explore how it can be amended and globally harmonized to provide sanction and backing to self-regulatory and *technical solutions*".[4] By 2004, the fact "that privacy protection has to be incorporated in most IT applications" was thought to be "one of the least controversial statements" (Gritzalis, 2004, p. 8). Towards the end of the 2000s, researchers described a vision of 'law by design', i.e., a new kind of law that involves the legislator requiring that data protection rules be inscribed into technological systems "making the violation of these rules difficult by means of design" (FIDIS, 2007, p. 28).

1 Supra Chapter 3 pp. 94–95
2 Infra Chapter 5.1.
3 Emphasis added.
4 Emphasis added.

Doubtless, a legal obligation to employ technical measures of data protection vested on marketplace providers must be a central element of an adequate legal response to the privacy risks associated with automated marketplaces. This is especially the case given that privacy-enhancing technologies can address the inherent weakness of legal 'data protection' rules, which, according to commentators (e.g., Edwards, 2003, p. 243; Bergkamp, 2002, pp. 37–38), relates to enforcement. Indeed, an encryption-adopting automated marketplace, for example, which technically prevents the interception of software contractual communications, can reduce the risk of privacy violations and, simultaneously, also the need wholly to rely on data protection authorities that often lack sufficient resources to protect privacy in such highly technical environments.

As for merchant risks relating to data protection, these arise post-contract conclusion, specifically, when consumer personal data gets into the systems of the merchant who is to perform contract by product delivery. These could again be addressed by an obligation technically to protect personal data, albeit vested on merchants. Moreover, they can further be reduced by an 'access control' mechanism[5] applied by the marketplace provider requiring potential participating merchants to demonstrate adherence to satisfactory privacy policies through the presentation of privacy-related credentials. Such approach could improve privacy both within and outside the marketplace, as a privacy-respecting merchant is likely to behave in a privacy-friendly manner in all settings. An access control mechanism is therefore an answer both to marketplace and merchant privacy-related risks. Accordingly, legal regimes obliging marketplace providers to apply such an access control mechanism can be accepted as entailing a welcoming response to the relevant risks.

TRUSTe (TRUSTarc, 2019a) is a US-based organization that monitors the privacy policies of online businesses ensuring compliance with its privacy standards. These standards are developed in accordance with legal requirements, including those in the GDPR (TRUSTarc, 2019b). Businesses can request the so-called 'letter of attestation', i.e., "a customized letter of attestation that your company . . . has undergone a review and alignment with TRUSTe's privacy program requirements", which "can be shared with clients and business partners". (TRUSTarc, 2019c).

One can see such letters of attestation or seals (i.e., digital credentials) being used for access to automated marketplaces, or in the context of the suggested access control mechanism. Importantly, automated marketplaces can technically support their use (Barlow, Hess, and Seamons, 2001, pp. 2–4). Given this readiness of both industry and technology to utilize privacy-related digital credentials, the law should not hesitate to exploit their privacy-enhancing potential by imposing requirements strengthening their value and encouraging their use. In fact, this could be an example of the "complicated interaction between technology and law in which technology also influences the law" referred to by Brazier et al. (2004a, p. 138).

More specifically, the provision of such credentials should be overseen by the law in response to voices claiming that they do not "necessarily provide full protection, as there is no formal control of the seal providing organizations" (Bain and Subirana, 2003b, p. 288).[6] Indeed, in 2014, TRUSTe settled an enforcement action taken by the FTC (USA Federal Trade Commission, 2014a; USA Federal Trade Commission, 2014b, para. 16), amongst

5 Access control has also been discussed by reference to fraud in Chapter 3.

6 Credential or certification providers are more generally often accused of insufficient monitoring and leniency towards merchants (Froomkin, 2000, pp. 1525–1526; Edwards, 2003, p. 238; Erlanger, n.d.).

others, on the ground that "from 2006 until January 2013, Respondent did not conduct annual recertifications for all companies holding TRUSTe Certified Privacy Seals" to ensure continuous compliance with privacy standards. Even though the incidence casted further doubt on the effectiveness of the seal (or certification) approach (Snyder, 2014), it has resulted in TRUSTe undertaking extra information duties towards the FTC regarding how it administers a certain certification program (USA Federal Trade Commission, 2014c, III–IV). It arises therefore that privacy credential providers can in fact be overseen by authorities ensuring real value in the provided credentials. Accordingly, legal regimes which ensure official control of credential providers can be accepted as entailing an enhanced response to privacy risks.

Froomkin (2000, p. 1527) considers the *voluntary* nature of seal programmes to be another serious weakness, resulting in limited merchant participation. Though self-regulatory measures are *by nature* voluntary, the law can play a role in boosting their use. One way is the previously suggested imposition of a legal obligation on marketplace providers to employ privacy-enhancing technologies. If, in discharging that obligation, the relevant parties only allow to their marketplace *certified* privacy-respecting merchants, resort to relevant certifications by merchants will inevitably be increased. Additionally, the law may reward merchant participation to relevant self-regulatory schemes by providing for a presumption of compliance with relevant legal requirements in favour of participating merchants. Legal regimes providing for such legal presumptions would address the relevant weakness of relevant certification schemes, thereby improving the adequacy of their response to the data protection risks associated with automated marketplaces.

4.3 User confidentiality (data protection risks): the EU legal response

4.3.1 General remarks

Having discussed the risks to consumer privacy or data protection in the relevant context (and the additional risk of fraud inherent in inadequate data protection), the discussion will now turn to whether EU law adequately responds to these risks. The preceding analysis can guide the relevant legal analysis, as it has also largely illustrated the appropriate content of an adequate legal response, too. More specifically, such legal response should entail the following elements: (a) an obligation on marketplace providers to respect (and protect) consumer personal data and apply existing privacy-enhancing technologies, in particular encryption (something that responds to marketplace privacy-related risks); (b) an obligation on marketplace providers to apply a privacy-related access control mechanism (something that responds to both marketplace and merchant privacy-related risks); (c) official control and/or oversight of providers of privacy credentials to be used in the context of the aforementioned access control mechanism; (d) effective encouragement of merchant participation in regulatory schemes leading to the award of privacy credentials and (e) the obligation described in point (a) above imposed on participating merchants, as those too, get to process consumer personal data on their own systems post-contract conclusion. A sixth element should have to do with the (practical) effectiveness of the obligations referred to in the aforementioned element (a), which partly depends on the number of parties burdened with them; as it will be explained, the more parties subject to data protection obligations in relation to *the same* personal data processing, the more effective such obligations will be.

Two European measures, namely the General Data Protection Regulation (GDPR) and the E-Privacy Directive (EPD), appear as directly relevant, though it should be recalled that the PSD2 discussed in Chapter 3 contains additional solutions relating to personal data in the form of consumer payment details (or payment security credentials) The relevant legal response will thus primarily be searched for within the said measures by reference to the aforementioned six elements of an adequate such response. Before doing so, however, two main questions should be answered first. As both of the said measures are only applicable to cases (or services) involving processing of data that is *personal*, the *first* of these questions is whether the data being processed by marketplace providers and marketplace-participating merchants qualifies as 'personal data'. Similarly, as the obligations flowing from the GDPR are addressed to *data controllers* (and some to *data processors*, too), the *second* question is whether the aforementioned parties qualify as data controllers and/or data processors. This question is very important for an additional reason. The GDPR governs the *legal relationship* between data controllers and processors as well as between joint data controllers; this relationship is particularly relevant to elements (b) and (f) of the previously suggested content of an adequate relevant legal response, as it will be explained.

After resolving the aforementioned two preliminary questions, the main question will be examined, namely the one relating to whether the GDPR and the EPD contain all of the elements of the adequate legal response. This necessitates a thorough analysis of some of the provisions of the said measures.

4.3.2 *Is it personal data?*

It is not difficult to conclude that most, if not all, of the data moving within automated marketplaces and eventually passing into the systems of participating merchants is 'personal data' for the purposes of the GDPR. The same holds true of the EPD, which similarly only applies to personal data[7] and adopts the same 'personal data' definition.[8] In Article 4(1), GDPR, 'personal data' is defined as follows:

> Any information relating to an identified or identifiable natural person ('data subject'); an identifiable natural person is one who can be identified, directly or indirectly, in particular by reference to an identifier such as a name, an identification number, location data, an online identifier or to one or more factors specific to the physical, physiological, genetic, mental, economic, cultural or social identity of that natural person.

The definition is evidently very broad and widely acknowledged as capable of covering most data (Hon et al., 2014, executive summary). Especially given that automated marketplaces enable contract conclusion, i.e., an activity normally necessitating personal data processing, it is unsurprising that the data processed in their context qualifies as personal data. It arises from the 'personal data' definition that data revealing the identity of a natural person, including consumer names, home addresses and payment details (normally used for the purpose of contract conclusion and performance) is clearly personal data. Personal data is also data that does not readily reveals identity but can lead to identity if combined with additional information. Thus, identification numbers, online identifiers, pseudonyms or

7 Article 3, EPD.

8 The EPD does not contain a relevant definition and explicitly refers to the definitions of the Data Protection Directive, see Article 2, EPD. The European Commission (2017b) has recently published a Proposal for a Regulation for e-Privacy to replace the EPD, amongst others to ensure compatibility with the GDPR. The proposal again does not contain a 'personal data' definition but Article 4(1)(a) states that the GDPR definitions shall apply.

other constructed identities, such as Consumer Software A, would also qualify as personal data. Accordingly, consumer full names need *not* be used in the marketplace for the data relating to consumers utilized within or outside the marketplace to qualify as 'personal data' triggering the application of the GDPR and the EPD.

More specifically, Recital 26 leaves no doubt that pseudonyms constitute personal data.[9] Interestingly, this is so not just because marketplace providers and participating merchants will most probably be able to use additional information (such as names provided at the point of registration with the marketplace), thereby establishing the identity of the consumer behind the pseudonym-bearing contracting software. Even without the use of consumer names, consumers behind contracting software distinguished through a pseudonym can still be reached and affected, meaning that they are in fact identified. Indeed, specific merchant-to-consumer communications (and contracting) would be impossible without pseudonyms or some other unique identifier being linked to individual consumers, thereby isolating the consumer, whom a given communication is aimed at. Pseudonyms and any other '"anonymous" identifier, such as a number, in fact enable the so-called 'isolate and affect' identification (as opposed to physical identification) and are therefore 'personal data'. As the Data Protection Working Party (DPWP) clarified in 2007, this kind of identification and *not just* (traditional) *physical* (or by name) identification renders data as 'personal' (Article 29, DPWP, 2007, p. 14).

Data comprising consumer instructions or parameters given to consumer software to guide its activity and even consumer software code containing negotiation strategies and/or tactics would also qualify as personal data, in most cases. Indeed, such data is highly unlikely to exist in isolation from personal data, such as a consumer name or pseudonym. It is data that must exist 'within' (or somehow accompany) the software acting for a given consumer, defining its activity and behaviour. Data comprising user instructions or software strategies *in isolation* of any consumer identifier is admittedly *not* personal data, yet such data could not affect the consumer and it thus merits no protection. Accordingly, there is no problem with it not qualifying as personal.

It follows that the data utilized or processed by marketplace providers and participating merchants would qualify as 'personal data', when it can somehow be linked to individual consumers rendering them vulnerable. Accordingly, when the consumer is in need for protection, both the GDPR and the EPD will be applicable.

4.3.3 Are they data controllers and/or processors?

4.3.3.1 Importance of the concepts and the relationship of the parties

Whether automated marketplace providers and marketplace-accessible merchants would qualify as data controllers, joint controllers and/or data processors is also a crucial question. Indeed, the said concepts serve "to allocate responsibility" (Article 29, DPWP, 2010a, p. 4) for compliance with the data protection obligations of the GDPR. Thus, this question, together with the related question as to the relationship between the different parties (and

9 Recital 26, GDPR: "Personal data which have undergone pseudonymisation, which could be attributed to a natural person by the use of additional information should be considered to be information on an identifiable natural person. To determine whether a natural person is identifiable, account should be taken of all the means reasonably likely to be used, such as singling out, either by the controller or by another person to identify the natural person directly or indirectly".

thus, between marketplace providers and participating merchants) under the GDPR, has significant ramifications on the adequacy of the relevant EU legal response.

4.3.3.2 Application of the concepts to automated marketplaces

According to Article 4(7), GDPR "a 'controller' means the natural or legal person, public authority, agency or other body which, alone or jointly with others, determines the purposes and means of the processing of personal data". Put simply, this refers to the party deciding why and how personal data is processed (DPWP, 2010a, p. 13). Unlike the GDPR, which contains no clarification on the definition, Recital 47, of the Data Protection Directive (now replaced by the GDPR) provided the following:

> Whereas where a message containing personal data is transmitted by means of a telecommunications or electronic mail service, the sole purpose of which is the transmission of such messages, the controller in respect of the personal data contained in the message will normally be considered to be the person from whom the message originates, rather than the person offering the transmission services; whereas, nevertheless, those offering such services will normally be considered controllers in respect of the processing of the additional personal data necessary for the operation of the service.

The question as to whether automated marketplace providers and marketplace-accessible merchants, and who (in particular) and in relation to which 'personal data' processing, qualify as 'data controllers' is not simple. The DPWP (2010a, p. 6) has recognized that the application of the relevant concepts has become "more urgent and also more complex than before", amongst others, because technology has facilitated "the use of subcontracting or outsourcing of services in order to benefit from specialisation and possible economies of scale". Automated marketplaces definitely constitute an example of such developments leading to the creation of highly complex environments within which multiple actors (specifically, marketplace providers and marketplace-accessible merchants) are involved in the processing of the same or different personal data.

Commentators have in the past opined that the 'data controller' in an automated marketplace will be the user and/or the provider of the software agent, i.e., the contracting software (Bygrave, 2001, p. 285; Basoli, 2002, sec. 5; Bettelli, 2002, sec. 3; Subirana and Bain, 2005, p. 215). Apparently, the term 'user' refers to a merchant using an automated marketplace to sell his products and the provider is the marketplace provider. Yet, as the said parties may assume differing roles in relation to different 'personal data' processing within a marketplace, the particular issue requires further analysis.

Marketplace providers and merchant users of contracting software would *both* qualify as data controllers if they are both involved in the determination of the purposes and means of the processing of the personal data provided by consumer users of the marketplace; a party need not determine the said purposes and means *alone* but can do so "jointly with others".[10] As it will be shown, marketplace providers are data controllers in relation to some 'personal data' processing and merchants are controllers of other such processing. Additionally, there may be 'personal data' processing in relation to which marketplace providers and merchants are *joint* controllers, though marketplace providers may appear to qualify as processors instead.

10 See relevant definition, supra.

The controller of any data provided by consumers *for registering with an automated marketplace* is clearly the marketplace provider; the said party is the one determining the means and purposes of the relevant data processing; the said data processing is evidently necessary for consumers to be able to use the service and hence for its operation. This view is also supported by the aforementioned Recital 47, DPD.[11] Marketplace-accessible merchants have no direct or substantial involvement (or role) in the relevant personal data processing. Definitely, therefore, they could not be regarded as 'data processors' defined in Article 4(8), GDPR as "a natural or legal person, public authority, agency or other body which processes personal data on behalf of the controller". They are probably not data controllers either; their general interest in the registration of consumers with the marketplace through which they are to sell their products does not seem sufficient to recognize them with an active role in the determination of the purposes and means of data processing inherent in marketplace registration. Thus, the protection of the registration-related data, amongst others, through technical measures of protection pursuant to Articles 24, 32 and 35, GDPR discussed later, will most likely be the exclusive responsibility of the (controller) marketplace provider.

If *data provided for registration purposes (for example, consumer names or other personal identifiers), accompanies each message originating from consumer software and transmitted to merchant software* for the purposes of contracting within the marketplace, *such* 'personal data' processing is different from the one performed solely for the purpose of registration with the marketplace. The same is true more generally of the *content of the messages* exchanged therein. In this case, by choosing to sell their goods or services through such marketplace and under such conditions, merchants determine the means and purposes of *this* data transmission or processing and, therefore, act as data controllers. Indeed, according to the DPWP (2010a, p. 8), "being a controller is primarily the consequence of the factual circumstance that an entity has chosen to process personal data for its own purposes": "one should look at the specific processing operations in question and understand who determines them, by replying in a first stage to the questions 'why is this processing taking place'" (DPWP, 2010a, p. 8).

Marketplace-accessible merchants choose to process the relevant personal data for their *own* purpose of selling products to consumers; this is the main reason why the said processing takes place. Admittedly, the relevant processing takes place solely on the systems of the marketplace provider, who seems therefore to be the one determining *the means of the processing* as is also required by the 'data controller' definition. Yet, as the DPWP (2010a, pp. 13–14) has clarified, in determining who is the controller, the emphasis should be placed *on the determination of the purposes* and that the determination of the means especially the technical ways of processing the data, can be delegated (or outsourced) to a processor, without the delegating party losing its capacity as a controller. Nor the fact that it is the marketplace provider who sets out the detailed terms of the co-operation between himself and participating merchants prevents controllership from being attached to the latter. As the DPWP (2010a, p. 26) has clarified:

> The fact that the contract and its detailed terms of business are prepared by the service provider rather than by the controller is not *in itself* a sufficient basis to conclude that the service provider should be considered as a controller, in so far as the controller has freely accepted the contractual terms, thus accepting full responsibility for them.

11 Supra p. 117

Thus, marketplace-accessible merchants are data controllers in relation to the personal data exchanged in the context of contractual communications within the marketplace.

Does it then follow that the marketplace provider will only be a processor in relation to the said data processing, i.e., a party processing the data on behalf of participating merchants as per Article 4(8), GDPR?[12] Though the GDPR does not explicitly exclude the possibility of a party being *both* a controller and a processor in relation to certain data processing, it would seem that such a (dual) capacity of a party is not possible.[13] Thus, marketplace providers would most probably be considered to be either controllers or processors. As it will be shown, there are strong arguments in favour of a finding that they do not meet the "two basic conditions for qualifying as processor" (DPWP, 2010a, p. 25); more specifically, though they are a *separate* legal entity from participating merchants, they do not really process personal data on their behalf. "Acting on behalf means serving someone else's interest" (DPWP, 2010a, p. 25), whereas, as is explained as follows, the marketplace provider certainly serves his own interest, too. Article 28(2) requires that a contract exist between the controller and the processor, stipulating that the latter shall "act only on instructions from the controller". However, the involvement of the marketplace provider is such that renders it difficult to accept that the said party acts *only* on instructions from the merchants.

The DPWP (2010a, p. 14) has spoken of "essential elements which are traditionally and inherently reserved to the determination of the controller, such as 'which data shall be processed?', 'for how long shall they be processed?', 'who shall have access to them?', and so on". Such issues therefore are not normally determined by mere processors, and marketplace providers have substantial involvement in their determination. Indeed, in setting up the marketplace, they certainly decide upon the rules according to which interactions are to take place. They decide the parties who are to have access to the data by choosing the merchants to be admitted in their marketplace and also by deciding upon the level of security to apply to data exchanged therein. They also have a role in the determination of the duration of the processing, as they are probably the ones deciding whether any communications are to be stored in their systems and for how long. They may additionally specify the *type* of information to be contained in the contractual communications (i.e., the offers or counter-offers exchanged in the marketplace) by providing the forms to be filled in by users in instructing and setting contracting software in operation. They also decide whether consumer names (instead of pseudonyms, for example) are to be transmitted to merchant software in the context of negotiations as well as whether payments are to be made with payment cards (as opposed to anonymous cash), thus requiring the processing of payment card data. The same is true of whether a street address must be provided for product delivery owing, for example, to the unavailability of escrow delivery.

With the previous in mind, the data exchanged within marketplaces appears closer to data necessary for the *operation of the marketplace service* in relation to which, Recital 47, DPD states that the service provider is the data controller. Additionally, as without the processing of such data, the marketplace service could *not* achieve its very purpose of facilitating contract conclusion, marketplace providers are clearly involved in the determination of the

12 Supra p. 118

13 The DPWP (2010a, p. 25) only recognizes the possibility of a party simultaneously being a processor in relation to certain processing and a controller in relation to certain *other* processing, while in all of the examples referring to a single processing, the DPWP strives to qualify actors as either controllers or processors. The impossibility of a dual capacity in this context may be taken to lie in the definition of the term 'processor', particularly the reference to the fact that he acts on behalf of the controller.

purpose of the data processing, this being the workability and availability of their service and the profit they derive from it. Given also that the processing occurs solely on their systems and primarily under their control, they also determine the means of the processing and, thus, qualify as controllers.

It is true that Recital 47, DPD states that the controller of the content of any messages exchanged *through e-mail* is not the 'e-mail service' provider but the originator of the messages.[14] Though the relevant text does not exist in the GDPR, the interesting question arises as to whether marketplaces designed to leave the content of the contractual communications in the absolute discretion of the contracting parties could escape a characterization as 'controllers' and be considered 'processors' instead. The question can safely be answered in the negative. The DPWP (2010a, p. 29) cites the example of a 'lost and found' website which assumed the role of a processor, the controllers being intended to be its users who were posting lost items. Though this arrangement seems consistent with Recital 47, the DPWP opined that the relevant website was, in fact, a controller:

> The website was set up for the business purpose of making money from allowing the posting of lost items and the fact that they did not determine which specific items were posted (as opposed to determining the categories of items) was not crucial as the definition of 'data controller' does not expressly include the determination of content. The website determines the terms of posting etc and is responsible for the propriety of content.

The same line of thinking could be applied to the case of marketplace providers reinforcing the conclusion that they are data controllers. Moreover, marketplace providers seem to bear additional controller characteristics, specifically "visibility/image given by the controller to the data subject, and expectations of the data subjects on the basis of this visibility" (DPWP, 2010a, pp. 12, 28). Given the strong visibility of marketplaces, such as eBay, to users[15] coupled with the fact that in the context of automated marketplaces, consumers will only *personally* interact with the marketplace, rather than with the participating merchants who are to communicate with consumer contracting software, automated marketplaces possess this visibility-related characteristic of controllership, too.

All in all, as the merchants participating in the marketplace are *also* controllers in relation to the processing inherent in the exchange of communications within the marketplace,[16] marketplace providers and marketplace-accessible merchants must be regarded as '*joint controllers*' in relation to all of the processing involved in the operation of automated marketplaces[17], except the one entailed in marketplace registration. As already seen, only the marketplace provider is the controller in the case of the latter.

When consumers do *not* use marketplace-provided contracting software but rather *software provided by an independent provider of their choice*, the controllers of personal data processed for the purposes of contracting within the marketplace remains unchanged.

14 Supra p. 117

15 Consumers tend to state that they bought something from eBay, rather than from the specific merchant selling on eBay.

16 Supra p. 120

17 This conclusion seems consistent with recent CJEU case law, in which merchants administering commercial Facebook Pages on the platform of Facebook have been considered to be data controllers jointly with Facebook, the platform provider (Case C-210/16 *Unabhängiges Landeszentrum für Datenschutz Schleswig-Holstein v Wirtschaftsakademie Schleswig-Holstein GmbH*, [2018], (CJEU), ECLI:EU:C:2018:388).

Subirana and Bain (2005, pp. 216–217) consider the independent software provider to be the data controller and the marketplace provider to be either a processor or a joint controller. The former is clearly a data controller in relation to the data processing occurring while the consumer instructs the software and sends it to the marketplace. It occurs on its own systems through means and for purposes that the said party mainly determines.

When that software enters the marketplace, it will have to follow the rules and procedures determined by the marketplace provider. Yet, the independent software provider probably remains a controller too, as any such processing occurs in the context (and actually consists) of the performance of its service. He thus seems to be involved in why and how personal data is processed. As for the role of the marketplace provider, that does not seem to be reduced to that of a processor. What has earlier been stated about the role of his role in the determination of the purposes and means of the processing would seem to remain unaltered by the fact that consumer personal data is not inputted in the marketplace directly by the consumer but through some independently provided software, which does so on the consumer's behalf. After all, this independently provided software has probably been designed on the basis of the rules and procedures established by the marketplace so that it can be compatible with it. Similarly, the position of the marketplace-accessible merchants clearly remains totally unaffected by the involvement of an additional party, namely the independent agent provider and therefore they are also data controllers on the basis explained earlier.[18] In the case of independently provided consumer software therefore, there will be three joint controllers (the independent software provider, the marketplace provider and the marketplace-accessible merchants).

4.3.3.3 Repercussions on the adequacy of the EU legal response

As it has been shown, automated marketplace providers and participating merchants will be joint controllers in relation to the main data processing involved in the operation automated marketplaces. The question now arises as to the implications of joint controllership on the effectiveness and/or enforcement of the data protection obligations imposed by the GDPR on controllers. As is illustrated in Chapter 4, section 4.3.4 of this book, the said data protection obligations are potentially capable of tackling the privacy-related risks inherent in automated marketplaces, yet the relevant potential cannot fully materialize in practice in the absence of rigorous enforcement and other strong incentives for compliance. This is particularly true in the area of data protection, where enforcement is notoriously problematic: "In practice, data protection authorities everywhere are rather strange 'beasts', given an impossible range of (some would say, incompatible) tasks, enormous powers – and too few resources to be truly effective" (Korff, 2002, p. 203).

An adequate legal response, therefore, necessitates not only appropriate and powerful substantive data protection obligations but also clear and satisfactory rules on *public enforcement, liability* and *the relationship between the obligation-bearing parties*, i.e., joint controllers and controllers and processors, that tend to maximize the potential of the substantive obligations actually having *practical* impact. Indeed, albeit to a lesser extent than public enforcement,[19] private enforcement and the inherent threat of being ordered to pay

18 Supra pp. 118–120

19 There is evidence that private redress is not sought often enough to operate as a liability threat capable of incentivizing compliance and controller-to-controller policing (Korff, 2002, p. 180). The said evidence relates to the DPD but the situation is unlikely dramatically to change in the context of the GDPR; time and costs are factors that always discourage private action for redress.

damages to aggrieved data subjects can also enhance the effectiveness of substantive data protection rules. For these reasons, the relevant provisions to be examined here are Articles 26, 28, 82 and 83, GDPR governing joint controllership, the relationship between controllers and processors, sanctions in the context of public enforcement and civil liability respectively.

All security-related (and other) obligations of the GDPR are addressed to the controller,[20] who is therefore the party having the heaviest burden under the particular measure. Accordingly, having *joint controllers* can effectively mean that more than one party is responsible for ensuring data protection. In the specific context of automated marketplaces where the one controller, specifically, a marketplace-accessible merchant processes personal data on the systems of the other controller, specifically, the marketplace provider, joint controllership can have major benefits on the effectiveness of 'data protection' rules. Indeed, the security of a marketplace is inevitably made a (legal) concern not only for the marketplace provider but also for marketplace-accessible merchants. The latter must thus take care to *choose privacy-compliant marketplaces*, as a way of reducing the possibility of facing enforcement action for failing to comply with the security-related obligations of the GDPR; being controllers themselves means that they are direct addressees of the said obligations, too. Obviously, this creates a *market* pressure towards automated marketplaces that comply with their legal obligations, which supplements the relevant *legal* pressure. Put otherwise, marketplace providers must seek to develop privacy-respecting and secure marketplaces not only to avoid enforcement action *but also* to be able to attract merchants who would be willing to offer their products through their marketplace. In this way, part of the enforcement burden shifts away from the struggling data protection authorities to the very parties whom the law seeks to regulate.

The aforementioned benefit, however, presupposes that joint controllership actually means joint responsibility and liability. Is this the case under the GDPR? In an attempt to enable "a clear attribution of the responsibilities under this Regulation, including where a controller determines the purposes, conditions and means of the processing jointly with other controllers or where a processing operation is carried out on behalf of a controller",[21] Article 26, GDPR expressly governs joint controllership.

Article 26, GDPR provides as follows:

1. Where two or more controllers jointly determine the purposes and means of processing, they shall be joint controllers. They shall in a transparent manner determine their respective responsibilities for compliance with the obligations under this Regulation, in particular as regards the exercising of the rights of the data subject and their respective duties to provide the information referred to in Articles 13 and 14, by means of an arrangement between them unless, and in so far as, the respective responsibilities of the controllers are determined by Union or Member State law to which the controllers are subject. The arrangement may designate a contact point for data subjects.
2. The arrangement referred to in paragraph 1 shall duly reflect the respective roles and relationships of the joint controllers vis-à-vis the data subjects. The essence of the arrangement shall be made available to the data subject.

20 Infra Chapter 4.3.4. Some are addressed to processors too.

21 Recital 62, Draft GDPR. This Recital is not in the (final) GDPR but the aim of a clear allocation of responsibilities especially in cases of joint controllership is mentioned in Recital 79, GDPR.

3. Irrespective of the terms of the arrangement referred to in paragraph 1, the data subject may exercise his or her rights under this Regulation in respect of and against each of the controllers.

The arrangement between controllers determining "their respective responsibilities for compliance with the obligations under this Regulation" as per Article 26(1) will most likely take the form of a private contract. As the Commission has noted, the said arrangement or contract "clarifies the responsibilities of joint controllers as regards their internal relationship and towards the data subject" (European Commission, 2012a, p. 10).The important question is whether a controller can avoid enforcement, private or public, on the grounds that relevant contract clearly refers to the other controller as the one responsible for complying with the security-related (and other) obligations of the GDPR. Understandably, if the answer is in the affirmative, the previously explained potential of market pressure towards GDPR-compliant marketplaces will greatly be weakened. Indeed, one should expect contracts between marketplace-accessible merchants and marketplace providers rendering the latter solely responsible for the security of the processing, privacy by design and other relevant obligations discussed later in this chapter.[22] Merchants are therefore likely to worry more about securing such contracts than choosing secure or law-abiding marketplaces.

Article 26(3), GDPR clarifies that the private contract between controllers does not essentially bind the data subject, who can therefore exercise her rights against *any* of them. Those rights, however, are the ones provided for in Chapter III of the GDPR, entitled 'the rights of the data subject' such as the right to information and the right of access to her personal data. Article 26(3) does not extend to the security-related obligations of the GDPR and does not therefore touch upon whether liability in the context of private and public enforcement under the GDPR is intended to be joint and severable.

Albeit in relation to the DPD, which made no reference to joint controllership or joint liability, the DPWP (2010a, pp. 22, 24, 33) has rejected 'joint and several liability' in *all* cases of joint controllership, opining that

> joint and several liability for all parties involved should be considered as a means of eliminating uncertainties, and therefore assumed *only* in so far as an alternative, clear and equally effective allocation of obligations and responsibilities has not been established by the parties involved or does not clearly stem from factual circumstances.
>
> (DPWP, 2010a, p. 24)

This (undesirable) approach penetrated the preparatory texts of the GDPR; Article 24 of the Draft Regulation (corresponding to Article 26, GDPR) expressly stated, "*In case of unclarity of the responsibility*, the controllers shall be jointly and severally liable".[23] Article 77 of the said Draft (corresponding to Article 82, GDPR) confined joint and several liability to cases where "an appropriate written agreement determining the responsibilities pursuant to Article 24" was absent.

Fortunately, these provisions do not exist in the GDPR and though, as already stated, Article 26, GDPR does not touch upon the relevant issue, Article 82(4), referring to cases where multiple controllers and/or processors are involved,[24] states that "each controller or

22 Infra Chapter 4.3.4
23 Article 24, DGDPR (LIBE text), emphasis added.
24 For more on Article 82, see infra Chapter 7 pp. 195–196

processor shall be held liable for the entire damage in order to ensure effective compensation of the data subject".[25] This certainly enhances the adequacy of the EU legal response towards the privacy risks associated with automated marketplaces; it creates a need for the policing of controllers by joint controllers translating into a market pressure towards the development of secure (and GDPR-compliant) marketplace systems, improving the effectiveness of security-related legal obligations.

The same question arises in relation to sanctions (particularly, in the form of administrative fines) in the context of public enforcement governed by Article 83, GDPR. The GDPR is not express regarding the implications of the privately agreed allocation of responsibilities as between controllers (as per Article 26) to administrative fines. However, Article 83(2), GDPR lists the factors that should be taken into account in the determination of the fine to be imposed in a given case. Amongst them is "*the degree of responsibility* of the controller or processor",[26] a factor that is generally relevant in contexts involving administrative fines.[27] The 'degree of responsibility' of each of the data controllers will inevitably be reflected and searched for in the Article 26 private arrangement, which will of course be checked against the factual circumstances. Given that the data processing involved mainly takes place on the systems of the marketplace provider, the factual circumstances are likely to coincide with the content of the private arrangement regarding responsibilities between the marketplace provider and marketplace-participating merchants. Obviously, the degree of responsibility of the latter is likely to be considered lesser than that of the former, resulting in an analogously lower administrative fine.

The particular result seems fair and logical, yet it should be applied with care so that it does not weaken the consequences of incompliance for certain (joint) controllers (in this context, the marketplace-participating merchants), so much as to result in indifference on their part as to their obligations under the GDPR. The responsibility of these parties, which is principally entailed *in their choice* of a given marketplace, through which to sell their products, should *not* be considered of a *minor* degree (leading to minor or insignificant fines), otherwise joint controllership would be rendered an escape route from the burden of discharging the security-related obligations of the GDPR effectively achieving *unaccountability*: the absence of "any risk of facing (unfavorable) consequences" could effectively mean *un*accountability (Alhadeff et al., 2012, p. 5).

By contrast, the GDPR places much emphasis on the exact opposite, namely accountability,[28] and explicitly ties it to the data controller through Article 5(2).[29] Moreover, the previous argument in favour of meaningful and effective sanctions for marketplace-participating merchants as joint controllers seems in accord with a related view of the DPWP (2010a, p. 22) that the inability *directly* to fulfil certain GDPR obligations excludes neither controllership nor responsibility under the GDPR,

25 See also Recital 146, GDPR.

26 Article 83(2), GDPR, emphasis added.

27 In the area of competition law for example, it has been emphasized by the CJEU that "where an infringement has been committed by several undertakings, the relative gravity of the participation of each of them must be examined" (Case T-62/02 *Union Pigments AS v Commission of the European Communities*, [2005], (General Court of EU), ECLI:EU:T:2005:430, *para. 118*).

28 Bovens (2007, p. 450) defines 'accountability' by reference to the possibility of consequences: "Accountability is a relationship between an actor and a forum, in which the actor has an obligation to explain and to justify his or her conduct, the forum can pose questions and pass judgement, *and the actor may face consequences*" (emphasis added).

29 See Article 24, GDPR, infra pp. 131–132

> especially in cases of joint control, not being able to directly fulfil all controller's obligations (ensuring information, right of access, etc.) does not exclude being a controller. It may be that in practice those obligations could easily be fulfilled by other parties, which are sometimes closer to the data subject. . . . *However, a controller will remain in any case ultimately responsible for its obligations and liable for any breach to them.*[30]

It follows, therefore, that despite the absence an *explicit* duty vested on controllers to police or vet a joint controller, the rules on joint controllership regarding private liability and public sanctions effectively impose a relevant duty indirectly. This enhances the effectiveness of the (GDPR) data protection obligations, as merchants will probably strive to use law-abiding marketplaces in order to avoid liability and sanctions. Additionally, marketplace providers have a strong incentive to vet merchants allowed in their marketplace, thereby reducing the risk of personal data processed on their systems to be misused by participating merchants resulting in liability or sanctions against themselves, too. Apart from enhancing the effectiveness of data protection obligations, thus entailing element (f) of an adequate legal response, as explained previously,[31] this latter effect also encompasses element (b) of such response,[32] as it essentially 'forces' marketplace providers to apply a privacy-relevant access control mechanism.

Notably, it would probably be better for the GDPR to impose an *explicit* duty of policing a joint controller. One such duty exists in relation to a processor. Article 28, GDPR, obliges data controllers to choose processors that respect data protection legal obligations and also employ adequate technical security measures meeting the requirements of the Regulation.[33] The obvious rationale behind this rule seems to apply to joint controllership, too. Just like controller-processor relationships, joint controllership often arises as a result of the one party seeking to have personal data processed on the systems and primarily under the physical control of another party. Automated (and other electronic) marketplaces provide an obvious example; the DPWP (2010a, pp. 19–20) also refers to a company seeking personnel on a job-finding website run by a different party and to a financial institution conducting its financial transactions through a third-party financial transaction carrier.

There seems to be no valid reason behind such controllers not being imposed with an *explicit* duty to ensure that their *chosen* co-controller is legally compliant. The fact that the party processing the data does not remain totally passive with absolutely no role in the determination of the 'processing' means and/or purposes so as to qualify as a mere processor (rather than a joint controller) does not convincingly explain this difference of approach. An explanation could be that being a controller, the (joint) controller is *directly* burdened by all of the obligations of the GDPR. However, processors are also *directly* subject to the security-related obligations of Article 32, GDPR[34] and yet, Article 28, GDPR explicitly requires controllers to choose processors who meet the said obligations. Moreover, as explained, such duty creates market pressures and inter-party policing and regulation that enhances the effectiveness of data protection obligations. It would thus be desirable if such duty was explicitly imposed in the context of not only relationships as between a controller and a processor but also as between (joint) controllers.

30 Emphasis added.
31 Supra pp. 121–122
32 Supra p. 114
33 See in particular, Article 28(1) and Article 28(3)(c), GDPR.
34 These and other relevant data protection obligations are discussed in Chapter 4.3.4.

4.3.4 The data protection obligations under the EU data protection legal regime

The most important of the elements of an adequate legal response to the privacy risks associated with automated marketplaces are elements (a) and (e),[35] namely an obligation on marketplace providers and participating merchants to respect (and protect) consumer personal data and apply existing privacy-enhancing technologies, in particular encryption. *Doubtless*, EU law contains one such obligation, which is imposed on *both* of the aforementioned parties given that as already explained, they both qualify as data controllers. Indeed, the GDPR is all about imposing a clear and detailed such obligation; this, of course, translates into various data protection principles that need to be respected and several specific relevant duties imposed on data controllers and, to a lesser extent, on data processors.

Though the following discussion can serve as an in-depth commentary on certain of the provisions of the GDPR, going through *all* of the substantive provisions of the GDPR is out of the scope of this book. After all, it is not necessary to do so in order to illustrate that EU law does contain an obligation to protect personal data. The (existence of the) GDPR, namely a law "on the protection of natural persons with regard to the processing of personal data and on the free movement of such data, and repealing Directive 95/46/EC (General Data Protection Regulation)"[36] speaks on its own. The said measure is explicitly intended to serve as "a strong and more coherent data protection framework in the Union, backed by strong enforcement"[37] to respond to recent technological developments[38] and to ensure, amongst others, "a consistent and high level of protection of natural persons"[39] including consumers.

As it is further emphasized in the GDPR, "effective protection of personal data throughout the Union requires the strengthening and setting out in detail of the rights of data subjects and the obligations of those who process and determine the processing of personal data".[40] The GDPR certainly actually does that. It sets out basic data protection principles which data controllers should observe when processing personal data,[41] specific rights such as rights of access to personal data for the data subjects[42] and multiple detailed obligations mainly for data controllers.[43]

It may be true that data protection laws, including the GDPR, are unable to give individuals full control over their data (Koops, 2014, pp. 3–6) given that enormous amounts of personal data are now processed in complex technological systems using techniques that are difficult to understand or predict. Yet, the GDPR is not just about putting individuals in control. As is shown in the following, it is, to an important extent, also about obliging those performing such processing to protect the personal data they process against unauthorized access, disclosure or loss. As already illustrated, this is very important in the context of automated marketplaces, where, in fact, the problem is *not* so much about the data subject staying in control of his personal data. Indeed, the latter relinquishes control, as the very purpose of automated marketplaces is to take over freeing him from contracting tasks. The primary issue is with *the data controller staying in control* of the personal data it

35 Supra p. 114
36 This is the very title of the GDPR.
37 Recital 7, GDPR.
38 Recital 6, GDPR.
39 Recital 10, GDPR.
40 Recital 11, GDPR.
41 See Article 5, GDPR. Two of those principles have been discussed in Chapter 2, infra at p. 48–49
42 Articles 12–22, GDPR.
43 Articles 24–38, GDPR.

receives from the data subject; the aforementioned elements (a) and (e) of an adequate legal response largely refer to this type of obligation, namely to an obligation to stay in control through adopting privacy-enhancing technologies, in particular, encryption. After all, 'data controller' control over personal data goes a long way towards ensuring 'data subject' control, too, at least *vis-à-vis* parties other than the controllers to whom the data subject entrusts his personal data. Accordingly, this book focuses on specific GDPR obligations that seek to ensure this controller control, namely, Articles 5, 24, 25, 32 and 35. These provisions will now be analysed in an attempt to ascertain whether they actually entail the elements (a) and (e) of an adequate legal response.

A mere glance at the GDPR reveals that at least, the raw material of these elements exists. Indeed, the previously discussed privacy-by-design approach finds specific representation in the GDPR and this is no longer just a best practice. Indeed, as it will be shown, the privacy-by-design approach is spelled out as a legal requirement in an operative provision of the particular measure.[44] The same is true of the technology of encryption which is referred to in one Recital and three operative provisions of the GDPR.[45]

The DPD, the predecessor of the GDPR contained explicit requirements of technical data protection, too. By virtue of Article 17(1), DPD data controllers, amongst others, had to employ, *technical* measures "to protect personal data against accidental or unlawful destruction or accidental loss, alteration, unauthorized disclosure or access, in particular where the processing involves the transmission of data over a network and against all other unlawful forms of processing". Such measures had to be appropriate to the level of any existing risk, taking into account the state of the art and the cost involved. Recital 46, DPD expanded upon these obligations clarifying that the required technical measures should be taken "*both at the time of the design of the processing system* and at the time of the processing itself", thus mirroring a 'privacy-by-design' approach.[46] Recitals, however, do not impose binding obligations.

Article 32, GDPR constitutes a far more detailed version of the Article 17, DPD. Thus, data controllers must employ technical and organizational measures ensuring "a level of security appropriate to the risk".[47] This general (and wide) obligation can, amongst others, be discharged through the adoption of measures achieving "the pseudonymisation and encryption of personal data"[48] as well as "the ability to ensure the ongoing confidentiality, integrity, availability and resilience of processing systems and services".[49] Encryption, therefore, which has been explained to be an appropriate response to the main privacy risks inherent in automated marketplaces, is explicitly referred to, something that certainly increases the possibility of its utilization by data controllers. Article 32 does not specifically mandate encryption in *all* cases. However, a recent relevant Statement issued by the DPWP (2018, p. 1) referring to encryption as being indispensable particularly in the online (digital) world, indirectly renders it a mandatory requirement in the said context, thereby greatly enhancing the relevant EU legal response to the risks associated with automated marketplaces:

44 Article 25(1), GDPR. See infra at pp. 129–130
45 See Recital 83 and Articles 6(4), 32(1) and 34(3), GDPR.
46 Infra p. 129
47 Article 32(1), GDPR.
48 Article 32(1)(a), GDPR.
49 Article 32(1)(b), GDPR.

> The widespread use of services enabled by information and communication technologies has made encryption a critical and widely used tool to help ensure that data are secured. Properly implemented encryption using appropriate algorithms offers a reasonable guarantee that activities like buying goods online. . . . Without encryption, individuals' privacy and security can be compromised every time they wish to undertake those everyday activities. . . . Encryption is therefore absolutely necessary and irreplaceable for guaranteeing strong confidentiality and integrity when data are transferred across open networks like the Internet.

Additionally, unlike in Article 17, DPD, the emphasis in Article 32, GDPR is not placed on the prevention of particular risks to personal data, such as loss or alteration but more generally, on the confidentiality, integrity, resilience and also availability[50] of *data processing systems and services*. Importantly, though others favoured reference to data as well (as opposed to systems and services only) (Hon et al., 2014, pp. 25, 26), this wider phraseology may prove helpful. More specifically, it may be taken to render it less important to insist in the 'personal' nature of the actual data compromised and, thus, on whether data comprising software source code, for example, qualifies as personal or not. From the moment, a personal data processing system or service (such as an automated marketplace) has been compromised and the said compromise was preventable, a violation of the security obligations of Article 32, GDPR can be established. No doubt this makes enforcement easier and enhances overall data protection.

Admittedly, the reference to specific harmful events to personal data in Article 17, DPD could assist controllers and authorities in ascertaining what would be considered a data breach (or security leak) and the actual technical measures, which would satisfy the relevant security obligation in a given case. Article 32(2), however, avails the said help by stating that

> in assessing data security risk, consideration should be given to the risks that are presented by personal data processing, such as accidental or unlawful destruction, loss, alteration, unauthorised disclosure of, or access to, personal data transmitted, stored or otherwise processed which may in particular lead to physical, material or non-material damage.

Another important feature of Article 32 is that it essentially imposes a *continuous* obligation to take care of security, as it also mandates "a process for regularly testing, assessing and evaluating the effectiveness of technical and organizational measures for ensuring the security of the processing".[51] This would seem to require systematic system monitoring, which the UK National Cyber Security Centre rightly considers as "a key capability needed to comply with legal or regulatory requirements" (National Cyber Security Centre, 2015).

Most importantly, unlike the DPD, the GDPR does not exhaust technological data protection to the security obligations of Article 32. Instead, it upgrades *technological* data protection to one of the "principles relating to processing of personal data" listed in Article 5, GDPR. The latter provision lists the *core* data protection rules applicable to all cases. According to Article 5(1)(f), GDPR, personal data shall be "processed in a manner that ensures

50 Notably, in relation to systems, such as marketplaces, where contracts are concluded, *availability* is paramount as service interruption can be damaging, as it may prevent the completion of a beneficial transaction which was about to be concluded before interruption.

51 Article 32(1)(d), GDPR.

appropriate security of the personal data, including protection against unauthorised or unlawful processing and against accidental loss, destruction or damage, using appropriate technical or organisational measures ('integrity and confidentiality')". Security (or technological data protection), therefore, is by no means a secondary or supplementary obligation vested on data controllers; it is a core data protection principle, compliance with which is likely to be considered a priority by data protection authorities.

An additional provision, namely Article 25, GDPR, leaves no doubt that EU law contains the obligation to employ technical means of data protection and hence, elements (a) and (e) of an adequate legal response. Article 25(1), GDPR[52] explicitly requires the adoption of the previously mentioned privacy-by-design approach.[53] As commentators explain, this is actually the approach lying behind privacy-enhancing technologies (which have earlier been explained to comprise the answer to the privacy risks associated with automated marketplaces). It dictates that "privacy should be built into systems from the design stage and should be promoted as a default setting of every ICT system" (Koops and Leenes, 2014, p. 3). Indeed, Article 25(1) is accompanied by a requirement of 'data protection by default' contained in Article 25(2), GDPR, which provides for data protection to be wired into systems *as a default* rather than a 'choice' setting.[54]

Given the existence of Article 32, GDPR (which already requires technical data protection), Article 25, GDPR cannot but be seen as an unequivocal clarification on the part of law that the utilization of privacy-enhancing technology must be a core ingredient of their business model and systems and thus by no means merely an add-on available to consumers in exchange of payment (which has earlier been explained as undesirable). Accordingly, EU law clearly encompasses elements (a) and (e) of the adequate legal response and as shown in the following, the adequacy of the relevant response is further improved by additional provisions in the GDPR.

Admittedly, there seems to be a lack of consensus regarding how effective Article 25 is to be in practice. Kuner (2012, p. 7) foresees "profound implications in particular for . . . data processing service providers and other companies that . . . process data intensively". These would evidently include marketplace providers and merchants using their systems to sell their products. Others, however, are sceptical and assert that "encoding data protection requirements in software or hardware shows that this is much easier said than done" (Koops and Leenes, 2014, p. 7). They explain five different factors rendering the particular task regarding *all* data protection requirements at least, extremely difficult, if not impossible (Koops and Leenes, 2014, pp. 4–6). Data protection authorities should certainly have such factors in mind when considering enforcement action for a violation of Article 25, but the relevant requirement should by no means be abandoned or rendered obsolete.

52 The provision reads as follows: "Taking into account the state of the art, the cost of implementation and the nature, scope, context and purposes of processing as well as the risks of varying likelihood and severity for rights and freedoms of natural persons posed by the processing, the controller shall, both at the time of the determination of the means for processing and at the time of the processing itself, implement appropriate technical and organisational measures, such as pseudonymisation, which are designed to implement data-protection principles, such as data minimisation, in an effective manner and to integrate the necessary safeguards into the processing in order to meet the requirements of this Regulation and protect the rights of data subjects". It is exemplified in Recital 78, GDPR.

53 Supra pp. 112, 127

54 Infra p. 155

It is submitted that a significant flaw of Article 25 is that it is addressed to data controllers *only* and *not* to data processors as well. Given that processors will often be the ones providing and administering the data processing system (that will have to adhere to the data protection by design approach), their non-inclusion in the direct addressees of the Article 25 is unfortunate. It is also difficult to explain given that Article 32 is addressed to *both* controllers and processors and an earlier version of the final Article 25, namely Article 23 of the Draft GDPR was addressed to processors too. As a result, in the event that marketplace providers are considered to be merely processors processing personal data on behalf of participating merchants (the latter acting as the only data controllers),[55] the former, though being the ones responsible for the design, administration and provision of the marketplace system, will not directly be burdened by the Article 25 obligation.

Recital 78, GDPR does call for *producers* of data processing systems to adhere to data protection by design, yet Recitals do not impose legally binding obligations. It is also true that by virtue of Article 28(1), GDPR controllers must choose processors "providing sufficient guarantees to implement appropriate technical and organisational measures in such a manner that processing will meet the requirements of this Regulation", yet the effectiveness of Article 25 would certainly be improved, if it could directly be enforced against two different parties. This rather indirect obligation of data processors to respect Article 25 is further weakened by the fact that Article 28(3), GDPR which lists a number of data protection obligations that controllers must *contractually* impose on their processors does *not* include the data protection by design obligation of Article 25. It includes the obligations of Article 32, which directly burdens data processors too, which makes the omission of Article 25 from Article 28(3) even more difficult to explain.

Fortunately, given that both marketplaces providers and participating merchants have earlier been explained to qualify as 'data controllers' in most cases at least, this is flaw does not significantly weaken the overall response of EU law towards the relevant risks.

The obligations of technological data protection of the GDPR are supplemented and further strengthened by Article 35, GDPR on data protection impact assessments (DPIAs). The latter are closely connected with Article 25, as their performance constitutes "an integral part of taking a privacy by design approach" (Great Britain ICO, 2014, p. 4). These assessments are important as they force controllers to inquire into (and understand) both the data processing they intend to perform and the privacy risks it involves and identify and implement appropriate solutions.[56] (GB ICO, 2014, pp. 4–5; Cranor, 2014, pp. 15–17). They effectively contribute in the creation of a 'data protection' culture, which is vital to the GDPR proving to be successful in practice. Moreover, the relevant requirement facilitates enforcement in the particular context, which is also vital to its success. More specifically, rather than having to perform the laborious task of investigating the design of data processing systems or the implementation of privacy-enhancing technologies in all cases, data protection authorities can impose sanctions on the ground that a DPIA has *not* been performed. This is fair and reasonable; a data controller who has not performed a DPIA, thereby identifying and understanding risks is unlikely to have implemented *appropriate* technical and other solutions.

55 An application of the relevant concepts to automated marketplaces has found both marketplace providers and participating merchants to be joint controllers (see supra at Chapter 4.3.3.2), however, in contexts involving a multiplicity of parties, the relevant question is complex and not always eligible to a definite answer. The possibility cannot be excluded of circumstances in which marketplace providers maintain a pure processor role, especially given that the relevant concept does not require a totally passive role in the processing of data.

56 See Recital 90, GDPR.

Of course, DPIAs are not required in all cases or in relation to all data processing but only "where a type of processing in particular using new technologies, and taking into account the nature, scope, context and purposes of the processing, is likely to result in a high risk to the rights and freedoms of natural persons".[57] The reference to 'a high risk' narrows down the range of situations in which a DPIA will be required, as favoured by commentators (Hon et al., 2014, p. 46). Still, it remains true that Article 35, GDPR requires the data controller carefully to review *all* types of data processing involved, as this is how he could identify processing entailing a high risk necessitating a DPIA.

In any event, the data processing within automated marketplaces would seem to trigger the DPIA obligation, which is good; as already explained, the relevant obligation can strengthen the impact of Articles 25 and 32 and further boost the adequacy of the relevant EU legal response. Though automated marketplaces are not (readily) covered by Article 35 (3), GDPR and the three cases listed therein in which a DPIA shall be performed, the relevant processing will most probably qualify as one "likely to result in a high risk to the rights and freedoms of natural persons", thereby necessitating a DPIA as per Article 35(1). Indeed, such processing is inherent in *legal-status-altering* communications and probably also includes consumer names and financial (or payment) details. The Council text of the provision on DPIA referred to "discrimination, identity theft or fraud, financial loss, damage to the reputation, (breach of pseudonymity), loss of confidentiality of data protected by professional secrecy or any other significant economic or social disadvantage" as examples of possible high risks.[58] Fraud and financial loss are definitely risks inherent in automated marketplaces, as already illustrated. Also, despite assertions to the effect that new technologies should not be deemed inherently risky (Hon et al., 2014, p. 46), Article 35(1) does imply that a 'high risk' is likely to exist in processing with the use of new technologies.[59] The processing inherent in automated marketplaces is definitely such processing, something that reinforces the view that a DPIA will be considered as warranted. This effectively boosts the adequacy of the EU legal response towards the privacy-related risks involved in the particular context.

Finally, the relevant legal response is further strengthened as a result of one of the most-discussed innovations of the GDPR, namely the principle of accountability embodied in Article 24, GDPR[60] and referred to in Article 5(2)[61] too. Basically, accountability means that compliance with the Regulation is *not* enough; what is needed is *proven* compliance and, therefore, data controllers "shall implement appropriate technical and organisational measures to ensure and *to be able to demonstrate that processing is performed in accordance with this Regulation*".[62] Indeed, this refers to 'accountability' as is generally understood, namely as embodying the ability to check and verify that there has indeed been compliance with relevant rules and policies (Weitzner et al., 2006, p. 1).

57 Article 35(1), GDPR.
58 For Council text, see EDRI (2015).
59 Article 35(1), GDPR reads as follows: "Where a type of *processing in particular using new technologies* . . . is likely to result in a high risk to the rights and freedoms of natural persons, the controller shall prior to the processing carry out an assessment of the impact of the envisaged processing operations on the protection of personal data" (emphasis added).
60 On the history and development of the principle of accountability across several data protection instruments worldwide, see Alhadeff et al. (2012).
61 "The controller shall be responsible for, and be able to demonstrate compliance with, paragraph 1 ('accountability')".
62 Article 24(1), GDPR, emphasis added.

Accountability improves the adequacy of the EU legal response to the privacy risks associated with automated marketplaces because it greatly facilitates enforcement.[63] Indeed, controllers will have to be in a position to illustrate compliance to the satisfaction of an inquiring data protection authority (DPA). Accordingly, DPAs will not have to engage in lengthy and difficult investigations, especially in relation to technical matters in highly technical environments, in an effort to ascertain whether the data controller has been compliant. If the latter cannot furnish a DPA with evidence of compliance, a DPA can readily find a violation of the 'accountability' rule without having to examine the application of more difficult or technical provisions such as the previously discussed Article 32. A substantial burden involved in enforcement is thus effectively passed to the data controllers themselves. Moreover, the rule conveys the important message that there *can* (and *will*) be strict enforcement of the GDPR. The enforcement-facilitating potential of Article 24 is reinforced by Article 24(3), which renders adherence to approved codes of conduct or certification mechanisms as an element demonstrating compliance with the Regulation. The provision embodies a mode of co-regulation that has widely recognized enforcement benefits, specifically because the enforcement burden is, to an important extent, transferred to self-regulation.[64]

Thus, the GDPR effectively answers criticisms against the pro-GDPR regulatory regime for "placing too much emphasis on recovering if things go wrong, and not enough on trying to get organizations to 'do the right thing' for privacy in the first place" (Pearson and Charlesworth, 2009, p. 141) and for lacking a general mechanism of evaluation of the compliance measures taken by data controllers, such as an accountability principle (Alhadeff, Alsenoy and Dumortier, 2012, pp. 21–22). It is thus not entirely true that the GDPR contributes only modestly in the tackling of the enforcement problem in the area of data protection, as Erdos (2016, p. 1) suggests.[65]

Overall, it would follow that the EU legal response to the privacy risks associated with automated marketplaces is largely adequate; the GDPR has introduced enriched explicit security-related obligations (Article 32) further enhanced by a legally mandated 'data protection by design' approach (Article 25) supported by an obligation for DPIAs (Article 35) and accompanied by clear accountability principles (Article 24). In this respect, it clearly embodies the suggested elements (a) and (e) of an adequate legal response as it explicitly imposes obligations for the adoption of technical means of data protection, in particular, encryption.

It is true that "the legal obligations maintain a level of normative abstraction, which necessitates further elaboration, with instruments that can be technology-specific and context-specific" (Kamara, 2017, sec. 5.1.3). These technology-specific instruments are the so-called technical standards,[66] which can add specificity to the GDPR technology-flavoured obligations, thereby

63 This relationship between enforcement facilitation and the adequacy of the legal response has also been mentioned earlier, see supra p. 121

64 On co-regulation see infra Chapter 4.3.5.2

65 Erdos (2016, pp. 24–25) seems to illustrate this view by reference to the DPA-specific provisions of the GDPR mainly referring to the tasks and powers of the DPAs. Yet, other provisions of the DPA such as data protection by design, the accountability principle and the codes of conduct have, as is illustrated in this book, strong enforcement-assisting properties.

66 A technical standard is "a technical specification, adopted by a recognised standardisation body, for repeated or continuous application, with which compliance is not compulsory", Article 2(1), Regulation 1025/2012 on European standardisation, amending Council Directives 89/686/EEC and 93/15/EEC and Directives 94/9/EC, 94/25/EC, 95/16/EC, 97/23/EC, 98/34/EC, 2004/22/EC, 2007/23/EC, 2009/23/EC and 2009/105/EC of the European Parliament and of the Council and repealing Council Decision 87/95/EEC and Decision No 1673/2006/EC of the European Parliament and of the Council (European Standardisation Regulation).

guiding data controllers towards the appropriate technical solutions. These have a prominent role in the GDPR, something that serves as further proof of the sufficient exploitation of technology by the particular legal measure in response to the data protection risks in highly technical or technologically advanced environments (including automated marketplaces). Though the Proposed GDPR contained several references to technical standards, such as in security-related and 'data protection by design' provisions, Kamara (2017, sec. 4) confirms that direct reference to standards now only exists in Articles 22[67] and 43,[68] GDPR. Yet, the previously illustrated *inherently technical* nature of several of the GDPR provisions renders the development of technical standards unavoidable and the absence of explicit references to standards merely allows for some flexibility regarding their content and the body which can initiate standardization (Kamara, 2017, sec. 4; Kosta and Stuurman, 2014, pp. 458–459). Indeed, the European Commission has, in accordance with Article 10 of the European Standardization Regulation[69] issued an Implementing Decision on standardization in the field of data protection and security policy requesting three European Standardisation Organisations to develop technical standards regarding the implementation of privacy-by-design provisions.[70]

Given the adequacy of the EU legal response (as embodied in the GDPR) towards the privacy-related risks associated with automated marketplaces, it is not of a great concern that another EU legal measure, namely the e-Privacy Directive (EPD) is largely inapplicable to automated marketplaces. The EPD contains security and other privacy-enhancing obligations. Article 4(1), EPD obliges 'electronic communications service' providers to take appropriate technical and organizational measures to safeguard the security of their services, including measures limiting access to the data by authorized personnel and for legitimate purposes and ensuring the implementation of a security policy in relation to data processing.[71] The EPD also imposes duties to notify the DPA and the concerned subscriber or user about a security breach affecting his or her personal data.[72]

Article 32, GDPR is sufficiently broad to encompass the aforementioned measures required by the EPD. Moreover, as already seen, it is accompanied by additional detailed obligations relating to privacy by design, DPIAs, accountability and also records of processing activities[73] that leave no room for controllers not implementing a security policy as per Article 4(1a), EPD. Even notification duties relating to 'personal data' breaches are now also contained in Articles 33 and 34, GDPR. Article 33 refers to notification to the DPA and Article 34 requires communication of a breach entailing a high risk to the rights and freedoms of the individual to the affected data subject. Despite increasing the workload for DPAs, such duties improve data protection in the sense that they "create a strong incentive for firms to improve their practices in order to avoid negative publicity and customer backlash" (Romanosky and Acquisti, 2009, p. 1068)

67 This refers to the right of the data subject to object to profiling and automated decisions concerning him or her.
68 Article 43 concerns with certification, which is discussed in more detail later, see infra pp. 143–145
69 Regulation No. 1025/2012
70 For a description of the background and content of this implementing decision, see Kamara (2017, sec. 5).
71 Article 4(1a), EPD.
72 Article 4(3), EPD.
73 Article 30, GDPR requires the keeping of records including, amongst others, the purposes of the processing, the categories of data subjects and recipients and a description of the technical and organizational measures applied in compliance with Article 32, GDPR.

Notably, the Proposed E-Privacy Regulation[74] purporting to replace the EPD contains *no* expanded security-related and breach notification obligations. Right on the contrary, it omits such obligations altogether on the ground that the GDPR sufficiently covers the data security element of data protection: "The alignment with the GDPR resulted in the repeal of some provisions, such as the security obligations of Article 4 of the ePrivacy Directive" (European Commission, 2017b, para. 2.1). This clearly confirms the view that the inapplicability of the EPD to automated marketplaces does not affect the adequacy of the legal response towards the privacy risks associated with them.

It is noteworthy that this inapplicability stems from the fact that the provisions of the EPD are largely addressed to "the provider of a publicly available electronic communications service". Automated marketplace services are 'information society services',[75] yet the concept of 'electronic communication services' is much narrower and excludes 'information society services' that are not *largely* confined to signal conveyance on networks or as put by Keuleers and Dinant (2005, p. 149) to the transmission of data or messages.[76] It arises from the relevant definition that apart from having to be the *only* or at the least, the *main* functionality of the service, such data transmission must also be conducted *passively*, i.e, without any material editorial control over the transmitted data. The UK Office of Communications (Ofcom) distinguishes between basic, advanced and enhanced electronic communications services. The latter category stretches the definition to its limits and still only includes services such as "telephone calls completed through interactive voice response boxes, TV transmission with MPEG compression supported by compression systems, 3-way conference calls supported by conference bridges, e-mail supported by e-mail servers and voice mail supported by voice mail servers" (Ofcom, n.d.). Moreover, the DPWP (2009, p. 5) has confirmed that the obligations addressed to electronic communications service providers "affect a very limited number of stakeholders".

The service entailed in automated marketplaces is much more complex and/or enriched than an enhanced message transmission service. Also, being provided online, the 'automated marketplace' service is provided "on top of existing network infrastructure and telecom-related services" (DLA Piper, 2009, p. 13) and cannot itself wholly or mainly consist of mere low-level signal transmission. Admittedly, the Proposed E-Privacy Regulation extends the rules to a wider range of services and particularly to over-the-top communications services, such as Facebook Messenger and WhatsApp (European Commission, 2016c, para. 2.1).[77] Still, automated marketplaces cannot be compared to an instant messaging service, as the type of content to be

74 Proposal for a Regulation of the European Parliament and of the Council concerning the respect for private life and the protection of personal data in electronic communications and repealing Directive 2002/58/EC (Regulation on Privacy and Electronic Communications).

75 Supra Chapter 2 p. 32

76 The relevant definition is contained in Article 2(c), Framework Directive: "'electronic communications service' means a service normally provided for remuneration which consists wholly or mainly in the conveyance of signals on electronic communications networks, including telecommunications services and transmission services in networks used for broadcasting, but exclude services providing, or exercising editorial control over, content transmitted using electronic communications networks and services; it does not include information society services, as defined in Article 1 of Directive 98/34/EC, which do not consist wholly or mainly in the conveyance of signals on electronic communications networks".

77 See also the relevant (enriched) definition of 'electronic communications services' in Article 4(1)(b), Proposed E-Privacy Regulation (European Commission, 2017b). It adopts the corresponding definition in Article 2(4) of the Proposal for a Directive of the European Parliament and of the Council establishing the European Electronic Communications Code (Recast) (European Commission, 2016e).

exchanged within them will, to a significant extent, be specified or affected by the provider. Accordingly, the enlarged ambit of the successor of the EPD is unlikely to encompass automated marketplaces.

4.3.5 Overseeing providers of privacy credentials and encouragement of merchant participation in self-regulatory schemes

4.3.5.1 General remarks

It has been shown that EU law, specifically through the GDPR actually encompasses four of the six elements explained[78] to be essential parts of an adequate legal response to the privacy-related risks associated with automated marketplaces. It now remains to be examined whether it also contains the remaining two relevant elements, namely elements (c) and (d). More specifically, are the privacy credentials to be used in the context of a 'marketplace access' control mechanism subject to sufficient official control ensuring their quality and/or reliability?[79] Does the law effectively encourage the participation of merchants in self-regulatory schemes leading to such credentials, thereby addressing the weakness of self-regulation relating to voluntary participation?[80]

When consumer personal data leaves the marketplace and gets into the systems of marketplace-accessible merchants who process it to perform the contract, the controller of the relevant processing will obviously be the merchant. The said party, being a controller, will be bound by the previously discussed security-related and other 'data protection' enhancing obligations of the GDPR, as previously explained. However, the marketplace provider who previously admits such merchants in the marketplace inevitably has a role to play regarding data protection, even during the processing occurring outside the marketplace. Indeed, as already explained,[81] a 'marketplace access control' mechanism combined with self-regulatory measures leading to the award of privacy seals or credentials, can keep out of the marketplace (and thus, away from consumer users), privacy-indifferent merchants. Such access control can greatly be facilitated by self-regulatory measures, which can undertake the burden of policing the privacy practices of merchants and certify those whose practices are consistent with the law, specifically the GDPR. By exploiting relevant self-regulation schemes, therefore, the law can effectively make available to marketplace providers effective and not overly burdensome ways of conducting access control. Before examining whether EU law effectively does so regarding data protection, thereby effectively containing elements (c) and (d) of a relevant adequate legal response, it is important to explain the various ways in which self-regulation can *legally* be exploited.

4.3.5.2 Legal exploitation of self-regulation (co-regulation) and its various forms

The legal exploitation of self-regulation is called co-regulation. As others explain (Rees, 1988; Rubinstein, 2011, pp. 357–358), between the two extremes of legal regulation and self-regulation, there exist other regulatory techniques essentially consisting of self-regulation,

78 Supra p. 114
79 This is element (c).
80 This is element (d).
81 Supra p. 113

albeit with a role for the government (or certain public bodies). Rees (1988, p. 10) calls the main relevant hybrid as "mandated self-regulation", which, as Rubinstein (2009, p. 13) suggests, can be divided into weakly and strongly mandated depending on the extent of governmental involvement and more specifically on "the extent of the government's role in approving and monitoring one (or both) of the regulatory functions of rulemaking and enforcement". Put simply, if the government or a public body sets out the minimum rules to be contained in the code and efficiently monitors its enforcement, the resulting regulatory method is strongly mandated self-regulation.[82]

As Howells (2004, p. 121) further clarifies, "The introduction of soft law into the legal framework can take on many forms". The various forms of code-law integration (or co-regulation) are not mutually exclusive. One form is the recognition of a presumption of conformity with legal rules to the benefit of businesses submitting to an officially approved code, as in the 'product safety' context (Howells, 2004, p. 122). Such presumption of conformity with the law creates "a legal incentive for the private sector to actively take its future into its own hands" (Liikanen, 2000, p. 5) and seems to encourage *both* the submission of codes for official approval, leading to legally compliant codes, and merchant submission to approved codes.

Caution should, however, be taken to combine such legal presumption with adequate code-enforcement monitoring by authorities;[83] if enforcement is wholly left to the self-regulatory body administering the code without adequate official monitoring, a legal presumption of conformity may end up rendering code submission a handy way of law evasion. Indeed, as Koops et al. (2006, p. 137) state, the issue of compliance is very often cited as "a primary concern with self-regulation". Also, as early as in 2000, it has been emphasized that "self-regulation does not mean self-enforcement" and that "it must be in conformity with, and backed by law. It must be enforceable, verifiable, auditable" (Liikanen, 2000, p. 5).

Another form of code-law integration (or co-regulation) involves official opinions on a code having "some persuasive force within the legal regime, so that it could be taken into account by enforcement officials and courts" (Howells, 2004, p. 126). As codes often exemplify general (and possibly vague) legal rules by transforming them into practical guidelines of compliance specific to particular sectors, an assurance that compliance with officially approved codes will be taken into account when applying or interpreting the law obviously incentivizes merchant participation (or submission) to codes. For the same reason, codes can also serve as "effective means to have the legislation applied" (Campisi, 2013, p. 341).

The accountability of self-regulatory bodies translated into the possibility of them facing legal or administrative consequences when their codes violate relevant laws is important to prevent legally incompliant codes from entering the market and comprises a third form of code-law integration. Rules embodying a similar approach to this type of integration, (albeit in relation to traders and standard contract terms rather than codes of conduct and self-regulatory bodies), can be found in the Unfair Contract Terms Directive (UCTD), specifically in Article 7(2) and 7 (3). These provide for the right of organizations protecting collective consumer interests to apply to the court against amongst others, trader associations[84] seeking a decision "as to whether contractual terms drawn up for general use are unfair, so that they can apply appropriate and effective means to prevent the continued use of such terms".[85]

82 For a thorough overview of the concepts of self-regulation and co-regulation and of relevant developments at European and International level as well as nationally, see Koops et al. (2006).
83 For more on this, see infra p. 137
84 Article 7(3), UCTD.
85 Article 7(2), UCTD.

A fourth form of code-law integration can be inspired by the system of supervision of certification providers that Member States were required to establish by Article 3(3) of the Electronic Signatures Directives (ESD). If applied to self-regulatory bodies (administering codes of conduct), the said approach again ensures code quality and most importantly, reserves a role for the government (or public authorities) in the 'enforcement' function of self-regulation. The ESD, however, did not preclude supervision by private sector entities[86] and did not decisively incentivize submission to supervision.[87] A more powerful supervision system is established in the eIDAS Regulation, which has repealed the ESD. Article 17, eIDAS requires the designation of supervisory bodies "to supervise qualified trust service providers established in the territory of the designating Member State to ensure, through ex ante and ex post supervisory activities, that those qualified trust service providers and the qualified trust services that they provide meet the requirements laid down in this Regulation".[88] Supervisory bodies should report to the Commission in relation to their activities[89] so that it is made possible for the Commission and the Member States "to assess the effectiveness of the enhanced supervision mechanism".[90] Submission to supervision is also powerfully legally encouraged; it is essentially mandatory for any *qualified* trust service provider to submit to the supervision of the supervisory body as only the said body can grant a provider the qualified status.[91] The eIDAS establishes benefits for the services provided by a qualified (as opposed to a non-qualified) providers,[92] thereby encouraging such submission to supervision.

As a fifth form of co-regulation (which can readily be characterized as 'strongly mandated self-regulation')[93] can be found in the Italian data protection regime. Approved data protection codes are published in the Official Journal of the State and are also incorporated in the Italian Code, thus becoming legally binding and enforceable (de Azevedo Cunha and Mario Viola, 2013, p. 182). The said commentators call for conferring on DPAs and/or the Commission, supervisory or enforcement powers over approved codes of conduct so that the latter can have binding effects (de Azevedo Cunha and Mario Viola, 2013, pp. 201–202). This approach essentially refers to the codification of self-regulatory schemes (Koops et al., 2006, pp. 140–141) and entails the involvement of private stakeholders in the development of detailed and sector-specific legal requirements that exemplify the general and 'all market' legal rules of the data protection legislation. Obviously, this blurs the distinction between self-regulation and legal requirements and seems to be a controversial approach; some seem to see "nothing distinctive or valuable" about it (Centre for Information Policy Leadership, Huntons & Williams LLC, 2011, p. 12).

The appropriate form (or combination of forms) of co-regulation for the EU data protection context can certainly be worked out, if the EU legislator *decisively* opts to think in terms of real 'code-law' integration. In the context of unfair commercial practices, the

86 Recital 13, ESD.
87 An exception was perhaps the case of third country certification providers who had to be accredited for their certificates to be considered as equivalent to certificates issued by EU-based providers (Article 7(1)(a), ESD).
88 Article 17(3)(a), eIDAS.
89 Article 17(6), eIDAS.
90 Recital 40, eIDAS.
91 Article 3(20), eIDAS. For more on the eIDAS and trust services that also include electronic signature services, see infra Chapter 5.3.3.2.3
92 On these benefits, see infra Chapter 5 p. 165, 168
93 On strongly mandated, as opposed to weakly mandated, self-regulation, see supra pp. 135–136

European Commission has been said "to think [rather] in terms of self-regulation than co-regulation " (Howells, 2004, p. 126). The important question now to be examined is whether the same holds true of the data protection context.

4.3.5.3 Co-regulation in the GDPR: elements (c) and (d) of an adequate legal response

Prior to the GDPR, Article 27, DPD expressly encouraged the drawing of codes of conduct concerning the implementation of the provisions of the Directive.[94] However, though seen as mirroring a combination of government regulation and self-regulation and as envisaging "a substantial role for both national and Community codes" (Lloyd, 2014, p. 78), it entailed no serious attempt to integrate those codes into law in any of the ways described previously. It provided for a freedom to submit codes for official opinion or approval by the Data Protection Working Party (DPWP)[95] but other than an obligation on the Commission to ensure publicity of approved Community codes,[96] there was no other specific incentive for exercising this freedom or for controllers to submit to an approved code.

Admittedly, a legal obligation to submit codes for official approval has its detractors. Lloyd (2014, p. 78) writes that the "novelty" of requiring supervisory authorities to opine on the conformity of submitted codes with data protection legislation "is coming close to giving an unelected agency law-making powers – a practice which has been traditionally resisted in the UK". Yet, this criticism loses some of its strength where code submission remains voluntary and non-submission is not legally penalized.

Moreover, under the DPD, official rejection (or non-approval) of a code did not mean that the self-regulation body could not still use that code. There was no accountability system for legally incompliant codes either. Also, there was absolutely no provision about the role of the government (or the DPAs) in the 'enforcement function' of code regulation, this being, as already explained, an unsatisfactory and even risky approach.[97] Finally, approved codes were not *expressly* furnished with legal relevance. The only other reference to codes in the DPD existed in Recital 26, which referred to them as a possible source of guidance on how personal data could be anonymized.

Of course, a code approved by enforcement authorities as complying with the law is *de facto* attached with legal relevance as it would seem unreasonable for a controller which complies with an approved code to face enforcement action on the ground that the controller violates data protection legislation, (at least regarding provisions addressed in the code). Even if enforcement action is taken, the compliance of the controller with one such code will be taken into account probably leading to no (serious) sanctions. Thus, despite the absence of an express provision to that effect, Hirsch (2013, p. 1057) presumes that compliance with a DPWP-approved code would result in "a legal safe harbor, valid with respect to the data protection laws of all twenty-eight E.U. member states". Similarly, Koops et al. (2006, pp. 121–122) write that the DPD provided for "stipulated self-regulation" as data protection authorities "declare that the code of conduct conforms with the law, thus giving legal effect to the code". Along similar lines, Yves Poullet (2001, pp. 21–22) has spoken of a synergy between private and state-established norms. It would seem therefore that even

94 Article 27(1), DPD.
95 Article 27(2) and (3), DPD.
96 Article 27(3), DPD.
97 Supra p. 136

though the DPD did not expressly provide for a presumption of compliance to the benefit of code-complying controllers, such presumption could be implied.

The exact nature (or extent) of this legal relevance, however, is difficult to assess, especially given that, as the European Commission (2010a, p. 12) confirms, the DPD provisions on self-regulation "have rarely been used". The lack of explicit provisions regarding the role of codes within the data protection legal regime is probably a relevant culprit. More generally, given the voluntary nature of submission to codes, clear legal incentives are necessary to enhance participation.

All in all, it could not be said that the DPD mirrored the EU legislator thinking in terms of co-regulation. The GDPR, however is different; though its relevant provisions are not without weaknesses, the GDPR must be credited for making a decisive turn towards real co-regulation.

More specifically, codes and certification are devoted a whole section, specifically Section 5 in Chapter IV, GDPR and are also mentioned in other provisions that explicitly furnish them with specific legal relevance. More specifically, Article 40, GDPR builds upon its predecessor, namely Article 27, DPD, urging the Member States and relevant EU institutions and bodies to encourage the drawing up of codes.[98] It *additionally* refers to "associations and other bodies representing categories of controllers or processors",[99] which "may prepare codes of conduct, or amend or extend such codes, for the purpose of specifying the application of this Regulation".[100] It also provides guidance regarding the content of such codes (European Commission, 2012a, p. 12) by listing a number of issues, such as data pseudonymization and enforcement and dispute resolution that may be governed by such codes.[101] This evinces a mild form of code-law integration (involving the law attempting to get involved in the content of self-regulation). Code-law integration in the GDPR, however, takes a much stronger form.

Indeed, the freedom of self-regulatory bodies to submit their codes for official approval existing in the DPD and also in the Draft GDPR[102] is replaced by *an obligation* to do so in Article 40(5), GDPR. This is evidently a decisive step towards code-law integration and can, in particular, work towards ensuring the quality and/or reliability of codes. The said provision is followed by provisions laying down procedures for approval and subsequent publication of approved codes, both national, concerning data processing occurring in a single Member State and Community, concerning data processing occurring in multiple Member States.[103] In the latter case, the process before and after approval involves not only the DPA but also the Data Protection Board and the Commission. Notably, Community codes are very important in the context of automated marketplaces; these are likely to attract consumers from across the EU and feature merchants directing their business to multiple Member States.

However, it is unfortunate that DPAs, the Board and the Commission are *not* imposed with an obligation to *act without delay* in the context of code approval; one such obligation was added by the Parliament in the Draft GDPR[104] but did not survive the final stages of the Regulation,[105] despite the fact that other provisions do impose an obligation to act

98 Article 40(1), GDPR.
99 Article 40(2), GDPR.
100 Ibid.
101 Article 40(2), GDPR.
102 Article 38(2), DGDPR (Parliament text).
103 Article 40(6)-(11), GDPR.
104 Article 38(2), DGDPR (Parliament text).
105 Such obligation is not imposed by Article 57(1)(m), GDPR either, which provides for the tasks of DPAs regarding code approval pursuant to Article 40(5), GDPR.

without delay in relation to other matters.[106] This obligation is important in relation to code approval: the procedure leading to the approval of the FEDMA Community Code submitted to the DPWP under Article 27(3), DPD lasted five years (DPWP, 2003, pp. 2–3) and the same is true of the approval of an Annex to the Code (DPWP, 2010b, pp. 2–3). This is an excessive period of time especially given that the DPWP did not have to examine numerous codes[107] and may have contributed in the rare use of the relevant DPD provisions.

Another weakness of the relevant GDPR provisions is that they are confined to the consequences of the approval of submitted codes; there is no reference to the implications of an official rejection (or non-approval) of a code (apart from the non-publication of such code). An accountability system to deal with legally incompliant codes comparably to the ones that could have been inspired by the UCTD as explained previously is therefore not established in the GDPR. Thus, legally incompliant codes are not guaranteed to be extinguished from the market. Moreover, DPAs are not in any way rendered accountable for their approval-related responsibilities and yet, an approved and hence, publicized code may influence the choices of data subjects leading them to contract with controllers, who have submitted to the code. Notably, even though Article 78(1) entitles data subjects to a judicial remedy against the supervisory authority, this is in respect of DPA decisions "concerning them"; it is therefore unlikely that the supervisory authority could (successfully) be sued on the ground of a mistaken approval and hence, publication of a code, unless of course, the relevant provision is very broadly interpreted so as to cover decisions that concern (or affect) data subjects only indirectly.

Turning to the core issue of the legal relevance of controller/processor submission to a code of conduct (which is very important if trader participation to codes is to be enhanced), Articles 40 and 41, GDPR on codes of conduct lay down no express legal presumption of conformity in favour of code-abiding controllers and/or processors and in no other way, provide for the legal relevance of code submission. The same was true of the Commission Proposal as a whole. Still, perhaps for the reason already explained,[108] commentators (Kuner, 2012, p. 9; Hirsch, 2013, p. 1058) presumed that adherence to such codes would be taken to mean compliance with the Regulation. Kuner (2012, p. 9), however, rightly called for this to be made more explicit in the text.

The parliamentary text of the Draft GDPR (DGDPR) referred to adherence to codes as a means to secure a right to transfer data as between different controllers belonging to the same group[109] and as proof of compliance with Article 26(1), DGDPR which required controllers to choose processors providing sufficient guarantees to implement privacy-protective technical and organizational measures.[110] This specific and limited recognition of legal relevance to codes is not ideal. Indeed, it may result to uncertainty regarding the *overall* legal relevance of codes, i.e., regarding their relevance to the rest of the obligations of the GDPR.

Thanks to the Council and the amendments it introduced in the text of the Draft GDPR,[111] the (final) GDPR does much better. First of all, legal relevance is expressly

106 See for example Article 64(4), GDPR.
107 Actually, the FEDMA code and its Annex were the only documents submitted for approval pursuant to Article 27(3), DPD.
108 Supra p. 138
109 Article 22(3a), DGDPR (parliamentary text).
110 See Article 26(3a), DGDPR (Parliamentary text).
111 See Articles 23, 26, 30 and 33, DGDPR (Council text).

attributed to codes in the context of the wide-ranging principle of accountability, which covers the totality of the obligations of the Regulation.[112] Thus, by providing that "adherence to approved codes of conduct as referred to in Article 40 or approved certification mechanisms as referred to in Article 42 may be used as an element by which to demonstrate compliance with the obligations of the controller" as required by Article 24 (1), Article 24(3), GDPR seems to be able to render approved codes and certification mechanisms legally relevant to the totality of the GDPR obligations. Though it does not go as far as to render code compliance sufficient proof of legal compliance (Korff, 2014), it clearly furnishes it with legal weight, which can in practice operate as sufficient proof of legal compliance at least in most cases. This can act as a powerful incentive for merchant submission to approved codes.

A provision identical to Article 24(3) exists in Article 32 (which contains the security-related obligations of controllers and processors),[113] Article 28 (which lays down the obligations of processors and the requirements that any processor chosen by a controller should meet)[114] and in Article 25, which refers to data protection by design and data protection by default.[115] In Article 25, however, *only* certification is mentioned probably because it seems to be a more appropriate method for demonstrating compliance with obligations requiring a detailed and in-depth analysis of the design of data processing systems. Despite the generality of Article 24, the repetition of the relevant provision in Articles 28 and 32 is justifiable, too; unlike Article 24, which is addressed to controllers only, Article 28 is addressed to processors and Article 32, both to controllers and processors.

The GDPR furnishes codes with an additional form of legal relevance, specifically in the context of DPIAs. Thus, compliance with approved codes "shall be taken into due account in assessing the impact of the processing operations performed by such controllers or processors, in particular for the purposes of a data protection impact assessment".[116] This renders approved codes a useful way for controllers to assess the risks involved in their data processing operations. In this respect, it further strengthens the incentive for controllers to submit to approved codes.

The legal relevance of approved multi–Member State (or Community) codes can be even more substantial, due to Article 40(9), GDPR empowering the Commission to confer on approved codes *general validity* through the adoption of implementing acts. Implementing and delegated acts are the new EU legal acts introduced by the Treaty of Lisbon currently provided for in Articles 290 and 291, TFEU respectively. These entail the Commission amending or supplementing a legislative act, thus exercising quasi-legislative power (in the case of delegated acts) or laying down, amongst others, procedures and sub-rules for the uniform implementation of legal rules (in the case of implementing acts). Implementing acts are explained by ClientEarth (2014, p. 2) as follows:

> An implementing act . . . is considered to be inherently more procedural (templates, procedures, deadlines), a pure, practical implementation of rules that already exist in the original legislation. In layman's terms, implementing acts should legislate upon the 'how' implementation should take place.

112 See Article 24(1), GDPR, emphasis added, supra at p. 131 (note in particular the phrase 'to ensure' in said provision)
113 Article 32(3), GDPR.
114 Article 28(3), GDPR.
115 Article 25(3), GDPR.
116 Article 35(8), GDPR.

Given that codes exactly aim at facilitating implementation by exemplifying general legal rules and transforming them into more specific guidelines, implementing acts constitute an appropriate tool in this context. Importantly, implementing acts are of general application and thus, legally binding (Craig and de Búrca, 2011, p. 116; Craig, 2004, p. 80). Accordingly, if the Commission decides to issue an implementing act furnishing an approved code with general validity and thus, legal force, the result will be comparable to the strong co-regulatory approach adopted in the Italian data protection regime explained previously.[117]

Most importantly, the GDPR also takes seriously the enforcement aspect of codes, which, as already explained,[118] is central to a *real* co-regulatory approach. More specifically, Article 41 is devoted to the bodies to which the monitoring of compliance with the code is assigned,[119] despite the fact that some Member States opposed their setting up, amongst others, because of the administrative burden involved.[120] Those bodies must be accredited by DPAs by reference to criteria relating to independence, impartiality, possession of expert knowledge in relation to the code and the existence of adequate procedures of handling complaints about code infringements.[121] The accredited enforcement-monitoring bodies are entrusted with powers to take action against incompliant controllers and processors, including suspension or exclusion from the code.[122] The accreditation of the said bodies is subject to revocation by the competent DPA, amongst others, where they cease meeting the aforementioned accreditation criteria.[123] Thus, code enforcers must be impartial and expert bodies possessing the capability of exercising code-enforcing duties. Moreover, the accreditation procedure in conjunction with the relevant de-accreditation rules effectively constitute an accountability system to which code enforcers are subject.

All in all, the GDPR on codes of conduct seems to reflect Rubinstein's (2009, p. 13) "strongly-mandated self-regulation" or *real* co-regulation, as the law is involved both in *rule-making* and in the *enforcement* of codes. Indeed, regarding rule-making, the content of (approved) codes that have legal relevance are industry-written but must comply with the Regulation, as they have to be submitted for official approval. Accordingly, a legal instrument sets out the minimum requirements. Additionally, a legal instrument gives the code legal relevance and/or force, thereby effectively incentivizing code submission. As for enforcement, the enforcers, namely the bodies provided for in Article 41(1) are subject to accreditation and monitoring by public authorities.

Of course, it remains to be seen if this will be a real co-regulatory approach *in practice*, too. More specifically, if, in practice, accredited enforcement bodies remain inactive towards code violations and data protection authorities ignore this inactivity omitting to revoke accreditation, self-regulation will end up a purely voluntary system of regulation. Indeed, albeit in relation to the US-EU Safe Harbour Agreement regarding the transfer of personal data to the US, Rubinstein (2011, p. 20) concluded that "while in theory the SHA is a

117 Supra p. 137

118 Supra p. 136

119 Moreover, to facilitate this monitoring of compliance with codes, Article 40(4) requires that codes of conduct contain mechanisms enabling the said bodies "to carry out the mandatory monitoring of compliance with its provisions by the controllers or processors which undertake to apply it".

120 Note 253, DGDPR (Council text).

121 Article 41(2), GDPR.

122 Article 41(4), GDPR.

123 Article 41(5), GDPR. According to this provision, accreditation can also be revoked if actions taken by the body infringe the GDPR. It would be wise to specify inactivity on the part of the body as a ground for accreditation revocation.

strongly mandated self-regulatory program (because the government sets the requirements both for rulemaking and enforcement), in practice the government monitoring of both functions is so weak as to render the SHA more like a purely voluntary program". Most certainly, this should not be the faith of the GDPR co-regulatory approach.

The GDPR is not confined to codes of conduct but exploits self-regulation further by providing for another self-regulatory technique, namely certification. This was totally absent from the DPD. Article 42(1), GDPR calls for the encouragement of "the establishment of data protection certification mechanisms and of data protection seals and marks, for the purpose of demonstrating compliance with this Regulation of processing operations by controllers and processors". Data protection certification, seals and marks can be an effective way of informing consumers about the level of data protection afforded by a particular trader (controller)[124] and could also be used as credentials taken into account by marketplace providers in the context of the suggested marketplace access control system applied to potential merchant participants. Yet, contrary to the intentions of the Parliament, which favoured a provision *obliging* DPAs to offer certification to interested controllers and processors,[125] Article 42 only calls for their encouragement and does not establish any relevant mechanisms or schemes.[126]

Controllers and processors can choose to submit details of their processing to a certification body or the competent DPA[127] which upon checking it against criteria approved either by the DPA or the European Data Protection Board[128] can issue certification for up to three years. Such certification can be renewed or revoked depending on whether the said criteria continue to be met or not.[129] According to Article 42(5), GDPR, if certification is issued based on harmonized criteria approved by the Board, it may result to the 'European Data Protection Seal'. If the certification procedure is handled by certification bodies, rather than the DPA, such bodies must be accredited by reference to specific criteria, comparably to the aforementioned context of the accreditation of enforcement monitoring bodies in relation to codes of conduct provided for in Article 40.[130]

The legal relevance of certification is the same with that of codes of conduct discussed earlier. It can be used as an element of demonstrating compliance but does not operate as a liability exemption or enforcement action bar, as made clear in Article 42(4), GDPR: "A certification pursuant to this Article does not reduce the responsibility of the controller or the processor for compliance with this Regulation and is without prejudice to the tasks and powers of the supervisory authorities which are competent pursuant to Article 55 or 56". This echoes the position of the DPWP, which warned against the possibility of the certification mechanism narrowing the playing field of DPAs when enforcing the Regulation: "The following situation must be avoided: in the case of a data controller's or processor's non-compliance, the DPA shall first have to prove that this non-compliance stems from a deviation from the model that was certified before any other action may be considered. This would in many cases make enforcement very difficult, if not impossible" (DPWP, 2014, p. 5). It is, however, uncertain whether, in practice, enforcement action will be taken against a *certified*

124 See Recital 100, GDPR.

125 See Article 39(1a) in conjunction with Article 52(1)(ja), Regulation (European Parliament text), the latter listing the tasks of DPAs.

126 Infra at p. 144

127 Article 42(3), 42(5) and 42(6), GDPR.

128 Article 42(5), GDPR.

129 Article 42(7), GDPR.

130 The relevant provision is Article 43, GDPR.

controller and/or processor without the need to explain why certification was previously issued. Most probably, despite the aforementioned Article 42(4), GDPR, a DPA taking enforcement action will inevitably have to pinpoint to a deviation from the model certified or admit a mistake during certification on the part of the certifying DPA or certification body. This is not necessarily undesirable. Especially when certification is performed by the DPA, it effectively forces a careful approach in conducting the certification, which, in turn, leads to *reliable* privacy seals that can safely be acted upon by consumers.

Importantly, during the preparatory stages of the GDPR, the Council has been accused of "trying to undermine privacy seals (and through this, the General Data Protection Regulation)" (Korff, 2014). The relevant criticism was partly based on the ground that the Council text of the Draft GDPR only required the encouragement of certification[131] rather than the establishment of a certification procedure. The criticism remains pertinent, as Article 42 of the GDPR does the same,[132] yet it seems answerable to some extent. Indeed, this 'laid back' approach towards certification allows Member States flexibility regarding whether, when and how they are to introduce and establish a certification mechanism. This flexibility may be necessary given that DPAs are often understaffed with limited resources, while certification entails a substantial burden, which may be impossible to discharge at least by some DPAs. Moreover, as already seen, the GDPR introduces an enhanced (and overall satisfactory) co-regulatory approach based on codes of conduct, which aims at serving the (same) purpose of facilitating compliance with (and/or enforcement of) the Regulation. This approach should be expected to work well in some Member States possibly rendering a certification mechanism less necessary.

Admittedly, 'approved code' compliance does not lead to the European Data Protection Seal, which is reserved by the GDPR to certification. Yet, as already seen,[133] seals (which can be used in the context of a marketplace access control mechanism) are commonly issued in the context of codes too and can certainly be awarded following successful submission to an approved Community (multi–Member State) code of conduct. Moreover, codes of conduct and certification could potentially be put to work together in a cost-effective manner, for example, by DPAs using the same accreditation system for both schemes. To the extent that certification entails a more thorough actual examination of the specific data processing operations of a given controller than submission to a relevant code of conduct, the co-existence of these two co-regulatory approaches may beneficial.

It should, of course, be acknowledged that where *no* certification mechanisms exist, controllers are precluded from using it as a way of demonstrating compliance with their privacy-by-design obligations of Article 25, GDPR. As already seen, certification only (and *not* codes of conduct, too) serves as an element to demonstrate compliance with the Article 25 obligations, as per Article 25(3), GDPR.[134] Accordingly, data controllers operating in Member States, which have not established a relevant certification mechanism may be placed in a disadvantageous position compared to controllers operating in Member States, which have done so.

The relevant problem can be remedied by the operation of the common certification mechanism leading to the (EU-wide) European Data Protection Seal as per Article 42(5),

131 See Article 39(1) in conjunction with Article 52(1)(gb)-(gc), DGDPR (Council text), the latter referring to DPAs having to promote certification and provide accreditation to certification bodies, only where applicable.

132 Supra p. 143

133 Supra pp. 113–114

134 Supra p. 141

GDPR.[135] This is important especially in contexts, such as automated marketplaces probably involving processing of personal data of consumers from across the EU. Article 42(5), GDPR clarifies that the said seal can be awarded following certification against criteria approved by the European Data Protection Board, meaning that such criteria will probably be common or recognized and accepted by all Member States. Moreover, the European Commission will be able to work further towards a common certification mechanism by laying down harmonized criteria through delegated acts by virtue of Article 43(8), GDPR. The latter provision seems to give the Commission wide powers, as it refers to the specification of "the requirements to be taken into account for the data protection certification mechanisms referred to in Article 42(1)". Referring to a similar provision in the Draft GDPR, Korff (2014) asserts that "these harmonising measures relate only to the parameters and technical details of the certification scheme". Yet, this role seems to be reserved to implementing acts by Article 43(9), GDPR referring to "implementing acts laying down technical standards for certification mechanisms and data protection seals and marks, and mechanisms".

In any event, the provisions of the GDPR on certification, though *not* establishing an operative certification system, national or pan-EU, they definitely construct one ready to be put in operation should DPAs or the relevant EU bodies decide they should do so. This is not an insignificant step forward, especially, in the light of the failure of a past Commission initiative about the creation of an accreditation system for trust seal providers (European Commission, 2004b, pp. 7–8) and the ineffective call of the European Parliament for its re-launching more than a decade ago (European Parliament, 2006, p. 2).

It has been argued previously that adequate self-regulatory schemes such as codes and certification seals can prove useful in the hands of marketplace providers in improving privacy and data protection both within and outside the marketplace to the benefit of consumer users. The EU data protection regime, specifically the GDPR has come a long way exploiting such schemes and thus, effectively empowering marketplace providers to protect consumer interests.

Notably, the law can further incentivize code submission and the use of seals by merchants by rendering such choices a strong competitive advantage, specifically through legal obligations of disclosing code participation to consumers. In this way, consumers can know and prefer marketplaces, which adhere to codes or have undergone certification. Especially after the introduction of Legal-XML language,[136] the same can apply to marketplace-participating merchants; consumer buying software can be technically capable of acting upon information on codes or seals, thereby being instructed to contract with selling software providing information as to a code or seal. EU law responds to this need too, as it contains one such information duty. More specifically, Article 10(2), E-Commerce Directive requires that an 'information society service' provider provide service recipients with information about "any relevant codes of conduct to which he subscribes". In the context of distance consumer contracts, a similar pre-contractual information duty is imposed by Article 6(1)(h), CRD[137] It is somewhat uncertain whether the codes mentioned in the aforementioned provisions cover ones relating to data protection practices. This is rather doubtful as regards

135 See supra p. 143

136 Supra n. 47

137 This obligation refers to codes as defined in Article 2(f), Unfair Commercial Practices Directive (UCPD), which refers to codes defining the behaviour of traders who undertake to be bound by the code in relation to one or more particular commercial practices or business sectors.

the latter provision at least. Thus, it would be preferable for a relevant information duty to be included in the information duties of the GDPR itself, specifically its Article 13 requiring the provision of certain information to the data subject at the time of data collection. Such provision should also include certification seals, as opposed to just codes.

4.4 Concluding remarks

It has been shown that given the very broad legal definition of 'personal data' in the EU data protection regime, the majority of the data processed in the context of automated marketplace services would qualify as 'personal data', thereby triggering the application of the GDPR and the EPD. Though being addressed to electronic communications service providers, the obligations of the EPD does not apply to most automated marketplaces, that does not leave any gap in data protection. The main data protection obligations in the EU are contained in the GDPR and the EPD (and even more so, the upcoming E-Privacy Regulation) do not go beyond the GDPR in any way. The obligations of the GDPR are mainly addressed to data controllers and, as it has been illustrated, marketplace providers and marketplace-participating merchants would seem to qualify as data controllers acting together as joint controllers in relation to the bulk of the data processing occurring within automated marketplaces. The GDPR is thus perfectly applicable to them and despite certain deficiencies in its various provisions, all six ingredients of an adequate solution to the privacy risks associated with automated marketplaces are provided for in the GDPR.

More specifically, though an explicit duty vested on controllers to police or vet a joint controller is absent, the GDPR rules on joint controllership regarding civil liability and public sanctions effectively impose a relevant duty indirectly. Thus, merchants will strive to use law-abiding marketplaces, thereby avoiding liability and sanctions themselves and marketplace providers will want to vet merchants allowed in their marketplace, thereby reducing data breaches for which they will also be liable. This greatly improves the practical effectiveness of the GDPR obligations and seems to entail two of the aforementioned six elements of an adequate legal response, namely elements (b) and (f). Elements (a) and (e), namely a clear obligation on marketplace providers and marketplace-participating merchants to protect personal data through the adoption of available *technical* privacy-enhancing measures, definitely also exists in the GDPR, particularly, Articles 5, 24, 25, 32 and 35, which have a strong technological flavour. Existing deficiencies have been illustrated to require minor drafting modifications while others, such as the fact that some of these obligations are only addressed to data controllers and do not burden data processors too, do not greatly affect data protection in automated marketplaces where both marketplace providers and marketplace-participating merchants qualify as data controllers.

As it has been illustrated, relevant self-regulation initiatives can greatly enhance data protection in automated marketplaces (and in general) if adequately exploited by the law in the context of a relevant co-regulatory approach. This is relevant to the aforementioned elements (c) and (d) of an adequate legal response, which have both been found in the GDPR, in particular its section governing codes of conduct and certification seals. Doubtless, the relevant provisions constitute a decisive step towards the adoption of an effective co-regulatory approach in the area of data protection and also encourage merchant participation in self-regulatory schemes, amongst others, by rendering such participation legally relevant. They do suffer from certain deficiencies (such as the absence of an information duty referring to codes or certification), which if addressed, would further improve the adequacy of the EU legal response in this context, but these do not greatly weaken the relevant EU legal response. Of course, whether the relevant co-regulatory approach will actually work well, thereby improving data protection, will largely depend on how rigorously DPAs perform their duties of approving codes and/or monitoring the administration and enforcement of relevant self-regulatory schemes.

It follows therefore that overall the EU legal response towards the risks referring to data protection (and privacy) associated with automated marketplaces is largely adequate.

5 Risks to data integrity, data authentication and non-repudiation (transactional security)

5.1 General remarks

This chapter looks into transactional security, which is a condition precedent to a viable automated marketplace allowing for the conclusion of binding contracts. This is different and broader than data protection (or data security) in the sense that it concerns not with the protection of *personal* data but, more generally, with the security of the *electronic transactions*. This effectively leads to ensuring that human participation in automated transactions will be safe (as opposed to potentially harmful to their interests). Unlike in the offline context, transactions within online automated marketplaces are inherently unsecure. The distance and lack of human participation together with the risks concerning the integrity of the data involved, the authentication of the other contracting party and the existence of sufficient proof of the transactional communications associated with highly technical environments operating on the internet, render automated marketplaces environments in need for effective transactional security measures.

The first part of this chapter will illustrate these risks and the existence of a need for the law to intervene, thereby imposing an obligation to ensure transactional security upon automated marketplace providers. It will do so by answering arguments against such an obligation and by illustrating that it is technologically possible (mainly, through encryption) to be met. Relevant to this exercise, are arguments against the introduction of encryption in online contractual contexts, hence the said arguments will also be discussed and answered. The second part of the chapter will identify the EU legal measures that are relevant to transactional security and examine them in search for the aforementioned legal obligation. As it will be shown, a relevant obligation can be found only in relation to the very big marketplaces. However, a number of relevant legal measures working in synergy potentially reduce the gap left by the absence of an express legal obligation to ensure transactional security burdening all automated marketplace providers.

5.2 Illustrating the 'transactional security' risks inherent in automated marketplaces and the appropriate legal response

Being places where binding contracts are negotiated and eventually concluded altering the legal status of human contracting parties, automated marketplaces must be subjected to strict security requirements if they are to comprise a viable alternative contracting method not associated with fraud and/or unintended contracts. The data travelling within automated marketplaces mainly consists of contractual offers, counter-offers and acceptances that make up the contracts from which rights and obligations flow. Contracts are notoriously all about the data they contain and the identity of the contracting parties against whom they may be enforced. Thus, there could be no (reliable) automated contracting, if (a) such data were vulnerable to accidental and/or malicious modification, (b) the identity of its sender could not be verified and (c) no evidence of the communication was produced and stored preventing contracting parties from simply denying having taken part in it.

As regards the first, "service-providers, other agents, or clones can easily change the personal data" (Borking et al., 1999, p. 36).[1] There is nothing that human consumers can do on their own to prevent or limit these technical risks, thereby ensuring *data integrity*. The second, which refers to *data authentication* is equally important. As Barofsky (2000, p. 150) quoting Robertson (1998, p. 796) emphasizes, the simple electronic signatures typically used online (such as a typed name), though "theoretically may satisfy the formality of signature", they lack many of the "inherent security attributes" of handwritten signatures, such as "the semipermanence of ink embedded in paper, unique attributes of some printing processes, watermarks, the distinctiveness of individual signatures, and the limited ability to erase, interlineate or otherwise, modify words on paper". Parties may thus need the assistance of security-enabling technology when acting online.

Regarding the third, the creation (and preservation) of evidence of a link between an action, such as the sending of a message and the identity of its sender is called '*non-repudiation*'[2] and is again of increased significance in automated marketplaces. Indeed, as in every online setting, software-represented contracting parties do not come in direct contract with each other and do not actively take part in the contractual process or get to receive any physical proof, such as a receipt. They are even unaware of the content of the communications leading to the binding contract. They are thus not in a position to provide any evidence proving the link between a communication and the actual person from whom it originated.[3]

Legal protection of the parties must thus be achieved *technically*, and it is on the technical capabilities of protection, namely, data integrity, authentication and non-repudiation, of the automated marketplace that the parties must fully rely. More generally, a *secure* marketplace will naturally not attract fraudsters and in this respect, the implementation of security technology can act as a general protection shield.

There are therefore plenty of reasons why 'transactional data' security technology should be obligatory for automated marketplace providers, at least those allowing for the sale of expensive products. Though, as others note (Subirana and Bain, 2005, p. 82), security-imposing legislation may render online contracting more burdensome than its offline counterpart, this would seem to be unavoidable. Indeed, through some believe that information

1 See also Barofsky (2000, p. 149).

2 'Non-repudiation' has been defined as "a service that provides proof of the integrity and origin of data" and as "a property achieved through cryptographic methods which prevents an individual or entity from denying having performed a particular action related to data" (W. Caelli, D. Longley and M. Shain, 1991. *Information Security Handbook*. London: Macmillan). An ISO standard states that the purpose of a non-repudiation service is "to provide irrefutable evidence concerning the occurrence or non-occurrence of a disputed event or action" (International Standards Organization. Information Technology – Open Systems Interconnection – Security Frameworks for Open Systems – Part 4: Non-repudiation. International Standard ISO/IEC 10181-4, 1996). Irrefutable in this context must be taken to mean concrete, strong or convincing but not absolutely infallible (Roe, 2010, pp. 37, 40–41).

3 As Mason (2006, p. 164) confirms when discussing electronic signatures that "the central issue will be how to prove the nexus between the application of the signature, whatever from it takes, and the person whose signature it purports to be".

security can be brought about by technology and the market (Boss, 1999, pp. 623–624), economic theory suggests that market forces could not be trusted to achieve an optimal level of information security and that any market-based solutions are likely to prove inefficient (Irion, 2012, pp. 5–6).

The need for legal intervention has repeatedly been recognized in technical literature (Brazier et al., 2003a, pp. 53–70; Brazier et al., 2003b, p. 5; Chiu et al., 2005, p. 724; Fasli, 2007, p. 7). The same literature also illustrates the *existence* of the technical means to meet a relevant legal obligation. Borking, van Eck and Siepel (1999, p. 37) refer to *integrity*-ensuring technologies, such as "parity-bits, checksums, or digital signatures". Digital signatures based on encryption can assist in *authentication* too (Tsvetovatty et al., 1997, p. 504; Brazier et al., 2003b, p. 5). Cryptographic *non-repudiation* protocols can ensure that the any action, such as the sending or reading of a contractual message is impossible without the generation of relevant digital evidence (Liew et al., 1999, secs. 3.2–3.3). Encryption thus seems capable of playing an important role in the development of *secure* and hence, *safe* automated marketplaces and indeed, Fasli (2007, pp. 21–22) illustrates that it can help with all three of the aforementioned security elements.

Various arguments, specifically against cryptographic non-repudiation (Ellison, n.d.; Gutmann, 2005; McCullagh and Caelli, 2000) are not convincing enough. These arguments can be summarized as follows:

a it is unachievable, as keys for encrypting and signing data can be stolen or infected by a virus, thereby operating against the will of the person they supposedly identify;
b it is anti-consumer, as high-level security means that consumers will face increased difficulty in proving that they have not authorized a transaction even when this is the case;
c it is anti-ecommerce: 'credit card' chargebacks and, more generally, withdrawal rights (which are allegedly the opposite of non-repudiation) constitute effective tools of consumer protection enabling e-commerce to thrive) and;
d it is potentially at odds with traditional contract law that allows repudiation on various grounds such as undue influence, fraud or unfair contract terms.

Regarding the first, handwritten signatures are vulnerable to misappropriation or misuse too and yet, they have always been (legally) recognized as a method of authentication and expression of contractual intent. Moreover, they often comprise a legal requirement, amongst others, in the context of transactions of high significance, such as those involving land. Siems (2002, pp. 18–19) further notes that handwritten signatures are easy to forge or, generally, to be misused *while* the risks to the reliability of digital signatures are comparably small and incapable of negating the fact that they can afford increased protection.

The second argument essentially says that a signatory may be held bound by his digital signature even though he has not wilfully used it, for example, because his private key has been stolen. It thus suggests that because cryptography can achieve *increased* but *not absolute* security, the overall benefits of increased security should be turned down for avoiding injustice in the few cases that cryptography may be compromised *and* the relevant systems in place will fail to record the compromise. It can thus readily be dismissed.

Moreover, the relevant injustice may only occur very rarely, if at all. The Second Payment Services Directive allows for a payee simply to deny having authorized a transaction and places the burden to prove that the transaction was in fact authorized on the payment service provider.[4] It thus lays down a presumption of non-authorization that needs to be rebutted by the party who has received the contested authorization and is thus best-equipped to offer evidence regarding the actual security of the relevant payment transaction. Where the cryptographic signature at issue relates to the contractual communications preceding payment, the E-identification Regulation (eIDAS), which has replaced the Electronic Signatures Directive (ESD)[5] lays down no presumptions of actual authorization (or non-repudiation); as Mason (2006, p. 163) notes presumptions in relation to digital signatures often follow those applicable in relation to handwritten signatures in the offline world. There is thus the possibility of the parties bringing evidence proving or disproving the validity of a digital signature, though admittedly it may particularly difficult (McCullagh and Caelli, 2000) or very expensive (Mason, 2006, p. 163) for this possibility to be exercised in practice.

Importantly, however, the application of cryptographic non-repudiation technology within electronic marketplaces effectively places between the two contracting parties *two* intermediaries, namely the marketplace provider and the trusted third party who is to issue and manage the digital signature affording non-repudiation. These two parties can either eliminate the possibility of digital signature misuse or ensure that relevant reliable evidence regarding whether security has been compromised will be available. The law can ensure that these intermediaries are effectively burdened with the relevant onus through imposing on them relevant security-related obligations associated with liability for their breach. Though the relevant EU legal response is examined later on, it is noteworthy here that EU law does respond to the relevant need. The now replaced ESD, upon which the provisions on digital signatures of the (new) eIDAS are built, necessitated the involvement of a trusted third party in the use of qualified advanced signatures (i.e., the ones equated with handwritten signatures). The said intermediary was required to use "trustworthy systems and products which are protected against modification and ensure the technical and cryptographic security of the process supported by them"[6] as well as signature-creation data (private keys) that were technologically protected against forgery. In this respect, the ESD required what appears to be the equivalent of 'trusted computing systems' that according to McCullagh and Caelli (2000) answer the relevant objection against cryptographic non-repudiation.

The remaining two arguments against cryptographic non-repudiation apparently rest on a misunderstanding regarding the intended role of cryptographic non-repudiation; in reality, it only seeks to prevent a party from denying the affixation of the signature comparably to what (offline) witnesses do.[7] It does not thus affect or even touch upon any of the other legal grounds upon which a party may seek to avoid a contract. It is certainly, ***not*** an opposite to withdrawal rights (or any of the other grounds upon which a contract may be avoided) either. Withdrawal rights or reliance on contract avoidance grounds, such as undue influence, inherently entail the party seeking to avoid the contract while *accepting, not denying* his participation in the transaction. Non-repudiation aims at preventing denial of participation, not legal withdrawal or a challenge of the validity of the provided consent.

4 Infra Chapter 6 p. 187
5 These measures are discussed infra Chapter 5.3.3.2.3.
6 Electronic Signatures Directive, Annex II, para. f.
7 Though witnessing operates at the time of affixing the signature while cryptographic methods may achieve their purpose via actions occurring at the post-signature stage (McCullagh and Caelli, 2000), it remains true that technical non-repudiation is confined to non-repudiation of the signature and does not extend to contract repudiation in general.

This chapter has so far illustrated the transactional security risks associated with the use of automated marketplaces and the need for as well as the justifiability of a legal obligation to ensure security imposed upon involved providers. The discussion will now turn to whether EU law responds to the relevant need, thereby addressing the risks involved.

5.3 'Transactional data' security risks associated with automated marketplaces: the EU legal response

5.3.1 General remarks

This part of Chapter 5 will examine whether EU law obliges automated marketplace providers to employ measures ensuring transactional security in their platforms. As it will be shown, though the security obligations of the GDPR go some way towards the particular aim, they are tied to 'personal data' protection and cannot therefore fully address transactional security as a purpose on its own. The relevant aim is assisted by measures, such as the CRD, which evince a very soft transactional security approach but more decisively by recent measures focusing on data and transactional security, namely the NISD and the eIDA Regulation. No express 'transactional security' obligation potentially burdening *all* automated marketplace providers can be found. However, *big* marketplaces inherently entailing greater risks (amongst others, due to the number of consumers affected) can be considered to be imposed with one such obligation. Moreover, the GDPR, the NISD and the eIDA Regulation can potentially work together to increase market acceptance and utilization of 'transactional security' technical solutions, thereby improving the overall security in automated marketplaces.

5.3.2 An early soft transactional security approach in a contractual context

Early signs of a (*very*) *soft* transactional security approach depicting a concern on the part of EU lawmakers about the ephemeral nature of online contractual communications can be found in the Distance Selling Directive (now replaced by the CRD) and in the E-Commerce Directive (ECD). Article 5(1) of the Distance Selling Directive (now Article 8(7), CRD) requires that merchants provide consumers with the pre-contractual information required under Article 4 (now Article 6, CRD) (which also form part of the contract),[8] on a *durable medium*, i.e., a medium enabling storage and unchanged reproduction.[9] Assuming that merchant users of (selling) software will want to comply with the said obligation through the automated marketplace rather than have to communicate the said information to the consumer directly outside the marketplace, this requirement can result in a market demand for marketplaces guaranteeing durability that will probably extend to all exchanged messages.[10] Durability certainly increases security in the sense that it entails some evidence of the concluded transaction, yet it does not seem to touch upon data integrity or authentication at all.

Subirana and Bain (2005, p. 82) also refer to Article 10(3), E-Commerce Directive as requiring preservation of "evidence or proof of *an agent-created contract* to provide higher levels of trust and certainty in agent-based ecommerce".[11] The said provision provides that

8 Article 6(5), CRD.
9 Article 2(10), CRD.
10 For a similar argument, ableit by reference to authentication, see supra Chapter 6 p. 106
11 Emphasis added.

"Contract terms and general conditions provided to the recipient must be made available in a way that allows him to store and reproduce them". Obviously, it does not mandate the preservation of the (pre)-contractual communications, which are invaluable in case of a dispute. Therefore, its potential role is very similar to that of Article 8(7), CRD, which only scratches the surface of rendering *highly secure* automated marketplaces *mandatory*.

5.3.3 A stronger security approach

EU law has gone much deeper into the ocean of information security. In 2004, the European Network and Information Security Agency (ENISA) has been established by the ENISA Regulation amongst others, to "assist the Commission and the Member States... cooperate with the business community, in order to help them to meet the requirements of network and information security".[12] The Regulation defines 'network and information security' as an essential characteristic *not* only of public networks or electronic communication services but also of any information system or service running on information networks and systems, something that would obviously include automated marketplaces:

> the ability of a network or an information system to resist, at a given level of confidence, accidental events or unlawful or malicious actions that compromise the availability, authenticity, integrity and confidentiality of stored or transmitted data and the related services offered by or accessible via these networks and systems.[13]

The definition clearly covers the transactional security elements of data integrity and data authentication,[14] which are also specifically defined in the Regulation.[15] Non-repudiation, however, is not specifically included and it is not entirely clear whether the reference to 'availability of stored or transmitted data'[16] would cover it. In 2013, the relevant Regulation has been replaced by Regulation 526/2013 concerning the European Union Agency for Network and Information Security (ENISA) and repealing Regulation (EC) No 460/2004. The new ENISA Regulation establishes an Agency to replace the initial ENISA, maintaining but strengthening its advisory and supporting role. Yet, up until very recently, the only legislative measures imposing security requirements, thus relating to the activities of ENISA were the Framework Directive,[17] particularly Article 13a, the E-Privacy Directive, specifically Article 4, the Data Protection Directive, particularly Article 17 (now Article 32, GDPR) and the Electronic Signatures Directive (now replaced by the eIDAS).

The Framework Directive[18] and, as already explained, the E-Privacy Directive are *not* addressed to information society service providers, including most automated marketplace

12 Article 1(2), ENISA Regulation.
13 Article 4(c), ENISA Regulation.
14 Integrity and authenticity are, as evident, specifically mentioned in the relevant definition.
15 Infra p. 154
16 Article 4(d), ENISA Regulation: "'availability'' means that data is accessible and services are operational".
17 Now part of the Directive (EU) 2018/1972 of the European Parliament and of the Council of 11 December 2018 establishing the European Electronic Communications Code.
18 "Member States shall ensure that *undertakings providing public communications networks or publicly available electronic communications services* take appropriate technical and organisational measures to appropriately manage the risks posed to security of networks and services", Article 13a, Framework Directive as amended by as amended by Directive 2009/140/EC and Regulation 544/2009 (emphasis added). See also Recital 10, Framework Directive.

providers; they only target providers of public communication networks and publicly available communication services.[19] It follows that the suggested obligation to ensure transactional security must be searched for in the EU data protection regime (specifically, the GDPR), the eIDAS and another recent relevant EU measure, namely the Network and Information Security Directive (NISD).[20]

5.3.3.1 The GDPR

The Data Protection Directive, the predecessor of the GDPR, was applicable to all marketplace providers, as data controllers,[21] yet its security obligations specifically referred to the adoption of measures against data destruction, loss, alteration, disclosure and "all other unlawful forms of processing".[22] These seem clearly to cover 'data integrity'[23] and perhaps indirectly 'soft' non-repudiation,[24] and albeit not as clearly, 'data authenticity' (or 'authentication'[25]), too. Cryptographic non-repudiation is quite difficult to be accepted as covered though.

The relevant provision seems to refer to measures affording protection *after* the data is collected or inserted in the system whereas data authentication presupposes confirmation (or verification) measures at the time of the input of (merchant) data. However, one way of ensuring data security is by controlling access to the data and more specifically, by ensuring that only parties of known and confirmed identity can access it. In this respect, given that marketplace-participating merchants will naturally have access to personal data held by consumer buying software, the taking of measures authenticating merchant identity could be seen as a measure required under Article 17, DPD. Kennedy and Millard (2015, p. 4) report that none of the six Member States surveyed required *multi-factor* authentication[26] in their non-sectoral guidance on the security obligations of the DPD, and that in relation to certain specific more sensitive sectors, three of those Member States required multi-factor, specifically two-factor authentication. This seems to confirm that data authentication was taken to be covered by the security obligations of Article 17, DPD. The fact that the strongest (three-factor) authentication was *not*

19 See supra pp. 134–135
20 Regulation 526/2013 has now also been replaced by the very recent EU Cybersecurity Act, which has renewed the mandate of ENISA and has introduced an EU-wide certification system through which the security of ICT products and services can be verified. Though this is an important development, it does not come close to imposing an obligation to employ cybersecurity solutions. The EU Cybersecurity Act is Regulation (EU) 2019/881 of the European Parliament and of the Council of 17 April 2019 on ENISA (the European Union Agency for Cybersecurity) and on information and communications technology cybersecurity certification and repealing Regulation (EU) No 526/2013 (Cybersecurity Act).
21 See supra Chapter 4 pp. 119–120
22 See Article 17(1), supra p. 127
23 "'data integrity' means the confirmation that data which has been sent, received, or stored are complete and unchanged", Article 4(f), ENISA Regulation. .
24 As already seen, this refers to evidence preservation (see supra p. 149) and in this respect, the obligation to take security measures against data destruction could perhaps indirectly be taken to require non-repudiation in appropriate cases.
25 "'authentication' means the confirmation of an asserted identity of entities or users", Article 4(e), ENISA Regulation.
26 This refers to authentication by three different factors, namely something that the person knows (such as a password), something that the person possesses (such as a token) and something that the person is (such as a fingerprint) (Kennedy and Millard, 2015, p. 3). This coincides with three-factor authentication required under the PSD2 discussed earlier (supra p. 99), through in that context, the focus is on the authentication of the consumer payer, not the merchant.

specifically required in *all* cases makes sense; Article 17, DPD, just like the corresponding Article 32, GDPR are subject to a proportionality criterion effectively requiring measures that are proportionate to the risk involved.

Cryptographic non-repudiation seems more difficult to derive from Article 17, DPD. As already seen, it pre-supposes the *production* of certaindata in the form of concrete and indisputable evidence regarding who has sent and/or received a message. This appears to require more than the obligations merely *to protect personal data* imposed by the Directive. Soft non-repudiation, however, would seem to require an effective system of audit logs tracking and storing all actions of the users on the marketplace, which is widely accepted as a standard security measure (Cobb, 2011) which can be derived from Article 17.

The GDPR imposes *enriched* security obligations,[27] and indeed, these are easier to be construed as covering the three transactional security elements of data integrity, data authentication and non-repudiation. More specifically, Article 32(1) imposes a *very broad* obligation to take measures "*to ensure a level of security appropriate to the risk*", the "accidental or unlawful destruction, loss, alteration, unauthorised disclosure of, or access to personal data transmitted, stored or otherwise processed" only being mentioned as risks to be taken into account by data controllers/processors "in assessing the appropriate level of security".[28] Moreover, unlike Article 17, DPD, Article 32 specifically refers to 'unauthorized access' as a risk that the required measures must address,[29] something that makes the earlier argument relating to the relationship between access control and data authentication[30] stronger. Interestingly, to the extent that Article 32 will be taken to require merchant identity authentication, the said provision can be taken to compensate to some extent[31] for the absence of a positive obligation to vet merchants discussed in Chapter 3. Similarly, the wide-ranging security obligation of Article 32(1) can more readily cover non-repudiation and given that encryption is now explicitly referred to,[32] *cryptographic* non-repudiation and *encryption-based* digital signatures can more readily be covered, too (in appropriate cases). A non-repudiation requirement (in the form of action logging leading an audit trail on what happens on the system) seems further to be assisted by the accountability principle of Article 24(1), GDPR.[33]

Others refer to the additional security obligations of the GDPR, namely data protection by design and data protection by default in Article 25,[34] stating that they "likely raise the overall 'base-level' for security measures" (Kennedy and Millard, 2015, p. 5). Indeed, as they report, some DPAs already referred to multi-factor authentication as a method of complying with data protection by default, the latter meaning that "a high level of security settings should be pre-set on relevant products and services" (Kennedy and Millard, 2015, p. 6). This is reinforced by the fact that privacy by default contained in Article 25(2), GDPR expressly refers to measures affecting the *accessibility* of personal data.[35]

27 Supra Chapter 4 p. 127
28 Article 32(2), GDPR.
29 Supra Chapter 4 p. 128
30 Supra p. 154
31 Authenticating merchants does not necessarily mean vetting them against criteria relating to their reliability and quality of business practices.
32 Article 32(1)(a), GDPR.
33 Supra Chapter 4 p. 131
34 This provision, mainly to the extent referring to privacy by design is discussed previously, supra Chapter 4 pp. 129–130
35 Article 25(2), GDPR reads as follows: "The controller shall implement appropriate technical and organisational measures for ensuring that, by default, only personal data which are necessary for each specific purpose of the processing are processed. That obligation applies to the amount of personal data collected, the extent of their processing, the period of their storage and their

However, though it may not be impossible to derive transactional security obligations from the GDPR security-related provisions, transactional security or the security of contractual communications must be seen a virtue of all relevant online environments *irrespective of the involvement of personal data.* Indeed, as the GDPR is inapplicable to data of legal persons,[36] most merchant data will escape the reach of the GDPR. Accordingly, whereas marketplace providers, as data controllers, will be obliged to ensure that consumer data is accurate and non-modifiable, there will be no such obligation regarding merchant data. Consequently, contractual communications sent by the consumer buyer should be non-modifiable, but the same is not rendered mandatory by the GDPR for the communications originating from merchants. Understandably, this paradox may result in 'holes' in the data security of automated marketplaces meaning that the GDPR *alone* cannot comprise a *fully* satisfactory EU legal response towards the relevant risks. A complete transactional security solution must thus be searched elsewhere.

5.3.3.2 *Security obligations* outside *the EU data protection regime*

5.3.3.2.1 THE LEGISLATIVE LOOPHOLE REGARDING THE SECURITY OF INFORMATION SOCIETY SERVICES

EU law lays down obligations to secure the 'security and integrity of networks and services' *independently of the involvement of any personal data*, specifically in the Framework Directive, Article 13a (ENISA, 2014, p. 9), yet those are of very limited application to automated marketplaces, which comprise 'information society services', rather than electronic communications services.[37] Up until very recently, it contained no security obligations addressed to information society services, though there seems to be no valid reason behind not explicitly requiring relevant providers to secure the security of their services, just like 'electronic communications service' providers. Expressing a similar concern regarding this difference in the legal treatment of the two 'digital service' categories, Rossi (2014, pp. 7, 10) proposed a new, all-inclusive category of 'digital services' that would absorb both of types of services and subject them to horizontal regulation (Rossi, 2014, pp. 10–12).[38]

The European Commission did not take up the particular solution but saw the relevant loophole. In fact, information security has been a main concern of the Commission for more than a decade. Indeed, a 2001 Communication detailing a proposal for a European policy

accessibility. In particular, such measures shall ensure that by default personal data are not made accessible without the individual's intervention to an indefinite number of natural persons".

36 Recital 14, GDPR.

37 See supra Chapter 4 p. 134–135

38 Rossi (2014, p. 11) sees a problem with the 'remuneration' criterion in the legal definition of an 'information society service', see supra p., which as she states, prevents the relevant definition from covering electronic services that derive revenue from advertisers instead from users. She cites in that respect, the Opinion of the Attorney-General in Google Spain (*C-131/12, para. 37*) where he concluded that Google search engine does not constitute an information society service because it does not charge searchers for its service. Yet, the said Attorney-General was wrong in that respect. The definition speaks of services '*normally* provided for remuneration' and does not thus exclude non-directly remunerated online services. This is expressly clarified in Recital 18, E-Commerce Directive, where it is stated that search and information-providing services fall within the definition, which covers services that constitute an economic activity even if they are directly paid by recipients. It has also been confirmed in *Sotiris Papasavvas, Case C-291/13, paras. 26–30.* On this issue, see also DLA Piper (2009, pp. 10–13).

approach in relation to network and information security (European Commission, 2001) has been followed by the adoption of a Strategy for a Secure Information Society (European Commission, 2006) and the 2010 Digital Agenda for Europe that called for measures enhancing network and information security (European Commission, 2010b). A 2009 Communication on Critical Information Infrastructure protection emphasized "the economic and societal role of the ICT sector and ICT infrastructures" on which governments, businesses and consumers heavily rely (European Commission, 2009b, p. 4). That Communication launched an action plan to support Member States in preventing and responding to cyberattacks against such infrastructures. It was subsequently acknowledged that cyber security could not be achieved at national level (European Commission, 2011a, p. 5).[39]

Given the long-lasting interest of the European Commission in cyber security, a more decisive step on its part was perhaps inevitable, even more so because there has not been any progress at national level (European Commission, 2013, p. 5). That step took the form of a Proposal for a Directive concerning measures to ensure a high common level of network and information security across the Union (European Commission, 2013). It led to the NISD, which was followed by the eIDAS. Both measures focus on information security and definitely enrich the relevant EU legal landscape.

5.3.3.2.2 THE NISD

The explanatory memorandum to the Proposal for the NISD stated that the aim of the proposed measure was to improve

> the security of *the Internet and the private networks and information systems* underpinning the functioning of our societies and economies . . . by requiring operators of critical infrastructures, such as energy, transport, *and key providers of information society services* (*e-commerce platforms, social networks, etc.*), as well as public administrations to adopt appropriate steps to manage security risks and report serious incidents to the national competent authorities.
>
> (European Commission, 2013, p. 2)[40]

Clearly, the proposed measure concerned with the security of the 'upper level of the internet' occupied by information society service providers, as opposed to the 'lower level', mainly consisting of public communication networks and electronic communications services. Had the proposed measure become law without any changes as to its scope, it would have been the first European legislative instrument imposing security obligations on providers of information society services. As is shown in the following, this was not meant to happen, yet, fortunately, the 2016 Network and Information Systems Security Directive (NISD) does cover certain specific information society services including automated marketplaces. Thus, the particular measure is very relevant to automated marketplaces and goes a long way towards boosting the adequacy of the EU legal response regarding the security risks associated with them. The route to this achievement, however, has been somewhat 'dramatic', with the EU legislator recognizing the sensitivity of marketplace services and doing the right thing literally the last minute.

39 On the security-related actions of the European Commission, see also European Commission (2013, pp. 4–5). Irion (2012, pp. 8–12) offers a comprehensive summary of EU governance activities in the domain of network and information security.

40 Emphasis added.

The NISD adopts the definition of 'network and information system' security found in the ENISA Regulation that clearly covers data authentication and integrity.[41] Article 1(2) of the Proposed measure stated that the Directive, amongst others, "(c) establishes security requirements for market operators and public administrations". The corresponding provision in the (final) NISD, namely Article 1(2)(d) refers to "security and notification requirements for operators of essential services and for digital service providers" instead. The latter apparently comprise a much narrower class than 'market operators', yet in any event, the NISD obligations were never intended to apply ***indiscriminately to all*** information society services. This is not problematic; the said services constitute a vast category of services, and security is not always an issue.[42]

In the Proposed NISD, the establishment of security requirements for market operators and public administrations was achieved through Article 14 in a way strongly resembling the legislative approach towards security in the GDPR, the EPD and the Framework Directive. Thus, Article 14(1) laid down obligations to adopt appropriate technical and organizational security-related measures "to manage the risks posed to the security of the networks and information systems which they control and use in their operations"[43]and notification duties in case of a security breach affecting their services.[44] The said obligations were addressed to public administrations and 'market operators', the latter being defined to include, apart from critical infrastructure operators,[45] "provider[s] of information society services which enable the provision of other information society services, a non-exhaustive list of which is set out in Annex II".[46] This list included six notorious internet players, namely e-commerce platforms ***and, hence, automated marketplaces,*** internet payment gateways, social networks, search engines, cloud computing services and application stores. The Commission was definitely right; the proposed measure was closing existing legislative loopholes relating to network information security (NIS),[47] one of which was, already explained, the absence of security obligations regarding information society service providers, such as automated marketplaces or platforms, that operate ***independently of whether personal data is involved.***

41 See supra p. 153 and Articles 4(2), NISD. Moreover, according to Article 4(1), 'network and information system' means: "(a) an electronic communications network within the meaning of Directive 2002/21/EC, and (b) any device or group of inter-connected or related devices, one or more of which, pursuant to a program, perform automatic processing of computer data, as well as (c) computer data stored, processed, retrieved or transmitted by elements covered under point (a) and (b) for the purposes of their operation, use, protection and maintenance". It thus covers networks, interconnected data processing devices and the transmitted and processed data as such. All these together would obviously cover any e-commerce platform, including an automated marketplace.

42 A website intending to provide information about a company and its services is an 'information society service' and yet, its availability poses no serious security risks and the provider needs not be imposed with any heavy security-related obligations.

43 Article 14(1), Proposed NISD.

44 Article 14(2), Proposed NISD.

45 These are those "essential for the maintenance of vital economic and societal activities in the fields of energy, transport, banking, stock exchanges and health, a non-exhaustive list of which is set out in Annex II", Article 3(8)(b), Proposed NISD.

46 Article 3(8)(a), Proposed NISD.

47 "A step-change is therefore needed in the way NIS is dealt with in the EU. Regulatory obligations are required to create a level playing field and close existing legislative loopholes. To address these problems and increase the level of NIS within the European Union, the objectives of the proposed Directive are as follows" (European Commission, 2013, p. 4).

Additionally, similarly to the GDPR,[48] the NISD obligations are applicable to providers offering services in the EU, irrespective of whether they are established and/or maintain their systems in the US, for example.[49] This evinces the response of EU to the global nature of the internet, and is very important in the context of automated marketplaces. Given the example of eBay and Amazon, automated marketplaces are likely to grow big in the US, with their services being offered worldwide, including in the EU.

However, during the preparatory stages of the NISD, the coverage of automated marketplaces became uncertain. This uncertainty and the route to the eventual coverage of the 'big' marketplaces by the NISD will now be explained, as this will effectively illustrate both the justifiability of marketplaces being imposed with security obligations through the relevant measure and the scope of application of the relevant measure regarding these particular actors.

The European Parliament had backed the Commission Proposal, albeit with 138 amendments. The 51st amendment deleted Article 3(8)(a) (European Parliament, 2014a), thus removing from the scope of the measure 'information society service' providers and "significantly water[ing] down the effect of the Directive, as such operators are central to the online world and the economy as a whole" (Arthur Cox, 2014, p. 4). Rather unconvincingly, the relevant amendment seems to have been proposed in the name of "proportionality and swift results of the Directive" (European Parliament, 2014b, sec. 2A). Indeed, Article 14(1), Proposed NISD *already* had a built-in proportionality element, which has remained intact in the corresponding Article 16(1), NISD; the required security measures have to "guarantee a level of security *appropriate to the risk presented*".

Another reason behind the said Parliamentary amendment, namely, "overlapping regulation" (Dekker, 2013, p. 24), specifically, 'double notification' duties, is not impossible to address, either. Recital 31, Proposed NISD clearly stated, "Member states shall implement the obligation to notify security incidents in a way that minimises the administrative burden in case the security incident is also a personal data breach", that must be notified under the GDPR.[50] Moreover, double notification duties also exist elsewhere in EU law[51] and there are therefore some interesting ideas regarding how the problem can be addressed.[52] Accordingly, the Parliament's sweeping amendment that removed *all* security obligations regarding information service providers was clearly a disproportionate response to double notification duties.

Lastly, the Proposed NISD and in particular, the security obligations of Article 14 (now Article 16, NISD) embodied an application of the 'Think Small First' principle,[53] effectively exempting small enterprises from certain EU legislation or choosing a lighter regime for them (European Commission, 2011b, p. 3, 7). The same is true of Article 16(11), NISD, which explicitly renders Article 16, i.e., the security obligations of digital service providers inapplicable to small and microenterprises. Considering that microenterprises account for 92% of SMEs, which in turn account for 99% of all enterprises (European Commission, 2011b, p. 2.), it becomes clear that the Parliamentary removal of information society

48 Article 3(2), GDPR.

49 Article 18(2), NISD.

50 Supra Chapter 4 p. 133. Notification duties exist in Article 16(3), NISD.

51 An example can be seen in Article 13a, Framework Directive and Article 4, EPD.

52 On this issue and the idea that ENISA develops a single notification template, see Dekker (2013, pp. 24–26). ENISA's proposal for one security framework for Article 13a and Article 4 (Dekker, Karsberg and Moulinos, 2013) is also relevant.

53 Article 14(8), Proposed NISD.

services from the scope of the Proposal would only lighten the relevant burden for the very few powerful businesses, which are in *no* need for such treatment and whose services pose serious security risks (amongst others, due to their big customer base).

When the Proposed NISD has been debated before the Council, some Member States insisted for some information society services to remain within the scope of the measure (Fleming, 2015). A possibility arose for information society services that provide vital services to critical infrastructure operators (Stokes, 2015) to be included; of course, a business-to-consumer automated marketplace is not one such service. The Council proposed that Member States are allowed to decide which critical infrastructure operators within the domains specified in Article 3(8)(b)[54] should be subjected to the obligations of the Directive (Stokes, 2015). The said solution was not any relevant to automated marketplaces, either. What is definite is that the exclusion of (at least) large scale technical contracting environments fully relying on network and information systems did not sit easily with the view that "in public policy, information and communications technology (ICT) infrastructures are typically regarded as critical information infrastructures" (Irion, 2012, p. 1).

Fortunately, the main security obligations of the (final) NISD are addressed to certain information society services through Article 16(1), NISD addressed to the so-called 'digital service providers':

> Member States shall ensure that digital service providers identify and take appropriate and proportionate technical and organisational measures to manage the risks posed to the security of network and information systems which they use in the context of offering services referred to in Annex III within the Union. Having regard to the state of the art, those measures shall ensure a level of security of network and information systems appropriate to the risk posed, and shall take into account the following elements: (a) the security of systems and facilities; (b) incident handling; (c) business continuity management; (d) monitoring, auditing and testing; (e) compliance with international standards.

Though this category of providers ('digital service providers') appears broad, it is defined rather restrictively in Article 4(5) as "a service within the meaning of point (b) of Article 1 (1) of Directive (EU) 2015/1535 of the European Parliament and of the Council (17) which is of a type listed in Annex III". Annex III is short and only includes online marketplaces, search engines and cloud computing services. Though their inclusion in the scope of application of the NISD seems to have been affected by a concern for businesses relying on the them and ultimately, the internal market,[55] there is certainly a direct benefit to consumer protection given that the relevant services are prominent examples of consumer services. Automated marketplaces clearly fall within the first of these three 'digital service' types; an online marketplace is broadly defined in a technology-neutral way as "a digital service that allows consumers and/or traders as respectively defined in point (a) and in point (b) of Article 4(1) of Directive 2013/11/EU of the European Parliament and of the Council to conclude online sales or service contracts with traders either on the online marketplace's website or on a trader's website that uses computing services provided by the online

54 These are domains such as energy and transport, see supra n. 45

55 Indeed, Recital 48, NISD, amongst others, states that "those digital service providers that are subject to this Directive are those that are considered to offer digital services on which many businesses in the Union increasingly rely".

marketplace". Evidently, the definition covers only marketplaces allowing for *actual* contract conclusion, and thus any services only involved in pre-contractual stages such as price comparison websites do not qualify as online marketplaces for the purposes of the NISD.[56] Given that transactional security issues mostly arise in the context of automated marketplaces,[57] this cannot be considered problematic. Moreover, it reflects a recognition of contract conclusion as a security-sensitive activity and of automated marketplaces as services entailing increased security risks. In this respect, the NISD greatly improves the response of the EU law to the said risks, thereby reducing the previously illustrated relevant gap.[58]

Of course, the NISD does not fully close the said gap. First of all, because of Article 16 (11), NISD and the 'Think Small First' principle,[59] only the few large- and medium-sized enterprises are obliged to take care of the security of their marketplaces in accordance with Article 16(1). Fortunately, the gap is not enormous as it is kept limited by the security obligations (with the limitations described earlier) flowing from the GDPR, which does not exclude small data controllers. This can, however, potentially lead to a multiplicity of levels of protection afforded to consumers transacting on marketplaces, depending on the size of the business running the marketplace utilized. This is undesirable, as relevant protection must mainly depend on the security risks involved in a given service, rather than on the size of the provider who provides it. Moreover, *all* consumers need to be able to rely on secure marketplaces for contracting. The built-in proportionality element in Article 16(1), NISD[60] was probably enough to account for the interests of small providers.

Another weakness of the NISD (regarding its ability to fully cover for the security issues associated with automated marketplaces) is that it is not tailored to contracting-related security. Rather, it is a general cybersecurity measure bound to miss some of the specific security aspects of contracting, such as non-repudiation. Indeed, as already explained,[61] the definition of security adopted in the NISD, including Article 16(1),[62] does not specifically account for non-repudiation. The concept of 'availability' in the relevant definition seems mostly to connote the availability or continuity of the service as such[63] whereas non-repudiation requires the availability of certain particular data that can serve as concrete or indisputable evidence of a concluded transaction. Accordingly, whether measures ensuring non-repudiation constitutes a requirement under Article 16(1), NISD is at the very least uncertain. Moreover, if it is true that measures achieving data authentication (an element explained previously as covered by the definition of information and network security) may not necessarily achieve non-repudiation, too (Pornin, 2011), one cannot hope that the former will be achieved through measures aiming at the latter.

Still, the fact that large automated marketplaces have been brought within the scope of application of the NISD, which extends security obligations to data regardless of it being personal or not, comprises a significant improvement of the EU legal response towards the relevant risks. As is shown, another EU measure, namely the eIDAS Regulation, can further

56 This is made clearer in Recital 15, NISD.
57 Supra Chapter 1 p. 16
58 Supra p. 156
59 Supra pp. 159–160
60 Supra p. 160
61 Supra pp. 153, 158
62 Supra p. 160
63 See supra p. 153. Article 16(2), NISD makes specific reference to availability requiring providers to take measures limiting the impact of security incidents on their services so as to ensure "with a view to ensuring the continuity of those services". See also Recital 48, NISD.

boost the adoption of security technology in automated marketplaces, thereby improving the adequacy of the relevant legal responsefurther. This is so especially given that the eIDAS focuses on security in contracting, as opposed to data (and system) security in general.

5.3.3.2.3 THE EIDAS

5.3.3.2.3.1 THE BACKGROUND TO THE EIDAS

The predecessor of the eIDAS Regulation is the Electronic Signatures Directive (ESD). The ESD was up until 2014 the only measure explicitly concerning with data authentication. Recognizing that "electronic communication and commerce necessitate electronic signatures and related services allowing data authentication",[64] the Directive intended to offer them a (legal) boost facilitating their use and contributing in their legal recognition.[65] It provided clear definitions for 'electronic signatures'[66] and 'advanced electronic signatures'[67] and sought to ensure that electronic signatures would not be deprived of legal effect as a result of their electronic nature or even due to not being *advanced* electronic signatures.[68] It thus avoided a discriminatory approach as between the various signature types,[69] recognizing that there may be low-risk relationships or transactions in relation to which the increased security[70] inherent in advance electronic signatures would constitute an unnecessary burden for parties.

Plain 'electronic signatures' cannot verify the real identity of the signatory.[71] A digitalized copy of a signature can be affixed on a document, and a contractual offer may be sent through a password-protected marketplace account, yet there is no guarantee that those 'data authenticating' acts have indeed been performed by the person whose name appears on the signature or the account. Without additional measures, anyone can make a digitalized copy of a signature. Similarly, anyone can apply for a password-protected online account, amongst others, to gain access to a marketplace. There is no established link between the data submitted and the identity of the party submitting it.

To afford an extra boost to secure signatures that *allow for real-identity authentication*, the ESD implemented a two-tier approach (Barofsky, 2000, p. 157; Spyrelli, 2002, sec. 3.3). Thus, if certain requirements were met, advanced electronic signatures were considered as *qualified* advanced electronic signatures and were given stronger legal effect. More

64 Recital 4, ESD.
65 Article 1, ESD.
66 "'electronic signature' means data in electronic form which are attached to or logically associated with other electronic data and which serve as a method of authentication", Article 2(1), ESD.
67 "'advanced electronic signature' means an electronic signature which meets the following requirements: (a) it is uniquely linked to the signatory; (b) it is capable of identifying the signatory; (c) it is created using means that the signatory can maintain under his sole control; and (d) it is linked to the data to which it relates in such a manner that any subsequent change of the data is detectable", Article 2(2), ESD.
68 Article 5(2), ESD.
69 Electronic signatures can take various forms including typing a name on a document, clicking on an 'I agree' button, affixing a digitalized copy of signature on a document, utilizing a password or PIN such as to withdraw money or encryption-associated private keys. See, amongst others, Mason (2006, pp. 157–158) and Barofsky (2000, p. 150).
70 See Article 2(2), ESD, supra n. 67.
71 As Mason (2006, pp. 155–156) states, an electronic signature within the meaning of Article 2(1) of the Directive "only serves to authenticate data. In contrast, a qualified certification is capable of identifying a person or entity". On certificates (including qualified ones) see infra p. 167

specifically, they were equated with handwritten signatures[72] and their legal admissibility as evidence was explicitly recognized.[73] For a signature to qualify as an 'advanced electronic signature', there had be a secure signature creation device involved[74] and a third party certifying the required link between the signature and the (real) identity of the signatory. The Directive additionally laid down security-enhancing requirements that such devices[75] and third parties (certification service providers)[76] could meet. If those requirements were all met, the signature was not merely an advanced electronic signature but a *qualified* advanced electronic signature enjoying the strongest legal recognition.

Both signature types enabled identity verification (or authentication) but the latter was capable of performing this function more reliably than the former. In fact, qualified electronic signatures are capable of achieving authentication, integrity, confidentiality and non-repudiation (de Andrade et al., 2014, p. 13), i.e., full transactional security. The non-repudiation capabilities of qualified electronic signatures are particularly important given that as illustrated previously, neither the GDPR nor the NISD clearly provide for this element of transactional security.

The Electronic Signatures Directive did not *impose* the use of the qualified or even of the non-qualified advanced (and thus, *authentication-enabling*) signature. It was not a measure from which security-related legal obligations were directly flowing. Besides, security-related *legal* obligations often entail a proportionality mechanism that allows the addressee of the obligation to choose the security solution by reference to the (level) of the risk involved. Indiscriminately requiring the use of advanced or qualified advanced signatures would thus be inappropriate. Moreover, qualified advanced signatures comprise one technological way in which data security could be achieved while laws must notoriously be technologically neutral. Notably, even without requiring the use of advanced signatures, the ESD did not manage this kind of neutrality (Barofsky, 2000, pp. 157–158); in practice, the underlying technology in the 'secure signature' definitions of the ESD was encryption-based public key infrastructure (PKI).[77]

In any event, the ESD evinced a strong emphasis on online transactional security and a willingness to encourage the employment of *effective* security measures in electronic transactions.[78] Its suitability in the context of automated marketplaces, however, was doubtful. As Subirana and Bain (2005, p. 86) observe, the ESD defined an advanced electronic signature by reference to a requirement that it be "created using means that the signatory can maintain under his *sole* control",[79] whereas in automated marketplaces, the signature creation means are to be handled by contracting software and, thus, by parties (specifically, marketplace providers) other than the signatory.

72 Article 5(1)(a), ESD.
73 Article 5(1)(b), ESD.
74 Recital 15, ESD.
75 Article 2(6), ESD.
76 Articles 2(9)–(11), ESD.
77 At the time, PKI was the only solution that could achieve the constituting security-related ingredients of the advanced electronic signature (Dumortier, 1999, p. 35) and hence, a security-oriented definition of signatures could not really be totally technology neutral. See also, Blythe (2005, p. 18).
78 As Blythe, 2005, p. 9 wrote "because of its emphasis on attainment of security, the Directive does seem to implicitly suggest the use of more sophisticated and security-minded technologies such as PKI".
79 Article 2(2)(c), ESD, emphasis added.

5.3.3.2.3.2 THE CONTRIBUTION OF THE EIDAS IN ADDRESSING THE TRANSACTIONAL SECURITY RISKS

The ESD failed fully to achieve the expected market boost in digital (or security-enabling) signatures; they had been enjoying limited use, specifically, only in the e-banking sector and for access to certain public services (European Commission, 2006, pp. 6, 10). Service providers were (and largely still are) developing their own often 'soft identification' mechanisms (such as passwords). The ESD has been repealed by the E-Identification, Authentication and Trust Services (eIDAS) Regulation, which recognizes that the ESD has failed to deliver "a comprehensive cross-border and cross-sector framework for secure, trustworthy and easy-to-use electronic transactions".[80] The eIDAS does not, however, achieve any dramatic breakthrough; just like the ESD, it does *not* impose an obligation on e-commerce platform (marketplace) providers to use any of the relevant security-enhancing measures.

Indeed, a main criticism against the eIDAS has been that in regulating website authentication services, it refrains from obliging website operators to use those services (Arnbak and van Eijk, 2012, p. 24; Asghari et al., 2013, p.25; Arnbak, 2015, p. 234).[81] However, as much as critics (Arnbak, 2015, p. 56) remain unconvinced by the reasons put forward by the EU Commission, namely that devising the relevant rules would be very complicated, the Regulation is intended to target the security services *as such* rather than the online actors who can utilize them. Moreover, legal security-related obligations on such actors cannot consist of patchworks. Indeed, obliging merchants effectively to authenticate themselves when conducting commerce through a website but *not* when they sell on the website of an intermediary, such as an automated marketplace provider, does not obviously add enough to security; the authentication of the website of the marketplace would be of limited significance if the authenticated entity behind that website does not authenticate the merchants who sell through its marketplace.

A legal obligation to ensure transactional security fits better within a measure intended to take a more direct approach towards online security, thereby addressing relevant obligations to the actors who can employ the various security-enhancing solutions. As illustrated previously, such a measure now exists at EU level; the NISD imposes a general security obligation on certain information society service providers, including large marketplace providers, yet it lacks elements specific to transactional security or security for *contracting* environments, particularly non-repudiation and is additionally inapplicable to small marketplaces, even when expensive products are traded.[82] Most certainly, these gaps in EU transactional security law cannot completely be filled in by the eIDAS, yet its specific solutions of contracting-related security that, as it will be shown, cover non-repudiation too, can be exploited by marketplace providers in the context of complying with their security obligations imposed by the NISD. In other words, the regulation of signatures by the eIDAS coupled with the imposition of relevant security obligations by the NISD significantly increases the chances of the adoption of the relevant security technologies ultimately resulting in large automated marketplaces affording full transactional security.

80 Recital 3, eIDAS.

81 Recital 67, eIDAS: "Website authentication services provide a means by which a visitor to a website can be assured that there is a genuine and legitimate entity standing behind the website. Those services contribute to the building of trust and confidence in conducting business online, as users will have confidence in a website that has been authenticated. *The provision and the use of website authentication services are entirely voluntary*" (emphasis added).

82 Supra p. 161

This possible beneficial synergy between the two measures is reinforced by the fact that similarly to the NISD, the eIDAS is not tied to personal data. The emphasis is on the security of *electronic transactions* as such,[83] and though the term 'security' is not defined (Arnbak, 2015, p. 56), nothing in the Regulation ties security to personal data protection. By referring to the Data Protection Directive,[84] the Regulation does not really intend a conceptualization of security as others (Arnbak, 2015, p. 56) suggest. It just responds to the notorious tension between privacy and data minimization on the one hand and security and identification on the other, clarifying that the eIDAS does not suggest the use of identification technologies where *not* necessary in the light of the existing risk.

Having shown that the eIDAS can in fact be very relevant to automated marketplaces, its provisions, particularly the ones referring to digital signatures and trust services, which play a vital role in transactional security will now be discussed. The aim is to understand how it regulates the relevant technologies or services and see whether there are any suitability or applicability issues in the context of automated marketplaces.

5.3.3.2.3.3 THE CONTENT OF THE EIDAS

The Regulation has three main pillars, namely electronic identification (e-identification), trust services and electronic signatures.[85] Regarding electronic signatures, the Regulation maintains the essence of the ESD but expands upon it in ways that certainly enhance the security and reliability of the digital signature that is equated with its handwritten counterpart. It thus goes further than the ESD in answering the objection against technical non-repudiation, namely that the latter is practically infeasible, thereby leading to false or unfair presumptions.[86]

More specifically, the Regulation explicitly introduces what existed implicitly in the ESD regime, namely a third type of electronic signatures called 'qualified electronic signature', defined as an advanced electronic signature[87] created by a qualified signature creation device and based on a qualified certificate for electronic signatures.[88] This is the signature recognized as equivalent to handwritten signature and must meet very detailed requirements of security ensuring that the signature indeed achieves *true authentication, integrity and non-repudiation*. The relevant requirements are long and complex, but they are divided into those concerning the device used to create the signature and those relating to the certificate for the signature.[89] The latter is further divided into two sub-categories, the first referring to the certificate as such and the other to the trust service provider issuing it.

83 See Recitals 1 and 2, eIDAS.

84 Recital 11, eIDAS: "This Regulation should be applied in full compliance with the principles relating to the protection of personal data provided for in Directive 95/46/EC. . . . In this respect, having regard to the principle of mutual recognition established by this Regulation, authentication for an online service should concern processing of only those identification data that are adequate, relevant and not excessive to grant access to that service online. Furthermore, requirements under Directive 95/46/EC concerning confidentiality and security of processing should be respected by trust service providers and supervisory bodies".

85 Article 1, eIDAS.

86 On this issue, see supra p. 150

87 The definition of 'advanced electronic signatures' in Articles 3(11) and 26, eIDAS remains essentially the same with that in the Directive, see supra pp. 162–163

88 Article 3(12), eIDAS.

89 "'certificate for electronic signature' means an electronic attestation which links electronic signature validation data to a natural person and confirms at least the name or the pseudonym of that person", Article 13(14), eIDAS.

The device-oriented requirements are listed in Annex II, eIDAS[90] and similarly to the ESD, they refer to the implementation of technical and procedural means ensuring the confidentiality of the signature creation data and preventing its forgery or unauthorized use.[91] The relevant requirements also restrict the freedom of trust service providers to duplicate signature generation data, thereby weakening its security, and permit such duplicating only for back-up purposes, to the extent absolutely necessary and provided that any duplicates are as secure as the originals.[92]

The requirement in paragraph 3 of Annex II stating that "generating or managing electronic signature creation data on behalf of the signatory may only be done by a qualified trust service provider" is of particular importance in the context of automated marketplaces. More specifically, it remedies a problem inherent in the ESD,[93] which did not recognize the possibility of the signature creation data not being generated and/or managed by the signatory *personally*. One such case is when the signatory delegates the handling of the contractual process to software within an automated marketplace. Paragraph 3 Annex II therefore opens up the way for the use of qualified digital signatures within automated marketplaces.

The Regulation states that signature creation devices shall undergo an evaluation against relevant security assessment standards to be listed by the Commission through an implementing act (or another evaluation process using comparable security levels) with the aim of ascertaining and certifying conformity with the previously stated requirements of Annex II.[94] The relevant evaluation shall be carried out by public or private bodies designated by Member States[95] in accordance with criteria that the Commission is empowered to introduce through delegated acts.[96] All certified signature-creation devices shall be notified to the Commission, which shall publish them in a relevant list.[97] The security standards against which signature creation devices must be evaluated have been published in the Commission Implementing Decision (EU) 2016/650. The Commission specifically takes up the requirement in paragraph 3, Annex II and usefully draws a clear distinction between the cases "when the signatory physically possesses a product and when a qualified trust service provider operates on behalf of the signatory",[98] recognizing that "the security requirements and their respective certification specifications are different".[99] Though the security standards included in the Decision are only those for the first of the two cases,[100] it is made clear in the Decision that the Commission intends to specify standards for the second case, too.[101] In the meantime, the security assessment and certification of relevant products "shall be based on a process that, pursuant to Article 30(3)(b), uses security levels comparable to those required by Article 30(3)(a) and is notified to the Commission by the public or private body referred to in paragraph 1 of Article 30 of Regulation (EU) No 910/2014".[102] In this respect, the Regulation clearly recognizes the need for the (increased) security afforded by

90 Article 29(1), eIDAS.
91 Annex II(1), eIDAS.
92 Annex II(4), eIDAS.
93 Supra p. 163
94 Article 30(3), eIDAS.
95 Article 30(1), eIDAS.
96 Article 30(4), eIDAS.
97 Article 31, eIDAS.
98 Recital 5, Commission Implementing Decision (EU) 2016/650.
99 Ibid.
100 Article 1(1), Commission Implementing Decision (EU) 2016/650.
101 Ibid.
102 Article 1(2), Commission Implementing Decision (EU) 2016/650.

qualified electronic signatures in environments where it is simply impracticable (or even unworkable) to require that the device is physically held and possessed by the signatory. Automated marketplaces certainly comprise such environments. Most importantly, it responds to the said need without failing to take into account the increased security-related vulnerabilities, which will have to be addressed through specifically designed standards.

As stated previously, apart from having to be created by a qualified signature device, a qualified signature must be based on a certificate, that is, "an electronic attestation which links electronic signature validation data to a natural person and confirms at least the name or the pseudonym of that person",[103] which must be qualified, too. To be 'qualified', a certificate must be issued by a qualified trust service provider and meet the requirements laid down in Annex I.[104] The certificate-oriented requirements of Annex I are largely taken from the ESD and mainly aim at the reliability and/or effectiveness of certificates by imposing rules of content; qualified certificates must for example, include an indication of their nature as qualified, the identity of the issuing trust service provider, their period of validity and location of services through which validity can be confirmed. A stronger security-oriented requirement arises from paragraphs (g)-(h), Annex I by virtue of which, qualified certificates must contain the *advanced* electronic signature (or seal) of the trust service provider issuing them as well as the location from which the certificate for that signature (or seal) can be checked out.

To be qualified, certificates must also be issued by a qualified trust service provider, i. e., "a trust service provider who provides one or more qualified trust services and is granted the qualified status by the supervisory body".[105] The Regulation responds to the need for sufficient supervision of trusted third parties and more generally, for a real co-regulatory approach.[106] Trusted third parties effectively act as private regulators regulating the process towards the conclusion of a transaction. The law (in this case, the eIDAS) is involved in the rule-making part of this private regulation, as it lays down detailed requirements that trusted services should meet and, in effect, the rules according to which the relevant private regulation should be conducted. It is also involved in the enforcement part of the said regulation by providing for the approval and ongoing supervision of trust service providers by accredited bodies which act in co-operation with a public authority. Moreover, it ensures publicity for those providers choosing to submit to the relevant system of detailed criteria and supervision and incentivizes submission by attaching greater legal weight to their services. It even establishes an accountability system for such providers and, thus, probably constitutes the most complete co-regulatory solution in EU law.

More specifically, the Regulation lays down detailed requirements that trust service providers and their services should meet to qualify as 'qualified'[107] and permits the award of the status only when compliance with them is assessed by an accredited conformity assessment body[108] and confirmed by the national supervisory body[109] to which the conformity assessment report of the former body must be submitted.[110] If the relevant status must be

103 Article 3(14), eIDAS.
104 Article 3(15), eIDAS.
105 Article 2(20), eIDAS.
106 On the necessary elements of co-regulation, see supra Chapter 4.3.5.2
107 Article 24, eIDAS.
108 Article 20(4), eIDAS.
109 Article 17, eIDAS.
110 Article 21(1), eIDAS.

awarded, the supervisory body must inform the trust service provider accordingly and also notify the national body managing the public lists of qualified trust service providers[111] so that the latter can update the said 'trusted list'. When the name of the qualified trust service provider is placed in the 'trusted list', the said provider can start providing its qualified trust services[112] and can use the EU trust mark, which links to the relevant trusted list[113] in order "to indicate in a simple, recognisable and clear manner the qualified trust services they provide".[114]

Supervision of qualified trust service providers is ongoing as, amongst others, they must submit a conformity assessment report to the supervisory body at least every 24 months.[115] This latter obligation can prompt the exercise of the supervisory powers, thereby enabling actual and meaningful supervision. Indeed, the long and detailed Articles 17 and 20, eIDAS confirm that unlike the ESD, which was confined to vaguely requiring the establishment of a system of supervision for qualified certification providers,[116] the Regulation seems to take supervision seriously, as it lays down specific duties and powers to be discharged or exercised by the relevant supervisory bodies. It thus leaves little room for a shallow or practically inactive supervision system. Another feature of the Regulation greatly assisting in meaningful supervision is the fact that a significant part of the cost of that supervision is expressly placed on the trust providers themselves.[117] Though the Regulation specifically states that "supervisory bodies shall be given the necessary powers and adequate resources for the exercise of their tasks",[118] shifting costs to the regulated industry is important. Public supervisory authorities notoriously often possess limited resources, something that is often the reason behind legally mandated, yet practically weak, supervision.

Of course, adopting such cost-shifting approach in a domain where there is a demonstrated 'incentive problem' (Asghari et al., 2013, pp. 23–24) mainly due to the voluntary nature of the use of the relevant services can threaten the overall success of the measure. In this respect, though the "prevailing economic rationale" of the Regulation has troubled commentators (Arnbak, 2015, p. 235), putting the emphasis on the internal market of trust services was a wise option. The eIDAS, unlike the ESD, contains an internal market clause obliging Member States to accept and recognize qualified electronic signatures, seals and time stamps issued in another Member State.[119] In this way, it opens up the economic benefits of the internal market to the businesses, which would invest in the trust services domain, thereby addressing the aforementioned incentive problem.

As the security-enhancing properties of qualified electronic signatures would be undermined in the absence of a procedure that relying parties could follow to validate the signature, the Regulation lays down requirements that must be met for a qualified electronic signature to be considered as validated[120] and also provides that the validation process must

111 Article 22(3), eIDAS.
112 Article 21(3), eIDAS.
113 Article 23(2), eIDAS.
114 Article 23(1), eIDAS.
115 Article 20(1), eIDAS.
116 Article 3(3), ESD.
117 Article 20(1), eIDAS reads as follows: "Qualified trust service providers shall be audited *at their own expense* at least every 24 months by a conformity assessment body" (emphasis added). The same is said in relation to additional audit that may specifically be requested by the supervisory body pursuant to Article 20(2), eIDAS.
118 Article 17(1), eIDAS.
119 Article 4, eIDAS
120 Article 32(1), eIDAS.

allow relying parties to detect any security defects.[121] Thus, Article 33, eIDAS provides that the validation process must be provided by a qualified trust service provider in accordance with the requirements of Article 32(1),[122] who must allow "relying parties to receive the result in an automated manner, which is reliable, efficient and bears the advanced electronic signature or advanced electronic seal of the provider of the qualified validation service".[123] By referring to the 'relying party', Article 33, eIDAS does not envisage the possibility of the validation result having to be communicated to software substituting the relying party. Yet, as the Regulation recognizes that a signature can be created *on behalf of* the human signatory, as explained previously,[124] it is not very difficult to interpret it as *not* requiring the *personal involvement* of the said human party in the signature validation process. The relying party will have to be taken to cover software acting on his behalf (capable of reading and acting upon the validation process result).

The eIDAS also regulates *all* trust service providers, including non-qualified ones; along similar lines to Article 32, GDPR, Article 19(1), eIDAS obliges relevant providers to "take appropriate technical and organisational measures to manage the risks posed to the security of the trust services they provide". However, the supervisory body does not have to audit or monitor compliance on the part of *non-qualified* providers[125] and only has to take action after the fact, "when informed that those non-qualified trust service providers or the trust services they provide allegedly do not meet the requirements laid down in this Regulation".[126] This 'light supervision' approach has caused negative criticism (Arnbak, 2015, p. 236), yet it is somewhat counterbalanced by the liability threat created by Article 13, eIDAS Regulation. The latter renders trust service providers, qualified *and* non-qualified, liable for damage caused intentionally or negligently due to a failure to comply with their obligations under the Regulation.[127] Unlike the ESD, therefore, which imposed liability only on qualified providers,[128] the Regulation imposes liability on non-qualified ones, too. A liability rule is all the more important in the light of past experience showing that damage-causing poor security practices employed by trust service providers may go unnoticed by independent audits.[129]

Article 13 also adopts a 'reversal of the burden of proof' approach, but only in relation to qualified providers. Thus, while the intention or negligence of the qualified provider is presumed unless the provider proves the lack of such intention or negligence, the intention or negligence of a non-qualified provider has to be proved by the aggrieved party[130] in accordance with national rules on liability.[131] A reversal of the burden of proof in this case seems

121 Article 32(2), eIDAS.
122 Article 33(1)(a), eIDAS.
123 Article 33(1)(b), eIDAS.
124 Supra p. 166
125 Recital 36, eIDAS.
126 Article 17(3)(b), eIDAS.
127 The obligations must be the security-related obligations of Article 19 for all trust service providers and those of Article 24 for qualified ones.
128 Article 6, ESD.
129 Arnbak (2015, pp. 211–213) describes how a Dutch trust service provider which has been hacked by an attacker who have issued hundreds of false SSL certificates causing significant damage had passed several independent security audits.
130 Article 13(1), eIDAS.
131 Article 13(3), eIDAS.

justified; a relevant consideration is the technical or organizational complexity of the activity of the defendant, which makes it particularly difficult for the plaintiff to discharge the onus of proof (Giesen, 2009, p. 52). Trust services, especially those involving the administration of advanced electronic signatures, are indisputably of increased technical complexity.

Other relevant considerations are

> the idea that he who benefits from a certain activity should also bear the extra burdens related to that activity (profit theory), the idea of channeling liability in a certain direction, the idea of promoting preventive effects of (a harsher form of) liability, the need to protect fundamental rights at stake, the wish to decrease the dependence of one party, the need to decrease the imbalance in information between the litigants, the existence of insurance coverage, or to serve the goal of being able to invoke a substantive rule despite evidential difficulties.
>
> (Giesen, 2009, p. 52)

Obviously, most of them apply to the case of trust service providers, whether qualified or non-qualified.

Insurance coverage is amongst the requirements that according to the Regulation, qualified providers must meet.[132] Moreover, by virtue of Article 23 of the Services Directive,[133] insurance may become obligatory for all trust service providers if their service is considered to qualify as one involving serious financial risk.[134] It is not unlikely for their service to be considered as such; in the context of arguing in favour of compulsory insurance in the trust services domain, Arnbak (2015, p. 239) points out that the damage caused by a security breach suffered by trust service providers may often be much larger than the value of the trust service provider.[135]

What is more difficult to explain is the decision of the EU legislator to retain the 'reversal of the burden of proof' mechanism only in the case of qualified service providers, thereby deviating from the Proposal for the Regulation, where there was no relevant distinction between the two categories of providers.[136] The relevant choice has led to criticism (Arnbak, 2015, p. 239), justifiably. The recipients of both categories of trust services have clearly sought out security and must be able to rest assured that they will enjoy it. Though the risk of damage associated with platforms utilizing qualified trust services will probably be more serious, it is not certain that this is capable of justifying such a drastic differentiation regarding the burden of proof. Moreover, given the absence of strict supervision and auditing of non-qualified providers, the relevant liability rule is the only main legal force towards the exercise of care and diligence in the provision of their services.

The eIDAS Regulation has also been attacked (Arnbak, 2015, pp. 239–240) on the grounds that it allows trust service providers to place a cap on the financial value of transactions in relation to which their services can be used and limit their liability to the

132 Article 24(2)(c), eIDAS.

133 On this provision, see also infra p. 171

134 Recognizing that certain services may entail financial risks to recipients, Article 23 of the Services Directive provides for the possibility of nationally imposed requirements that relevant service providers be covered by professional liability insurance.

135 Arnbak (2015, p. 239) cites Baldwin et al. (2011, p. 127) who explain the relevant argument by reference to oil tankers and the damages of a spill which often exceed the value of the company that transports the oil.

136 See Article 9, Proposal (European Commission, 2012b).

corresponding amounts provided they inform their users accordingly.[137] The intention is to enable some predictability in the financial risk to which the liability rule exposes trust service providers and also assists in the insurability of the risk,[138] which is generally very relevant to the collectability of damage and the imposition of liability (Baker, 2006, p. 4; Lewis, 2005; Wagner, 2005).[139]

Central to insurability is the ability of the insurer to predict or assess the risk and most importantly, the damage that can be brought about if the risk materializes (Vate and Dror, 2002, pp. 126, 131; Faure, 2016, p. 619). A liability rule making no effort to facilitate insurability may discourage or even prevent the taking up of the activity, whereas the EU legislator in the context of trust services aimed at exactly the opposite,[140] hence the possibility for the liability limitation in Article 13(2), eIDAS. Besides, the European Commission knows about insurability problems, specifically, from the context of the insurance requirement of Article 23(1) of the Services Directive (European Commission, 2014b, pp. 4, 7, 11, 21), where insurance may be required but is unavailable to service providers.

As already said, unlike the ESD, the Regulation does not merely deal with electronic signatures but instead creates an overall framework for all services that in addition to the electronic signature (and website authentication services[141]) are important to "ensure the security and legal validity of an electronic transaction" (European Commission, 2018f). This perfectly illustrates that the eIDAS comprises a response to the issues of transactional security described at the beginning of this chapter.

Electronic seals are merely the equivalent of electronic signatures for legal persons. This is reflected in the provisions of the Regulation on electronic seals which either reproduce the provisions referring to electronic signatures discussed previously (with the necessary linguistic variations) or specifically state that those provisions apply *mutatis mutandis* to electronic seals.[142] The specific coverage of electronic seals is important especially in Member States in which company laws require the use of a company seal in the context of conclusion of corporate transactions. Moreover, electronic seals seem a suitable option in automated marketplaces, as they sweep away the need to inquire into the authorization of a natural person who purports to use an electronic signature on behalf of a legal person. This latter practice remains acceptable,[143] yet it would normally involve some relevant offline proof such as a company resolution and/or a power of attorney authorizing the natural person to bind the company, which is not consistent with full automation.

The eIDAS additionally contains provisions on time stamping, "i.e. the date and time on an electronic document which proves that the document existed at a point-in-time and that it has not changed since then" (European Commission, 2015). Also, it regulates electronic delivery, "i.e. a service that, to a certain extent, is the equivalent in the digital world of registered mail in the physical world" (European Commission, 2015). More specifically, it

137 Article 13(2), eIDAS.
138 See Recital 37, eIDAS.
139 It should be noted that there is no relevant consensus on whether this is or ought to be the case, as certain commentators think insurability does not and should not have an impact on tort rules regarding liability.
140 Supra p. 168
141 Supra p. 164
142 Articles 35, 36, 37 and 38, eIDAS on electronic seals correspond to Articles 25, 26, 27 and 28, eIDAS on electronic signatures. Articles 39 and 40, eIDAS on electronic seals state that Articles 29–34 on electronic signatures apply in the same way in the context of electronic seals.
143 Recital 58, eIDAS.

seeks to ensure that these contracting-related tools will not be denied legal effect or admissibility by reason of being electronic[144] at the same time laying down security-related requirements that relevant qualified service providers must meet,[145] so that they can be secure enough to deserve such treatment. Qualified service providers also enjoy presumptions of accuracy and integrity of relevant data such as the time that a document has been created, sent or received.[146] Finally, Article 46 confirms that the electronic form of documents must not deprive them of legal effect or admissibility.

All in all, it is clear that the eIDAS comprehensively provides for the electronic counterparts of all offline contracting tools and practices, thereby creating suitable conditions for electronic, including fully automated, contracting to thrive. More importantly, it makes available to automated marketplace providers everything they would need to provide *secure* contracting services and more generally, meet their security obligations flowing from other measures such as the GDPR and the NISD.

5.4 Concluding remarks

This chapter has focused on the risks associated with automated marketplaces that pertain to transactional security and the current EU legal response to the said risks. First, it has illustrated the need for effective transactional security, i.e., data integrity, authentication and non-repudiation in fully automated contracting environments where the contracting parties, including consumers, do not have personal involvement in the contractual process and, thus, fully rely on the software systems of the marketplace provider. After showing that it is technologically possible for relevant providers to offer *secure* contracting services that take into account all three of the aforementioned transactional security elements, it has been suggested that the law should not hesitate to require that they in fact have relevant security obligations that of course take into account the gravity of the risk involved. It has been argued that such automated contracting services are inherently risky (as they can alter the legal status of users), so there can be no provision of contracting services without an obligation that these are secure. However, the more serious the risk involved, the more stringent (or advanced) the transactional security measures that should be required for any security obligations to be considered as discharged.

The chapter then looked into relevant EU law in search for its response to the aforementioned need and has, in that context, discussed in detail some important new EU legal measures including the NISD and the eIDAS. It mainly found that the general security obligations contained in Article 32, GDPR burden *all* automated marketplace providers as data controllers and are subject to a proportionality criterion relating to the risk involved. Those obligations cover data integrity and albeit less directly, also authentication, but it is rather difficult to derive from them an obligation to adopt *technical* non-repudiation measures, too. Moreover, the said security obligations do not focus on transactional security but are tied to the involvement of *personal* data, something which may result in security gaps, especially when a contractual communication comes from the merchant, a legal person and may contain no personal data. It has been suggested that transactional security should be

144 Article 41(1) and Article 43(1) for electronic time stamps and electronic registered delivery respectively.

145 Article 42 and Article 44 for qualified electronic time stamps and qualified electronic registered delivery services respectively.

146 Article 41(2) and Article 43(2) for electronic time stamps and electronic registered delivery respectively.

seen by the law as a virtue in its own right, something which was not the case for quite some time in the EU legal landscape; information society services (including automated marketplaces) were not subject to any obligation to take care of the security of their services in general and thus, irrespective of whether personal data was involved.

The NISD came to reduce this gap by imposing general security obligations on certain information service providers (again) subject to a proportionality criterion relating to the risk involved. The said obligations, however, are not addressed to all automated marketplace providers, as small businesses and microenterprises are excluded. Moreover, similarly to the security obligations of the GDPR, they do not focus on transactional security but rather on general data and network security. Whether the non-repudiation element of transactional security is covered by the NISD obligations is, as a result, again uncertain.

The puzzle of the relevant EU legal response is completed by the eIDAS, which definitely focuses on the security of transactions and is therefore not subject to the aforementioned limitations of the GDPR and the NISD. However, though this measure regulates all of the services necessary for a secure contracting environment and accounts for all transactional security elements, it does not (and was not intended to) impose any (direct) obligation on marketplace providers to utilize those services. Of course, amongst others, by establishing their legal validity, it powerfully encourages their use and most definitely deprives relevant providers of any justification for not using them, thereby discharging their obligations imposed by the GDPR and the NISD, when necessary. There is therefore a great potential for a synergy between the GDPR, the NISD and the eIDAS (and as it arises from Chapter 3, the PSD2 too), which can make up for the imperfections of each one of the said measures, thereby leading to a recognized obligation on marketplace providers (particularly those entailing a high risk, for example, because of the value of products traded thereon) to exploit the services of increased transactional security provided for in the eIDAS. If market forces further boost this potential, resulting in its materialization, the EU legal response towards the transactional security risks associated with automated marketplaces will be able to be considered as fully adequate. For the time being, it can be said that EU law definitely contains the raw material of an adequate relevant solution, but only time will show how this combination of the relevant legal measures will work in practice and the results to be achieved.

6 Automated-contract validity and contractual liability in cases of mistaken contracts

6.1 General remarks

This chapter explores two legal issues that go at the heart of the service provided by automated marketplaces. The first refers to the legal validity of the contracts concluded on automated marketplaces. This is guaranteed by EU law, however the legal approach explaining validity is not specified at EU level. The result is (legal) uncertainty, specifically regarding the liability implications of automated contracting for the parties involved. This chapter goes through all possible approaches towards 'automated contract' validity and reaches conclusions as to the most suitable one. It also illustrates that some of the alternatives are very unlikely to be adopted by an EU Member State, something that greatly reduces the uncertainty problem.

The second important issue relates to the liability of consumers for the loss arising out of a mistaken (or erroneous) contract concluded by contracting software. Not all mistaken contracts can be avoided by operation of the doctrine of unilateral mistake, whereas consumer protection dictates that being an innocent party, the consumer must be able to avoid or recoup relevant losses. Mistaken contracts can be divided into those caused by a malfunction of the contracting software and those caused by a mistake of the consumer user in using the contracting software. This distinction seems consistent with Coteanu (2005, p.118) recognizing technological defects and consumer lack of knowledge on the technological abilities of contracting software as two causes of unequal bargaining power between traders and consumers. EU law responds well to the relevant risks, as one can unearth relevant solutions in multiple measures, including the CRD and the UCTD in relation to the first category concerned. As far as the second category is concerned, the ECD contains provisions specifically tackling errors in the use of online contracting tools and also make available to consumers an escape route when merchants do not comply with certain error-preventive obligations. Yet, those have not been devised with automated contracting in mind and suffer from relevant applicability problems.

6.2 Automated-contract validity: illustrating the issue

This is a core issue, as it affects the very purpose of automated marketplaces, namely contract conclusion. If automated contracts were not legally valid or their enforceability was uncertain, the opportunities offered by the relevant technology would be missed; very few would choose to contract on automated marketplaces. As Kerr (1999, p. 208) rightly points out, "In order to fully enjoy the benefits of automation, legislation must include a mechanism that will adequately cure contractual defects so as to ensure that the transactions generated by and through computers are legally enforceable". It would thus be a serious problem if EU law was not clearly providing for the legal validity of automated contracts. Fortunately, as is explained later,[1] this is not case.

1 Infra Chapter 6.3.4

However, the validity of fully automated contracts cannot be explained by traditional 'contract law' principles because, having *no personal* involvement in the transaction, the human contractors cannot be said to have been in agreement (Allen and Widdison, 1996, p. 32). This is true especially when the contracting software is allowed some discretion in closing a deal. For example, this is when it is instructed to buy a digital camera at a maximum price of EUR500.00 to be delivered within a month, and does not act upon rigidly pre-defined user specifications, for example, a Canon EOS 20D Digital SLR Mfg Part No: 9442A002 for EUR265.89 associated with a two-year guarantee to be dispatched in three days.

Traditional solutions such as the objective theory of consent (Weitzenboeck, 2001, p. 221) and the 'unread contract' principle (Allen and Widdison, 1996, pp. 44–45) cannot readily furnish relevant contracts with validity. Admittedly, as Weitzenboeck (2001, pp. 221–222) explains, the first places all of the emphasis on the external appearance of consent and is indifferent as to the actual intentions of the contracting parties: "If whatever a man's real intention may be he so conducts himself that a reasonable man would believe that he was assenting *to the terms proposed by the other party* . . . the man thus conducting himself will be equally bound as if he had intended to agree *to the other party's terms*".[2] Yet, the objective theory of consent requires an external appearance of consent '*to the other party's terms*' and may not therefore permit the "generalised and indirect intention to be bound by computer-generated agreements" (Allen and Widdison, 1996, p. 44) that may arise out of the mere use of contracting software. A reasonable man who contracts (through software) on an automated marketplace *knowing that the process is wholly handled by software* would not really believe that the other party assents to the *specific* terms of the transaction; a reasonable man would know that the other party is *not* aware of those exact terms.

The 'unread contract' principle, according to which a person who signs a written contract, is normally bound by its terms even if he has not read that contract (Allen and Widdison, 1996, p. 44) is similarly unsuitable. Allen and Widdison (1996, p. 44) consider it "a sound basis for treating the agreement as a legally binding contract" and Kerr (1999, p. 232) sees its extension to automated contracting as "simple". However, whereas an unread contract is always available for review by a contracting party and it is therefore reasonable for the other party to assume that it has indeed been read, an automated contract may not be similarly available and the other party may actually know that the contract has *not* in fact been read.

The aforementioned solutions would perhaps be viable in relation to contracts concluded in Kasbah-like automated marketplaces,[3] which allow users to instruct contracting software to seek their approval before finalizing a potential transaction. When this option is technically available but is nevertheless not exercised by the user, an analogy with unread contracts evidently becomes stronger. Likewise, under such circumstances, there may indeed be an external appearance of consent; it may be reasonable for a contracting party to assume that the other party has seen and agreed to the terms of the transaction.

Still, objective consent and the 'unread contract' principle are common law rules not recognized in every EU legal system. Furthermore, not all automated marketplaces will come with a 'prior approval' option. Most importantly, the relevant option runs counter to the very concept of *full* automation, which is the opposite to offering the user the option to approve each and every transaction intended by the contracting software substituting her. Put otherwise, the relevant two principles do not really solve the problem, as they will only

2 *Smith v Hughes (1871) I.R. 6 Q.B. 597*, emphasis added.
3 Supra Chapter 1 p. 12

work in the context of *semi*-automated contracting and thus, if the idea of *fully* automated contracts is abandoned.[4]

6.3 Possible legal approaches for solving the validity issue

6.3.1 General

The problem is not eligible to a simple solution. It is thus only natural that there is rich relevant literature discussing the different approaches towards establishing automated contract validity (Solum, 1992; Wein, 1992; Allen and Widdison, 1996; Kerr, 1999; Lerouge, 1999; Bellia, 2001; Kerr, 2001; Weitzenboeck, 2001; Bagby, 2004; Kis, 2004; Andrade, Novais and Neves, 2005; Jurewicz, 2005; Subirana and Bain, 2005, pp. 68–76; Dahiyat, 2006; Teubner, 2006; Al-majid, 2007; Andrade et al., 2007a; Andrade et al., 2007b; Chopra and White, 2009). It arises that there are four relevant approaches, namely: (a) the 'legal personality' approach, which involves deeming contracting as a legal person; (b) the 'agency' approach, which requires treating such software as an agent in law; (c) the 'legal fiction' approach, which involves pretending that contracting software is nothing but passive means of communication and (d) the 'relaxation of contractual intention' approach, which considers the general intention of users to be bound by contracts concluded by software sufficient to satisfy the 'consent' or 'intention' requirement of contract validity.[5]

It is submitted that apart from factors relating to "legal complexity and convenience of each" (Allen and Widdison, 1996, p. 41), the main criterion by reference to which the suitability of each of these approaches must be examined should be their interoperability with rules determining liability. Thus, the chosen approach must not only be able to explain contract validity (preferably without dramatically upsetting the deeply rooted traditional contract law principles) but also allow for a sound basis for rules governing contractual liability where the software fails to act as anticipated or otherwise malfunctions. Additionally, it should not have undesirable implications regarding the liability of consumers for unlawful acts such as a privacy violation committed by the contracting software representing them.

6.3.2 The 'legal fiction' and 'relaxation of intention' approaches

The approach that scores higher than the others when examined against the aforementioned criteria is the 'legal fiction' one.[6] Doubtless, it explains contract validity in the simplest possible way: "It would involve no change whatsoever to contract doctrine itself" (Allen and Widdison, 1996, p. 46) Commentators, however, worry about its consequences in cases of unintended contracts (and perhaps tortious acts) possibly resulting from malfunctioning software. If everything originating from the software is deemed to originate from its human user, the latter will have to bear the consequences of a malfunction and also be bound by a mistaken contract even if the mistake were or should have been obvious to the other party (Allen and Widdison, 1996, p. 47; Kerr, 1999, p. 235; Weitzenboeck, 2001, p. 10; Andrade et al., 2007b, p. 219).

4 A similar argument has been made in relation to the problem of compatibility of the information duties of the CRD in the context of automated contracting, see Chapter 2 supra pp. 64–65. On this matter and the various degrees of automation in contracting, see also Markou (2017b, pp. 5, 12).
5 This latter one is mainly only considered by Allen and Widdison (1996, pp. 43–45).
6 For further explanation of this approach, see Kerr (1999, p. 219).

Yet, by disregarding the autonomy of contracting software, the 'legal fiction' approach does not preclude the possibility of avoiding liability on the ground of mistake. It treats it as mere communication means, such as telephones and fax machines; the mistake doctrine is perfectly applicable to those cases offering an escape route to the mistaken party. Cavanillas (2001, sec. 2.5) writes that "contractors using an electronic agent would not be liable if they proved that a technical mistake occurred that was not due to their negligence", and he is not wrong; the doctrine of unilateral mistake can relatively easily be extended to cover malfunction-caused mistakes.

Admittedly, the particular doctrine traditionally required a *human* mistake of fact or of law rather than 'technical mistakes'. This is also apparent from Section 7:201(1), DCFR, which largely codifies the common law doctrine of unilateral mistake: "The general rule at common law is that if one party has made a mistake as to the terms of the contract and that mistake is known to the other party, then the contract is not binding".[7] A software malfunction effectively results in the user being mistaken as to how his intentions have been communicated and ultimately, as to the content of the resulting contract terms. This does not seem difficult to qualify as a mistake as to the contract terms and indeed, Section 7:202 (2), DCFR reinforces this view by stating that "an inaccuracy in the expression or transmission of a statement is treated as a mistake of the person who made or sent the statement." Moreover, in the US, the law on automated contracts empowers courts to grant relief when a contract has resulted from electronic mistake by applying the doctrine of mistake "even though an electronic agent cannot actually be said to have been . . . mistaken".[8]

Of course, for the doctrine to operate towards invalidating an erroneous contract, it is necessary that "the other party knew or could reasonably be expected to have known of the mistake".[9] It is difficult to attribute knowledge or constructive knowledge of a mistake to software, (specifically, the software handling the contracting process on behalf of the other party). As Kis (2004, p. 61) notes, "When the contract is formed by electronic agents, discovering the assumptions of the parties at that time may be problematic". However, the mistake doctrine could be applied through ignoring the involvement of autonomous contracting software and inquire into whether the mistake *would have been obvious* to the other party. Unreasonable terms or terms that given the content of the exchanged messages are manifestly mistaken or unintended could be deemed to have been known to the other contracting party, thus satisfying the relevant requirement. In fact, a Singaporean court has applied the relevant doctrine to a case involving electronic automated contracts considering the contracts that the plaintiffs were seeking to enforce as void on the ground of unilateral mistake.[10] Most importantly, the judgement confirms that the relevant doctrine should not quickly be dismissed as inapplicable in the context of automated contracts:

> Inevitably mistakes will occur in the course of electronic transmissions. This can result from human interphasing, machine error or a combination of such factors. Examples of such mistakes would include (a) human error (b) programming of software errors and (c) transmission problems in the communication systems. Computer glitches can cause

7 *Statoil A.S.A. v Louis Dreyfus Energy Services L.P. (The "Harriette N") [2008] EWHC 2257 (Comm.) [2008] 2 Lloyd's Rep. 685, para. 87.*

8 Section 206(a), UCITA and Comment 3 to Section 206(a), National Conference of Commissioners on Uniform State Laws (NCCUSL), Prefatory Note: Uniform Computer Information Transactions Act (UCITA).

9 Section 7:201(1)(a)(ii), DCFR.

10 *Chwee Kin Keong and others v Digilandmall.com Pte Ltd [2004] 2 SLR(R) 594.*

> transmission failures, garbled information or even change the nature of the information transmitted…Such errors can be magnified almost instantaneously and may be harder to detect than if made in a face to face transaction or through physical document exchanges. Who bears the risk of such mistakes? It is axiomatic that normal contractual principles apply but the contractual permutations will obviously be sometimes more complex and spread over a greater magnitude of transactions. The financial consequences could be considerable. The court has to be astute and adopt a pragmatic and judicious stance in resolving such issues.[11]

Thus, the doctrine of unilateral mistake could operate to invalidate the contract where, for example, consumer buying software buys an item at a price significantly higher than normal or where it closes a deal at terms evidently different from those evidenced in the exchanged pre-contractual communications. It is true that the mistake doctrine makes available no escape route in cases of mistaken contracts that are *not* manifestly so, yet this is *not* an unsatisfactory result. Certainty in automated contracting requires that parties should be able to rest assured that the other contracting party will be bound by the contracts concluded by contracting software. Moreover, the party whose software has malfunctioned is better equipped to turn against the software provider to recover the loss inherent in a non-obviously mistaken contract.

Finally, in most EU legal systems, a party cannot avoid a contract for mistake if the mistake was inexcusable or the risk of the mistake was assumed or should be borne by him (Lando and Beale, 2000, p. 241).[12] A mistake would be inexcusable and/or the risk assumed when the consumer misuses the software causing it to malfunction but hopefully, *not* when the consumer simply uses contracting software as Daniel (2004, pp. 342–343) implies by reference to US case law on telegraph transmission errors. Such approach would automatically render automated marketplaces particularly risky and undesirable contracting environments. Fortunately, in most EU countries, a transmission or expression error that is known or obvious to the non-mistaken party is not binding (Lando and Beale, 2000, pp. 242–243). Even in the US, the matter regarding liability for telegraph transmission errors is not uncontroversial.[13]

It has been shown that the 'legal fiction' approach towards automated contract validity is interoperable with the mistake doctrine mainly because it disregards software autonomy or involvement, thereby allowing for the doctrine to be applied *as if* the parties were negotiating and contracting directly. By contrast, the alternative 'relaxation of intention' approach is not similarly interoperable. By expressly recognizing that the whole process is handled by software, it does not really allow for the problematic inquiry into the 'state of mind' of the said *software*, simply to be avoided.

Most importantly, the 'legal fiction' approach also enables avoiding consumer liability for possible unlawful acts committed by malfunctioning contracting software, as it seems compatible with the view of consumer users as mere service recipients. This is not the case with alternative approaches, as is shown in the following. Automated marketplaces clearly comprise services available to consumers (and merchants interested to market their products through them). Consumers are thus mere *service recipients*, the hardware and software supporting the operation of an automated marketplace, including the contracting software, being tools *in the*

11 Ibid para. 102.
12 Section 7:201(2), DCFR.
13 See no author (1918, pp. 932–935).

hands of automated providers, who utilize them to conduct their business. Accordingly, unlike the employer of a tool (van Haentjens, 2002, sec. 4.2; Andrade et al., 2007b, p. 219), consumer users, being recipients of a service provided by (another) employer of a tool, cannot reasonably be liable for damage caused by a defect, malfunction or other failure of those tools; aggrieved parties must be able to turn against marketplace service providers for redress. This view is supported by literature acknowledging that users are not in full control of relevant software and should not therefore be considered liable (Heckman and Wobbrock, 1999, p. 94; Sartor, 2002, sec. 2).

6.3.3 The 'legal personality' and 'agency' approaches

The other two approaches, namely the 'legal personality' and the 'agency' ones[14] should be rejected as unnecessarily complex and even dangerous to the consumer user. Scholars who have inquired into the suitability of the 'legal personality' approach by reference to the three main justifications behind conferring legal personality on entities, namely moral entitlement, social reality and legal convenience seem to doubt that these, could readily apply to contracting software (Allen and Widdison, 1996, pp. 35–43; Kerr, 1999, pp. 214–219; Coteanu, 2005, p. 112). Moreover, certain practical problems, such as the need for procedures to identify such software, have led other commentators to conclude that there are "undoubtedly major difficulties in the attempt of 'personification' of such software agents" (Andrade et al., 2007b, p. 220).

One main idea behind the 'legal personality' approach is that, as only *persons* can contract, deeming contracting software as legal persons will furnish them with contractual capacity and, hence, with the ability to conclude valid contracts. Yet, as Kerr (1999, p. 210) rightly observes, contractual capacity requires not only personhood but also a certain degree of intellect that is higher than that possessed by minors or persons of unsound mind who lack contractual capacity. It would be difficult to measure the intellect of the various contracting software, thereby deciding whether they should be recognized with contractual capacity. Moreover, they will probably have varying degrees of intellect, the result being that some will have such capacity while others will not. This complicates things and further suggests that the relevant approach is not able to solve the problem in *all* cases in any event.

Teubner (2006, pp. 511–512) refers to the idea of "hybrids", i.e., associations between humans and non-humans which, if legally personified, could become new political, social and economic actors and asserts that the non-human component of a hybrid can be software.[15] Obviously, if that software is software contracting for the consumer, the consumer will naturally be the human component of the hybrid. In that case, the consumer could not be disassociated from the software component of the hybrid, and the patrimony of the hybrid would inevitably be that of the consumer. In effect, it would probably be difficult for the consumer user to avoid the negative consequences of malfunctioning software that causes damage to another party. In this respect, the particular approach is clearly unsuitable for the case of contracting software offered as a consumer shopping service in the context of automated marketplaces.

As for the agency approach, agency law recognizes contracts concluded by agents on behalf of their principals as valid on the ground that the latter have authorized the related

14 Supra p. 176
15 Allen and Widdison (1996, p. 40) also refer to the idea of human-computer hybrids asserting that it would be easier for the law to confer legal personality on them than on pure machines.

acts of the former (Bradgate, 1995, p. 98). Thus, deeming contracting software as agents in law of their users is tempting, as the former are in fact utilized (and are therefore also authorized) to act on behalf of the latter concluding contracts in their name. Moreover, the aforementioned problem with contractual capacity is avoided as agents need to be persons but contractual capacity is not required (Kerr, 1999, pp. 239–240). Moreover, as Kerr (1999, pp. 243–247) nicely illustrates, certain doctrines of agency law, such as apparent authority, ratification and undisclosed principal are perfectly adjustable to software-concluded contracts.

Indeed, according to the principle of apparent authority, "a person may also be bound by acts done by another on his behalf without his consent or even in breach of an express prohibition if his words or actions give the impression that he has authorized them" (Bradgate, 1995, p. 103). The common law principle of estoppel by representation of fact on which the one of apparent authority is based (Bradgate, 1995, pp. 104–105) dictates that "it must have been reasonable to rely on the representation" (Wilken and Villiers, 2003, para. 9:02). This 'reasonableness' requirement also exists in the principle of apparent authority as codified in the DCFR.[16] Thus, a consumer who instructs software to buy an item on his behalf, he will be bound by a resulting contract, even a mistaken one, unless it would not be reasonable for the other party to have relied on the contractual messages communicated by the software. Apparently, the 'agency' approach can produce the sound results regarding obvious and non-obvious mistakes described earlier by reference to the 'legal fiction' approach. Why then the latter should be preferred over the former? The answer lies with the way the 'agency' approach would deal with other liability issues.

According to agency law, the principal and third parties may have a cause of action against an agent who disobeys instructions or commits an unlawful act (Bradgate, 1995 pp. 133, 144). Thus, a contracting software user found himself bound by a non-obviously mistaken contract (or a third party harmed by an unlawful act committed by such software) will be able to turn against the software for compensation. Yet, unlike a *human* agent, a *software* agent, cannot be imposed with legal liability and also lacks patrimony, thereby being unable to pay compensation. Contracting software would have to be recognized with legal personality to be accepted as 'agents' under agency law and be imposed with liability. However, that would not *also* address the 'lack of patrimony' problem, i.e., the fact that software has no assets to pay compensation.

Commentators suggest furnishing agents with patrimony through special insurance schemes or money deposits (Karnow, 1996, pp. 195–196; Wettig and Zehendner, 2003 sec. IV.4) to be paid by the software owner or provider (Karnow, 1996, p. 194). This seems a suitable and fair allocation of the risk of loss involved, yet, if a *human being* is to bear the risk of loss and eventually pay, there may be no valid reason for furnishing software with legal personality (Bellia, 2001, p. 1067; Fasli, 2007, p. 32). Others counter-argue that the particular approach would limit the loss arising from a contracting software malfunction, as the insurance premiums would be lower than the actual damage possibly to be caused (Al-Majid, 2007, p. 5; Andrade et al., 2007b, p. 220). Such loss limitation is certainly desirable, but there are much simpler ways in which it can be achieved. Indeed, if the relevant risk of loss is placed on the shoulders of marketplace providers, the said parties will be free to take insurance to limit the possible loss. Insurance and its benefits do not necessitate the complexity the combination of 'legal personality' and 'agency' approaches. Besides, the 'insurance' concept is not a stranger to claims relating to failures of traditional software. It has even influenced the legal approach

16 II. 6:103(3), DCFR.

towards liability, specifically by serving as a factor justifying the imposition of the relevant risk on software developers who, because of their access to insurance, are increasingly found liable despite relevant exclusion clauses (Lloyd, 2000, p. 527). Moreover, as is explained in Chapter 7,[17] there is room for the introduction of a legal obligation of insurance for automated marketplace providers.

Apart from the unnecessary complexity it would introduce, the 'agency' approach would inevitably render the consumer user of contracting software, *a principal*, thereby distancing him from the 'innocent' capacity of a mere service recipient that utilizes a contracting service. More specifically, its adoption would bring into play the rules governing the liability of principals for the torts committed by their agents in the course of the exercise of their duties.[18] Even if consumers could turn against the insured contracting software to recover any loss arising from such liability, they would still not want this. Moreover, the possibility of the insurance company going out of business or otherwise failing to cover a damage could not be excluded.

Kerr (1999 pp. 239, 241) suggests an approach of diffused agency, which concentrates on the 'external aspect' alone, namely the relationship between the principal and the third party and ignores the internal principal-agent relationship, which would necessitate software legal personality and patrimony. Yet, this is worse for consumer users; while it renders them principals, thereby exposing them to the aforementioned liability risk, it fails to ensure the availability of a source of recovery, should that risk materialize. Weitzenboeck (2001, p. 13) thus rightly refers to failure of the particular approach to produce satisfactory results, amongst others, where contracting software performs an unlawful act.

6.3.4 The EU legal response towards the contract validity issue

All in all, the 'legal fiction' approach arises to be the most appropriate for the purpose of explaining the legal validity of software-concluded contracts; it does so without disturbing traditional contract law principles or introducing any practical problems and appears to operate well with traditional liability rules, giving rise to fair and logical results. It is therefore unsurprising that foreign legislators who have specifically embarked upon automated contract validity have opted for this approach. More specifically, the US Uniform Electronic Transactions Act (UETA, 1999) deems electronic agents as tools in the hands of users who will be bound by their agents' actions even if they have not reviewed them[19] and refers to the doctrine of mistake as the solution to software-made (or system) errors.[20] In the Prefatory Note of the Act, it is stated, "In these ways the Act permits electronic transactions to be accomplished with certainty under existing substantive rules of law".[21]

17 Infra Chapter 7 pp. 208–209

18 See *Hamlyn v John Houston & Co [1903] 1 KB 81 and Poland v Parr (John) & Sons [1927] 1 KB 236*. See also *McGowan & Co. v Dyer (1873) L.R. 8 Q.B. 141, 143*: "'In Story on Agency', the learned author states, in section 452, the general rule that the principal is liable to third persons in a civil suit 'for the frauds, deceits, concealments, misrepresentations, torts, negligences, and other malfeasances or misfeasances, and omissions of duty of his agent *in the course of his employment*, although the principal did not authorise, or justify, or participate in, or indeed know of such misconduct, or even if he forbade the acts, or disapproved of them'".

19 Sections 2(6) and 14, UETA and corresponding comment (NCCUSL, 1999, pp. 8–9, 43).

20 Section 10, UETA and corresponding comment (NCCUSL, 1999, pp. 33–36).

21 NCCUSL, 1999, p. 3. For more on relevant US law, see Coteanu (2005, pp. 122–123).

The European legislator has not been similarly *explicit* on the validity of fully automated contracts, but Article 9(1) of the E-Commerce Directive unequivocally asserts that contracts concluded through electronic means must *not* be denied validity by reason of their electronic nature. Contracting software and automated marketplaces clearly qualify as 'electronic means'. Indeed, Section 2(6), UETA defines an 'electronic agent' as "a computer program or an *electronic* or other automated *means*".[22] Consequently, Member States or EU national courts *have to* accept (and explain) automated contract validity in one way or another where the exchange of the relevant contractual communications would give rise to a valid contract in a non-electronic context.

Of course, maximum certainty is not achieved for automated contracting (or the conclusion of 'automated transactions'[23]). Unlike the UETA, the European Directive does not specify the approach towards contractual validity to be adopted, leaving the choice to the substantive contract law of each Member State. Given that automated contracting would know no geographical borders, users would not know whether they act as principals of an agent or as mere users of a tool (or service recipients) when using an automated marketplace. As already explained, the exact approach towards contractual validity may have repercussions on their liability for any (unlawful) software acts. Therefore, under EU law, as it now stands, they can be certain as to the validity of their contracts but not equally certain regarding the wider liability implications of their decision to engage in automated contracting.

By setting the law of the habitual residence of the consumer as the applicable law to most consumer contracts, the EU Rome I Regulation does not remedy the uncertainty. Article 6(2) of the Regulation permits the contractual parties to choose the applicable law as long as the said choice does not prevent the application of the mandatory rules of the law of the habitual residence of the consumer if they afford higher protection to the consumer than the corresponding ones of the chosen law. Yet, mandatory rules, i.e., rules that cannot contractually be excluded, are normally those which provide for consumer rights, such as the right of withdrawal from distance contracts derived from the Consumer Rights Directive or the right to free repair or replacement when the goods are not in conformity with the contract of the Consumer Sales Directive. The rules providing for the substantive or formal validity of contracts are not normally mandatory and therefore, it is those of the chosen law that will apply, which almost invariably is that of the merchant who sets the terms of the contract. Consumers will, in most cases, not know the identity, let alone the habitual residence, of the merchant with whom their contracting software has closed a contract.

It should be stated, however, that given that the issue of legal validity is addressed by EU law, which guarantees the legal validity of automated contracts through the E-Commerce Directive, as explained previously, the uncertainty resulting from the fact that the legal approach explaining validity is *not* specified at EU level may not constitute a major problem. The 'agency' and 'legal personality' approaches are so complex (perhaps even far-fetched), that it may be safe to assume that similarly to other non-EU countries, all Member States will most probably adopt the 'legal fiction' or, perhaps, the (not dramatically different) 'relaxation of intention' approach.

22 Emphasis added.

23 UETA apparently classifies agent-concluded contracts as 'automated transactions', see Section 2 (2) and corresponding comment by NCCUSL (1999, p. 7).

6.4 Liability in cases of mistaken (or unintended) contracts

6.4.1 Malfunction-caused mistaken contracts: the EU legal response

Reliance on software for contract conclusion inevitably places the consumer at risk of loss arising from the conclusion of a mistaken or unintended, yet binding, contract as a result of the contracting software malfunctioning. There is no need to go at length to illustrate this risk. The description of automated marketplaces in Chapter 1 evinces the fact that the relevant services fully rely on technical equipment and techniques which may fail.[24] There are several solutions to this issue available in EU law, namely the CRD and the UCTD, and their combination effectively leads to an adequate relevant legal response, though the latter at least, needs to be recognized or unearthed. The refund rights of the PSD2 are explained also to be able to assist the consumer in this context, even though consumer charges resulting from malfunction-caused mistaken contracts are not classical cases to which these rights apply.

As already shown, the chosen approach to contract validity will inevitably assist in resolving the issue of contractual liability where a mistaken contract arises, specifically through the traditional doctrine of unilateral mistake. Though it requires a mistaken belief by one party and (constructive) knowledge of that mistake by the other, i.e., cogitations or reasoning that could not readily be attributed to mere software, it is possible to achieve its application in the context of automated contracting. Importantly, however, the relevant solution is only available to *obvious* mistakes, meaning that according to basic contract law, the consumer will be bound by malfunction-caused mistaken contracts that would not be obvious to the other contracting party.[25] This is fair to the other contracting party and necessary to ensure certainty in automated transactions but consumer protection dictates that the (innocent) consumer must have an opportunity to avoid such contract or recover any loss from the marketplace provider.

A powerful solution exists in the Consumer Rights Directive (CRD), which would also render unnecessary that the consumer resort to the more complex doctrine of unilateral mistake, even in cases where the latter would be available. Though it is not available in relation to all distant (including automated) consumer contracts, it can effectively solve the problem of mistaken automated contracts in a considerable number of cases. Another solution is found in the Unfair Contract Terms Directive (UCTD), but is 'hidden', requiring a specific (suitable) interpretation to unearth it. The Second Payment Services Directive (PSD2) also contains certain relevant provisions, yet their application to this problem may cause certain questions.

Starting from the first, Article 9(1), CRD furnishes consumers with the right to withdraw from a distant contract without reason and without penalty. This right can be exercised as a method of avoiding mistaken or unintended automated contracts, given that the latter clearly qualify as 'distant' ones.[26] There are exceptions to this right, specifically listed in Article 16, CRD; these include contracts concerning "a newspaper, periodical or

24 See also infra Chapter 7, p. 199
25 Supra pp. 177–178
26 A 'distant contract' is defined by Article 2(7), CRD as "any contract concluded between the trader and the consumer under an organised distance sales or service-provision scheme without the simultaneous physical presence of the trader and the consumer, with the exclusive use of one or more means of distance communication up to and including the time at which the contract is concluded".

magazine"[27] and "goods made to the consumer's specifications or clearly personalized"[28] or which "are liable to deteriorate or expire rapidly".[29] Additional exceptions exist for contracts for digital content, such as CDs and DVDs, when unsealed after delivery,[30] as well as contracts concerning "accommodation other than for residential purpose, transport of goods, car rental services, catering or services related to leisure activities if the contract provides for a specific date or period of performance".[31] Understandably, in all of these cases,[32] the right of withdrawal cannot serve as a solution to the problem of mistaken automated contracts, yet these do not cover the majority of consumer contracts in which the relevant solution will be available. Given that in automated marketplaces, contracting software may conclude contracts through bidding in auctions, it is important to note that another exception in Article 16(k), CRD, referring to contracts concluded at public auctions, does not apply to online platforms adhering to an auction-like system.[33]

Of course, there is a time limit within which the withdrawal right must be exercised. In the DSD, that was a minimum of seven (7) days from the day of receipt or of the conclusion of the contract, in relation to contracts of goods and contracts of services respectively.[34] As consumer users of automated marketplaces are not *personally* involved in transactions, they may only become aware of certain mistakes *after* the particular time limit has lapsed. Fortunately, the CRD extended this time limit to fourteen (14) days in all Member States[35] improving the efficiency of the right and rendering it a robust solution to the problem of mistaken automated contracts.

As mentioned previously,[36] when the trader fails to inform the consumer of the existence of the right of withdrawal pre-contractually, i.e., before a binding contract comes into being, in compliance with Article 6(1)(h), CRD the period of withdrawal is extended dramatically to 12 months and 14 days.[37] Though in automated marketplaces contract conclusion is handled by software (rather than by the consumer personally), it is highly unlikely for this provision to lead to such prolonged withdrawal period in all cases in the particular context. As explained, there are ways, including communicating the required information to the consumer by e-mail, enabling traders to keep the withdrawal period to its minimum 14-day duration.[38]

The second solution to malfunction-caused mistaken automated contracts is contained in the UCTD. This Directive renders void and non-binding for the consumer *unfair* contract terms and is applicable to all consumer contracts, regardless of the manner they have been concluded[39] and thus to automated contracts, too. The general criterion of unfairness is contained in Article 3(1), UCTD which provides as follows:

27 Article 16(j), CRD.
28 Article 16(c), CRD.
29 Article 16(d), CRD.
30 Article 16(i), CRD.
31 Article 16(l), CRD.
32 There are additional exceptions. For a full list, see Article 16, CRD.
33 Recital 24, CRD.
34 Article 6(1), DSD.
35 The CRD is a maximum harmonization measure, see Article 4, CRD.
36 Supra Chapter 2 pp. 63, 69–70, 72
37 Article 10, CRD.
38 See supra Chapter 2 p. 70
39 Articles 1(1) and 6(1), UCTD.

> A contractual term which has not been individually negotiated shall be regarded as unfair if, contrary to the requirement of good faith, it causes a significant imbalance in the parties' rights and obligations arising under the contract, to the detriment of the consumer.

If consumer contracting software has not negotiated the offering of the merchant contracting software, the terms of the resulting contract will be subject to the fairness control of the UCPD. Admittedly, the need to establish procedural unfairness, i.e., a contractual process that is 'contrary to the requirement of good faith', necessitating an inquiry into how fairly the process has been conducted, would cause problems in the context of automated marketplaces, where this process is handled automatically by software. However, if the unfairness of a contractual term can be established on substantive grounds alone, i.e., by reference to the term as such (and to a significance imbalance mirrored in it),[40] the Directive could be used in cases of *obviously* mistaken automated contracts. More specifically, it can render obviously mistaken terms void effectively availing the consumer of an escape route from any relevant unfair contractual obligations.

Notably, according to Article 4(2), terms defining *the main subject matter of the contract* or *relating to the adequacy of the price* shall not be subjected to relevant fairness 'control' if they are in plain and intelligible language. In the Member States, which have transposed Article 4(2) into their national laws,[41] the relevant role of the Directive will be limited to cases *other than* those where consumer contracting software agrees to purchase the wrong product or a product at an unreasonably high price. As these will probably be common mistaken automated contracts, the relevant limitation is significant. Still, it does not affect cases, such as where the contracting software has agreed to an unreasonably long delivery time. Thus, if the contract provides for a standard product to be shipped in two years, for example, the consumer will be able to assert that the relevant term is unfair and therefore not binding upon him; *unfair* contract terms under the UCTD must be treated as non-existing (producing no legal effects at all).[42] In such a case, the consumer will be considered entitled to delivery within 30 days from the time of the order as per Article 18, CRD. The latter provision specifies the said time limit for delivery in cases where delivery time has *not* been agreed in the contract and allows consumers to terminate the contract where the trader does not deliver within the particular time period or shortly thereafter.

Most importantly, the UCTD can, albeit *indirectly*, prove of much greater help to the consumer whose software concludes a mistaken contract due to a malfunction assisting her to avoid the relevant adverse consequences in all relevant cases, including cases of *non-obvious* mistakes. This is because it does *not* exclude from its fairness control contract terms comprising 'exclusion of liability' clauses. Merchants engaging in traditional online contexts (i.e., through websites) often utilize contract terms (or clauses) reserving the right to avoid a contract when *technical* failures result in *erroneous* prices or other terms (Wearden, 2005; Groebner, 2004, paras. 6–7). Such clauses are unlikely to be considered unfair or otherwise invalid given that they only seek to invalidate a contract that has never been intended and has only arisen out of (technical) error.

40 A 'substantive unfairness' approach is possible in Member States which have not included the 'good faith' requirement (Ebers, 2008, p. 344) and also in the UK, where it seems to be assisted by the House of Lords in *The Director General of Fair Trading v First National Bank plc [2001] UKHL 52, [2002] AC 481 (HL)*, paras. 17, 33, 36 and 37.

41 The Directive is a minimum harmonization measure and as a result, not all Member States exclude terms as to subject-matter or price from the fairness requirement.

42 *Case C-618/10, Banco Español de Crédito SA v Joaquín Calderón Camino, 14 June 2012.*

Presumably, merchants operating in automated marketplaces will resort to similar exclusion clauses to deal with malfunction-caused mistaken contracts. Crucially, unlike in traditional e-commerce, where *only* merchants rely on technical equipment to communicate the details of their contractual intentions,[43] in the context of automated marketplaces, the same is true of consumers, who rely on software to contract on their behalf, thus communicating their contractual intentions to the other party. Thus, a term allowing the merchant, but *not* the consumer, to withdraw from a mistaken contract could be said to create a significant imbalance between the rights of the parties, thus being unfair under the UCTD. Indeed, a similarly imbalanced term "permitting the seller or supplier to retain sums paid by the consumer where the latter decides not to conclude or perform the contract, *without providing for the consumer to receive compensation of an equivalent amount from the seller* or supplier where the latter is the party cancelling the contract"[44] is contained in the list of the Directive with terms "which may be regarded as unfair".[45] The same is true of a term "authorizing the seller or supplier to dissolve the contract on a discretionary basis *where the same facility* is not granted to the consumer".[46]

As merchants would most likely want to avoid unfairness of exclusion of liability clauses pertaining to technical errors, thereby keeping the relevant escape route open to them, they are essentially 'forced' to make it available to consumers, too, thus using clauses granting the same facility (*equal* avoidance rights) to consumers. In this respect, the Directive affords relevant consumer protection by implicitly requiring that relevant '*consumer* liability' exoneration be provided for in the contract.

Interestingly, if software negotiations on automated marketplaces extend to such exclusion clauses,[47] these would be considered as *individually negotiated* and thus excluded from the reach of the UCTD fairness control.[48] As a result, the aforementioned benefit of the UCTD would be lost (though being able to understand or act upon an 'exclusion of liability' clause does not necessarily mean the clause will in fact be negotiated).[49] Thus, though Kis (2004, p. 66) is apparently troubled by the fact that current contracting software can mainly decide on the basis of price and quality and may, therefore, conclude "a contract that excludes all warranties ", it is actually the opposite that should be considered troublesome, at least in the context of consumer contracts. Indeed, especially contractual clauses 'excluding legal warranties' are often void and non-binding on the consumer not only by operation of the UCTD[50] but also (explicitly) by the Consumer Sales Directive,[51] in the latter case, even if individually negotiated. In this respect, it would be preferable for consumer contracting software not to touch upon any exclusion of liability clauses, thereby keeping them within the fairness control of the UCTD.

Sartor (2009, p. 284) specifically refers to merchant contracting software negotiating an exclusion of liability clause in return of availing the consumer a price reduction. As already

43 Typically, consumers just respond to such communications by using 'Submit Order' buttons.
44 Paragraph (d) of the Annex, UCTD, emphasis added.
45 Article 3(3), UCTD.
46 Paragraph (f) of the Annex. UCTD, emphasis added.
47 Subirana and Bain (2005, p. 187) mention Legal-XML, a technical proposal for a mark-up language enabling machines including software agents to understand and act upon legal clauses.
48 Article 3(1), supra pp. 184–185
49 Schreurs and Hildebrandt (2005, p. 49) suggest that Article 5, UCTD, requiring that contract terms be in plain and intelligible language could be taken to require that software agents or contracting software be technologically capable of considering *all* terms.
50 Paragraphs (a) and (b) of the Annex, UCTD.
51 Article 7(1), CSD.

explained, even if negotiated, such clauses, to the extent that they seek to exclude legal warranties, will be void. Hopefully, however, such offers will not be made in relation to clauses relating to technical errors or consumers will *not* instruct their software to accept them, thus blocking the 'fairness' control of the UCTD. Consumers should therefore be educated to use contracting software well; in fact, this case can serve as another example of the potential of "*well-used*" software agents (Lerouge, 1999, p. 433) that can improve the position of consumers *vis-à-vis* merchants.[52]

Another EU measure, namely the Second Payment Services Directive (PSD2), also contains provisions relevant to mistaken automated contracts, though these seem to suffer from some uncertainty. More specifically, it allows consumers to revoke a payment order at any time *before* it has been received by their payment service provider.[53] However, given that it normally only takes a few seconds for payment accounts to be charged after a consumer initiates payment, there will probably be no time for consumers successfully to revoke a payment order. Indeed, especially on automated marketplaces, consumers may not know of the conclusion of the automated contract until much later on.

The PSD2 also entitles consumers to an immediate refund of debited sums where the payment transaction has been unauthorized,[54] i.e., without their consent.[55] Crucially, this entitlement remains applicable for the sufficiently long period of 13 months from the debit date.[56] Moreover, the fact that the use of a payment instrument has been recorded is not sufficient evidence of the existence of authorization.[57] Additionally, the onus of proving that a payment transaction was in fact authorized lies with the payment service provider:

> Where a payment service user denies having authorised an executed payment transaction or claims that the payment transaction was not correctly executed, it is for the payment service provider to prove that the payment transaction was authenticated, accurately recorded, entered in the accounts and not affected by a technical breakdown or some other deficiency *of the service provided by the payment service provider*.[58]

Though these are certainly payer-friendly provisions, it arises that the 'technical breakdown or some other deficiency' that the payment service provider must prove that it has not affected the transaction, is of the payment service *as such* and not of some other service, such as that of the automated marketplace. After all, the payment service provider having to provide the refund,[59] namely the so-called, 'account servicing payment service provider' defined under the PSD2 as "a payment service provider providing and maintaining a payment account for a payer"[60] has no access to or control over the marketplace systems.

52 Lerouge (1999, p. 433) makes a different but interesting and valid point: "By creating an instrument that allows the consumer to indicate the minimum of protection he wishes in the terms and conditions of a contract, sellers will be encouraged to create clear, and protective terms and conditions. Well-used electronic agents may actually help consumers not familiar with disclaimers and therefore reduce the imbalance between buyers and sellers".
53 Article 80(1), PSD2.
54 Article 73, PSD2. See also Chapter 7.2.2.
55 Article 64(1)-(2), PSD2. Consent by contracting software will probably constitute consent of the user of the software.
56 Article 71(1), PSD2.
57 Article 72(2), PSD2.
58 Article 72(1), emphasis added.
59 Recital 73, PSD2.
60 Article 4(17), PSD2.

Moreover, Article 93, PSD2 exempts the refund liability of the payment service provider in cases of unavoidable and beyond his control "abnormal and unforeseeable circumstances". What happens on automated marketplace systems may be beyond the control (and even knowledge) of the responsible payment service provider. A payment authorization derived from a malfunction-caused automated contract would probably appear a perfect one (i.e., "authenticated, accurately recorded ") on the 'payment service provider' systems.

Yet, according to the PSD2, even if a payment initiation service provider is involved and is responsible for the unauthorized transaction, the payment service provider servicing the consumer payment account of the consumer *still* has to refund the consumer immediately, subject to a right to recover relevant sums by the latter.[61] If automated marketplaces qualify as initiation payment service providers (a question visited earlier),[62] it will fall on them to prove that there has not been a malfunction on their systems affecting the payment transaction. As the payment part of transactions is likely to be executed on systems that are different from those on which negotiations and contract conclusion operations are performed, the marketplace provider may be able to deny any responsibility proving that the transaction has been authenticated and probably recorded and executed on the systems supporting its payment service. However, as this is a matter concerning the allocation of the relevant loss between the payment service providers involved, the consumer will in most cases receive the refund, thereby recovering his loss. In this respect, though *ex-post*, the PSD2 provides an additional powerful solution to the problem of malfunction-caused mistaken contracts, especially if the automated marketplace choses to operate as a payment initiation service provider.

6.4.2 Consumer-caused mistaken contracts

Mistaken contracts need not arise from contracting software malfunction and may result from consumers making some mistake while instructing the software, such as pressing the wrong keys or buttons. The solution inherent in the withdrawal right of the CRD will be available to consumers also in this case but this is only an *ex-post* solution. Sufficient consumer protection dictates that such errors should be prevented from arising in the first place and indeed, the ability of consumers correctly to manage contracting software depends upon the provision of adequate relevant means and information. Thus, a relevant omission on the part of marketplace providers should comprise an escape route from mistaken contracts.

European law recognizes the need for the provision of *error-preventive* information and technical means to the users of electronic contracting services. Specifically, Article 10, ECD requires, *inter alia*, that "prior to the order being placed by the recipient of the service" the 'information society service' provider must provide the service recipient with clear and comprehensive information on "the different technical steps to follow to conclude the contract"[63] and on "the technical means for identifying and correcting input errors".[64] Article 11(2) mandates that "the service provider makes available to the recipient of the service appropriate, effective and accessible technical means allowing him to identify and correct input errors, prior to the placing of the order". In the UK, the failure to provide the technical means enabling the identification and correction of input errors gives rise to a right to

61 Article 72(1), 73(2) and 92(1), PSD2. On Article 92(1), see Chapter 3 supra p. 106
62 Supra Chapter 3.3.5.2.3
63 Article 10(1)(a).
64 Article 10(1)(c).

rescind the contract[65] and therefore results in a relevant escape route from mistaken electronic contracts.

As Cavanillas (2001, sec. 2.3.1) observes, the content of these provisions is influenced by the "technical asymmetry" of web-based e-commerce: "One of the contractors (usually the seller or the service provider) prepares his own e-commerce platform on his server or on a host server, while the other contractor is circumscribed to following the other's instructions from his 'client' computer". Indeed, the ECD is mainly intended for cases where consumers or service recipients use the systems set up and managed by merchants or service providers. This is confirmed not only by the restrictive wording of Articles 10 and 11[66] but also by Articles 10(4) and 11(3), which exempt from the aforementioned duties "contracts concluded exclusively by exchange of electronic mail or by equivalent individual communications", i.e., where each party uses his own system of communication or that of a service provider of his choice.

If merchants use third-party services enabling e-contracting, such as automated marketplaces, they remain 'information society service' providers,[67] and therefore subject to the aforementioned error-preventive duties. Indeed, it is broadly stated in Recital 10 that "selling goods online" consists of an information society service. Thus, merchants will have to choose automated marketplaces that possess the error-related features enabling them to comply with the said duties. This makes sense when consumers use *marketplace-provided* contracting software; they are clearly circumscribed to follow the directions (and use the systems) of the third party chosen by the merchant to enable and support its 'online sales' activity.

By contrast, where consumers (or both contracting parties) use software provided by an independent provider of their choice and the software meet in a marketplace to negotiate and contract, consumers do not follow the instructions or procedures of merchants (or of the merchant-chosen marketplace provider). Instead, both merchants and consumers follow the instructions of the independent software provider of their choice and it is mainly the systems of that provider that they use. Under such circumstances, the parties, through their software, may be taken to exchange "individual communications", thus triggering the Article 10(4) exception, which frees merchants from the error-preventive obligations. Again, this is reasonable given that merchants (or their chosen marketplace provider) cannot obviously assist consumers in avoiding button mistakes. Albeit by reference to software buying from websites, Lodder and Voulon (2002, p. 285) would seem to agree: "If an agent is ordering something from another agent, the paragraphs 1 and 2 [of Article 10] do not apply". Subirana and Bain (2005, p. 176) refrain from decisively reaching a similar conclusion in relation to the exchange of communications between merchant-controlled and consumer-controlled mobile devices, yet chances are that the particular provisions will not apply to that case either.

Thus, when consumers use marketplace-provided software, the error-related obligations of the ECD are applicable and burden merchants selling through automated marketplaces, whereas when consumers use software provided by an independent agent provider of their choice, these obligations are probably not applicable (as the Article 10(4) and 11(3), ECD exceptions are triggered). In the latter case, consumers should still receive error-preventive information and means, albeit from the independent software provider, who is the one in a position to discharge a relevant duty. Indeed, any button errors made by consumers while instructing independently provided software can lead to unintended contracts in the same

65 Regulation 15(b), Electronic Commerce (EC Directive) Regulations 2002.
66 Infra pp. 190–191
67 Supra Chapter 2, n. 41.

way in which errors made during the instruction of marketplace-provided ones can. As it has not been devised with such contracting scenarios in mind, the E-Commerce Directive does not contain relevant information duties. The relevant gap in consumer protection can probably be filled in by other EU legal measures imposing information duties on services providers, who must, as a result, offer consumers sufficient information enabling them correctly to use their service. This matter has been discussed earlier in this book, where it has been shown that certain EU law provisions can be interpreted so as to be taken to require the provision of information as to risks and user instructions.[68] This is however only an indirect and perhaps also uncertain solution.

When consumers utilize marketplace-provided software and the Articles 10(4) and 11(3) exceptions are *not* triggered, Articles 10 and 11, though applicable, are not fully compatible with automated contracting. Being tied to traditional website contracting,[69] the said provisions lack the neutrality necessary to enable them to cover other kinds of electronic contracting. First of all, the remedy of contract rescission, which is available to the service recipient in case of a violation of the obligation to provide error-corrective technical means,[70] is justifiable only where the party violating the particular obligation and contributing in the mistake is the other contracting party and not a third-party service provider, such as a marketplace provider, who will remain totally unaffected by it. Though the involvement of such a third party may not have been envisaged by the legislator at the time, the rescission remedy does not create any applicability problems, given that the (appropriate) addressee of the relevant duties will be the 'merchant' *contracting party* (who must simply utilize marketplaces enabling compliance with the relevant duties).[71]

A second characteristic of the relevant provisions is more problematic. The time "prior to the order being placed"[72] is not, in the context of automated marketplaces, the appropriate time at which any error-preventive information or means should be provided. It is software, not the consumer, that will place an order and the software cannot obviously make any button mistakes. Any such mistakes leading to an unintended contract are to be made by consumers while instructing the software and therefore it is prior to the finalization of the relevant instructions and the contracting software being set into operation that any error-preventive information or means must be provided. The "prior to placing an order" component would have to be interpreted (very) liberally to be taken to refer to this (appropriate) point in time in the context of automated marketplaces.

Even more problematic is a third issue relating to the suitability of the ECD error-preventive provisions to the automated marketplace context. Commentators suggest that consumers may stand as 'offerees', the 'contractual offer' being communicated by merchant contracting software (Bain and Subirana, 2003b, p. 285; Kerr, 2004, p. 288, Subirana and Bain, 2005, p. 80). Given that when a contractual communication is sufficiently specific it normally qualifies as an 'offer',[73] consumers buying on automated marketplaces may communicate an acceptance and never an offer. Indeed, in response to a consumer looking to buy a digital camera,[74] merchant contracting software may address to the software of that consumer a

68 Supra Chapter 2 pp. 45–48
69 Indeed, Lodder (2017, p. 43) discusses the said provisions by reference to orders being placed through clicking 'OK' and 'Buy Now' buttons.
70 Supra pp. 188–189
71 Supra p. 189
72 Articles 10(1)(a) and 10(1)(c), supra p. 188
73 Watnick (2004, p. 183) addresses the 'offeror/offeree' distinction in various different settings, not including automated marketplaces.
74 Such information may be in the form of a relevant listing in an agent-readable directory that forms part of an automated marketplace system.

relevant communication that is specific enough to qualify as an offer. If the consumer software 'decides' to buy, thus placing an order, it will do so by submitting an acceptance, *not* an offer. This makes sense; referring to shop or website displays of products, Cleff (2005, p. 61) explains that they are normally considered as 'invitations to treat' because they are not addressed to specific persons and can be accessed by an indefinite number of potential buyers; if they were offers, sellers would run the risk of finding themselves bound by an indefinite number of contracts exceeding their stock or geographical limitations. In the previously automated marketplace scenario, the merchant addresses a *specific* contractual communication to *specific* consumer software, thereby communicating an offer.

In such cases, the ECD error-related provisions would be wholly unsuitable, as there may not be a point "prior to the placing of an order" *at all.* Of course, the ECD does not define the term 'order' as being the contractual offer and does not interfere with the rules regarding offer and acceptance (Winn and Haubold, 2002, p. 11). Yet, such an '*order as offer*' definition is adopted by the relevant UK transposition measure. Specifically, Regulation 12 of the Electronic Commerce (EC Directive) Regulations 2002, provides that for the purposes of the provisions requiring the supply of information and means enabling error correction prior to the placing of the order, the 'order' means the 'contractual offer'. If or when consumers act solely as 'offerees', Articles 10(1)(c) and 11(2) will be very difficult to read, at least in Member States, which define 'orders' as 'offers'.

All in all, the EU legal response towards the risk pertaining to consumer-caused mistaken contracts could have been better. Despite the existence of the CRD right of withdrawal, error prevention in contracting is also important and the relevant provisions of the ECD which specifically tackle this issue, should perhaps be amended to accommodate more advanced modes of electronic contracting, including contracting on automated marketplaces.

It is noteworthy that the rest of the information duties of Article 10(1) are similarly not fully compatible with automated marketplaces. The duty to offer information relating to whether the contract is to be filed with the service provider[75] should also prescribe the filing of the consumer-given instructions, which would be very relevant to an allegation regarding a mistaken contract. Also, the duty to offer information on the languages available for contract conclusion[76] should refer to the languages in which contracting software can be instructed, as the language for contract conclusion will normally be the non-natural software communication language.

6.5 Concluding remarks

This chapter has discussed two risks associated with automated marketplaces, namely the possible invalidity of contracts concluded on such marketplaces and mistaken or unintended automated contracts. As it has been shown, the first is addressed by EU law, specifically by Article 9, ECD which guarantees that electronic contracts (including automated ones) cannot to be denied validity by reason of being electronic. Though the theory explaining validity is not specified at EU level (most probably, as a result of the absence of European substantive contract law), it is very important that validity is guaranteed; automated contracting would have no future, if automated contract validity was uncertain.

75 Article 10(1)(b), ECD.
76 Article 10(1)(d), ECD.

The absence of an established EU-wide legal approach towards contractual validity does lead to some uncertainty regarding the wider liability implications of automating contracting. This is because the rules regarding validity inevitably affect liability in cases of mistaken contracts and for any unlawful acts committed by the contracting software. Yet, the relevant problem is not very serious; most likely, all Member States will adopt the 'legal fiction' approach that simply ignores the involvement of an autonomous software and treats automated contracts as akin to those concluded through basic technologies such as the telephone. As it has been illustrated, this approach scores higher than the alternative ones of treating contracting software as a legal person or an agent in law, as it lacks complexity and is compatible with traditional liability rules, such as the doctrine of unilateral mistake. Moreover, it mirrors consumer users as mere service recipients who cannot be liable for unlawful acts committed due to the equipment of the service provider malfunctioning or otherwise behaving unexpectedly.

The second issue of mistaken or unintended contracts is a serious risk associated with automated marketplaces. It has been shown that the relevant EU legal response is satisfactory in the case of *malfunction-caused* mistaken contracts but not similarly so, where the mistaken contract results from some consumer error in the use of the contracting software. More specifically, in the first case the mistake doctrine can apply to automated contracting, (despite the peculiarities of the latter) and the right of withdrawal in the CRD additionally provides a powerful solution in the majority of cases of mistaken contracts, even when the mistake would not have been obvious to the other contracting party. Moreover, the UCTD effectively 'forces' the use of contract terms allowing *both* parties an escape route from malfunction-caused mistaken or erroneous contracts. An additional solution exists in the PSD2 and its refund rights which can result in the consumer recovering relevant losses especially if the automated marketplace qualifies and operates as a payment initiation service provider.

The CRD right of withdrawal serves as a satisfactory legal response to the problem of *consumer-caused* mistaken automated contracts, too. Yet, an additional solution towards such contracts exists in the ECD and operates not only *ex-post* (by allowing for the avoidance of the contract) but also *ex-ante* seeking to prevent consumer errors from leading to mistaken contracts in the first place. The relevant provisions, however, are not eligible to a clear application to contracts concluded on automated marketplaces, as they are tied to traditional (website) contracting. Thus, there is significant room for improvement of the relevant EU legal response; consumer button errors (while giving instructions to contracting software) can lead to mistaken *automated* contracts in the same way in which such errors in completing web-based order forms can lead to unintended traditional electronic contracts. As the ECD has been conceived at a time when only traditional web contracting existed (and was still at its infancy), it is only natural that its relevant provisions only address the problem in the second case and are not fully compatible with the specificities of automated contracting. Yet, as there is no valid justification behind this resulting differentiation, the error-preventive provisions of the ECD should be amended so that they at least get rid of ingredients, such as 'the time prior to the placing of the order', which render their application to automated contracting difficult or uncertain. Relevant national laws, too, should ensure that the consumer buyer is not deemed to be the offeror in all cases of online contracts, as this may not be the case in all cases in the context of automated marketplaces. When parties use independently-provided software, the ECD permissions are wholly unsuitable. Though the relevant gap could be reduced by more general information duties derived from other consumer protection measures, the EU should consider introducing wider error-preventive information duties, capable of being applied to more advanced modes of online contracting.

7 Defective or damage-causing platform services and damage recoverability

7.1 General remarks

As the participation of merchants and consumers in automated marketplaces entails the potential of causing these parties damage (or harm), the issue of damage recoverability, broad as it is, merits particular attention. Uncontestably, parties who utilize a commercialized service, including one consisting of the provision of contracting software, must have an available route to compensation should things turn out differently than expected leading to damage. The same is true of the case of shopping agent platforms, as albeit to a lesser extent,[1] damage may be caused to users of shopping agents, too. Rules of liability should thus be in place to afford a viable route to compensation.

The question as to whether such rules exist at EU level or how they should be devised is not an easy one, particularly because the relevant services are peculiar and may give rise to multiple and peculiar kinds of damage. Moreover, there may be multiple parties involved, namely the contracting software provider, the provider of the marketplace (if different from the former), the developers of their systems, if different,[2] the merchant user of contracting software and the consumer user who is need for protection. This complexity has prompted commentators to put forward drastic solutions involving affording contracting software legal personality, thus rendering it the necessary source of compensation. As it will be explained, the 'legal personality' approach is unnecessary in most cases, and it is also not a panacea in the cases for which it is mainly proposed.

The issue of 'damage' recoverability, and that of liability with which it is integrally associated, requires a holistic approach. The first question to be answered relates to the types and/or sources of damage that are relevant in the context of shopping agents and automated marketplaces. Some 'damage' types are recoverable in accordance with specialized liability rules existing in various legislative instruments. For those for which no such specialized liability regime exists, an inquiry into the legal concept of 'damage' in laws (or even model laws) at EU level is warranted. The aim is to ascertain whether the particular damage type is in fact recognized by the law as recoverable and, if yes, which area of law does so (contracts or tort). Finally, the 'liability' rules under which the relevant types of damage are recoverable must be examined in an attempt to ascertain whether the said rules can apply to

1 Infra p. 194
2 These will not in most case be different from the providers; given the experience with eBay and Amazon, automated marketplace providers are likely to develop and use their own software and/ or technical equipment rather than software or equipment developed by or marketed under the name of a different party.

shopping agents and/or automated marketplaces without problem. If problems exist, an inquiry is warranted into how they could be overcome.

The discussion in this chapter will unfold mainly by reference to automated marketplaces, as they can *directly* cause a wide array of damage to consumers, while shopping agents have limited harmful potential. More specifically, they can cause direct damage by misleading the consumer towards a bad purchase decision or infecting the consumer's device with a virus due to insufficient security measures. Less direct damage can be caused as a result of them linking to a rogue merchant or a virus-infected merchant website.

7.2 Types and/or sources of damage and the existence of a relevant liability regime

7.2.1 Privacy-related damage

In the context of automated marketplaces, damage can be monetary or non-monetary, arising out of *a privacy violation* that occurred in the marketplace. More specifically, there can be an unauthorized disclosure of consumer 'payment' details and consequent fraud, or an accidental disclosure of the contact details of a consumer who starts receiving (harassing) unsolicited commercial communications.[3] It is true that fraud can occur without a misappropriation of the credit card details of a consumer or, more generally, without interference with classical 'personal data'. Instead, it could be effected through a malicious alteration of software code causing the contracting software to buy unwanted products or to buy products at high prices. Yet, it should be recalled that such code most likely qualifies as 'personal data'. Consumer contracting software definitely serves as a consumer contact point, and as the DPWP has clarified, data which discloses a contact point through which the individual can be reached and affected constitutes personal data.[4]

In many cases, therefore, economic loss and non-monetary damage suffered on an automated marketplace will have a privacy violation or a 'personal data' security breach as its primary cause. This is particularly important, as the issue of liability for harm resulting from data protection violations is governed by a specialized legal regime laid down in the GDPR.

More specifically, Article 23(1), DPD rendered the data controller the source of compensation, and Article 23(2) reversed the relevant burden of proof requiring that the controller prove his *non*-responsibility for the damage. The data controller could escape liability in cases, such as "where he establishes fault on the part of the data subject or in case of force majeure".[5] Liability is clearly fault based (Gellert, 2015, p. 10), but the relevant reversal of the burden of proof greatly facilitated the pursuance of relevant claims, especially in the context of automated marketplaces, where it would be difficult for the consumer (or data subject) to prove that the violation has been due to the fault of the marketplace provider or a given marketplace-participating merchant. Especially, if the aggrieved consumer has dealt

3 In fact, privacy or data protection violations can result in a great variety of other (more traditional or tangible harm): "Breaches can also result in various types of identity theft (ranging from fraudulent unemployment claims to fraudulent tax returns, fraudulent loans, home equity fraud, and payment card fraud, which can impose financial, psychological, and other costs on the victims. Consumer costs can be indirect, too. For instance, in response to a breach notification, consumers must process the information and decide a course of action" (Romanosky and Acquisti, 2009, pp. 1065–1066).

4 Supra Chapter 4 p. 116

5 Recital 55, DPD.

with several marketplaces, commercial websites or more generally, online providers, it would be difficult to prove that the compromise of his personal data in fact originated from one particular data controller as opposed to another.

Still, there had been a very limited use of Article 23, DPD due to the difficulty in identifying a party responsible for the data protection breach (Linskey, 2014, p. 598). However, data protection was also less known or important during the pre-GDPR period. Additionally, in the context of automated marketplaces at least one data controller, namely the marketplace provider, will be known and identifiable. Additional data controllers will be the merchants who happened to interact with consumer contracting software, thereby processing personal data.[6] This situation may give rise to joint liability,[7] boiling down to multiple sources of compensation and thus, increased damage recoverability.

The term 'damage' was not defined in the DPD, but Recital 55 referred to "*any* damage".[8] With this in mind and given also that privacy is notoriously associated with non-tangible harms, such as mental distress, inconvenience and reputational harm, Article 23 was most probably *not* confined to monetary damage. In the UK, the term 'damage' in Section 13 of the (UK) Data Protection Act 1998, which transposed Article 23, DPD, was narrowly considered only to include monetary damage; compensation for distress was only available if monetary damage was *also* present under Section 13(2)(a) of the Act.[9] A more recent ruling by the Court of Appeal, however, acknowledged that the term 'damage' in the DPD was not confined to monetary damage and also covered emotional distress and that to the extent that Section 13(2)(a) of the Act stated otherwise, it would have to be considered as incompatible with the DPD and thus, inapplicable.[10] Given that under general tort law, consumers would face difficulty in claiming damages for *psychological* harm (such as for the distress inherent in having to worry about identity theft following a data protection breach),[11] the relevant liability rule in the EU data protection regime was invaluable.

Fortunately, the GDPR retains a privacy-specific liability rule and also sweeps away the uncertainty regarding the type of recoverable damage. Thus, Article 82(1), GDPR states, "Any person who has suffered *material or non-material damage* as a result of an infringement of this Regulation shall have the right to receive compensation from the controller or processor for the damage suffered".[12]

Moreover, Recital 146, GDPR specifically states that the concept of damage should broadly be interpreted. One remaining point of uncertainty relates to whether the concept is

6 See supra Chapter 4 pp. 119–120
7 Ibid.
8 Emphasis added.
9 *Johnson v Medical Defence Union [2007] 96 BMLR 99; Halliday v Creation Consumer Finance [2013] EWCA Civ 333* (where it was held that even nominal monetary damage was sufficient to trigger Section 13(2)(a) and thus, a right to compensation for distress).
10 *Vidal-Hall v Google, Inc. [2015] EWCA Civ 311 at paras. 72–77.* The Court of Appeal referred to CJEU case law (*Leitner v TUI Deutschland GmbhH & Co KG ECR [2002] ECR 1-1631*) and in particular to the Opinion of the Attorney-General who pointed towards a tendency at EU level to extend the term 'damage' to encompass non-monetary damage as well.
11 Romanosky and Acquisti (2009, pp. 1078–1081) illustrate this difficulty by reference to US law.
12 Emphasis added. It has been claimed (O'Dell, 2017, p. 9) that the term 'shall' means that Article 82 does not actually create a private cause of action for damage and only instructs Member States to introduce one. Despite the imperfect drafting however, this view does not seem to be supported by the nature of the GDPR as a Regulation and Recital 146, GDPR amongst others, stating that "the controller or processor should compensate any damage which a person may suffer".

intended to be as broad as also to encompass consequential economic losses, such as the expenses that a data subject may incur in his attempt to fix the problems created as a result of the infringement of the Regulation. Unlike Singaporean data protection legislation (Seng, 2014, p. 100), Article 82 does *not* explicitly confine recoverable damage to damage *directly* resulting from the infringement. Consequential losses can thus be considered as covered especially given the call for a broad interpretation in Recital 146.

The 'liability' rule in the GDPR remains fault based and associated with a reversal of the burden of proof. Thus, Article 82(3), GDPR states that "a controller or processor shall be exempt from liability under paragraph 2 if it proves that it is not in any way responsible for the event giving rise to the damage". The reference to 'the event giving rise to the damage' is unfortunate, as an event giving rise to the damage can be a virus attack or any other event for which the controller and/or processor are not responsible. Yet, the damage may occur because of the failure of the controller and/or processor to comply with Article 32, GDPR, thus implementing sufficient security measures to prevent the damage. The provision should more appropriately have referred to 'damage' (rather than 'an event giving rise to the damage'), just like Recital 146, which states, "The controller or processor should be exempt from liability if it proves that it is not in any way responsible *for the damage*".[13] That would prevent attempts by data controllers and/or processors to avoid liability and relevant uncertainty.

Other than that, Article 82, GDPR is much friendlier to the interests of the aggrieved data subject than Article 23 DPD. Indeed, liability extends to processors who breach their obligations under the GDPR or act outside the authority of the controller.[14] Accordingly, even if the marketplace provider is considered a processor (as opposed to a controller), consumers will still be able to turn against the particular party, too, given that controllers and processors alike are under an obligation to employ technical and other measures ensuring that the personal data they process is sufficiently secured.[15] Additionally, given that marketplace providers and participating merchants are bound to be involved in the same data processing,[16] it is important that the GDPR states that *each* of the controllers and/or processors responsible for the damage caused as a result of an infringement of the Regulation shall "be held liable for the entire damage in order to ensure effective compensation of the data subject".[17] This provision significantly eases the route to compensation and leaves it up to the responsible parties to figure out the extent of each other's responsibility and the corresponding amount of damage; Article 82(5), GDPR provides for the right of the party who has compensated the data subject to turn against other responsible parties to recover "that part of the compensation corresponding to their part of responsibility for the damage".

7.2.2 Monetary damage resulting from identity fraud

In relation to the recoverability of direct monetary loss resulting from a compromise of personal data consisting of consumer *payment details*, namely, a main aspect of "identity fraud" (European Commission, 2004a, p. 3), the GDPR is not alone in assisting damage recoverability. Recall that Article 73, PSD2 obliges payment service providers to refund any

13 Emphasis added.
14 Article 82(2), GDPR.
15 Article 32(1), GDPR.
16 Supra pp. 119–120
17 Article 82(4), GDPR. Rather strangely, the purpose underlying the choice of joint and several liability, namely effective compensation, is stated in the provision itself.

money debited from the account of the user as a result of unauthorized transactions.[18] The refund must be made by the payment service providers servicing the payment account of the consumer payer, meaning that this route to damage recoverability is pursuable against a party who will always be known and identifiable. The said provider must proceed with the refund "immediately, and in any event no later than by the end of the following business day, after noting or being notified of the transaction".[19] The only exception is when the payment service provider has reasonable grounds to suspect fraud, which must be communicated them in writing to the relevant national authority.[20] Importantly, the relevant right is not confined to any particular type of payment card or even to payment cards in general but extends to electronic money, too. Thus, it is much broader than the voluntary schemes of charge backs in place by all major payment card companies, such as VISA, and available in the majority of EU Member States.[21] Moreover, the refund obligation burdens not only credit institutions, i.e., banks, but also 'payment institutions'[22] like PayPal.[23] This is important as several online payments are now made through PayPal and the relevant provider will be the only one capable of providing the refund if the unauthorized payment has been made out of money held in the payer's PayPal account.[24]

Additionally, by virtue of Article 73(2), PSD2, the 'refund' obligation explicitly applies even when there has been a 'payment initiation service provider'[25] involved.[26] To the extent that automated marketplaces would qualify as 'payment initiation service providers' as explained earlier,[27] it should certainly be welcomed that the explicit language of Article 73(2), PSD2 prevents the uncertainty that would probably arise in relation to refunds as a result of their involvement in the payment transaction.

Admittedly, this 'refund' right is not unlimited. According to Article 74(1), PSD2, the payer (including a consumer payer) "shall be obliged to bear the losses relating to any unauthorized payment transactions, up to a maximum of EUR 50, resulting from the use of a lost or stolen payment instrument or from the misappropriation of a payment instrument". Though in the PSD1, the said maximum amount per transaction was EUR 150,[28] EUR 50 is still high for the majority of consumer transactions, which are typically of low value. Importantly, however, by virtue of Article 74(1)(a), PSD2, this derogation from the 'refund' right does *not* apply when "the loss, theft or misappropriation of a payment instrument was not detectable to the payer prior to a payment, except where the payer has acted

18 Supra Chapter 6 p. 187
19 Article 73(1), PSD2.
20 Ibid.
21 On these chargeback schemes or rights enabling payers to reverse unauthorized transactions, see ECC-NET (2013).
22 See definitions in Articles 4(3) and 4(4) in conjunction with Article 11 and Annex I as well as Article 4(11) in conjunction with Article 1(1), PSD2. These confirm that payment institutions qualify as payment service providers and are thus subject to the 'refund' obligations of the PSD2.
23 On PayPal as a 'payment institution', see supra Chapter 3 p. 103. PayPal is registered as an e-money institution in some Member States such as the UK (Valcke et al., 2015, pp. 57–58). Still, by virtue of Article 1(1)(b), PSD2, e-money institutions comprise payment services providers and are thus subject to the relevant refund obligations. This is confirmed by the European Commission, albeit by reference to the PSD1 (European Commission, 2008, pp. 53, 314).
24 See Chapter 3 supra p. 103 in relation to the so-called PayPal Balance.
25 See relevant definition in Article 4(15) and added explanation in Recital 27, PSD2, supra Chapter 3 p. 104
26 For more on this, see Chapter 6 supra p. 188
27 Supra Chapter 3.3.5.2.3
28 Article 61, PSD1.

fraudulently". This is very relevant to automated marketplaces; it will be impossible for consumers contracting through software to notice any misappropriation of their payment instruments before realizing that a payment has been made from their account. As a result, the Article 74(1) limitation to the 'refund' right will not affect consumer users of automated marketplaces.

7.2.3 The recoverability of other types of damage

It has been shown that when the damage suffered by consumer users of an automated marketplace consists of monetary or non-monetary damage arising from a data protection violation and/or an unauthorized payment transaction, there are clear and specific EU rules as to liability enabling the recoverability of the said damage contained in the GDPR and the PSD2. These permit a conclusion to the effect that there is a satisfactory EU legal response towards the issue of the recoverability of the relevant kinds of damage. These, however, are not the only types or sources of damage possibly to be suffered on automated marketplaces.

7.2.3.1 The types of damage and their cause

Damage to property, in particular to the hardware and data or software of the consumer user of an automated marketplace, cannot be excluded. Even when automated marketplaces or shopping agents will be accessible online (through a website), rather than in the form of software or an app installed or downloaded on the device of the user, viruses or, more generally, malware can infect a marketplace or shopping agent website (like any other website) and pass to the devices of the users of that website.[29]

Even more relevant to the specific context of automated marketplaces is (purely) economic damage or loss, that is as Barrows (2004, p. 253) explains, loss other than personal injury, damage to property and economic damage stemming from such injury or property damage. This may result from a malfunctioned-caused automated contract, in particular, if it cannot be avoided through resort to any of the relevant legal solutions discussed earlier in this book.[30] It may also be damage resulting from the contracting software closing a contract that is not the best deal available in the marketplace or failing to close a contract, thereby securing an item needed by the consumer. Such damage will normally be recoverable if the provider has represented that the contracting software was intelligent enough to close the best available deal or has guaranteed the purchase of the product that the software has been instructed to buy. In the latter case, the damage may be economic or non-economic, specifically, in the form of distress, inconvenience and/or loss of satisfaction that would arise from the use of the product or a failure adequately to prepare for an exam because the product (a required book) has not been bought.

Finally, economic damage may also result from misleading representations in or in relation to the listings displayed on shopping agent platforms or within communications sent to consumer contracting software by merchant contracting software on automated marketplaces.

It is not difficult to identify the party responsible for the loss or damage. Those of the previously described causes of damage relating to misleading representations will be attributed to the makers and/or promoters of those representations, who, in the particular context, will be the merchants featured on shopping agent platforms or selling through automated

29 On this possibility see Provos et al. (2007).
30 Supra Chapter 6.4.1

marketplaces and in most cases, the relevant platform providers too. As for the causes of actions relating to malfunctions or insufficient security measures, those may be regarded as 'software failures', i.e., "a deviation of software from its expected delivery or service" (Singh, 2009) or operational errors. Software failures are caused by software faults which are often the result of errors (Ko and Myers, 2005, pp. 43–44). These errors usually originate from the humans involved in the development or programming of the software and their failure, for example, to incorporate appropriate strategies and protocols.[31] Indeed, human mistakes such as the misreading of a specification, the omission of necessary facts from the software code and the incorrect implementation of an algorithm are common examples of causes of software failures, as experts confirm (Ko and Myers, 2005, pp. 47–48, Inacio, 1998, para. 2). Operational errors, namely "configuration errors, procedural errors and miscellaneous accidents" are alternative causes of a failure of a web application (Pertet and Narasimhan, 2005, p. 4). Most operational errors seem to be attributable to human fault, too. The possibility also exists of relevant damage being the result of a virus (or other security violation) and Denial of Service (DOS) attacks, particularly, if they cause the marketplace system either to go down during contract conclusion or behave strangely leading to unintended outputs. Indeed, security violations are mentioned as yet another cause of 'web application' failures (Pertet and Narasimhan, 2005, p. 5). Though such violations are committed by third parties, human fault linked to the provider of the automated marketplace may be in the form of a failure to apply adequate security measures. It arises that it is the provider of the automated marketplace, who will primarily be responsible for marketplace performance and hence, marketplace failures leading to consumer damage.

7.2.3.2 The EU legal response towards damage recoverability (in relation to these other types of damage)

The EU currently lacks a legal regime for 'service' liability, which means that there is no defined route to compensation for damage arising out of a 'defective' service, comparably to what exists in relation to product liability, in the Product Liability Directive. Of course, rules on liability for defective services, including liability for damage arising due to a failure of products or equipment used in the context of service provision,[32] may exist at national level.[33] EU law currently also lacks a contractual liability regime for defective services, comparable to the one existing in the Consumer Sales Directive in relation to goods, which has already been shown to be inapplicable to platform services.[34] However, the absence of general EU contractual and non-contractual liability regimes relating to service liability does not mean that EU law totally lacks solutions to the issue of damage recoverability in the context of shopping agents and automated marketplaces when the aforementioned kinds of damage are involved. As is illustrated in the following, such solutions can be found in the Proposed Supply of Digital Content Directive[35], the PLD and the UCPD. Moreover, a

31 Supra Chapter 1 p. 14

32 This case is not covered by the Product Liability Directive, see *Centre hospitalier universitaire de Besançon v Thomas Dutrueux, Caisse primaire d'assurance maladie du Jura, Case C-495/10, 21 December 2011.*

33 Greek law for example essentially reproduces and applies the system of strict liability of the Product Liability Directive to the context of services. This is in Article 8(1) of the (Greek) Law 2251/94. See also infra n. 56

34 Supra Chapter 3 p. 92

35 This has recently become a Directive, see supra n. 96

relevant comprehensive solution should most appropriately be derived from a tortious, rather than a contractual regime, though national contract regimes can also assist with the recoverability of some of the damage types.

7.2.3.2.1 THE PROPOSED SUPPLY OF DIGITAL CONTENT DIRECTIVE AND THE PLD

The European Commission (2015) has published a Proposal for a Directive on certain aspects concerning contracts for the supply of digital content, which essentially introduces a legal guarantee for digital content[36] analogous, but more favourable, to the consumer than the one applicable to goods through Consumer Sales Directive.[37] The relevant Proposal mainly refers to contracts for the supply of digital content such as movies, music, mobile apps and the like, yet its scope is broader. Indeed, in Article 2 (1) of the Proposal[38] the concept of 'digital content' is not defined solely by reference to such 'traditional' digital content[39] but very broadly by reference, amongst others, to "services which allow the creation, processing and storage of data".[40] "Cloud storage, social media or visual modelling files for 3D printing" (European Commission, 2015) are stated as examples of services covered, yet the relevant definition seems eligible to cover more online services. Though, as explained in the following, the said definition is not as broad as it seems, automated marketplace services at least, would seem to be covered.[41]

The Proposal applies to services offered for free; Article 3(1) states that "this Directive shall apply to any contract where the supplier supplies digital content to the consumer or undertakes to do so and, in exchange, a price is to be paid *or the consumer actively provides counter-performance other than money in the form of personal data or any other data*".[42] As is exemplified by Recital 14, "this Directive should apply *only* to contracts where the supplier requests and the consumer actively provides data, such as name and e-mail address or photos, directly or indirectly to the supplier *for example through individual registration or on*

36 See Articles 6, 7 and 8 of the Proposal. Article 6(1) provides as follows: "In order to conform with the contract, the digital content shall, where relevant: (a) be of the quantity, quality, duration and version and shall possess functionality, interoperability and other performance features such as accessibility, continuity and security, as required by the contract including in any pre-contractual information which forms integral part of the contract; (b) be fit for any particular purpose for which the consumer requires it and which the consumer made known to the supplier at the time of the conclusion of the contract and which the supplier accepted; (c) be supplied along with any instructions and customer assistance as stipulated by the contract; and (d) be updated as stipulated by the contract".

37 For example, the burden of proof lies with the supplier throughout the period of liability, see Article 9(1) of the Proposal. Under the Consumer Sales Directive, the burden of lies with the seller only within the first six months of the period of liability. Then, it is transferred to the consumer.

38 According to Article 2(1) of the Proposal, "'digital content' means (a) data which is produced and supplied in digital form, for example video, audio, applications, digital games and any other software, (b) a service allowing the creation, processing or storage of data in digital form, where such data is provided by the consumer, and (c) a service allowing sharing of and any other interaction with data in digital form provided by other users of the service".

39 Article 2(1)(a) of the Proposal, ibid.

40 Recital 11 of the Proposal. In the final Directive, such services form part of a distinct category, namely that of 'digital services', which are covered by the particular measure. The definition is broader in the final Directive, as the data processed or stored does not seem limited to data provided by the consumer. See Article 2(2) of the Directive and also Chapter 2 supra p. 41n98

41 See supra n. 38 and n. 40.

42 Emphasis added.

the basis of a contract which allows access to consumers' photos".[43] Given that consumers will most likely have to register to be able to participate in an automate marketplace, the contract between the provider of an automated marketplace and consumer users would qualify as a *contract* subject to the Directive, despite being offered for free.[44]

As for shopping agents, these can often be used without any requirement for registration in the context of which the consumer actively provides data; that is more often the case when the shopping agent is web based, rather than app based. Yet, the consumer does provide data, specifically about his browsing activity and in effect, about his likes, dislikes, preferences and interests (Riefa and Markou, 2014, pp. 397–398; Markou, 2016, pp. 215–216). This data has an important economic value, as providers can exploit it, thereby providing targeted advertising or market research services. Under EU law, the collection of browsing (clickstream) data by websites (often assisted by cookies and other tracking technologies) cannot be performed without prior consumer consent.[45] To comply with the relevant requirement, online businesses usually display a notice stating that their website uses cookies and that by using the website, the user consents to their use. Though it is doubtful that this should qualify as valid consent in all cases (Riefa and Markou, 2014, pp. 404–406; Markou, 2016, pp. 225–227), if the consumer continues using the shopping agent website (and even more so, if he clicks to accept cookies), that could amount to a contract and an active provision of consumer browsing data. This line of thinking would effectively bring shopping agents within the ambit of the proposed Directive.

An important positive feature of the Proposed Directive is that the liability of the provider of the service exists for the whole of the period during which the service is being provided to consumers,[46] something which is important for services such as online platforms, which are not provided once-off but for an indeterminate period.

Of course, the Proposed measure does not fully address the 'damage recoverability' issue currently under discussion, which refers to damage to property, pure economic loss and non-economic loss. Similarly to the Consumer Sales Directive,[47] the remedies available under the Proposed Directive[48] do not cover pure economic loss but are confined to (a) bringing the digital content in conformity with the contract (fixing the problem), (b) reducing the price, (which may never have been paid if the service was provided for free) and (c) contract termination.

Importantly, Article 14 of the Proposed Directive provides for another remedy, namely damages:

> The supplier shall be liable to the consumer for any economic damage *to the digital environment of the consumer* caused by a lack of conformity with the contract or a failure to supply the digital content. Damages shall put the consumer as nearly as possible into the position in which the consumer would have been if the digital content had been duly supplied and been in conformity with the contract.[49]

43 Emphasis added.

44 However,the final Directive would seem to leave out of its scope contracts for the use of automated marketplaces, if the provider does not use consumer-supplied data for any purpose (such as marketing) other than just to supply the service, see Article 3(1) of the Directive.

45 Article 5(3), EPD.

46 Article 10(c), Proposed Directive, now Article 11(3) of the final Directive.

47 Supra Chapter 3 p. 92

48 Article 12, Proposed Directive now Article 14 of the final Directive.

49 The term 'damages' is defined in Article 2(5) of the Proposed Directive as "'damages' means a sum of money to which consumers may be entitled as compensation for economic damage to their digital environment".

The digital environment of the consumer refers to the hardware and software of the consumer, i.e., damage to property discussed earlier, with specific reference to security breaches leading to malware being transferred to and harming consumer hardware and/or software.[50] Notably, security is explicitly referred to as an element of conformity with the contract in Article 6(1)(a) of the Proposed Directive[51], meaning that consumers would clearly be able to invoke the relevant measure seeking recovery of this kind of damage. Accordingly, EU law would have had an adequate and specific response to the issue of damage recoverability regarding this type of damage in the context of shopping agents and automated marketplaces, unfortunately however the aforementioned provision does not exist in the final Directive.

Thankfully, for the same type of damage, the consumer may additionally have a cause of action under the PLD, provided of course that the software comprising the marketplace is to be considered a 'product' for the purposes of the said measure.[52] In that case, a security defect leading to viruses damaging the property of the consumer would seem to render the software 'defective' within the meaning of the Directive, i.e., a product that "does not provide the safety which a person is entitled to expect".[53] This view seems to be shared by commentators arguing that software will be 'defective', if its design "in some way made it easily exposed to attack by viruses" (Howells et al., 2017, p. 192). Such *damage to property* primarily intended for private use, as opposed to economic loss, is recoverable under the Directive,[54] though only to the extent exceeding the amount of EUR 500.[55]

7.2.3.2.2 NATIONAL CONTRACT LAW

Economic loss in the form of the difference in price between the deal closed by the contracting software and the best deal available in the marketplace, for example, will generally be recoverable in contract (if there has been a breach of a representation or term guaranteeing otherwise). Indeed, contract law primarily concerns with the *economic* interests of the parties, hence as Burrows (2004, p. 207) explains, in the context of awarding damages in contract, the focus is on the failure of the party in breach to benefit the aggrieved party, i.e., to fulfil what was promised.

Non-economic losses in the form of physical inconvenience directly caused by a contractual breach, such as when the aggrieved party has to walk to work because the car he ordered has not arrived on time are generally recoverable: "Damages are . . . recoverable for physical inconvenience and discomfort caused by the breach and mental suffering directly related to that inconvenience and discomfort" (*Watts v Morrow [1991] 1 WLR 1421, 1445*). These, however, are rather exceptional cases, and national contract laws do not readily recognize a general right to recover non-economic loss[56] (Study Group on a European Civil Code and the Research Group on EC Private Law, 2009, n. 47).

50 Supra p. 198
51 Now Article 8(1)(6) of the final Directive.
52 For more on this question, see supra Chapter 3 p. 93
53 Article 6(1), PLD.
54 Article 9, PLD, see also supra Chapter 3 p. 93
55 Article 9(b), PLD.
56 Under Greek law for example, non-pecuniary (or non-economic) loss is only recoverable when the law prescribes and there is no law rendering such losses recoverable. An exception (which happens to be very relevant in this context) is Article 8(1) of the (Greek) Law 2251/94, which specifically states that the consumer is entitled to seek compensation, amongst others, for 'moral damage' against the provider of a service who causes the consumer that damage in the course of providing the service. However, this liability for non-pecuniary damage is tortious rather than contractual.

In the UK, non-economic loss is recoverable only in certain circumstances.[57] Apart from the aforementioned case of physical inconvenience directly resulting from the breach (which would seem to cover the inconvenience inherent in having to search for alternative ways to acquire a book required for an exam), there is another recognized case of recoverability of such losses. This is when "the very object of the contract is to provide pleasure, relaxation, peace of mind or freedom from molestation" as is the case with holiday contracts (*Farley v Skinner [2001] UKHL 49, para. 19*). Damages for "distress, frustration, anxiety, displeasure, vexation, tension or aggravation" can be recovered also when the matter is of importance to the aggrieved party and that was made clear to the other party whose required action in relation to the said matter was also clearly specified in the contract (*Farley v Skinner [2001] UKHL 49, para. 54*).

The object of the contract between automated marketplace providers and consumer users or the matter that requires the action of marketplace providers, is *the enabling of contract conclusion* or more simply, shopping. One could certainly view shopping-related contract conclusion as an object offering peace of mind or, at least, a matter understood by both parties to be of importance. However, even if that view were to be accepted, recovery of the non-economic loss resulting from the failure of the contracting software to conclude a contract requested by the consumer may still be difficult or at least, uncertain.

This is because of the possible remoteness or non-foreseeability of damage.[58] According to the DCFR, "the debtor in an obligation which arises from a contract or other juridical act is liable only for loss which the debtor foresaw or could reasonably be expected to have foreseen at the time when the obligation was incurred as a likely result of the non-performance, unless the non-performance was intentional, reckless or grossly negligent".[59] Given that the object of the contract between marketplace providers and consumers is the facilitation of contract conclusion in general, i.e., the conclusion of an *unknown number* of contracts of *unknown objects* (rather than the conclusion of any *specific* contract), an automated marketplace provider may be difficult to be deemed as being able to foresee all possible resulting damage. On the other hand, the requirement of foreseeability does not apply to the breach itself and most importantly, it only applies to the *type*, not the extent or other details, of the loss; it is sufficient that "the general type of consequence was within reasonable anticipation" (Harris, Campbell and Halson, 2005, pp. 95, 103). Arguably, if a marketplace allows for the conclusion of *any* contract, for example, the marketplace provider can reasonably contemplate that a breach (in the form of contracting software failing to strike a deal or the best deal) might cause consumers a wide range of damages including non-pecuniary losses. Foreseeability will certainly be easier to establish in relation to marketplaces allowing for the purchase of specific or a limited range of

57 "A contract-breaker is not in general liable for any distress, frustration, anxiety, displeasure, vexation, tension or aggravation which his breach of contract may cause to the innocent party. This rule is not, I think, founded on the assumption that such reactions are not foreseeable, which they surely are or may be, but on considerations of policy" (*Watts v Morrow [1991] 1 WLR 1421, 1445*).

58 In the UK, the principle of recoverability of damage that is not too remote has been formulated in *Hadley v Baxendale [1854] 156 ER 145, 152*: "Now we think the proper rule in such a case as the present is this: Where two parties have made a contract which one of them has broken, the damages which the other party ought to receive in respect of such breach of contract should be such as may fairly and reasonably be considered either arising naturally, i.e., according to the usual course of things, from such breach of contract itself, or such as may reasonably be supposed to have been in the contemplation of both parties, at the time they made the contract, as the probable result of the breach of it".

59 III-3:703, DCFR.

products, especially when their nature renders physical inconvenience or emotional distress relevant. The recovery of non-economic losses in contract could not therefore totally be excluded in all cases but it is, at the very least, uncertain in general.

7.2.3.2.3 THE UCPD

Interestingly, a solution pertaining to contractual recovery of damage may also arise from the Unfair Commercial Practices Directive (UCPD) and relates both to economic and non-economic loss caused by the platform service failing to achieve the results guaranteed or represented as comprising a purpose or benefit of the service. As already explained, the UCPD is not only confined to goods but covers commercial practices regarding services and digital content as well.[60]

The said measure does not currently provide for a private right of action against the traders who employ misleading or aggressive commercial practices while promoting, supplying or selling their product.[61] However, as enforcement has been left to the Member States,[62] some national laws do provide such right. An example is Ireland (Great Britain, The Department for Business Innovation and Skills, 2014a, p. 2) and the UK, which in 2014, introduced a relevant amendment of the Consumer Protection from Unfair Trading Regulations. More specifically, the Consumer Protection (Amendment) Regulations 2014[63] have introduced into the relevant Regulations a new Part 4A allowing consumers who, amongst others, have entered into a contract with a trader who has employed a misleading action[64] or an aggressive commercial practice to sue that trader seeking remedies if the practice has been "a significant factor in the consumer's decision to enter into the contract".[65]

The new rules do not apply to financial services as defined in Section 22 of the Financial Services and Markets Act 2000,[66] however payment service providers such as payment initiation service providers under the PSD2 do not qualify as 'financial services' within the meaning of the Act.[67] Thus, even if automated marketplaces are accepted to qualify as 'payment service providers' under the PSD2,[68] there will be a right to private redress against them for misleading actions or aggressive practices.

The remedies that can be sought by the consumer are the standard contractual remedies, namely the right to unwind the contract and receive the paid price back[69] or keep the product but claim a price discount.[70] Given that automated marketplaces and shopping agents

60 Supra Chapter 2 p. 44
61 This is about to change as there is an upcoming relevant amendment in a Proposal for a Directive amending, amongst other, the UCPD (European Commission, 2018a, Article 1(4)).
62 Article 11, UCPD.
63 S.I. 2014/870.
64 Misleading omissions discussed (supra Chapter 2 pp. 45–46) do not give rise to a private right of distress, see Article 27B, Consumer Protection from Unfair Trading Regulations 2008 as amended.
65 Sections 27A and 27B, Consumer Protection from Unfair Trading Regulations 2008 as amended.
66 Section 27D, Consumer Protection from Unfair Trading Regulations 2008 as amended.
67 This can be inferred from Section 22 of the Financial Services and Markets Act 2000 in conjunction with the separate regulatory regime for payment services providers introduced by the UK in transposing the PSD2. This latter regime exists in the Payment Services Regulations 2009, S.I. 2009/209.
68 On this matter, see supra Chapter 3.3.5.2.3
69 Sections 27E and 27F, Consumer Protection from Unfair Trading Regulations 2008 as amended.
70 Section 27I, Consumer Protection from Unfair Trading Regulations 2008 as amended.

will most probably be offered to consumers for free, the third remedy available under the UK Regulations, namely damages,[71] is more relevant. Importantly, not only (consequential) economic losses but also non-economic damage can be claimed. It seems clear though that in relation to the latter, only "*physical* inconvenience or discomfort"[72] is recoverable, something that makes the 'damages' remedy narrower than the one existing under the UK traditional contract law principles discussed previously.[73] Section 27J(b) also refers to damages for "alarm" and "distress", yet as is stated in the official guidance to the new rules, "damages for distress are most likely to be appropriate in respect of aggressive practices" (GB, The Department for Business Innovation and Skills, 2014b, p. 15).[74]

Moreover, it seems that a 'foreseeability of damage' test also applies to claims under the Regulations meaning that consumers will not be able to recover any non-pecuniary (or even pecuniary) damage that would *not* be recoverable under previously discussed traditional contract law principles: "In accordance with general principles, only reasonably foreseeable losses are covered" (GB, The Department for Business Innovation and Skills, 2014b, p. 15). Accordingly, the right to damages under the UCPD is *not* free from the hurdle inherent in or uncertainty surrounding damage recoverability in this context under traditional contract law. Additionally, there is an escape route available to traders, who can avoid liability for damages if they can demonstrate that the damage-causing unfair commercial practice was, amongst others, the result of a mistake or a factor beyond their control[75] or that the trader "took all reasonable precautions and exercised all due diligence to avoid the occurrence of the prohibited practice".[76] These are similar to the defences to criminal liability under the same Regulations[77] and would seem relevant to a merchant falsely represented by a shopping agent provider as being the cheapest without his knowledge, participation or control.[78] They will, however, most probably be unavailable to automated marketplace providers who intentionally, recklessly or even negligently misrepresent the capabilities of the contracting software or guarantee outcomes (such as the conclusion of every contract desired by the user).

In relation to damage possibly to be caused by shopping agents, for example as a result of the provider falsely representing that only reliable and tested merchants are featured or that a specific offering is the cheapest available, contractual recovery of damage, including under the UCPD, may not be possible. This will clearly be the case when shopping agents are not supplied under a contract.[79] For the UCPD cause of action to arise, the consumer must enter into a *contract* and not with *any* trader but with the trader who has employed the misleading action or aggressive practice resulting into that contract. The relevant Regulations subject the private right to conditions, two of which, are that "the consumer enters into a contract with a trader for the sale or supply of a product by the trader"[80] and "the trader engages in a prohibited practice in relation to the product".[81] The Department for

71 Section 27J, Consumer Protection from Unfair Trading Regulations 2008 as amended.
72 Section 27J(b), Consumer Protection from Unfair Trading Regulations 2008 as amended, emphasis added.
73 Supra Chapter 7.2.3.2.2
74 See Article 27J(4), Consumer Protection from Unfair Trading Regulations 2008 as amended.
75 Article 27J(5)(a), Consumer Protection from Unfair Trading Regulations 2008 as amended.
76 Article 27J(4)(b), Consumer Protection from Unfair Trading Regulations 2008 as amended.
77 Supra Chapter 3 p. 95
78 See the practice of 'smart buy' seals, supra Chapter 2 pp. 60–61
79 On this question, see supra Chapter 2 p. 38
80 Article 27A(2)(a), Consumer Protection from Unfair Trading Regulations 2008 as amended.
81 Article 27A(4)(a), Consumer Protection from Unfair Trading Regulations 2008 as amended.

Business Innovation and Skills (2014b, p. 10) confirms that it can be exercised against *the other contracting party*. Thus, even when the shopping agent is provided under a contract, if the misleading practice is solely employed by the provider and cannot be attributed to the merchant with whom the consumer enters into a contract as a result (as may be the case with 'smart buy' representations), there can be no private action against the platform provider under the UCPD.

Of course, as explained earlier in this book,[82] commercial practices displayed by shopping agents can, in most cases, be attributed to the merchants featured in the said practices. This is when those merchants willingly participate in the relevant platforms and have an active role in the making of the relevant practices. The same is evidently true of the commercial practices communicated to consumers within automated marketplaces. In such cases, the right cannot be exercised against the platform provider who may enter into *no* contract with the consumer as a result of the relevant misleading practices. It can, however, be exercised against the merchant with whom the consumer has contracted through the shopping agent platform or the automated marketplace. Tough in the latter case, it may be difficult to argue that the consumer contracting *software* has been misled by a misleading action of the merchant contracting software, one can resort to the adoption of a legal fiction approach similarly to what can be done in relation to the application of the doctrine of unilateral mistake.[83] Thus, when consumer damage arises out of representations inherent in listings or communications on the relevant platforms, the UCPD can greatly assist in recoverability. This is so especially given that in such cases relevant contracts (between a merchant and a consumer) will be of one specific object[84] making foreseeability easy to be examined and in appropriate cases, established.

All in all, economic and in some cases, even non-economic losses arising from 'automated marketplace' and 'shopping agent' providers failing to deliver what they have promised may be recoverable from the said parties under traditional contract law principles and under the UCPD. This is so provided that these platforms are offered under a contract and damage has been foreseeable. Moreover, some of the damage caused on such platforms can be recoverable under the UCPD (and perhaps traditional contract law principles) from the merchants selling thereon. It would seem, though, that the UCPD private redress (as introduced by the UK at least) does not add anything substantial to traditional contract law (such as, the principles governing misrepresentation). Indeed, recoverable non-economic losses are not defined more widely, and the contractual 'damage foreseeability' requirement explicitly applies to the UCPD context, too. It would perhaps be better if the UCPD private right was a (*tortious*) right of action. It could be exercised against *any* trader involved in a harmful commercial practice, whether in a contractual relationship with the consumer or not. Most importantly, damage recoverability would be easier in a tortious context, as is illustrated in the following section.

82 Supra Chapter 2 p. 56

83 Supra Chapter 6 p. 177. Thus, if consumer software is instructed to buy a product at a maximum price of EUR100,00 and merchant software communicates an offering at that price only to achieve contract conclusion and then, the consumer is asked to pay additional money, it could be argued that the offering communicated to the contract software was a misleading action. The consumer contracting software is considered to be the consumer, its involvement in the process essentially being ignored.

84 This is unlike contracts with the platform provider which have an object a very general contract conclusion service, as explained previously.

7.2.3.2.4 TORT LAW (COUPLED WITH INSURANCE) AS A BETTER ROUTE TO DAMAGE RECOVERABILITY

There are several reasons why a tortuous liability regime (supported by specific insurance duties) would be more appropriate than a contractual one, to provide for a route to compensation, despite the fact that suing in contract has the advantage of not having to prove the defendant's negligence. Indeed, tort law is notorious for having the flexibility necessary to achieve justice. As Lord Bingham has put it (*Fairchild v. Glenhaven Funeral Services Ltd [2002] UKHL 22, [2002] 3 All ER 305 (HL)*, para. 9),

> The overall object of tort law is to define cases in which the law may justly hold one party liable to compensate another. . . . If the mechanical application of generally accepted rules leads to such a result [i.e., unjustly leaving the victim without a remedy], there must be room to question the appropriateness of such an approach in such a case.

This flexibility is particularly useful in complex technological contexts, including automated marketplaces, where it is often difficult to prove fault and/or causation.[85]

More specifically, common law has long ago devised solutions for cases where the damage has multiple possible causes (*Wilsher v Essex Area Health Authority [1988] 1 AC 1074 (HL)*) or where the defendant may be taken only to have increased the risk of harm (*McGhee v National Coal Board [1972] 3 All ER 1008 (HL)*). The same principles appear in the Draft Common Frame of Reference (Study Group on a European Civil Code and the Acquis Group, 2009, sec. VI., 4:102–4:103) and can operate to relax the requirement of proving causation, thereby avoiding leaving aggrieved parties without a remedy (Burton et al., 2007, p. 26). These principles can certainly prove helpful in the context of automated marketplaces, where software systems operate online and can thus be affected by multiple different factors such as a design defect *and* a malicious act by a third party unrelated to the marketplace provider.

In appropriate cases, tort law also allows for the relaxation of the requirement to prove fault. More specifically, the tortious principle *Res Ipsa Loquitur* (*Henderson v Henry E Jenking & Sons [1970] AC 282 (HL); Ward v Tesco Stores Ltd [1976] 1 WLR 810 (CA)*) effectively reverses the burden of proof so that when the damage arose under circumstances outside the sphere of knowledge of the plaintiff, it is the defendant who has to prove that he has not been negligent. A simplified version of this principle that is moreover adjusted to technological contexts can be found in the Principles of European Tort Law, which render a party liable for damage caused while he pursues an economic enterprise using technical equipment (European Group of Tort Law, 2005, Article 4:202(1)). Obviously, this principle can lift the burden of proving negligence off the shoulders of consumers and place a burden of proving non-negligence on marketplace providers. Clearly, the latter know their systems better and are thus very well equipped to understand and explain their behaviour, unlike the consumer user who usually knows nothing about what lies behind the user interface. Interestingly, in discussing reversal of the burden of proof in relation to 'data protection' violations, commentators have described it as potentially "interesting in a much broader context" (Kosta et al., 2006, p. 41).

Additionally, though remoteness (or foreseeability) of damage is "a major limitation on recovery" in tort, too (Deakin, Johnston and Markensinis, 2013, p. 247), the degree of foreseeability of damage required in the context of the relevant requirement *in tort* is lower

85 Lloyd (2000, p. 497) demonstrates the increased difficulty in proving design defects even in simple software such as word processors that operate while confined in the relatively simple environment of personal computers.

than the degree required in the context of the corresponding foreseeability or remoteness test *in contract* (Harris, Campbell and Halson, 2005, p. 96). Accordingly, marketplace providers would more readily be accepted as being in contemplation of the damage caused to consumers in the context of an action in tort than in the context of an action in contract. This effectively means that the recovery of damage would be easier for them in tort than in it would be in contract.

As for the type of damage involved, tort law is certainly 'friendlier' to non-pecuniary (or non-economic) losses than contract.[86] Also, inconvenience, discomfort and distress can be claimed as a separate head of damages when *no* physical injury is involved (Oliphant, 2011, p. 557). It is true that tort law, and in particular, the law of negligence, is (notoriously) unsympathetic to pure economic loss (*Spartan Steel & Alloys Ltd v Martin [1972] 3 WLR 502*). Again, however, more than 50 years ago, it was established that pure economic loss can be recoverable in negligence when there is reasonable reliance of the plaintiff on a negligent misstatement made by the defendant (*Hedley Byrne & Co Ltd v Heller & Partners Ltd [1963] 2 All ER 575 (HL)*). There is a line of cases extending this principle to cases involving negligent performance (or provision) of a service (Furst, 2006, paras. 3, 4 and 13). Though, the existence of a special relationship between the parties justifying the assumption of responsibility is required (*Henderson v Merrett Syndicates [1995] 2 AC 145, 180*), it may be that such a special relationship *does* exist in the context of automated marketplaces; a professional party, i.e., the marketplace provider invites consumers to entrust him (and his systems) with the closing of contracts and thus with the altering of their legal status. As was stated in another case, "where the plaintiff entrusts the defendant with the conduct of his affairs, in general or in particular, the defendant may be held to have assumed responsibility to the plaintiff, and the plaintiff to have relied on the defendant to exercise due skill and care, in respect of such conduct" (*Spring v Guardian Assurance [1995] 2 AC 296, 318*).

Moreover, in the context of automated marketplaces, the consumer who accepts the relevant invitation indirectly commercially benefits the professional party; recall that without participating consumers, marketplace providers cannot benefit from paying merchants. In any event, the extended *Hedley Byrne* principle applies also in relation to services rendered gratuitously (*Hedley Byrne & Co. Ltd. v. Heller & Partners Ltd. [1964] AC 465, 526; Henderson v Merrett Syndicates [1995] 2 AC 145*). Accordingly, liability in tort cannot be denied on the ground that automated marketplace services are not directly paid by the consumer.

More generally, despite the historical and policy justifications behind the exclusion of pure economic loss, the validity or soundness of the distinction in protection between property and financial interests is somewhat questionable and commentators favour an approach that is open to examine the recovery of pure economic loss on a case-by-case basis without applying any harsh rule of total exclusion (Deakin et al. 2013, pp. 140–143). It may therefore be the case that courts will resort to the inherent flexibility of tort law and perhaps begin more easily to adopt even wider extensions of the *Hedley Byrne* principle.

A possible objection to an enhanced (or 'easy') recoverability of economic losses arising on automated marketplaces is a policy one and relates to the fear of stifling innovation by exposing the providers of innovative services to unpredictable or unlimited liability. Insurance, however, can allow for the spreading of the relevant risk of loss amongst multiple parties, i.e., everybody involved in the provision of the relevant service and in a position to affect the operations of an automated marketplace; such parties may be marketplace

86 As is put by McGregor (2009, para. 3-002), non-pecuniary losses flourish" in tort.

providers and companies providing hosting services, if different. This risk-spreading effect in conjunction with potential losses being translated into known and specific insurance premiums would go a long way answering the aforementioned objection.

An insurance solution in this context has been proposed in combination with an approach involving furnishing software with legal personality and thus, attaching to it liability (Solum, 1992, p. 1245; Karnow, 1996, pp. 195–196; Al-Majid, 2007, pp. 4–5). The insurance solution proposed here is different and involves EU law rendering automated marketplace insurance compulsory, just as motor insurance is.[87] The law regarding motor insurance could also inspire the introduction of an 'Automated Insurance Fund' analogous to the one that Member States are obliged to set up in relation to motor accidents.[88] The existence of such a fund would ensure that damage caused by uninsured marketplaces can still be recoverable. Such approach would create trust in the use of such services by consumers and would indirectly benefit providers who would in this way offset the burden inherent in insurance premiums.

The EU law already contains the material of one such insurance obligation, specifically, in Article 23 of the Services Directive mentioned earlier in this book.[89] Moreover, the insurance market definitely already knows *team* and even fault-independent insurance schemes. The Single Point Project (Financial Loss) Insurance (SPPI), for example, has been used in the construction industry with the support of the UK government for quite some time now (Reed Business International Ltd, 2006). All of the professionals working together to deliver a construction project, i.e. consultants, contractors and sub-contractors, are insured *as a team*. The focus is on the extent of the potential financial loss while the question as to the *specific* party who has been at fault is immaterial (Millet, 2006a, paras. 8–14). Apart from the fact that such team insurance schemes "facilitate integrated working" (Strategic Forum for Construction, 2002; cited in Millet, 2006b, para. 5) and can thus even reduce the possibility of damage arising in the first place, they also seem to constitute attractive solutions in contexts, such as automated marketplaces, to the extent that it may not always be possible to pinpoint to the *specific* party at fault.

7.3 Concluding remarks

This chapter has looked into the damage that can be caused to consumer users in the course of utilizing automated marketplace and, to a lesser extent, shopping agent services seeking to ascertain whether EU law avails of a relevant liability regime through which consumers can recover such damage. As it has been shown, such damage can be of various types and causes. More specifically, it can be a data protection violation causing economic and/or non-economic damage. In relation to this type of damage, there is a clear liability regime in the GDPR, which recognizes the right of consumers as data subjects to turn against marketplace providers and participating merchants as data controllers seeking compensation. Where the data breach involves personal data in the form of payment credentials and leads to an unauthorized payment transaction, the PSD2 complements the GDPR and avails an additional route to compensation from the payment service provider, which is readily identifiable and can enable damage recovery (in the form of a refund) more easily. Both the GDPR and the PSD2 reverse the burden of proof, which is thus placed on the data controller and the payment service provider respectively;

87 Article 3, Motor Insurance Directive.
88 Article 10, Motor Insurance Directive.
89 See Chapter 5 supra p. 170

the consumer is therefore greatly assisted in pursuing relevant claims, something that significantly enhances damage recoverability.

Things are more complicated in relation to other types or causes of damage, namely damage to property as well as economic and non-economic loss, such as inconvenience and discomfort resulting from defective security measures or design and/or operational errors in the systems supporting the relevant platforms. In relation to the first, compensation can be recovered through the liability regime of the Product Liability Directive. Though the question of whether the said measure covers software products is not uncontroversial, there are strong arguments in favour of an affirmative answer, in which case, the producer of the platform (who will in most cases be the provider) will be recognized with strict liability for the arising damage to the hardware and/or software of the consumer. A Proposed Directive on contractual liability for digital content was expected to lead to the establishment of a contractual liability regime through which consumers would be able to recover damage to property when the digital content lacks conformity with the contract, such as when it does not entail sufficient security. The very recent final Directive however, does not allow for this possibility.

None of the aforementioned measures can assist the consumer in recovering economic and non-economic losses, i.e., damage other than damage to property. In the absence of a (harmonized) EU contract or tort law regime, this chapter has first searched for damage recoverability solutions in traditional contract law principles. It found that an action for breach of contract against marketplace providers can in fact lead to the recovery of economic and even non-economic losses, though the requirement of foreseeability of damage may present problems. This is true especially in relation to non-economic losses, the recoverability of which are subject to special rules rendering their recovery to some extent exceptional even in non-technical (traditional) settings. The resulting uncertainty is not swept away by the (additional) private right of redress in cases of misleading representations (i.e., false or inaccurate information on price or delivery time) arising from the UCPD. Though it specifically covers economic and, even, some non-economic losses, specifically physical inconvenience, and could be useful in cases where contracting software fails to conclude a contract contrary to representations about its ability to do so, it is subject to the same foreseeability of damage requirement. Moreover, it can only be exercised against the party who has employed the misleading action leading to the damage provided that there has been a resulting contract between that party and the consumer. As it has been explained, the question as to whether (at least) some shopping agents are provided under a contract is not straightforward. More generally, the relevant route to compensation will not be available against the provider of the platform in some of the cases and will have to be followed as against merchants who participate in the platform. In those cases, i.e., when the damage is caused by misleading representations inherent in listings or communications on the platform, it can readily only be used against merchants on shopping agent platforms, as it would be difficult to argue that a misleading action has affected the 'mind' of the contracting software, which acts on behalf of the consumer on automated marketplaces. This is so unless a 'legal fiction' approach is adopted towards the application of the UCPD.

Finally, given the absence of a more general (harmonized) EU legal solution to the issue of damage recoverability of economic and non-economic losses, this chapter has illustrated that the relevant solution is best to be provided for in a tortious rather than a contractual regime. There will be a wider number of parties against which a right to compensation can be exercised and moreover, the area of tort law already encompasses principles, amongst others, relaxing the requirements of proving fault and causation that can be very useful to the consumer in the complex technical context of automated marketplaces. Any policy objections to an easy compensation route against providers of innovative services, such as automated marketplaces, can effectively be answered by resorting to the introduction of associated insurance obligations, especially given EU law, specifically the Services Directive, already knows of insurance obligations for certain (risky) services.

8 Conclusion

8.1 General

This book has looked into the aspects of consumer protection pertaining to two online shopping platforms, namely shopping agents, which find and compare available product offerings on the internet, and automated marketplaces, which allow for the task of finding *and buying* a product to be performed by software on behalf of the consumer. The latter have not been made commercially available as yet, but they have been shown probably to comprise the next step in the evolution of online shopping platforms. Given that the law is notoriously lagging behind technology, the legal inquiry into automated marketplaces is likely to prove particularly useful, when full automation suddenly hits e-commerce.

The 'consumer protection' aspects of the said two online platforms include issues pertaining to data protection and transactional (and payment) security; the consumer user of such platforms cannot be considered as protected if her personal data, which is intensively processed on such platforms, does not receive sufficient protection or when the transactions concluded thereon are not secure enough to prevent fraud. Thus, the legal inquiry conducted by this book has not been confined to traditional 'consumer protection' issues such as product liability or unfair commercial practices but extended to risks pertaining to data protection and security, which fall traditionally within a different area of law, namely data protection and information security law.

8.2 Risks and issues associated with shopping agents and automated marketplaces

Using knowledge derived from the use of commercialized shopping agents and other platforms, such as eBay, as well as from legal, technical, economic and consumer behaviour literature on shopping agents and automated marketplaces, this book has, as a first step, identified and illustrated the main consumer risks or issues associated with the use of the relevant platforms. It came up with seven risk/issue categories encompassing specific risks or issues, as follows:

- Bad or unintended purchase decisions and frustration of consumer expectations: information about the platform service
- Misleading marketing representations relating to the platform service, its benefits or capabilities
- Non-disclosure of information on risks, limitations and other characteristics of the service including instructions of use

This first category of risks and issues relates *both to shopping agents and automated marketplaces* and has been covered in Chapter 2. It is generally derived from the fact that the relevant services suffer from limitations, such as biases, inaccurate or incomplete information and inherent privacy risks and at the same time, are innovative, technical and even peculiar services, which may not easily be understood by consumers. Accordingly, there is an acute need for adequate information disclosure (and the avoidance of statements that can be misleading) so that the consumer is enabled to make an informed decision as to whether to use the service, how to use it and to what extent to rely on it in the context of searching for products or concluding contracts. It has been emphasized that some of the required information, particularly information helping consumers to make correct use of the platforms or their output needs, to be provided not only pre-contractually, i.e., while the consumer considers using the platform but also post-contractually, in particular while she is making use of it.

- Bad or unintended purchase decisions and frustration of consumer expectations: information provided by or exchanged on the platform
    - Incomplete or inaccurate information on vital purchase-related factors, such as delivery time in product offerings (or merchant listings) displayed and compared on shopping agent platforms
    - Incomplete or inaccurate information on vital purchase-related factors in the communications exchanged between consumer and merchant contracting software on automated marketplaces

This category of risks/issues again *relates to both shopping agents and automated marketplaces.* It has been covered in the second part of Chapter 2 and refers not to the information referring to the platform service (as the previous category) but to the information comprising the 'product' or output of the said service. This information forms the basis upon which consumer contracts are concluded and must, therefore, be accurate and complete, otherwise an unintended or undesirable consumer contract may arise. It has been emphasized that in the context of shopping agents, any accuracy or completeness requirements must target the information displayed on the shopping platform as such and not just the information that may be provided to consumers after leaving the platform and arriving on the individual merchant website. In relation to automated marketplaces, consumer purchase decisions must again be made on the basis of complete and accurate information, but the question additionally arises as to what pieces of information must be provided to the consumer contracting *software*, given that it 'thinks' and 'decides' differently than human consumers.

- Fraud or unreliable transactions: controlling or vetting merchant access to the platform

This risk has been covered in Chapter 3 and *relates to both shopping agents and automated marketplaces.* It focuses on the role of the two relevant platforms as gateways to merchants who sell their products online or as intermediaries bringing such merchants and consumers together. As it has been argued, they must be responsible for ensuring that this role does not effectively facilitate fraud or unreliable transactions, thereby causing harm to consumers or increasing costs for them, rather than the opposite. They should undertake a guardianship role keeping out of their 'doors' fraudulent or unreliable merchants. This is so especially given that technology makes available the means through which such access control can be performed and relevant platform providers should be expected to utilize them (proportionately to the risk involved), rather than being allowed to profit from a service that is not safe for consumers. This risk does not cover electronic fraud but situations in which merchants fail to deliver ordered products or do not comply with their contractual obligations, such as those relating to delivery because they are disorganized or unreliable.

- Risks pertaining to data protection (and privacy)
    - Data protection risks on the marketplace (marketplace risks)
    - Data protection risks arising after consumer personal data leaves the marketplace and gets in the hands of merchants with whom consumers have concluded contracts (merchant risks)

A 'personal data' breach leads to intangible privacy harms such as harassment and it can also expose consumers to additional risks such as identity theft and electronic fraud, which entail (tangible) financial harm. This risk category, which is ***applicable to automated marketplaces only***, has been the focus of Chapter 4, which illustrates that platform providers must adopt measures of *technological* data protection to reduce marketplace risks. Merchant risks can be addressed by privacy-enhancing measures both by the relevant merchants and the platform provider, who must ensure that only privacy-respecting merchants are allowed on its platform and hence, near consumers. It has been illustrated that the means of such *technological* data protection certainly exist and that privacy-related self-regulatory initiatives can be exploited so that data protection (and thus, consumer 'safety') on such marketplaces is further enhanced.

- Risks relating to transactional security: electronic fraud and unsecure transactions
    - Issues relating to data authentication
    - Issues relating to data integrity
    - Issues relating to non-repudiation

Chapter 5 discussed 'transactional security' issues, which are ***relevant to automated marketplaces only*** by reference to all of the ingredients of transactional security, except from data protection that has been the subject-matter of Chapter 4. These ingredients of transactional security, namely data authentication, data integrity and non-repudiation, concern the security of transactions *per se*, regardless of the involvement of personal data. It has been explained that transactional security must be considered as critical in technical environments enabling contracting; reliable transactions cannot be ensured if the origin of contractual communications cannot be verified (data authentication) and their content cannot be guaranteed as real and unaltered (data integrity). The same is true when the parties to a transaction can simply falsely deny their involvement in the said transaction and there is no concrete evidence disproving such untrue allegation (non-repudiation). Arguments against non-repudiation have been shown to be unconvincing. Again, the technical means of achieving transactional security have been illustrated to exist and marketplace providers must be expected to use them, at least when expensive products are traded or risks are high. Contracting is *de facto* a security-sensitive activity and contracting services must be inherently secure; they cannot be provided in isolation from security.

- Automated contract validity and liability for mistaken automated contracts
  - Legal validity of contracts concluded on automated marketplaces
  - Liability for malfunction-caused mistaken contracts
  - Liability for consumer-caused mistaken contracts

These issues are *only relevant to automated marketplaces* and have been discussed in Chapter 6. They are core issues, as the viability of automated marketplaces as contracting environment presupposes that there will be no doubt regarding the validity (and enforceability) of automated contracts. It also presupposes that there will be a way to avoid the effects of contracts, which are unintended or erroneous, whether caused by a technical malfunction or by a consumer mistake in utilizing the platform that can be attributed to an omission of the provider.

- Recoverability of damage arising from the use of the platform
  - Liability for damage arising out of a data protection breach (privacy-related harm)
  - Liability for monetary damage resulting from identity fraud
  - Liability for damage to property due to a defect in the marketplace
  - Liability for economic loss due to a defect in the marketplace
  - Liability for non-pecuniary loss, such as physical inconvenience and distress due to a defect in the marketplace.

Chapter 7 has emphasized that there must be a clear and viable route to compensation for damage that arises due to the use of an automated marketplace, otherwise their use will be a risky and potentially harmful consumer choice. It has also illustrated the different types of damage that may arise in this context, as well as the possible causes of each 'damage' type. *Automated marketplaces are more likely to cause damage to consumers than shopping agents*; as the latter do not host contract conclusion, their use may only mainly cause economic loss as a result of the consumer being directed towards a bad purchase decision (due to inaccurate or misleading information) or damage to property, in particular, hardware and software, if they are infected by some 'virus', which passes to consumer equipment.

A central conclusion is that automated marketplaces raise more issues and/or pose more risks than shopping agents; all of the aforementioned risk categories are applicable to automated marketplaces whereas only the first three, and, to a limited extent, the seventh category, apply to shopping agents, too. Even if one accepts that shopping agents raise data protection issues, too (mainly relating to the tracking of consumer browsing behaviour and behavioural advertising, which are common to commercial websites in general and have thus been left out of the scope of this book),[1] the issues and risks associated with automated marketplaces remain substantially more than those relating to shopping agents. It would seem that the greater the automation or reliance on the (technical) platform, the more the consumer risks and the issues that need to be resolved. This is perhaps only natural; as human consumers distance themselves from the actual shopping setting, entrusting legally binding activities to technical equipment, more effort is needed for such equipment (and its providers) to achieve the increased trust required.

1 See Chapter 1 pp. 4–5

8.3 The EU legal landscape within which the legal response has been searched for

As is illustrated in this book, the law has a central role to play in facilitating consumer trust and supporting the shift to automation in shopping, particularly by providing for sufficient consumer safeguards. If the current legal regime is not mature enough to accommodate the 'consumer protection' needs of such innovative contracting-related services, the consumer user will be at risk and the development of such services hindered. Thus, the main question that this book has sought to answer is whether EU law pertaining to consumer protection (including data protection and security) responds adequately to the risks and issues associated with the use of shopping agents and automated marketplaces. The relevant exercise involved an examination of a variety of EU legislative measures that are relevant to the electronic (or online) context, as is shown in the following list by reference to each of the identified risk/issue categories:

- Bad or unintended purchase decisions and frustration of consumer expectations: information about the platform service
    - The E-Commerce Directive
    - The Consumer Rights Directive
    - The Unfair Commercial Practices Direction
    - To a lesser extent, the General Data Protection Regulation, the Product Safety Directive and the Services Directive
- Bad or unintended purchase decisions and frustration of consumer expectations: information provided by or exchanged by the platform
    - The Consumer Rights Directive
    - The Unfair Commercial Practices Directive
- Fraud or unreliable transactions: control or vetting of merchant access to the platform
    - The E-Commerce Directive
    - The Consumer Sales Directive
    - The Product Liability Directive
    - The Unfair Commercial Practices Directive
- Risks pertaining to data protection (and privacy)
    - The General Data Protection Regulation
    - The Second Payment Services Directive (also relevant to the previous risk category)
    - The E-Privacy Directive
    - To a lesser extent, the Consumer Rights Directive and the E-Commerce Directive
- Risks relating to transactional security: electronic fraud and unsecure transactions
    - The General Data Protection Directive
    - The Electronic Identity and Trust Services for Electronic Transactions Regulation
    - The Network and Information Security Directive
- Automated contract validity and liability for mistaken automated contracts
    - Traditional contract law principles, particularly, the doctrine of unilateral mistake, and the Draft Common Frame of Reference (the latter not a legislative instrument)

  - The Consumer Rights Directive
  - The Unfair Contract Terms Directive
  - The E-Commerce Directive

- Recoverability of damage arising from the use of the platform

  - The General Data Protection Regulation
  - The Second Payment Services Directive
  - The Proposed Supply of Digital Content Directive (now a Directive)
  - The Product Liability Directive
  - The Unfair Commercial Practices Directive
  - The Principles of European Tort Law (not a legal instrument)
  - To a lesser extent, the Services Directive

Fourteen (14) pieces of EU secondary legislation, mainly in the form of Directives and to a lesser extent, Regulations, have been found to be directly relevant to shopping agent and automated marketplace platforms and in effect, to online platforms in general. The two model laws, namely the Draft Common Frame of Reference and the Principles of European Tort Law have briefly been considered alongside relevant English law, when resort was necessary to traditional contract and tort law principles given that there is no (harmonized) European contract or tort law as yet. More recent measures, such as the New Deal for Consumers, which have only briefly mentioned are not listed above.

Reference to the predecessors of some of the relevant Directives and Regulations, such as the Data Protection Directive now replaced by the General Data Protection Regulation and the Distance Selling Directive now replaced by the Consumer Rights Directive, has also been made to facilitate the understanding of the measures now in force or to flag significant differences between prior and current EU regulation. Some additional measures such as the Motor Insurance Directive, the Payment Accounts Directive and the Radio Equipment Directive have also been mentioned to draw analogies or support arguments, where appropriate. When necessary to ascertain the effects of the application of some of the Directives, there has been resort to the relevant UK transposition measures, such as the Consumer Protection from Unfair Trading Regulations 2008 (transposing the Unfair Commercial Practices Directive into UK law) and the Electronic Commerce (EC Directive) Regulations 2000 (implementing the E-Commerce Directive). Such past EU legislation or national transposition measures are not listed previously; their discussion only intended to assist in the examination of the previously listed currently in force EU legal measures in search for the EU legal response towards the risks and issues associated with shopping agents and automated marketplaces.

Though the number of EU legal measures within which the relevant EU legal response had to be searched for is quite large, the applicability or usefulness of half of them, namely the Consumer Sales Directive, the Product Safety Directive, the Product Liability Directive, the Proposed Directive on the Supply of Digital Content, the Unfair Contract Terms Directive, the Services Directive and the E-Privacy Directive is limited and in relation to some of them, even marginal.

In effect, the bulk of the current EU legal response towards the relevant risks and issues is contained in the following legal measures:

- The Unfair Commercial Practices Directive
- The Consumer Rights Directive

- The General Data Protection Regulation,

which are significantly complemented or greatly assisted by:

- The Second Payment Services Directive
- The Network and Information Security Directive
- The Electronic Identity and Trust Services Regulation
- The E-Commerce Directive,

though some of the provisions of the latter can potentially undermine, rather than assist in, the adequacy of the relevant EU legal response.

The extensive role of the Unfair Commercial Practices Directive to this highly technical context is notable. It appears as relevant to four out of the seven risk/issue categories and, as it has been shown, it often does a very good job in filling in gaps left by other measures, thereby improving and sometimes even completing the solution afforded by EU law. Given that this is a measure of the early days of the internet that lacks any technological flavour and applies to all markets indiscriminately, its high performance in the technologically advanced context of shopping agents and automated marketplaces, which also mirrors innovative marketing techniques, highlights the importance of general and/or neutral legal duties or rules. The general idea of treating consumers fairly underpinning all of the provisions of the Unfair Commercial Practices Directive, especially in conjunction with the general idea of respecting (and protecting) their personal data that underpins the provisions of the General Data Protection Regulation, which also plays a role in four out of the seven identified risk/issues categories, go a long way towards constructing an adequate EU legal response to the arising risks and issues associated with the relevant platforms.

8.4 The EU legal response towards the risks and issues associated with shopping agents and automated marketplaces

The search for the relevant EU legal response, mainly in the aforementioned fourteen (14) EU legal measures undertaken in this book, has produced the following results in each of the relevant risk/issue categories:

- Bad or unintended purchase decisions and frustration of consumer expectations: information about the platform service

The EU legal response towards the issues of misleading marketing representations relating to the nature and capabilities of the relevant platform services and the issue referring to need for disclosure on the risks, limitations and instructions for use is mainly contained in the ECD, the CRD and the UCPD and is complemented by relevant provisions in the SD and the GDPR. The ECD, in particular, Article 6(a), would only cover one specific limitation, namely, the lack of impartiality of shopping agents and thus, addresses the need for the provision of information on their business model as well as the proper identification of merchant listings. It does not, however, seem also to require the disclosure of different kinds of *paid* listings or their separation from one another. Article 6(1)(c), UCPD is a more demanding relevant provision and could be interpreted, as it has been shown, so as to give rise to one such requirement and thus lead to a complete legal solution to this specific aspect of the relevant issue.

A solution to the broader issue of information disclosure is contained in the CRD, in particular, the detailed information duties of Article 6(1). Those do not contain an explicit duty to inform as to the risks inherent in a product similarly to the one existing in Article 5 (1), PSD or less directly, in Article 6(1), PLD, which can be of no use in the particular context. However, the CRD information duties, specifically Articles 6(1)(a), 6(1)(r) and 6 (1)(s), have been shown to be capable of being interpreted so as to require the provision of information on risks, limitations and other important characteristics of the platform services. User instructions are not mandated by the said provisions though. Most importantly, though they have been shown to apply to automated marketplaces and app-based shopping agents, they may not be similarly applicable to web-based shopping agents, which are difficult to be considered as provided under a contract; as it has been explained, this difference regarding the applicability of the CRD between app-based and web-based shopping agents is difficult to explain. Moreover, the CRD only imposes *pre-contractual* information duties or duties that do *not* take account of the fact that such platform consumers need most of the relevant information while they actually use the service, i.e., post-contractually and at appropriate places on the platform. This gap is not filled in by additional provisions of the CRD, such as Article 8(7)(a), nor by Article 22(1)(j), SD, which is also a pre-contractual duty.

The UCPD, however, effectively closes these gaps: the implicit general information duty in Article 7(1), UCPD in combination with the list of information pieces of Article 6(1), UCPD have been shown as capable of being taken to require the provision of information on risks, limitations, other characteristics of the service and also on correct use. Also, the relevant provisions are applicable to both platform types with no exception; though, they require the involvement of a 'transactional decision', something that may cause questions regarding their applicability to free platform services, it has nevertheless been shown that they should be considered as perfectly applicable both to shopping agents and automated marketplaces; this is due to the close proximity between the decision to use the platform service and a purchase, i.e., a classic transactional decision. Finally, because of Article 7(2), UCPD, the information needs to be provided in a timely manner (and hence, on the platform) rather than merely pre-contractually.

Perhaps the only aspect of the information disclosure issue to which the UCPD does not clearly afford a solution relates to the provision of information and guidance on privacy- and security-enhancing features of automated marketplaces. This role has, however, been shown to be performed by the GDPR, in particular through a suitable interpretation of certain of its provisions, namely Articles 5(1)(c), 5(1)(f), 6(a) and 32, though the GDPR should have contained an explicit relevant information duty.

The related issue of misleading or inaccurate marketing representations in regard to the platform service and its capabilities is fully addressed by EU law, specifically by Article 6(1), UCPD, which effectively prohibits misleading actions. As far as automated marketplaces and app-based shopping agents are concerned, the relevant issue is also addressed by Article 6 (1), CRD in conjunction with relevant CJEU case law.

All in all, the EU legal response to this first risk/issue category can be considered as **largely satisfactory**; the material of the appropriate solutions certainly exists in the provisions of various relevant Directives, which can work together fully to address the relevant issues, though these need **careful and suitable interpretation** to achieve the said result. As it also arises, most of the work in this respect is performed by the UCPD assisted by the CRD and to a lesser extent, the ECD and the SD.

- Bad or unintended purchase decisions and frustration of consumer expectations: information provided by or exchanged by the platform

The solution to this risk/issue category, in particular, the omission by the relevant platforms of information on certain vital purchase-related factors such as delivery time, has been searched for and found in two EU Directives, namely the UCPD and the CRD. In relation to shopping agents, the pre-contractual duties of the CRD are not suitable to address the relevant issue mainly because they cannot be interpreted as requiring the relevant information to be provided on the shopping agent platform *as such*. The UCPD, however, is eligible to one such interpretation. The product offerings or merchant listings displayed on shopping agent platforms qualify as 'invitations to purchase'. As such, they are subject to specific information duties imposed by the UCPD both on shopping agent providers and the individual merchants listed on their platform (to the extent that the latter pay or otherwise, have consented to be listed). These duties, contained in Article 7(4), UCPD, require that invitations to purchase include all of the necessary purchase-related information, including delivery time. A relevant exception provided for by Article 7(3), UCPD has been explained not to be applicable to shopping agents.

There is a problem with Article 7(4), however; more specifically, it mandates information, amongst others, on delivery time *only when the relevant arrangement is not in accord with professional diligence*. As it has been explained, this qualification is not appropriate in the online context and may result in uncertainty regarding whether information on delivery time is required. A relevant (unqualified) requirement can be derived from Article 7(1), UCPD through a suitable interpretation, and if the uncertainty caused by the relevant explicit qualification in Article 7(4) is swept away (perhaps by the CJEU), the relevant EU legal response could readily be accepted as adequate.

The UCPD also provides an adequate solution to the problem of misleading 'smart buy' seals that may be attached to merchant listings by shopping agent providers; those qualify as commercial practices employed by the said providers as 'traders' and as such, they should not be misleading. The fact that the provider does not profit from the said practice does not affect his capacity as a 'trader' for the purposes of the UCPD. Actually, as it has been explained, a misleading smart buy seal is likely to be considered a more serious violation of the Directive (leading to stricter sanctions) than misleading merchant listings bearing no such seal.

The solution to the possible omission of information on all vital purchase-related factors on automated marketplaces had to be searched in the CRD, given that the communications exchanged between selling and buying contracting software are clearly pre-contractual communications triggering the CRD pre-contractual information duties. Those information duties (contained in Article 6(1), CRD) are detailed enough to require *all* of the information that needs to be considered by a consumer when contemplating a purchase, yet they are not fully compatible with automated contracting; some of the required information is totally unsuitable, as the provided information is not to be considered by a human consumer at all but by software acting on her behalf. This book has considered five different approaches towards the application of the CRD information duties to automated marketplaces. Having rejected two of them, namely the ones requiring communication of all of the required information to the consumer contracting software or directly to the human consumer respectively, it has shown that the CRD can be taken to require that some of the required information pieces be provided to the consumer contracting software while others, specifically those that could be totally useless to 'software minds', centrally on the website through which the marketplace is made accessible. The relevant exercise is by no means easy, as the relevant solution should not be achieved simply by abandoning the idea of fully automated contracting. Thus, solutions that insist in the provision of the required information directly to the *human* consumer are not in fact solutions.

This book has also advocated the adoption of a more drastic approach entailing the removal of some of the information pieces required by Article 6, CRD. The CRD cannot currently accommodate that approach, and its adoption may, in any event, be pre-mature at this stage while automated marketplaces are still at their infancy and have not been put to work in practice. However, when the time comes, it can be adopted without resulting in a discount to consumer protection through effecting certain relatively minor amendments to some of the provisions of the CRD.

Another arising issue relates to whether the CRD is addressed to automated marketplace providers too, as opposed to being confined to the merchants selling on such platforms. Though the European Commission seem to have answered the said question in the affirmative, which is a desirable approach, the issue is not entirely clear given that the 'trader' definition in the CRD does not readily support such an interpretation.

All in all, the EU legal response to the relevant issue as entailed in the UCPD in relation to shopping agents and the CRD in relation to automated marketplaces, can be considered as **adequate,** mainly in the sense that the provision of information on all vital purchase-related factors is mandated. However, the application of the relevant provisions realizing the said solution is bound to prove problematic and/or uncertain, especially in the context of automated marketplaces. They thus need **special (and careful) interpretation** to be able to produce the required effects. Moreover, in the future, when the full automation inherent in automated marketplaces is fully realized, resorting to a more automation-compatible approach may be merited. Such an approach would entail the removal of some information pieces from the pre-contractual duty Article 6(1), CRD coupled with certain adjustments to other CRD provisions, such as Article 6(6), to ensure the maintenance of a satisfactory level of consumer protection.

- Fraud or unreliable transactions: control or vetting of merchant access to the platform

The risk of fraud or of transactions with unreliable merchants has been shown as capable of being tackled by a legal obligation on relevant platform providers to control merchant access to their systems, thus ensuring that only real and reliable merchants will reach consumers. As it has been explained, no alternative legal approach, such as the 'notice and take down', could effectively respond to the relevant risk. The search for one such legal obligation conducted by this book has *not* led to any EU legal measure from which it could be derived directly. The provisions on intermediary liability of the ECD, in particular, Article 14, ECD, can be interpreted as covering both 'shopping agent' and 'automated marketplace' providers. In such a case, not only they will be exempted from liability for the fraud committed through their services but also Article 15, ECD may even prohibit the imposition of the suggested fraud-preventive obligation on them. Of course, a suitable interpretation of the relevant ECD provisions should exclude the relevant platform providers from their scope, yet national case law has not consistently been following that direction and the European Commission seems to consider a relevant obligation as prohibited. This book has suggested ways in which this undesirable result can be avoided (or the relevant uncertainty resolved), including officially flagging the intended (and appropriate) restrictive interpretation of the relevant provisions.

A relevant obligation has been found not to arise indirectly from any of the liability-related Directives. The CSD is wholly inapplicable to the relevant platform providers, whereas the PLD and the PSD, though potentially applicable, are not concerned at all with the type of damage, namely economic loss inherent in the risk of fraud. However, a fraud-preventive obligation has been shown indirectly to arise from the UCPD, which can tackle both traditional fraud in the form of deceptive merchant listings or contractual communications and less traditional fraudulent techniques, such as a malicious alteration of consumer software code. More specifically, as platform providers qualify as 'traders' for the purposes of the UCPD, they are effectively obliged to take measures to limit or eliminate unfair commercial practices on their systems, thereby avoiding relevant sanctions themselves. It has been explained, however, that the said potential of the UCPD, at least as far as an obligation to vet promoted or selling merchants is concerned, remains unrecognized so far. Moreover, the relationship between this measure and the ECD provisions on intermediary liability may need to be clarified; though the ECD should not be taken to prevent the fraud-preventive obligation indirectly arising from the UCPD, it is not clear that this is not in fact the case. Additionally, the effectiveness of the UCPD-derived obligation will very much depend on how effective enforcement will be. The fact that it is mainly up to the consumer to uncover fraudulent practices, thereby triggering enforcement, has been said to comprise an important relevant weakness, particularly, in the context of automated marketplaces in which consumers have no active involvement in the contractual process or sufficient knowledge of how merchants act or behave.

In relation to automated marketplaces, any gap in protection created by the absence of a direct or explicit legal fraud-preventive obligation in the form of 'platform access' control is somewhat reduced by the PSD2; as this measure concerns with payments, it has no role to play in the context of shopping agents, which do not host or support payments. The PSD2 has been explained to afford powerful protection against consumer fraud not only *ex-post* but also *ex-ante*. Its refund rights, which are triggered in cases of unauthorized transactions resulting in consumer financial harm, only provide for a partial solution, however; in the context of automated marketplaces, fraud will not always be in the form of unauthorized payment transactions for the purposes of the refund-related PSD2 provisions. However, its *ex-ante* controls in the form of demanding payment security obligations and the obligation for strong customer authentication have a great potential of significantly enhancing the security of automated marketplaces, thereby protecting consumer payers against fraud. It has been shown that the ingredients of strong customer authentication may not be compatible with automated marketplaces, thus resulting in payment service providers administering payment instruments and/or servicing payment accounts 'blocking' consumer use of such marketplaces. Yet, the said problems are not impossible to overcome, mainly because automated marketplaces would in many cases qualify as 'payment service providers', specifically PISPs. Accordingly, not only are payment service providers prohibited from refusing to co-operate with automated marketplace providers but also the latter are subject to the detailed security obligations of the PSD2 themselves, something that directly (and indirectly as it has been explained) renders their service largely fraud-proof. Moreover, it strongly encourages the use of technical measures of increased security, such as digital signatures regulated by the eIDAs Regulation.

All in all, the EU legal response to risk of fraud associated with shopping agents and automated marketplaces is **not fully adequate**, mainly due to the lack of a direct and/or explicit fraud-preventive obligation imposed on platform providers. Any work performed by EU law in this respect is again potentially done by the UCPD, which may somewhat reduce the relevant gap, particularly if Article 15, ECD is not allowed to hinder its relevant role. The problem is more serious in relation to shopping agents, as in relation to automated marketplaces, the PSD2 further reduces the adverse effects of the lack of the suggested fraud-preventive obligation.

- Risks pertaining to data protection (and privacy)

The use of automated marketplaces also entails data protection risks to which the appropriate response has been illustrated to consist of certain specific elements, namely (a) an obligation on marketplace providers to respect (and protect) consumer personal data and apply existing privacy-enhancing technologies, in particular encryption (something that responds to marketplace privacy-related risks); (b) an obligation on marketplace providers to apply a privacy-related access control mechanism (something that responds to both marketplace and merchant privacy-related risks); (c) official control and/or oversight of providers of privacy credentials to be used in the context of the aforementioned access control mechanism; (d) effective encouragement of merchant participation in regulatory schemes leading to the award of privacy credentials; (e) the obligation described in point (a) above imposed on participating merchants, as those, too, process consumer personal data on their own systems *post*-contract conclusion and (f) a *multiplicity* of parties as addresses of the obligations referred to in the aforementioned element (a) for increased effectiveness.

These elements have primarily been searched for in the EU data protection regime, namely the GDPR and the EPD, though it has been illustrated by this book that additional data protection is afforded by the PSD2, when it comes to the specific case of personal data in the form of consumer payment details such as passwords Though the data processed by marketplace providers and marketplace-participating merchants have been illustrated to qualify as 'personal data', which is very broadly defined, the obligations of the EPD, being addressed to electronic communications service providers, will not apply to most automated marketplaces. This is not a problem, as the EPD (and the Regulation soon to replace it) does not go beyond the obligations of the GDPR. The latter are mainly addressed to data controllers. In relation to the main data processing involved in an automated marketplace service, marketplace providers and marketplace-participating merchants would both qualify as data controllers (acting together as joint controllers). The GDPR is thus perfectly applicable to them.

Most importantly, it provides for all six ingredients of the appropriate solution. Though an *explicit* duty vested on controllers to police or vet a joint controller is absent (something which is perhaps unfortunate), the rules on joint controllership regarding civil liability and public sanctions effectively impose a relevant duty *indirectly*. Thus, merchants will strive to use law-abiding marketplaces, thereby avoiding liability and sanctions themselves (provided care is taken not to consider merchants as having a marginal degree of responsibility due to the data processing occurring on the systems of the marketplace provider). Similarly, marketplace providers will want to vet merchants allowed in their marketplace, thereby reducing data breaches for which they will also be liable. This greatly improves the practical effectiveness of the GDPR obligations and seems to entail two of the aforementioned six elements of an adequate legal response, namely elements (b) and (f).

Elements (a) and (e), namely, a clear obligation on marketplace providers and marketplace-participating merchants respectively to protect personal data through the adoption of technical privacy-enhancing measures, also exist in the GDPR, particularly, Articles 5, 24, 25, 32 and 35. These have a strong technological flavour and should be expected to be given further specificity facilitating compliance through technical standards.

As it has been illustrated, relevant self-regulation initiatives can greatly enhance data protection in automated marketplaces (and in general) if adequately exploited by the law in the context of a relevant co-regulatory approach, as evinced in elements (c) and (d) of the adequate legal response. Both of these elements have again been found in the GDPR, in particular its section governing codes of conduct and certification seals. Doubtless, the relevant provisions comprise a decisive attempt on the part of EU law to adopt an effective co-regulatory approach in the area of data protection and also encourage merchant participation in self-regulatory schemes, amongst others, by rendering such participation legally relevant and thus beneficial to participants. Whether the relevant co-regulatory approach will actually work well, thereby improving data protection, will of course largely depend on how rigorously DPAs perform their duties of approving codes and/or monitoring the administration and enforcement of relevant self-regulatory schemes. Self-regulation could further be exploited by an information duty obliging controllers to disclose their certification or participation in a relevant code of conduct. Unfortunately, the GDPR lacks one such information duty, and relevant duties in the CRD and the ECD do not cover seals. Moreover, it is uncertain whether they could be interpreted as covering codes of conduct relating to data protection.

Overall, the EU legal response towards the data protection risks associated with automated marketplaces, mainly entailed in the provisions of the GDPR, is **largely satisfactory**. These provisions do suffer from certain deficiencies. The deficiencies consisting of the fact that Articles 24 and 25, GDPR are not addressed to processors do not affect automated marketplaces, as all of the parties involved are, as illustrated, controllers. However, the deficiencies relating to the provisions on self-regulation, such as the lack of consequences for the use of rejected codes or an obligation on DPAs to act without delay when examining a code for approval, are important and if addressed, the adequacy of the EU legal response in this context will certainly further be improved.

- Risks relating to transactional security: electronic fraud and unsecure transactions

As automated contracting services are inherently risky (as they can alter the legal status of users while relying on technical equipment operating on the internet), providers should be obliged to make use of available technologies affording transactional security, in particular data authentication, data integrity and non-repudiation. It has arisen that the general security obligations contained in Article 32, GDPR burden *all* automated marketplace providers as data controllers and are appropriately subject to a proportionality criterion relating to the risk involved. Those obligations cover data integrity and albeit less directly, data authentication too, but it is somewhat to difficult and, at the very least, uncertain also to derive an obligation to adopt technical non-repudiation measures as well. Moreover, the said security obligations do not focus on transactional security, which should be considered a virtue in its own right but are inevitably tied to the involvement of *personal* data. This may result in security gaps, especially when a contractual communication comes from the merchant, which is a legal person and thus contains no personal data.

The NISD reduces these gaps by imposing general security obligations on certain information service providers (subject to a proportionality criterion relating to the risk involved). The said obligations, however, are not addressed to all automated marketplace providers, as small businesses and microenterprises are excluded. Moreover, similarly to the security obligations of the GDPR, they do not focus on *transactional* security but rather on general data and network security. Whether the non-repudiation element of transactional security is covered by the NISD obligations is, as a result, again uncertain.

By contrast, the eIDAS focuses on the security of transactions as such. However, though it regulates all of the services necessary for a secure contracting environment, such as digital signatures, it does not impose any (direct) obligation on marketplace providers to utilize those services. Of course, amongst others, by confirming their legal validity, it powerfully encourages their use and, most definitely, deprives relevant providers of any justification for not using them, thereby discharging their obligations imposed by the GDPR and the NISD. There is therefore a great potential for a synergy between the GDPR, the NISD and the eIDAS; such a synergy can cover for the imperfections of each one of the said measures (as far as transactional security is concerned) and lead to a recognized obligation on marketplace providers (particularly those entailing a high risk due to the high value of products, for example) to exploit the 'transactional security' services regulated by the eIDAS. If market forces further boost this potential, resulting in its materialization, the EU legal response towards the transactional security risks associated with automated marketplaces will be able to considered as adequate.

All in all, to the extent that there is no direct and clear obligation to adopt 'transactional security' measures, at least when there is a high risk involved, the EU legal response towards the relevant risks associated with automated marketplaces is **not fully adequate**. EU law however definitely contains the raw material of an adequate relevant solution, though certain deficiencies, such as the reversal of the burden of proof only in relation to the liability of the qualified trust service providers in the eIDAS, do exist. Of course, only time will show how the combination of the existing relevant legal measures will work in practice and what results will be achieved. The fact that online marketplaces have been included in the addressees of the security obligations of the NISD at the last minute, coupled with the fact that those comprise only the minority of big marketplaces, cannot leave one very optimistic regarding the extent of the adoption of digital signatures and other eIDAS trust services, Of course, the PSD2 which may be applicable to more automated marketplaces and also pushes for the adoption of security-enhancing technologies governed by the eIDAS can be of assistance.

- Automated contract validity and liability for mistaken automated contracts

Possible legal solutions to two further risks associated with automated marketplaces, namely the possible invalidity of automated contracts and mistaken or unintended contracts, have been found in the ECD in relation to the first and the CRD, the UCTD and the PSD2 in relation to the second. Any uncertainty regarding the validity (and hence, enforceability) of contracts concluded on automated marketplaces is bound to hinder their development and it is therefore very important that the relevant issue is fully addressed by EU law. Though unlike in other jurisdictions, fully automated contracts are not specifically regulated, Article 9, ECD is unequivocal that electronic contracts, which clearly include automated ones, should not be denied validity by reason of being electronic. The theory explaining validity is not specified at EU level (most likely as a result of the absence of European substantive contract law), something that leads to some uncertainty regarding the wider liability implications of automating contracting; the validity-related rules have been explained inevitably to affect liability in cases of mistaken contracts and for unlawful acts committed by the autonomous contracting software.

Yet, the relevant problem is not a major one. Indeed, this book has gone through the four possible approaches by reference to which validity could be explained, namely 'legal fiction', relaxation of the contractual intention requirement, software legal personality and software as an agent in law. It has concluded that the most appropriate one is the 'legal fiction' approach, which simply ignores the involvement of an autonomous software and treats automated contracts as akin to those concluded through basic technologies such as the telephone. Indeed, unlike the last two, at least, it lacks complexity and works well with traditional liability rules, such as the doctrine of unilateral mistake, without leading to absurd or undesirable results relating to consumer liability. Most probably, therefore, no Member State will adopt an alternative approach leading to a lack of uniformity and consequent uncertainty.

As for the risk of mistaken contracts, these are divided into ***malfunction-caused*** and ***consumer-caused*** mistaken contracts, the latter arising from some consumer error in the use of the contracting software. Apart from the fact that the mistake doctrine can, as it has been shown, apply to automated contracting (despite the peculiarities of the latter), the right of withdrawal in the CRD, effectively allowing consumers a 14-day period within which they can withdraw from a distant contract without having to show reason, provides a powerful solution in the majority of cases of mistaken contracts, whether caused by malfunction or consumer. Additionally, the UCTD has been explained effectively to 'force' the use of contract terms allowing ***both*** parties an escape route from malfunction-caused mistaken contracts, if appropriately interpreted. Additional solutions in the PSD2, particularly refund rights, could also be helpful to the consumer in practice, particularly if automated marketplaces operate as payment initiation service providers.

The CRD right of withdrawal serves as a satisfactory legal response to the problem of ***consumer-caused*** mistaken automated contracts, too. Yet, an additional solution towards such contracts exists in the ECD, specifically, Article 11(2), and operates not only *ex-post* (by permitting the avoidance of the contract) but also *ex-ante* seeking to prevent consumer errors from leading to mistaken contracts in the first place. The said provision obliges service providers to make available to consumers the technical means of correcting any button errors before they submit their order. However, it is tied to traditional web contracting and does not seem eligible for a clear and/or unproblematic application to contracts concluded on automated marketplaces. As consumer button errors (while giving instructions to contracting software) can lead to mistaken contracts in the same way in which such errors in the context of completing web-based order forms can, EU law should address the relevant issue in both cases.

All in all, the EU legal response towards this risk/issue category is largely satisfactory, though the solution in the UCTD pre-supposes a suitable interpretation unearthing it. Moreover, the response towards consumer-caused mistaken contracts merits further improvement, specifically by an extension of the approach regarding consumer button errors of Article 11(2), ECD to automated contracts; not only will this avail consumers of an additional escape route from a mistaken or unintended contract but also it will reduce such contracts, which is certainly desirable.

- Recoverability of damage arising from the use of the platform

The answer to the question regarding whether EU law contains appropriate rules as to liability to enable consumers to recover damage arising from the use of an automated marketplace or a shopping agent depends on the type or cause of the damage involved. When there is a data protection violation causing economic and/or non-economic damage, there is a clear liability regime in the GDPR, which recognizes the right of consumers as data subjects to turn against marketplace providers and participating merchants as data controllers seeking compensation. Where the data breach involves consumer payment credentials and leads to an unauthorized payment transaction, the PSD2 complements the GDPR and provides for an additional route to compensation against the payment service provider, which is readily identifiable and can enable damage recovery (in the form of a refund) more speedily (or easily). Both the GDPR and the PSD2 reverse the burden of proof, thereby placing it on the data controller and the payment service provider, respectively. The consumer is therefore greatly assisted in pursuing relevant claims, something that significantly enhances relevant damage recoverability and enables one to consider the relevant EU legal response as adequate.

The position is not as straightforward in relation to damage to property as well as economic and non-economic loss, such as inconvenience and discomfort, resulting from defective security measures and/or design or operational errors in the systems supporting the relevant platforms. In relation to the first, compensation can be recovered through the liability regime of the Product Liability Directive. Though the question of whether the said measure covers software products is not uncontroversial, there are strong arguments in favour of an affirmative answer, in which case the producer of the platform (who will in most cases be the provider) will be imposed strict liability for the arising damage to the hardware and/or software of the consumer. The Directive on certain aspects concerning contracts for the supply of digital content and digital services has led to the establishment of a contractual liability regime as well, yet pure economic losses are not recoverable and consumers will not be able to recover damage to property when the digital service (the platform service) lacks conformity with the contract, such as when it does not entail sufficient security, either.

The PLD cannot assist the consumer in recovering economic and non-economic losses, i.e., damage other than damage to property. In the absence of a (harmonized) EU contract or tort law regime, this book has first searched for damage recoverability solutions in traditional contract law principles. It found that an action for breach of contract against marketplace providers can in fact lead to the recovery of economic and even non-economic losses, though the requirement of foreseeability of damage may present problems, especially in relation to non-economic losses. Indeed, the recoverability of such losses is subject to special rules rendering their recovery to some extent exceptional even in non-technical (traditional) settings.

The resulting uncertainty is not resolved by the (additional) private right of redress in cases of misleading representations (i.e., false or inaccurate information on price or delivery time) based on national implementations of the UCPD. In the UK, though the relevant right specifically covers economic and even some non-economic losses, specifically physical inconvenience, it is subject to the same 'foreseeability of damage' requirement. Moreover, it can only be exercised against the party who has employed the misleading action leading to the damage and provided that there has been a resulting contract between that party and the consumer. As a result, the relevant route to compensation will not be available against the provider of the platform where the platform is not provided under a contract; this may be the case in relation to some shopping agents. It will also be unavailable in cases where the misleading action cannot be attributed to the merchant with whom the consumer has concluded a contract; this will mainly be the case in relation to 'smart buy' commercial practices. Even when this is not the case and the right can thus be exercised against the merchant, difficulties may arise in relation to one of the platforms, namely automated marketplaces; it would be difficult to argue that a misleading action has affected the 'mind' of contracting software, unless of course, a legal fiction approach (ignoring the software involvement) is adopted towards the application of the UCPD. Overall, the UCPD right (at least, as implemented in the UK) appears be very narrow to be considered as evincing an adequate legal response towards damage recoverability.

At a more general level, this book has illustrated that the solution to the issue of recoverability for economic and non-economic loss is best to be provided for in a tortious rather than a contractual regime, mainly because several tort law principles, amongst others, relating to causation, the burden of proof and the type of losses recoverable, can handle the difficulties inherent in establishing liability in technical environments. Any policy objections to an easy compensation route against providers of innovative services, such as automated marketplaces, can effectively be answered by resorting to the introduction of associated insurance obligations; insurance can ensure the manageability of the financial consequences of liability. EU law, specifically Article 23, SD, already contains an insurance obligation, which should be recognized as highly relevant in the particular context.

Overall, the EU legal response towards the issue of damage recoverability is adequate to the extent that the damage arises from or can be linked to a data protection or payment credential violation (or compromise) or when it consists of damage to property. There is also a sufficient response in most cases where the damage arises from misleading actions attributable to merchants participating on the platform. This is not the case when defects in the marketplace systems, for example, lead to economic or non-economic loss. It should be noted, however, that as such liability issues are not currently regulated at EU level, any relevant failure could not fully be attributed to EU law. Even the private right of redress based on the UCPD is not, at this stage at least, a creature of the Directive itself. It has been explained that a tort liability regime would be more appropriate to accommodate the needs of consumer users in this context than a contractual one, but this is an option to be taken up primarily by Member States. The insurance obligation that is necessary to support a relevant tort liability rule does exist in EU law, but again needs to be exploited by Member States. With these in mind, though EU law does not afford a comprehensive solution to the issue of damage recoverability, its response, in relation to the types and/or sources of damage regulated at EU level, is adequate. Moreover, it contains an insurance obligation that can prove useful in relation to types or sources of damage not so regulated. In this respect, the relevant EU legal response can be considered as largely satisfactory.

8.5 Overall conclusions

The EU legal response towards the consumer protection risks and issues associated with shopping agents and automated marketplaces, though not comprehensive or fully adequate, can be considered as largely satisfactory, especially given that online platforms are relatively new e-commerce actors and automated marketplaces have not been commercialized as yet. Perhaps the most notable gaps relate to the lack of an obligation vested on platform providers to prevent fraud by controlling platform access and to employ transactional security measures proportionate to the risk involved. An indirect fraud-preventive obligation and multiple data protection and security obligations, however, can somewhat reduce the relevant gap, though only in the case of automated marketplaces, which allow for contracting and payments. EU law has been found to afford direct and adequate solutions in relation to some of the risks involved, such as in relation to data protection risks while in relation to the other risks and issues, the legal response has been found to be largely satisfactory or as encompassing the raw material of appropriate solutions. Accordingly, the EU is not in need of a wholly new (that needs to be built from scratch) for e-commerce. Quite often, the relevant provisions need special (or suitable) interpretation or adjustments to be able to realize the intended or desirable results in some cases resulting in uncertainty. Yet, this is only natural when laws not devised with a particular technology (or innovative business model) in mind are called upon to regulate one such technology or business model. Such regulation requires knowledge and understanding of the relevant technology and/or business model by legislators and enforcers and, of course, some insight or guidance, which this book has sought to offer in relation to the two relevant online platforms.

Bibliography

1. Legislation

1.1 European Union

Council Directive 85/374/EEC of 25 July 1985 on the approximation of the laws, regulations and administrative provisions of the Member States concerning liability for defective products ('Product Liability Directive' (PLD)) [1985] OJ L 210/29.

Council Directive 86/653/EEC of 18 December 1986 on the coordination of the laws of the Member States relating to self-employed commercial agents ('Commercial Agents Directive') [1986] OJ L 382/17.

Council Directive 93/13/EEC of 5 April 1993 on unfair terms in consumer contracts ('Unfair Contract Terms Directive' (UCTD) [1993] OJ L 95/29.

Directive 95/46/EC of the European Parliament and of the Council of 24 October 1995 on the protection of individuals with regard to the processing of personal data and on the free movement of such data ('Data Protection Directive' (DPD)) [1995] OJ L 281/0031.

Directive 97/7/EC of the European Parliament and of the Council of 20 May 1997 on the protection of consumers in respect of distance contracts ('Distance Selling Directive') [1997] OJ L 144/19.

√Directive 98/34/EC of the European Parliament and of the Council of 22 June 1998 laying down a procedure for the provision of information in the field of technical standards and regulations ('Technical Standards Directive') [1998] OJ L 204/37.

√Directive 98/48/EC of the European Parliament and of the Council of 20 July 1998 amending Directive 98/34/EC laying down a procedure for the provision of information in the field of technical standards and regulations [1998] OJ L 217/18.

Directive 1999/5/EC of the European Parliament and of the Council of 9 March 1999 on radio equipment and telecommunications terminal equipment and the mutual recognition of their conformity ('Radio Equipment Directive') [1999] OJ L 91/10.

Directive 1999/44/EC of the European Parliament and of the Council of 25 May 1999 on certain aspects of the sale of consumer goods and associated guarantees ('Consumer Sales Directive' (CSD)) [1999] OJ L 171/0012.

Directive 1999/93/EC of the European Parliament and of the Council of 13 December 1999 on a Community framework for electronic signatures ('Electronic Signatures Directive' (ESD)) [1999] OJ L 013/0012.

Directive 2000/31/EC of the European Parliament and of the Council of 8 June 2000 on certain legal aspects of information society services, in particular electronic commerce, in the Internal Market ('Directive on electronic commerce') ('E-commerce Directive (ECD)) [2000] OJ L 178/1.

Directive 2001/95/EC of the European Parliament and of the Council of 3 December 2001 on general product safety ('General Product Safety Directive') [2001] OJ L 11/4.

Directive 2002/21/EC of the European Parliament and of the Council of 7 March 2002 on a common regulatory framework for electronic communications networks and services (Framework Directive) [2002] OJ L 108/33.

Directive 2002/22/EC of the European Parliament and of the Council of 7 March 2002 on universal service and users' rights relating to electronic communications networks and services ('Universal Service Directive' (USD)) [2002] OJ L 108/51.

Directive 2002/58/EC of the European Parliament and of the Council of 12 July 2002 concerning the processing of personal data and the protection of privacy in the electronic communications sector (Directive on privacy and electronic communications) [2002] OJ L 201/37.

Directive 2005/29/EC of the European Parliament and of the Council of 11 May 2005 concerning unfair business-to-consumer commercial practices in the internal market and amending Council Directive 84/450/EEC, Directives 97/7/EC, 98/27/EC and 2002/65/EC of the European Parliament and of the Council and Regulation (EC) No 2006/2004 of the European Parliament and of the Council ('Unfair Commercial Practices Directive' (UCPD)) [2005] OJ L 149/22.

Directive 2006/123/EC of the European Parliament and of the Council of 12 December 2006 on services in the internal market ('Services Directive') [2006] OJ L 376/36.

Directive 2007/64/EC of the European Parliament and of the Council of 13 November 2007 on payment services in the internal market amending Directives 97/7/EC, 2002/65/EC, 2005/60/EC and 2006/48/EC and repealing Directive 97/5/EC ('First Payment Services Directive' (PSD)) [2007] OJ L 319/0001.

Directive 2009/103/EC of the European Parliament and of the Council of 16 September 2009 relating to insurance against civil liability in respect of the use of motor vehicles, and the enforcement of the obligation to insure against such liability ('Motor Insurance Directive') [2009] OJ L 263/11.

Directive 2009/110/EC of the European Parliament and of the Council of 16 September 2009 on the taking up, pursuit of and prudential supervision of the business of electronic money institutions amending Directives 2005/60/EC and 2006/48/EC and repealing Directive 2000/46/EC ('E-Money Directive') [2009] OJ L 267/7.

Directive 2009/136/EC of the European Parliament and of the Council of 25 November 2009 amending Directive 2002/22/EC on universal service and users' rights relating to electronic communications networks and services, Directive 2002/58/EC concerning the processing of personal data and the protection of privacy in the electronic communications sector and Regulation (EC) No 2006/2004 on cooperation between national authorities responsible for the enforcement of consumer protection laws [2009] OJ L 337/11.

Directive 2010/13/EC of the European Parliament and of the Council of 10 March 2010 on the coordination of certain provisions laid down by law, regulation or administrative action in Member States concerning the provision of audiovisual media services (Audiovisual Media Services Directive) [2010] OJ L 95/1.

Directive 2011/83/EU of the European Parliament and of the Council of 25 October 2011 on consumer rights, amending Council Directive 93/13/EEC and Directive 1999/44/EC of the European Parliament and of the Council and repealing Council Directive 85/577/EEC and Directive 97/7/EC of the European Parliament and of the Council ('Consumer Rights Directive' (CRD)) [2011] OJ L 304/64.

Directive 2013/11/EU of the European Parliament and of the Council of 21 May 2013 on alternative dispute resolution for consumer disputes and amending Regulation (EC) No 2006/2004 and Directive 2009/22/EC (Directive on consumer ADR) [2013] OJ L 165/63

Directive 2014/92/EU of the European Parliament and of the Council of 23 July 2014 on the comparability of fees related to payment accounts, payment account switching and access to payment accounts with basic features ('Payment Accounts Directive' (PAD)) [2014] OJ L 257/214.

√Directive (EU) 2015/1535 of the European Parliament and of the Council of 9 September 2015 laying down a procedure for the provision of information in the field of technical regulations and of rules on Information Society services, [2015] OJ L 241/1.

Directive (EU) 2015/2366 of the European Parliament and of the Council of 25 November 2015 on payment services in the internal market, amending Directives 2002/65/EC, 2009/110/EC and 2013/36/EU and Regulation (EU) No 1093/2010, and repealing Directive 2007/64/EC ('Second Payment Services Directive' (PSD2)) [2015] OJ L 337/35.

Directive (EU) 2016/1148 of the European Parliament and of the Council of 6 July 2016 concerning measures for a high common level of security of network and information systems across the Union ('Network and Information Security Directive' (NISD)) [2016] OJ L 194/1.

Directive (EU) 2018/1972 of the European Parliament and of the Council of 11 December 2018 establishing the European Electronic Communications Code (Recast) [2018] OJ L 321/36.

Directive (EU) 2019/770 of the European Parliament and of the Council of 20 May 2019 on certain aspects concerning contracts for the supply of digital content and digital services, (PE/26/2019/REV/1), [2019] OJ L 136/1.

Regulation (EC) No 544/2009 of the European Parliament and of the Council of 18 June 2009 amending Regulation (EC) No 717/2007 on roaming on public mobile telephone networks within the Community and Directive 2002/21/EC on a common regulatory framework for electronic communications networks and services, [2009] OJ L 167/12.

Regulation (EU) No 1025/2012 of the European Parliament and of the Council of 25 October 2012 on European standardisation, amending Council Directives 89/686/EEC and 93/15/EEC and Directives 94/9/EC, 94/25/EC, 95/16/EC, 97/23/EC, 98/34/EC, 2004/22/EC, 2007/23/EC, 2009/23/EC and 2009/105/EC of the European Parliament and of the Council and repealing Council Decision 87/95/EEC and Decision No 1673/2006/EC of the European Parliament and of the Council ('European Standardization Regulation') [2012] OJ L 316/12.

Regulation (EU) No 526/2013 of the European Parliament and of the Council of 21 May 2013 concerning the European Union Agency for Network and Information Security (ENISA) and repealing Regulation (EC) No 460/2004, [2013] OJ L 165/41.

Regulation (EU) No 910/2014 of the European Parliament and of the Council of 23 July 2014 on electronic identification and trust services for electronic transactions in the internal market and repealing Directive 1999/93/EC ('Electronic Identity and Trust Services for Electronic Transactions Regulation' (eIDAs Regulation)) [2014] OJ L 257/73.

Regulation (EU) 679/2016 of the European Parliament and of the Council of 27 April 2016 on the protection of natural persons with regard to the processing of personal data and on the free movement of such data, and repealing Directive 95/46/EC (General Data Protection Regulation) [2016] OJ L 119/1.

Regulation (EU) 2019/881 of the European Parliament and of the Council of 17 April 2019 on ENISA (the European Union Agency for Cybersecurity) and on information and communications technology cybersecurity certification and repealing Regulation (EU) No 526/2013 (Cybersecurity Act) (PE/86/2018/REV/1), [2019] OJ L 151/15.

Commission Regulation (EC) No 460/2004 of the European Parliament and of the Council of 10 March 2004 establishing the European Network and Information Security Agency ('ENISA Regulation') [2004] OJ L 077/0001.

Commission Implementing Decision (EU) 2016/650 of 25 April 2016 laying down standards for the security assessment of qualified signature and seal creation devices pursuant to Articles 30(3) and 39(2) of Regulation (EU) No 910/2014 of the European Parliament and of the Council on electronic identification and trust services for electronic transactions in the internal market C/2016/2303 [2016] OJ L 109/40.

1.2 Great Britain

Consumer Protection from Unfair Trading Regulations 2008 (SI 2008/1277).

Consumer Protection (Amendment) Regulations 2014 (S.I. 2014/870).

Electronic Commerce (EC Directive) Regulations 2002 (SI 2002/2013).

Great Britain. *Data Protection Act 1998: Elizabeth II. Chapter 29.* (1998) London: The Stationary Office.

Financial Services and Markets Act 2000 (S.I. 2000/8)
Payment Services Regulations 2009 (S.I. 2009/209).

1.3 United States of America

√United States of America. Uniform Computer Information Transactions Act, 7 U.L.A. 208 (2002): National Conference of Commissioners on Uniform State Laws.

√United States of America. Uniform Electronic Transactions Act (1999) (UETA): National Conference of Commissioners on Uniform State Laws. Available at: http://euro.ecom.cmu.edu/program/law/08–732/Transactions/ueta.pdf [Accessed 5 April 2019].

2. Case law

2.1 European Union

Case C-412/06 *Annelore Hamilton v Volksbank Filder eG*, [2008], (CJEU), ECLI:EU:C:2008:215.

√Case C-618/10 *Banco Español de Crédito SA v Joaquín Calderón Camino*, [2012], (CJEU), ECLI:EU:C:2012:349.

Case C-360/10, *Belgische Vereniging van Auteurs, Componisten en Uitgevers CVBA (SABAM) v Netlog NV*, [2012], (CJEU), ECLI:EU:C:2012:85.

Case C-352/85 *Bond van Adverteerders and others v The Netherlands State*, [1988], (CJEU), ECLI:EU:C:1988:196.

√Case C-495/10 *Centre hospitalier universitaire de Besançon v Thomas Dutrueux and Caisse primaire d'assurance maladie du Jura*, [2011], (CJEU), ECLI:EU:C:2011:869.

√Case C-49/11 *Content Services Ltd v Bundesarbeitskammer*, [2012], (CJEU), ECLI:EU:C:2012:419.

Cases *Google France SARL and Google Inc. v Louis Vuitton Malletier SA (C-236/08), Google France SARL v Viaticum SA and Luteciel SARL (C-237/08) and Google France SARL v Centre national de recherche en relations humaines (CNRRH) SARL and Others (C-238/08)*, Joined cases C-236/08 to C-238/08 [2009], (CJEU), ECLI:EU:C:2009:569, Opinion of the Advocate General Poiares Maduro delivered on 22 September 2009.

√Cases C-236, 237 & 238/08 *Google France SARL and Google Inc. v Louis Vuitton Malletier SA, Google France SARL v Viaticum SA and Luteciel SARL, Google France SARL v Centre national de recherche en relations humaines (CNRRH) SARL, Pierre-Alexis Thonet, Bruno Raboin and Tiger SARL* [2010] All ER (D) 23 (Apr).

Case *Google Spain*, [2014] (C-131/12), (CJEU), ECLI:EU:C:2013:424, Opinion of the Advocate-General.

√Case C-122/10 *Konsumentombudsmannen v Ving Sverige AB*, [2011], (CJEU), ECLI:EU:C:2011:299.

Case C-168/00 *Leitner v TUI Deutschland GmbhH & Co KG* ECR [2002] (CJEU) ECLI:EU:C:2001:476, Opinion of the Advocate-General.

√Case C-324/09 *L'Oréal SA and Others v eBay International AG and Others*, [2011], (CJEU), ECLI:EU:C:2011:474.

Case C-70/10 *Scarlet Extended SA v Société belge des auteurs, compositeurs et éditeurs SCRL (SABAM)*, [2011], (CJEU), ECLI:EU:C:2011:771.

√Case C-291/13 *Sotiris Papasavvas v O Fileleftheros Dimosia Etaireia Ltd and Others*, [2014], (CJEU), ECLI:EU:C:2014:2209.

√Case C-281/12, *Trento Sviluppo srl, Centrale Adriatica Soc. coop. arl v Autorità Garante della Concorrenza e del Mercato*, [2013], (CJEU), ECLI:EU:C:2013:859

√ Case C-484/14 *Tobias Mc Fadden v Sony Music Entertainment Germany GmbH*, [2016], (CJEU), ECLI:EU:C:2016:170, Opinion of the Advocate-General.

Case C-210/16 *Unabhängiges Landeszentrum für Datenschutz Schleswig-Holstein v Wirtschaftsakademie Schleswig-Holstein GmbH*, [2018], (CJEU), ECLI:EU:C:2018:388.

√Case T-62/02 *Union Pigments AS v Commission of the European Communities*, [2005], (General Court of EU), ECLI:EU:T:2005:430.

2.2 Germany

BGH, Urteil vom 12.7.2007, Az. I ZR 18/04, 2007 – Jugendgefährdende Medien bei eBay
BGH, Urteil vom 19.4.2007, Az. I ZR 35/04 – Internet-Versteigerung II.
BGH, Urteil vom 16.7.2009, Az. I ZR 140/07 – Versandkostenangabe in Preisvergleichslisten

2.3 Great Britain

√*Bunt v Tilley* [2006] EWHC 407 (QB), [2006] 3 ALL ER 336 (QB).
√*Dramatico Entertainment Ltd v British Sky Broadcasting Ltd* [2012] EWHC 1152 (Ch).
Halliday v Creation Consumer Finance [2013] EWCA Civ 333.
Hamlyn -v- John Houston & Co [1903] 1 KB 81.
Hedley Byrne & Co Ltd v Heller & Partners Ltd [1963] 2 All ER 575 (HL).
Hedley Byrne & Co. Ltd. v. Heller & Partners Ltd. [1964] AC 465, 526.
Henderson v Henry E Jenking & Sons [1970] AC 282 (HL)
Henderson v Merrett Syndicates [1995] 2 AC 145.
Fairchild v. Glenhaven Funeral Services Ltd [2002] UKHL 22, [2002] 3 All ER 305 (HL).
Farley v Skinner [2001] UKHL 49.
Johnson v Medical Defence Union [2007] 96 BMLR 99.
McGhee v National Coal Board [1972] 3 All ER 1008 (HL).
McGowan & Co. v. Dyer (1873) LR. 8 QB 141,143.
Poland -v- Parr (John) & Sons [1927] 1 KB 236.
The Director General of Fair Trading v First National Bank plc [2001] UKHL 52, [2002] AC 481 (HL).
√*Twentieth Century Fox Film Corp v British Telecommunications plc* [2011] EWHC 1981 (Ch).
Statoil A.S.A. v. Louis Dreyfus Energy Services L.P. (The "Harriette N") [2008] EWHC 2257 (Comm.) [2008] 2 Lloyd's Rep. 685.
Vidal-Hall v Google, Inc. [2015] EWCA Civ 311.
Ward v Tesco Stores Ltd [1976] 1 WLR 810 (CA).
Watts v Morrow [1991] 1 WLR 1421, 1445.
Wilsher v Essex Area Health Authority [1988] 1 AC 1074 (HL).

2.4 Ireland

J20 v Facebook Ireland Ltd [2016] NIQB 98.

2.5 Singapore

Chwee Kin Keong and others v Digilandmall.com Pte Ltd [2004] 2 SLR(R) 594.

2.6 United States of America

Ticketmaster Corp. v Tickets.com, Inc., 2000 U.S. Dist. Lexis 12987 (C.D. Cal., Aug. 10, 2000). Internet Library [Online. Available at: http://www.internetlibrary.com/pdf/Ticketmaster-Tickets.com-CD-Ca-mtnp relim-injunction.pdf [Accessed: 10 October 2009].

3. Governmental and other official publications

√Article 29 Data Protection Working Party (2000) *Privacy on the internet: an integrated EU approach to on-line data protection* [Online]. Available at: http://ec.europa.eu/justice/policies/privacy/docs/wpdocs/2000/wp37en.pdf [Accessed: 11 May 2009].

√Article 29 Data Protection Working Party (2003) *Opinion 3/2003 on the European code of conduct of FEDMA for the use of personal data in direct marketing of 13 June 2003* (10066/03/EN final WP 77) [Online]. Available at: https://ec.europa.eu/justice/article-29/documentation/opinion-recommendation/files/2003/wp77_en.pdf [Accessed: 3 April 2019].

√Article 29 Data Protection Working Party (2007) *Opinion 4/2007 on the concept of personal data of 20th June* (01248/07/EN WP 136) [Online]. Available at: https://ec.europa.eu/justice/article-29/documentation/opinion-recommendation/files/2007/wp136_en.pdf [Accessed: 3 April 2019].

√Article 29 Data Protection Working Party (2009) *Opinion 1/2009 on the proposals amending Directive 2002/58/EC on privacy and electronic communications (e-Privacy Directive) of 10 February 2009* (00350/09/EN WP 1590) [Online]. Available at: https://ec.europa.eu/justice/article-29/documentation/opinion-recommendation/files/2009/wp159_en.pdf [Accessed: 3 April 2019].

√Article 29 Data Protection Working Party (2010a) *Opinion 1/2010 on the concepts of "controller" and "processor" of 16 February 2010* (00264/10/EN WP 169) [Online]. Available at: https://ec.europa.eu/justice/article-29/documentation/opinion-recommendation/files/2010/wp169_en.pdf [Accessed: 3 April 2019].

√Article 29 Data Protection Working Party (2010b) *Opinion 4/2010 on the European code of conduct of FEDMA for the use of personal data in direct marketing of 13 July 2010* (00065/2010/EN WP 174) [Online]. Available at: https://ec.europa.eu/justice/article-29/documentation/opinion-recommendation/files/2010/wp174_en.pdfhttp://ec.europa.eu/justice/data-protection/article-29/documentation/opinion-recommendation/files/2010/wp174_en.pdf [Accessed: 3 April 2019].

√Article 29 Data Protection Working Party (2014) Statement on the results of the last JHA meeting, 17 September 2014 (14/EN WP 222) [Online]. Available at: https://ec.europa.eu/justice/article-29/documentation/opinion-recommendation/files/2014/wp222_en.pdf [Accessed: 3 April 2019].

√Article 29 Data Protection Working Party (2018) *Statement of the WP29 on encryption and their impact on the protection of individuals with regard to the processing of their personal data in the EU,* [Online]. Available at: http://ec.europa.eu/newsroom/article29/document.cfm?action=display&doc_id=51026 [Accessed: 3 April 2019].

ASA: Advertising Standards Authority (2004) *ASA non-broadcast adjudication: Freeserve plc,* Complaint Ref: 38095, 16 June 2004. [Online]. Available at: http://www.asa.org.uk/Complaints-andASA-action/Adjudications/2004/6/Freeserve-plc/CS_38095.aspx [Accessed: 10 May 2009].

√Banking Stakeholder Group (2016) *Draft BSG Response to EBA/DP/2015/03 on Future Draft Regulatory Technical Standards on Strong Customer Authentication and Secure Communication under the Revised Payment Services Directive (PSD2): General Comments and Replies to Questions,* London, February 7, 2016, [Online]. Available at: https://www.eba.europa.eu/documents/10180/1303936/BSG+response+to+Consultation+Paper+(EBA-DP-2015–03)%20-+08+February+2016.pdf [Accessed: 3 April 2019].

√EBA: European Banking Authority (2015) *Discussion Paper on future Draft Regulatory Technical Standards on strong customer authentication and secure communication under the revised Payment Services Directive (PSD2),* (EBA/DP/2015/03) 8 December 2015 [Online]. Available at: https://www.eba.europa.eu/documents/10180/1303936/EBA-DP-2015–03+(RTS+on+SCA+and+CSC+under+PSD2).pdf [Accessed: 3 April 2019].

√EBA: European Banking Authority (2016) *Consultation Paper On the draft Regulatory Technical Standards specifying the requirements on strong customer authentication and common and secure communication under PSD2,* (EBA-CP-2016–11) 12 August 2016 [Online]. Available at: https://www.eba.europa.eu/documents/10180/1548183/Consultation+Paper+on+draft+RTS+on+SCA+and+CSC+(EBA-CP-2016–11).pdf [Accessed: 3 April 2019].

EBA: European Banking Authority (2018) *Opinion of the European Banking Authority on the implementation of the RTS on SCA and CSC*, (EBA-Op-2018–04) 13 June 2018 [Online]. Available at: https://eba.europa.eu/documents/10180/2137845/Opinion+on+the+implementation+of+the+RTS+on+SCA+and+CSC+%28EBA-2018-Op-04%29.pdf [Accessed: 21 June 2019].

ENDRI (2015) 'Comparison of the Parliament and Council text on the General Data Protection Regulation'. Edri.org [pdf]. Available at: https://edri.org/files/EP_Council_Comparison.pdf [Accessed: 12 March 2019].

√European Commission (1988) Answer of the commission on 15 November 1988 to written question No. 706/88 [1989] OJC 144/42.

√European Commission (2001) *Communication from The Commission to the Council, the European Parliament, the European Economic and Social Committee and the Committee of the Regions: Network and Information Security: Proposal for a European Policy Approach.* 6 June, COM (2001) 298 final, [Online]. Available at: http://ec.europa.eu/transparency/regdoc/rep/1/2001/EN/1-2001-298-EN-F1-1.Pdf [Accessed: 3 April 2019].

√European Commission (2003a) *Proposal for a Directive of the European Parliament and of the Council concerning unfair business-to-consumer commercial practices in the Internal Market and amending directives 84/450/EEC, 97/7/EC and 98/27/EC (the Unfair Commercial Practices Directive)* COM (2003) 356 final, 18 June. [Online]. Available at: http://eurlex.europa.eu/LexUriServ/LexUriServ.do?uri=COM:2003:0356:FIN:EN:PDF [Accessed: 3 April 2019].

√European Commission (2003b) *First report on the application of Directive 2000/31/EC of the European Parliament and of the Council of 8 June 2000 on certain legal aspects of information society services, in particular electronic commerce, in the Internal Market (Directive on Electronic Commerce)*, COM (2003) 702 final, 21 November. [Online]. Available at: http://eur388lex.europa.eu/LexUriServ/LexUriServ.do?uri=COM:2003:0702:FIN:EN:PDF [Accessed: 13 October 2008].

√European Commission (2004a) *Communication from the Commission to the Council, the European Parliament, the European Economic and Social Committee, the European Central Bank and Europol: A New EU Action Plan 2004–2007 to Prevent Fraud on Non-Cash Means of Payment*, COM (2004) 679 final, 20 October, [Online]. Available at: http://ec.europa.eu/transparency/regdoc/rep/1/2004/EN/1–2004-679-EN-F1-1.Pdf [Accessed 3 April 2019].

√European Commission (2004b) *Consumer confidence in e-commerce: lessons learned from the e- confidence initiative* (Commission Staff Working Document), SEC(2004) 1390, 8 November. [Online]. Available at: http://ec.europa.eu/consumers/cons_int/e-commerce/e-conf_working_doc.pdf [Accessed: 10 February 2009].

√European Commission (2005) *Privacy Incorporated Software Agent: Building a privacy guardian for the electronic age: Enhancing privacy and security for e-transactions*, 18 September, [Online]. Available at: https://cordis.europa.eu/project/rcn/53640/brief/en [Accessed: 5 April 2019]

√European Commission (2006) *Report from the Commission to the European Parliament and the Council: Report on the operation of Directive 1999/93/EC on a Community framework for electronic signatures*, COM (2006) 120 final, 15 March [Online]. Available at: https://eur-lex.europa.eu/legal-content/EN/TXT/PDF/?uri=CELEX:52006DC0120&from=EN [Accessed: 21 June 2019].

√European Commission (2008) *Your questions on PSD Payment Services Directive 2007/64/EC Questions and answers*, [Online]. Available at;

https://ec.europa.eu/info/system/files/faq-transposition-psd-22022011_en.pdf [Accessed: 3 April 2019].

√European Commission, (2009a) *Commission Staff Working Document Guidance on the Implementation/Application of Directive 2005/29/EC On Unfair Commercial Practices Accompanying the Document Communication from the Commission to the European Parliament, The Council, The European Economic and Social Committee and The Committee of the Regions: A comprehensive approach to stimulating cross-border e-Commerce for Europe's citizens and businesses.* (No longer available online due to 2016 updated guidance).

√European Commission (2009b) *Communication from the Commission to the European Parliament, the Council, the European Economic and Social Committee and the Committee of the Regions on*

Critical Information Infrastructure Protection "Protecting Europe from large scale cyber-attacks and disruptions: enhancing preparedness, security and resilience", COM (2009) 149 final, 30 March, [Online]. Available at: https://eur-lex.europa.eu/LexUriServ/LexUriServ.do?uri=COM:2009:0149:FIN:EN:PDF [Accessed: 3 April 2019].

√European Commission (2010a) *Communication from the Commission to the European Parliament, the Council, the Economic and Social Committee and the Committee of the Regions: A comprehensive approach on personal data protection in the European Union*, Brussels, 4.11.2010 COM (2010) 609 final, 4 November. [Online]. Available at: https://eur-lex.europa.eu/LexUriServ/LexUriServ.do?uri=COM:2010:0609:FIN:EN:PDF [Accessed: 3 April 2019].

√European Commission (2010b) *Communication from the Commission to the European Parliament, the Council, the European Economic and Social Committee and the Committee of the Regions: A Digital Agenda for Europe*, COM (2010) 245 final, 19 May, [Online]. Available at: https://eur-lex.europa.eu/LexUriServ/LexUriServ.do?uri=COM:2010:0245:FIN:EN:PDF [Accessed: 3 April 2019].

√European Commission (2011a) *Communication from the Commission to the European Parliament, the Council, the European Economic and Social Committee and the Committee of the Regions: on Critical Information Infrastructure Protection 'Achievements and next steps: towards global cyber-security'*, COM (2011) 163 final, 31 March, [Online]. Available at: https://eur-lex.europa.eu/LexUriServ/LexUriServ.do?uri=COM:2011:0163:FIN:EN:PDF [Accessed: 3 April 2019].

√European Commission (2011b) *Report from the Commission to the Council and the European Parliament: Minimizing regulatory burden for SMEs, Adapting EU regulation to the needs of micro-enterprises*, COM (2011) 803 final, 23 November, [Online]. Available at: http://eur-lex.europa.eu/LexUriServ/LexUriServ.do?uri=COM:2011:0803:FIN:EN:PDF [Accessed: 3 April 2019].

√European Commission (2012a) *Proposal for a Regulation of the European Parliament and of the Council on the protection of individuals with regard to the processing of personal data and on the free movement of such data (General Data Protection Regulation)*, COM (2012) 11 final, 25 January [Online]. Available at: https://eur-lex.europa.eu/LexUriServ/LexUriServ.do?uri=COM:2012:0011:FIN:EN:PDF [Accessed: 3 April 2019].

√European Commission (2012b) *Proposal for a Regulation of the European Parliament and of the Council on electronic identification and trust services for electronic transactions in the internal market*, COM (2012) 238 final, 4 June [Online]. Available at: https://eur-lex.europa.eu/LexUriServ/LexUriServ.do?uri=COM:2012:0238:FIN:en:PDF [Accessed: 3 April 2019].

√European Commission (2013) *Proposal for a Directive of the European Parliament and of the Council concerning measures to ensure a high common level of network and information security across the Union*, COM (2013) 48 final, 7 February, 2013/0027 (COD) [Online]. Available at: https://eur-lex.europa.eu/legal-content/EN/TXT/PDF/?uri=CELEX:52013PC0048&from=EN [Accessed: 3 April 2019].

√European Commission (2014a) *Justice Guidance Document concerning Directive 2011/83/EU of the European Parliament and of the Council of 25 October 2011 on consumer rights, amending Council Directive 93/13/EEC and Directive 1999/44/EC of the European Parliament and of the Council and repealing Council Directive 85/577/EEC and Directive 97/7/EC of the European Parliament and of the Council*, (DG JUSTICE, June 2014 1 DG) [Online]. Available at: https://ec.europa.eu/info/sites/info/files/crd_guidance_en_0.pdf [Accessed: 3 April 2019].

√European Commission (2014b) *Commission Staff Working Document: Access to insurance for services provided in another Member State*, SWD (2014) 130 final, 31 March, [Online]. Available at: http://ec.europa.eu/DocsRoom/documents/15037/attachments/1/translations/en/renditions/pdf [Accessed: 3 April 2019].

√European Commission (2015) *Proposal for a Directive of the European Parliament and of the Council on certain aspects concerning contracts for the supply of digital content*, COM (2015) 634 final, 9 December, [Online]. Available at: http://eur-lex.europa.eu/legal-content/EN/TXT/HTML/?uri=CELEX:52015PC0634&from=EN [Accessed: 3 April 2019].

√European Commission (2016a) *Communication from the Commission to the European Parliament, the Council, the European Economic and Social Committee and the Committee of the Regions: Online Platforms and the Digital Single Market Opportunities and Challenges for Europe*, COM (2016) 288 final, 25 May, [Online]. Available at: http://eur-lex.europa.eu/legal-content/EN/TXT/PDF/?uri=CELEX:52016DC0288&from=EN [Accessed: 3 April 2019].

√European Commission (2016b) *Commission Staff Working Document on Online Platforms, accompanying the document "Communication on Online Platforms and the Digital Single Market"* (COM (2016) 288), [2016], 25 May, [Online]. Available at: https://ec.europa.eu/digital-single-market/en/news/commission-staff-working-document-online-platforms [Accessed: 3 April 2019].

√European Commission (2016c) *Commission Staff Working Document: Guidance on the Implementation/Application of Directive 2005/29/EC on Unfair Commercial Practices, SWD(2016) 163 final, Accompanying the Document Communication from the Commission to the European Parliament, the Council, the European Economic and Social Committee and the Committee of the Regions: A Comprehensive Approach to Stimulating Cross-Border E-Commerce for Europe's Citizens and Businesses,* {COM(2016) 320 final} 25 May, [Online]. Available at: https://eur-lex.europa.eu/legal-content/EN/TXT/PDF/?uri=CELEX:52016DC0320&from=EN [Accessed: 3 April 2019].

√European Commission (2016d) *Evaluation and Fitness Check (FC) Roadmap: Evaluation of the Directive 85/374/EEC concerning liability for defective products* [Online]. Available at: http://ec.europa.eu/smart-regulation/roadmaps/docs/2016_grow_027_evaluation_defective_products_en.pdf [Accessed: 5 April 2019]

European Commission (2016e) *Proposal for a Directive of the European Parliament and of the Council establishing the European Electronic Communications Code (Recast)*, COM (2016) 590 final, 12 October [Online]. Available at: https://eur-lex.europa.eu/legal-content/EN/TXT/HTML/?uri=CELEX:52016PC0590&from=EN [Accessed: 5 April 2019]

√European Commission (2017a) *Communication from the Commission to the European Parliament, the Council, the European Economic and Social Committee and the Committee of the Regions: Tackling Illegal Content online, towards an enhanced responsibility of online platforms,* COM(2017) 555 final, 28 September, [Online]. Available at: http://eur-lex.europa.eu/legal-content/EN/TXT/HTML/?uri=CELEX:52017DC0555 [Accessed: 3 April 2019].

√European Commission (2017b) *Proposal for a Regulation of the European Parliament and of the Council concerning the respect for private life and the protection of personal data in electronic communications and repealing Directive 2002/58/EC (Regulation on Privacy and Electronic Communications)*, COM (2017) 10 final, 10 October, [Online]. Available at: https://eur-lex.europa.eu/legal-content/EN/TXT/PDF/?uri=CELEX:52017PC0010&from=EN [Accessed: 3 April 2019].

European Commission (2018a) *Proposal for a Directive of the European Parliament and of the Council amending Council Directive 93/13/EEC of 5 April 1993, Directive 98/6/EC of the European Parliament and of the Council, Directive 2005/29/EC of the European Parliament and of the Council and Directive 2011/83/EU of the European Parliament and of the Council as regards better enforcement and modernisation of EU consumer protection rules,* COM(2018) 185 final, 2018/0090 (COD), 11 April [Online]. Available at: https://eur-lex.europa.eu/legal-content/EN/TXT/?qid=1523880940100&uri=COM:2018:185:FIN [Accessed: 21 June 2019].

√European Commission (2018b) *Proposal for a Regulation of the European Parliament and of the Council on promoting fairness and transparency for business users of online intermediation services,* (COM (2018) 238 final), 26 April. Available at: https://eur-lex.europa.eu/legal-content/EN/TXT/?uri=CELEX%3A52018PC0238 [Accessed: 3 April 2019].

√European Commission (2018c) *Commission Recommendation of 1.3.2018 on measures to effectively tackle illegal content online* (COM (2018) 1177 final), 1 March, [Online]. Available at: https://ec.europa.eu/digital-single-market/en/news/commission-recommendation-measures-effectively-tackle-illegal-content-online [Accessed: 3 April 2019].

European Commission (2018d) *COMMISSION STAFF WORKING DOCUMENT Evaluation of Council Directive 85/374/EEC of 25 July 1985 on the approximation of the laws, regulations and administrative provisions of the Member States concerning liability for defective products Accompanying the document Report from the Commission to the European Parliament, the Council and the European Economic and Social Committee on the Application of the Council Directive on the approximation of the laws, regulations, and administrative provisions of the Member States concerning liability for defective products (85/374/EEC)*, SWD/2018/157 final, 7 May 2018 [Online]. Available at: https://eur-lex.europa.eu/legal-content/EN/TXT/?uri=SWD:2018:157:FIN [Accessed: 21 June 2019].

European Commission (2018e) *Commission Delegated Regulation (EU) 2018/389 of 27 November 2017 supplementing Directive (EU) 2015/2366 of the European Parliament and of the Council with regard to regulatory technical standards for strong customer authentication and common and secure open standards of communication*, C/2017/7782 [2018] OJ L 69/ 23.

√European Commission (2018f) *Digital Single Market, Policy, Trust Services* [Online]. Available at: https://ec.europa.eu/digital-single-market/trust-services [Accessed: 3 April 2019].

√ECME Consortium (2013) *Study on the coverage, functioning and consumer use of comparison tools and third-party verification schemes for such tools Final report prepared by ECME Consortium (in partnership with DELOITTE)* EAHC/FWC/2013 85 07 [Online]. Available at: https://ec.europa.eu/info/sites/info/files/final_report_study_on_comparison_tools_2013_en.pdf [Accessed: 3 April 2019].

√Europe Economics (2011) *Digital Content Services for Consumers: Assessment of Problems Experienced by Consumers* (Lot 1) Report 4: Final Report, 15 June 2011, [Online]. Available at: http://www.europe-economics.com/publications/eahc_final_report_+_appendices.pdf [Accessed: 3 April 2019].

√European Parliament (2006) *Working Document on consumer confidence in the digital environment* (INI/2006/2048), PE 378.891v01.00 [Online]. Available at: http://www.europarl.europa.eu/meetdocs/2004_2009/documents/dt/634/634241/63441en.pdf [Accessed: 10 August 2009].

European Parliament (2014a) *European Parliament legislative resolution of 13 March 2014 on the proposal for a directive of the European Parliament and of the Council concerning measures to ensure a high common level of network and information security across the Union* (COM(2013)0048 – C7-0035/2013 – 2013/0027(COD)) (Ordinary legislative procedure: first reading) [Online].Available at: http://www.europarl.europa.eu/sides/getDoc.do?type=TA&language=EN&reference=P7-TA-2014–0244 [Accessed: 3 April 2019].

√European Parliament (2014b) *Report on the proposal for a directive of the European Parliament and of the Council concerning measures to ensure a high common level of network and information security across the Union* (12 February 2014) (COM (2013)0048 – C7-0035/2013 – 2013/0027(COD)) [Online]. Available at: http://www.europarl.europa.eu/sides/getDoc.do?type=REPORT&reference=A7-2014–0103&language=EN [Accessed: 3 April 2019].

√European Parliament (2015) *Resolution of 16 February 2017 with recommendations to the Commission on Civil Law Rules on Robotics* (2015/2103(INL)) [Online]. Available at: http://www.europarl.europa.eu/sides/getDoc.do?pubRef=-//EP//TEXT+TA+P8-TA-2017–0051+0+DOC+XML+V0//EN#BKMD-12 [Accessed: 3 April 2019].

√European Payments Council (2015) *PSD2: Almost final – a state of play* [Online]. Available at:http://www.europeanpaymentscouncil.eu/index.cfm/blog/psd2-almost-final-a-state-of-play/ [Accessed: 3 April 2019].

European Union Agency for Network and Information Security (ENISA) (2014) *Technical Guideline on Security measures for Article 4 and Article 13a*, Version 1.0 December [Online]. Available at: https://resilience.enisa.europa.eu/article-13/guideline-on-security-measures-for-article-4-and-article-13a/TechnicalGuidelineonSecuritymeasuresforArticle4andArticle13a_version_1_0.pdf [Accessed 3 April 2018]

Great Britain. Department for Business Innovation and Skills, (2014a) *Explanatory Memorandum to the Consumer Protection (Amendment) Regulations 2014* (2014 No.870) [pdf]. Available at: http://www.legislation.gov.uk/uksi/2014/870/pdfs/uksiem_20140870_en.pdf [Accessed: 5 April 2019]

√Great Britain. Department for Business Innovation and Skills, (2014b) *Misleading and Aggressive Commercial Practices: New Private Rights for Consumers, Guidance on the Consumer Protection (Amendment) Regulations 2014*. Department for Business, Energy & Industrial Strategy (July 2018) [pdf]. Available at: https://www.gov.uk/government/uploads/system/uploads/attachment_data/file/409334/bis-14–1030-misleading-and-aggressive-selling-rights-consumer-protection-amendment-regulations-2014-guidance.pdf [Accessed: 5 April 2019]

√Great Britain. Department of Trade and Industry (2006) *Consultation Document on the Electronic Commerce Directive: the liability of hyperlinkers, location tool services and content aggregators –*

government response and summary of responses [Online]. Available at: http://www.berr.gov.uk/files/file35905.pdf [Accessed: 8 April 2009].

√Great Britain. Financial Services Authority (2008) *Review into general insurance comparison websites – May 2008* [Online]. Available at: http://www.fsa.gov.uk/pages/Doing/Regulated/Promo/thematic/review_gi_comparison.shtml [Accessed: 30 July 2010].

√Great Britain. ICO (2014) *Conducting privacy impact assessments code of practice, Data Protection Act*, [pdf]. Available at: https://www.pdpjournals.com/docs/88317.pdf [Accessed 3 April 2019].

Great Britain. Office of Fair Trading (OFT) (2007) *Internet shopping*. Available at: http://webarchive.nationalarchives.gov.uk/20140402163042/http://oft.gov.uk/OFTwork/markets-work/internet [Accessed: 3 April 2019].

Great Britain. Office of Fair Trading (OFT) (2009) *Opinions and observations: intermediaries and complexity* [Online]. Available at: http://www.oft.gov.uk/news-and-updates/events/activeconsumers/opinions/ [Accessed: 30 July 2010].

√Great Britain. Office of Fair Trading (OFT) (2010) *Annex E, Statistical analysis* [Online]. Available at: http://webarchive.nationalarchives.gov.uk/20140402173005/http://oft.gov.uk/shared_oft/market-studies/AoP/Annexe-E.pdf [Accessed 3 April 2019].

√Great Britain. Office of Fair Trading (OFT) (2010) *Annexe K Price comparison site trawl summary*. Available at: http://webarchive.nationalarchives.gov.uk/20140402173021/http://oft.gov.uk/shared_oft/market-studies/AoP/Annexe-K.pdf [Accessed: 3 April 2019].

√Great Britain. Office of Fair Trading (OFT) (2012) *Price Comparison Websites: Trust, choice and consumer empowerment in online markets*, (OFT/1467) [Online]. Available at: http://webarchive.nationalarchives.gov.uk/20131101205826/http://www.oft.gov.uk/shared_oft/706728/Tool-landing-pages/consumer-protection/pcw-items-banners/PCWs-report.pdf [Accessed: 3 April 2019].

√UK Law Commission (2008) *A private right of redress for unfair commercial practices? Preliminary advice to the Department for Business, Enterprise and Regulatory Reform on the issues raised* [Online]. Available at: https://s3-eu-west-2.amazonaws.com/lawcom-prod-storage-11jsxou24uy7q/uploads/2015/04/rights_of_redress_advice12.pdf [Accessed 3 April 2019].

United States of America. Federal Trade Commission (2002) *Commercial alert complaint requesting investigation of various internet search engine companies for paid placement and paid inclusion programs* [Online]. Available at: http://www.ftc.gov/os/closings/staff/commercialalertattatch.htm [Accessed: 26 March 2009].

√United States of America. Federal Trade Commission (2014a) '*TRUSTe Settles FTC Charges it Deceived Consumers Through Its Privacy Seal Program: Company Failed to Conduct Annual Recertifications, Facilitated Misrepresentation as Non-Profit*', November 17, 2014 [Online]. Available at: http://www.ftc.gov/news-events/press-releases/2014/11/TRUSTe-settles-ftc-charges-it-deceived-consumers-through-its [Accessed: 3 April 2019].

√United States of America. Federal Trade Commission, (2014b) *In the Matter of: TRUE ULTIMATE STANDARDS EVERYWHERE, INC., a corporation, Cd/b/a TRUSTe, Inc.*, Docket No. C. Complaint [Online]. Available at: https://www.ftc.gov/system/files/documents/cases/141117trustecmpt.pdf [Accessed: 3 April 2019].

√United States of America. Federal Trade Commission, (2014c) *In the Matter of: TRUE ULTIMATE STANDARDS EVERYWHERE, INC., a corporation, d/b/a TRUSTe, Inc.*, Agreement Containing Consent Order, Docket No. [Online]. Available at: https://www.ftc.gov/system/files/documents/cases/141117trusteagree.pdf [Accessed: 3 April 2019].

√UNITED STATES OF AMERICA. National Conference of Commissioners on Uniform State Laws (NCCUSL), Prefatory Note: Uniform Computer Information Transactions Act (UCITA), [Online]. Available at: https://www.uniformlaws.org/HigherLogic/System/DownloadDocumentFile.ashx?DocumentFileKey=2a359b5d-32f2-ab70-60f9-85698f7b6125&forceDialog=0 [Accessed: 3 April 2019].

4. Web pages and online business reports and releases

√123PriceCheck. (2017) *Guardians of the Galaxy Vol. 2 DVD* [2017]. Available at: http://www.123pricecheck.com/Product-283926/B072L435Z1-Guardians+of+the+Galaxy+Vol+2.html [Accessed 5 April 2019].

√Abercrombie Online (2001) *EZ sniper pricing*. Available at: http://www.ezsniper.com/cost.php3 [Accessed 5 April 2019].

√AddAll.com (2018) *Book Search and Price Comparison*. Available at: http://www.addall.com/ [Accessed 5 April 2019].

√Amazon.com Inc. (2017) *Sell on Amazon*. Available at: https://services.amazon.co.uk/services/sell-online/pricing.html [Accessed 5 April 2019].

√Apple Store, (2017) *iTunes*. Available at: https://itunes.apple.com/us/app/mona-personal-shopping-assistant-for-1–300-brands/id935514186?mt=8 [Accessed 5 April 2019].

√Best-dvd-price.co.uk (2017b) *Guardians of the Galaxy Vol. 2 [DVD] [2017]*. Available at: http://best-dvd-price.co.uk/Product-283926/B072L435Z1-Guardians+of+the+Galaxy+Vol+2.html [Accessed 5 April 2019].

√Business Wire (2016). *Research and Markets: Global Online Comparison Shopping Trends Report 2015*. Available at: https://www.businesswire.com/news/home/20160104006225/en/Research-Markets-Global-Online-Comparison-Shopping-Trends [Accessed: 5 April 2019].

√ClientEarth (2014) *Introduction to Delegated and Implementing Acts*. Available at: http://www.arc2020.eu/wp-content/uploads/2017/06/introduction-to-delegated-and-implementing-acts.pdf [Accessed: 5 April 2019].

√Connexity (2017a) *Shopzilla*. Available at: http://www.shopzilla.com/ [Accessed: 5 April 2019].

√Connexity (2017b) *Handbags & Totes*. Available at: http://www.shopzilla.com/handbags-totes/10010600/products [Accessed: 5 April 2019].

√Connexity (2017c) *You want buyers, we'll find them*. [Online] Connexity commerce. Available at: http://connexity.com/cpc-listings/retailer-listings/ [Accessed: 12 March 2019].

√Connexity (2017d) *Bellino The Compact Laptop Roller*. Available at: http://www.shopzilla.com/bellino-the-compact-laptop-roller/7004782915/compare [Accessed: 5 April 2019].

√Connexity (2017e) *Shopzilla, Store Directory*. Available at: http://www.shopzilla.com/store-directory [Accessed: 5 April 2019].

√Consumer Focus (2013) *Comparing comparison sites: Price comparison website mystery shopping report for Consumer Focus by eDigitalResearch*. Available at: http://webarchive.nationalarchives.gov.uk/20140522160227/http://www.consumerfutures.org.uk/files/2013/05/Comparing-comparison-sites.pdf [Accessed: 5 April 2019].

Cygnus Software Ltd (2017) *fetchbook*. Available at: http://www.fetchbook.info/ [Accessed: 18 June 2017]

√eBay Inc. (2007) *Annual report* [Online]. Available at: http://www.annualreports.com/HostedData/AnnualReportArchive/e/NASDAQ_EBAY_2007.pdf [Accessed: 5 April 2019].

√eBay Inc. (2017a) *Apple iPod nano 2nd generation black (8 GB) MP3 player*. [Online] Available at: http://uk.shopping.com/xPO-Apple-iPod-nano-Second-Gen-Black-8-GB [Accessed: 5 April 2019].

√eBay Inc. (2017b) *Dealtime, Millions of Deals on SALE*. Available at: http://www.dealtime.com/digital-picture-frames/products [Accessed 3 April 2019]

√eBay Inc. (2017c) *Your User Agreement*. Available at: http://pages.ebay.co.uk/help/policies/user-agreement.html#scope [Accessed 3 April 2019]

√eBay Inc. (2018a) *All about bidding*. Available at: http://pages.ebay.com/help/buy/bidding-overview.html#auto [Accessed 3 April 2019]

√eBay Inc. (2018b) *Store selling fees*. Available at: http://pages.ebay.com/help/sell/storefees.html [Accessed 3 April 2019].

ECC-NET (2013) *Chargeback in the EU/EEA: A solution to get your money back when a trader does not respect your consumer rights*. [pdf]. Available at: https://www.eccireland.ie/wp-content/uploads/2013/07/Chargeback-report.pdf [Accessed 21 June 2019].

√ECC-NET (2017) *Fraud in cross-border e-commerce*, [Online]. Available at: https://ec.europa.eu/info/sites/info/files/online_fraud_2017.pdf [Accessed 3 April 2019].

√EmoneyAdvice.com (2015) *Does your e-commerce marketplace need a payments licence?*. Available at: http://emoneyadvice.com/psd2-commercial-agent-marketplace/ [Accessed 3 April 2019].

√FIDIS (2007) *Future of Identity in the Information Society*, "D7.9: A Vision of Ambient Law" Editors: Mireille Hildebrandt (VUB), Bert-Jaap Koops (TILT) [Online]. Available at: http://www.fidis.net/fileadmin/fidis/deliverables/fidis-wp7-d7.9_A_Vision_of_Ambient_Law.pdf [Accessed 3 April 2019]

√Google Inc. (2017a) *Maximum CPC bid: Definition*. Available at: https://support.google.com/adwords/answer/6326?hl=en [Accessed 3 April 2019]

√Google Inc. (2017b) *The ad auction*. Available at: https://support.google.com/adwords/answer/1704431 [Accessed 3 April 2019]

√Google Inc. (2017c) *Google Shopping*. Available at: https://www.google.com/shopping [Accessed 3 April 2019]

√Google Inc. (2017d) *Ads you can count on*. Available at: https://www.google.com/adsense/start/#/?modal_active=none [Accessed 3 April 2019]

√Google Inc. (2019) *How Google Search Works*. [Online]. Available at: http://www.google.com/support/webmasters/bin/answer.py?hl=en&answer=70897 [Accessed 3 April 2019]

√Ingenico Group (2017) *Ingenico ePayments announces complete and PSD2-compliant solution for marketplaces*. Available at: https://www.ingenico.com/press-and-publications/press-releases/all/2017/06/psd2-compliant-solution-for-marketplaces.html [Accessed 3 April 2019]

√Kelkoo (2017a) *Kelkoo, Find. Compare. Save*. Available at: http://www.kelkoo.co.uk/ [Accessed: 3 April 2019].

√Kelkoo (2017b) *About Kelkoo*. Available at: http://www.kelkoo.co.uk/company-pages/about-kelkoo [Accessed: 12 March 2019].

√Kelkoo (2017c) *Convert every visit into a sale!* Available at: https://www.kelkoogroup.com/merchants/ [Accessed: 12 March 2019].

√Kelkoo (2017d) *Apple iPhone 5S 16GB*. Available at: https://www.kelkoo.co.uk/p-sim-free-mobile-phones-100020213/apple-iphone-5s-16gb-19873920 [Accessed: 3 April 2019].

√Lifewire.com (2019) *Hypertext Transfer Protocol Explained*. Available at: https://www.lifewire.com/hypertext-transfer-protocol-817944 [Accessed 3 April 2019]

Microsoft (2018) *Safeguard individual privacy with the Microsoft Cloud*. Available at: https://www.microsoft.com/en-us/trustcenter/privacy/gdpr/solutions [Accessed 3 April 2019]

√National Cyber Security Centre (2015) *Guidance:10 steps to cyber security* [Online]. Available at: https://www.ncsc.gov.uk/guidance/10-steps-monitoring [Accessed 3 April 2019]

√Osborne Clarke (2015) *Revision of the Payment Services Directive: quasi-banking regulation for e-commerce platforms?* [Online]. Available at: https://www.osborneclarke.com/insights/revision-of-the-payment-services-directive-quasi-banking-regulation-for-e-commerce-platforms/ [Accessed: 3 April 2019].

√PayPal Inc. (2017) *About Payment Methods*. Available at: https://www.paypal.com/us/webapps/mpp/popup/about-payment-methods [Accessed 3 April 2019]

√Pricerunner International AB (2017a) *About us*. Available at: https://www.pricerunner.com/info/about-pricerunner [Accessed: 3 April 2019].

√Pricerunner International AB (2017b) *Apple iPad (2018) 9.7" 32GB*. Available at: https https://www.pricerunner.com/pl/224-4540493/Tablets/Apple-iPad-(2018)-9.7-32GB-Compare-Prices [Accessed: 7 August 2019].

√Pricerunner International AB (2017c) *Pricerunner*. Available at: https://www.pricerunner.uk/ [Accessed: 3 April 2019].

√Shopping.com (2017) *shopping.com, iphone 7*. Available at: http://uk.shopping.com/laptop-and-tablet-accessories/iphone-7/products?KW=iphone+7 [Accessed: 3 April 2019].

√Fortune (2017) *About Your Privacy on this Site*. Available at: http://fortune.com/2017/04/28/5-reasons-amazon-physical-stores/ [Accessed: 3 April 2019].

√Master of Code Global (2017) *How to Develop a Personal Shopper App Based on Artificial Intelligence.* Available at: https://medium.com/master-of-code-global/how-to-develop-a-personal-shopper-app-powered-by-data-intelligence-and-humans-4dc8787a957 [Accessed: 3 April 2019].

√Sofort GmbH (2017) *Who or what is SOFORT GmbH.* Available at: https://www.klarna.com/pay-now-with-direct-banking/business/merchant-support/questions-sofort-gmbh/who-or-what-is-sofort-gmbh/ [Accessed: 3 April 2019].

√True Fit Corporation (2018) *What We Do.* Available at: https://www.truefit.com/about-us/what-we-do [Accessed: 3 April 2019].

√TRUSTe (TRUSTarc, 2019a) *TrustArc simplifies privacy compliance for the GDPR, CCPA, and other data protection regulations with an unrivaled combination of technology and privacy expertise.* Available at: https://www.trustarc.com/about/ [Accessed: 3 April 2019].

√TRUSTe (TRUSTarc, 2019b) *TRUSTe privacy certifications and verifications help organizations demonstrate compliance.* Available at: https://www.trustarc.com/privacy-certification-standards/ [Accessed: 3 April 2019].

√TRUSTe (TRUSTarc, 2019c) *Align your privacy practices with regulatory and industry standards.* Available at: https://www.trustarc.com/products/download-certification/ [Accessed: 3 April 2019].

√Ofcom (n.d.) *The definition of "relevant activity" for the purposes of administrative charging.* Guidelines issued by Ofcom [Online]. Available at: http://stakeholders.ofcom.org.uk/binaries/consultations/designation/statement/guidelines.pdf [Accessed 3 April 2019].

5. Books, articles, studies, reports, academic projects and other

√Alhadeff J., Alsenoy B.V. and Dumortier J. (2012) '*The Accountability Principle in Data Protection Regulation: Origin, Development and Future Directions*' in Neyland, D., Hempel, L., Ilten, C, Kroener, I., Guagnin, D., Postigo, H.(eds), Managing Privacy through Accountability, Palgrave Macmillan, pp. 49–82.

√Allen, T. and Widdison, R. (1996) 'Can computers make contracts?', *Harvard Journal of Law and Technology*, 9, pp. 25–52. [Online]. Available at: http://jolt.law.harvard.edu/articles/pdf/v09/09HarvJLTech025.pdf [Accessed: 10 June 2017].

Allgrove, B. and Ganley, P. (2007) '*Search engines, data aggregators and UK copyright law: a proposal*' [Working paper]. SSRN [Online]. Available at: http://ssrn.com/abstract=961797 [Accessed: 8 April 2017].

√Al-Majid, W. (2007) 'Electronic agents and legal personality: time to treat them as human beings' in *22nd BILETA Annual Conference*, Hertfordshire, 16–17 April. BILETA [Online]. Available at: http://www.bileta.ac.uk/Document%20Library/1/Electronic%20Agents%20and%20Legal%20Personality%20-%20Time%20to%20Treat%20Them%20as%20Human%20Beings.pdf [Accessed: 12 May 2018].

√Andrade, F., Novais, P. and Neves, J. (2005) '*Will and declaration in acts performed by intelligent software agents: preliminary issues on the question*', in Oskamp, A., and Cevenini, C. (eds) Proceedings of the 4th international workshop on the law of electronic agents (LEA 2005) Nijmegen: Wolf Legal Publishers, pp. 53–56, University of Minho. Department of Informatics [Online]. Available at: http://www.di.uminho.pt/~pjn/Projectos/AIRJ/Docs/2005%20-%20LEA.pdf [Accessed: 20 May 2017].

√Andrade, F., Novais, P., Machado, J. and Neves, J. (2007a) 'Contracting agents: legal personality and representation', *Artificial Intelligence and Law*, 15(4), pp. 357–373, SpringerLink [Online]. Available at: http://www.springerlink.com/content/n368028l51115513/ [Accessed: 10 April 2018].

√Andrade, F., Novais, P., Machado, J. and Neves, J. (2007b) '*Intelligent contracting: software agents, corporate bodies and virtual organizations*', in Camarinha-Matos, L., Afsarmanesh, H., Novais, P. and Analide, C. (eds) Establishing the foundation of collaborative networks. IFIP Advances in Information and Communication Technology, vol. 243. New York: Springer, pp. 217–224.

√Angeles, S. (2017) '*Artificial Intelligence is revolutionizing the retail industry. Here's how it's being used and what the future of retail looks like.*'. [Online] Business.com. Available at: https://www.business.com/articles/retail-artificial-intelligence/ [Accessed: 12 March 2019].

√Arnbak A.M. and Van Eijk N.A.N.M. (2012) 'Certificate authority collapse: regulating systemic vulnerabilities in the HTTPS value chain' in *TPRC 2012: the research conference on communication, information and internet policy*. Available at: http://papers.ssrn.com/sol3/papers.cfm?abstract_id=2031409

√Arnbak A.M. (2015) '*Securing private communications: Protecting private communications security in EU law: fundamental rights, functional value chains and market incentives*', University of Amsterdam, UvA-DARE (Digital Academic Repository) [pdf]. Available at: http://dare.uva.nl/document/2/166342 [Accessed: 12 March 2019].

√Asghari H., Arnbak A.M., Van Eeten M.J.G. and Van Eijk N.A.N.M. (2013) '*Security Economics in the HTTPS Value Chain*', a Workshop on the Economics of Information Security 2013 [pdf]. Available at: https://www.econinfosec.org/archive/weis2013/papers/AsghariWEIS2013.pdf [Accessed: 12 March 2019].

√Bagby, J.W. (2004) '*Reconciling the promise of agency law doctrine with contract, tort and property law restrictions on electronic agent deployment*'. [Huber Hurst Research Seminar], 14 February. [Online]. Available at: https://www.researchgate.net/publication/228525487_Reconciling_the_Promise_of_Agency_Law__Doctrine_with_Contract_Tort_and_Property_Law_Restrictions_on_Electronic_Agent_Deployment [Accessed: 20 June 2019].

√Bailey, P.J. and Bakos, Y. (1997) 'An explanatory study of the emerging roles of electronic intermediaries', *International Journal of Electronic Commerce*, 1(3), pp. 7–20, CiteseerX [Online]. Available at: http://citeseerx.ist.psu.edu/viewdoc/summary?doi=10.1.1.7.5389 [Accessed: 2 May 2009].

√Bain, M. and Subirana, B. (2003a) 'E-commerce oriented software agents: legalising autonomous shopping agent processes', *Computer Law & Security Report*, 19(5), pp. 375–387.

√Bain, M. and Subirana, B. (2003b) 'E-commerce oriented software agents: some legal challenges of advertising and semi-autonomous contracting agents', *Computer Law & Security Report,* 19(4), pp. 282–288.

√Bain, M. and Subirana, B. (2003c) 'E-commerce oriented software agents: towards legal programming: a legal analysis of ecommerce and personal assistant agents using a process/IT view of the firm', *Computer Law & Security Report,* 19(3), pp. 201–211.

√Bainbridge, D. (2000) '*Introduction to computer law*'. 4th ed. Harlow and London: Pearson Education.

√Baker, T. (2006) 'Liability Insurance as Tort Regulation: Six Ways That Liability Insurance Shapes Tort Law in Action' [comments], Essay, *Connecticut Insurance Law Journal*, 12(1), (2005–2006), pp. 1–16. Available at: https://core.ac.uk/download/pdf/13529151.pdf [Accessed: 3 April 2019].

√Bakos Y. (1997) '*Reducing Buyer Search Costs: Implications for Electronic Marketplaces*', ACM Digital Library [Online]. Available at: http://dl.acm.org/citation.cfm?id=2797328 [Accessed: 3 April 2019].

√Barlow, T., Hess, A. and Seamons, E.K. (2001) '*Trust negotiation in electronic markets*', in Schoop, M. and Walczuch, R. (eds) Proceedings of the eighth research symposium on emerging electronic markets (RSEEM 01): Maastricht, The Netherlands, September 16–18, 2001. RWTH Aachen University. Computer Science 5. Available at: https://www.researchgate.net/profile/Kent_Seamons/publication/239653105_Trust_Negotiation_in_Electronic_Markets/links/59512635458515a207f49181/Trust-Negotiation-in-Electronic-Markets.pdf [Accessed: 20 June 2019].

√Barofsky, A. (2000) 'The European Commission's Directive on Electronic Signatures: Technological "Favoritism" Towards Digital Signatures', *B.C. Int'l & Comp. L. Rev.* 24(145) (2000). Available at: http://lawdigitalcommons.bc.edu/iclr/vol24/iss1/5 [Accessed: 5 April 2019].

√Bartolini, C., Preist, C. and Jennings, N.R. (2005) 'A software framework for automated negotiation', in Choren, R., Garcia, A., Lucena, C. and Romanovsky, A. (eds) Software engineering for multi-agent systems III: research issues and practical applications. Lecture Notes in *Computer Science*, 3390. Berlin and Heidelberg: Springer-Verlag, pp. 213–235, ECS EPrints [Online]. Available at: http://eprints.ecs.soton.ac.uk/10807/1/selmas04.pdf [Accessed: 29 April 2019].

Bassoli, E. (2002) 'Intelligent agents & privacy', *LEA 2002 workshop on the law of electronic agents.* Bologna 13 July. University of Bologna. Interdepartmental Research Centre in History of Law, Philosophy of Law, Computer Science and Law. Available at: http://citeseerx.ist.psu.edu/viewdoc/download?doi=10.1.1.202.6000&rep=rep1&type=pdf [Accessed: 20 June 2019].

√Baye, R.M., Morgan, J. and Scholten, P. (2004) 'Price dispersion in the small and in the large: evidence from an internet price comparison site', *Journal of Industrial Economics*, 52(4), pp. 463–496, JSTOR [Online]. Available at: http://www.jstor.org/pss/3569859 [Accessed: 28 July 2018].

√BBC (2009) 'Have your say: comparison websites'. *BBC News*, 17 July [Online]. Available at: http://news.bbc.co.uk/2/hi/programmes/moneybox/8156955.stm [Accessed: 21 June 2019].

√Beer, A., d'Inverno, M., Luck, P., Jennings, P., Preist, C. and Schroeder, M. (1999) 'Negotiation in multi-agent systems', *Knowledge Engineering Review*, 14(3), pp. 285–289. [Online] DOI: 10.1017/S0269888999003021

√Bellia, J.A. (2001) 'Contracting with electronic agents', *Emory Law Journal*, 50, pp. 1047–1092, SSRN [Online]. Available at: http://ssrn.com/abstract=910210 [Accessed: 1 May 2019].

√Bergkamp, L. (2002) 'EU data protection policy: the privacy fallacy: adverse effects of Europe's data protection policy in an information-driven economy', *Computer Law & Security Report*, 18(1), pp. 31–47. [Online] DOI: 10.1016/S0267-3649(02)00106-1 [Accessed: 18 May 2018].

Berkes, E.J. (2003) '*Decentralized peer-to-peer network architecture: Gnutella and Freenet*', University of Manitoba, Canada. SysDesign archive [Online]. Available at: https://www.researchgate.net/publication/228694133_Decentralized_peer-to-peer_network_architecture_Gnutella_and_Freenet [Accessed: 20 June 2019].

√Bettelli, V.A. (2002) '*Agent technology and on-line data protection*', LEA 2002 workshop on the law of electronic agents. Bologna 13 July. University of Bologna. Interdepartmental Research Centre in History of Law, Philosophy of Law, Computer Science and Law. Available at: http://www.cirfid.unibo.it/~agsw/lea02/pp/Villecco.pdf

√Blythe, S. (2005) 'Digital Signature Law of the United Nations, European Union, United Kingdom and United States: Promotion of Growth in E-Commerce with Enhanced Security', *Richmond Journal of Law and Technology*, 11(2). Available at: https://scholarship.richmond.edu/cgi/viewcontent.cgi?referer=&httpsredir=1&article=1238&context=jolt [Accessed: 5 April 2019].

√Body of European Regulators for Electronic Communications, (BEREC) (2012) '*Article 28(2) Universal Service Directive: A harmonised BEREC cooperation process – Consultation paper*' (BoR (12) 85) [Online]. Available at: https://berec.europa.eu/eng/document_register/subject_matter/berec/download/0/979-consultation-paper-on-article-282-univer_0.pdf [Accessed: 3 April 2019].

√Boonk, M.L. and Lodder, A.R. (2006) '"Halt, who goes there?": on agents and conditional access to websites' in the *21st BILETA conference on globalisation and harmonisation in technology law*. Malta 6–7 April. BILETA. Available at: https://www.researchgate.net/publication/237552532_Halt_who_goes_there_On_agents_and_conditional_access_to_websites [Accessed: 20 June 2019].

√Boonk, M.L., de Groot, D.R.A., Brazier, F.M.T. and Oskamp, A. (2005) '*Agent exclusion on websites*' in Cevenni, C. and Oskamp, A. (eds) LEA 2005: the law of electronic agents: proceedings of the workshop "LEA 2005". Amsterdam: Wolf Legal Publishers, pp. 13–20, Vrije Universiteit Computer/Law Institute [Online]. Available at: https://research.vu.nl/en/publications/agent-exclusion-on-websites [Accessed: 5 June 2019].

√Borking, J.J., van Eck, B.M.A. and Siepel, P. (1999) '*Intelligent Software Agents and Privacy*'. The Hague: Registratiekamer [Online]. Available at: https://autoriteitpersoonsgegevens.nl/sites/default/files/downloads/av/av13.pdf [Accessed: 5 April 2019].

√Boss, A. H. (1999) 'Searching for Security in the Law of Electronic Commerce', *Nova Law Review*, 23 (2), 1999 Article 3, Nova Law Review is produced by The Berkeley Electronic Press (bepress) [Online]. Available at: https://core.ac.uk/download/pdf/51081619.pdf [Accessed: 5 April 2019].

√Bovens, M. (2007) 'Analysing and Assessing Accountability: A Conceptual Framework' European Law Journal, Review of European Law in Context, 13(4), pp. 447–468 [Online]. Available at: https://onlinelibrary.wiley.com/doi/abs/10.1111/j.1468–0386.2007.00378.x [Accessed: 5 April 2019].

Bradgate, R., White, F., Fennell, S. (1995) '*Commercial Law*', Blackstone Press.

√Bradgate, R. (1997) 'The EU Directive on distance selling', *Web Journal of Current Legal Issues*, 4 [Online]. Available at: https://www.researchgate.net/publication/277105706_The_distance_selling_directive_consumer_champion_or_complete_irrelevance [Accessed: 10 December 2017].

Bradshaw J.M. (1997) '*An introduction to software agents*', in Bradshaw J.M. (ed). Software agents. Cambridge, MA: MIT Press, pp. 3–46, CiteseerX [Online]. Available at: http://citeseerx.ist.psu.edu/viewdoc/summary?doi=10.1.1.39.640 [Accessed: 20 July 2017].

√Brazier F.M.T., Oskamp, A., Prins, J.E.J., Schellekens, M.H.M., Schreuders, E., Wijngaards, N.J.E., Apistola, M., Voulon, M.B. and Kubbe, O. (2003a) '*ALIAS: analyzing legal implications and agent information systems*'. Technical Report No. IR-CS-004.l, Delft University of Technology. Intelligent Interactive Distributed Systems Group [Online]. Available at: https://nlnet.nl/project/alias/alias-final.pdf [Accessed: 13 June 2019].

√Brazier F.M.T., Oskamp, A., Schellekens, M.H.M. and Wijngaards, N. (2003b) '*Can agents close contracts?*' in Oskamp, A and Weitzenböck, M.E. (eds) LEA 2003: the law and electronic agents: proceedings of the second LEA workshop: Edinburgh, 24 June 2003. Oslo: Norwegian Research Center for Computers and Law, pp. 9–20, Delft University of Technology. Intelligent Interactive Distributed Systems Group [Online]. Available at: https://www.researchgate.net/publication/2919640_Can_Agents_Close_Contracts [Accessed: 20 May 2017].

√Brazier, F., Oskamp, A., Prins, C., Schellekens, M. and Wijngaards, N. (2004a) 'Anonymity and software agents: an interdiscplinary challenge', *AI & Law*, 12(1–2), pp. 137–157, SpringerLink [Online]. Available at: http://www.springerlink.com/content/h25w62q6326242m8/[Accessed: 7 May 2019].

√Brazier F.M.T., Oskamp, A., Prins, J.E.J., Schellekens, M.H.M., Schreuders, E. and Wijngaards, N.J.E. (2004b) 'Law-abiding & integrity on the internet: a case for agents', *AI & Law*, 12(1–2), pp. 5–37, SpringerLink [Online]. Available at: http://www.springerlink.com/content/hn4u90m4649ju447/ [Accessed: 27 March 2019].

√Burkert, H. (1998) '*Privacy-Enhancing Technologies: Typology, Critique, Vision*', in Agre, P.E., Rotenberg, M. (eds), Technology and Privacy: The New Landscape, pp.125–142.

√Burrows, A. (2004) '*Remedies for Torts and Breach of Contract*', Third Edition, Oxford University Press. Available at: https://global.oup.com/academic/product/remedies-for-torts-and-breach-of-contract-9780406977267?cc=cy&lang=en& [Accessed 3 April 2019].

√Burton, F., Cory-Wright, C., Levene, S. and Mead, P. (2007) *PIBA personal injury handbook*. 3rd edition (rev.). Bristol: Jordan Publishing.

√Bush D. (2016). 'How data breaches lead to fraud', *Network Security*, 2016, (7), pp. 11–13 [Online]. Available at: https://ac.els-cdn.com/S1353485816300691/1-s2.0-S1353485816300691-main.pdf?_tid=5bc66cca-f446-11e7-9a3b-00000aab0f6c&acdnat=1515397048_3eb19fa24bea74321bf49fd20e136eb8 [Accessed 3 April 2019].

√Bygrave, A.L. (2001) 'Electronic agents and privacy: a cyberspace odyssey 2001', *International Journal of Law and Information Technology*, 9(3), pp. 275–294. [Online] DOI: 10.1093/ijlit/9.3.275.

√Caelli, W., Longley D. and Shain, M. (1991) *Information Security Handbook*. London: Macmillan.

√Calliess, G-P. (2008) '*Transnational consumer law: co-regulation of B2C-e-commerce*', CLPE Research Paper No. 3/2007. CLPE Research Paper Series, 3(3), SSRN [Online]. Available at: http://ssrn.com/abstract=988612 [Accessed: 2 May 2019].

√Calkins, M. (2001) '*My Reputation Always Had More Fun Than Me: The Failure of eBay's Feedback Model to Effectively Prevent Online Auction Fraud*', RICH. J.L. & TECH. 7(33) (Spring 2001). [Online]. Available at: http://jolt.richmond.edu/jolt-archive/v7i4/note1.html#h4b [Accessed 5 April 2019].

√Campisi, P. (2013) '*Security and Privacy in Biometrics*', Springer – Verlag London.

Cate, F.H. and Mayer-Schönberger, V. (2013) 'Notice and consent in a world of Big Data', *International Data Privacy Law, 3*(2), pp. 67–73.

Cavanillas, S. (2001) '*An introduction to web contracts*', in Walden, I. and Hornle, J., E-commerce Law and Practice in Europe, Section 2, Woodhead Publishing.

Cavoukian, A. and Jonas, J. (2012) *'Privacy by design in the age of big data'*, Information and Privacy Commissioner of Ontario, Canada, pp. 1–17. Available at: https://www.ipc.on.ca/wp-content/uploads/Resources/pbd-pde.pdf [Accessed 5 April 2019].

√Center for Democracy and Technology (CDT) (2010) '*Intermediary Liability: Protecting Internet Platforms for Expression and Innovation*', April 2010. [Online]. Available at: https://www.cdt.org/files/pdfs/CDT-Intermediary%20Liability_(2010).pdf [Accessed 5 April 2019].

√Center for Democracy and Technology (CDT) (2012) '*Shielding the Messengers: Protecting Platforms for Expression and Innovation*', Version 2, updated December 2012 [Online]. Available at: https://www.cdt.org/files/pdfs/CDT-Intermediary-Liability-2012.pdf [Accessed 5 April 2019].

√Centre for Information Policy Leadership, Huntons & Williams LL.C (2011) '*Accountability: A Compendium for Stakeholders*', [Online]. Available at: http://informationaccountability.org/wp-content/uploads/Centre-Accountability-Compendium.pdf [Accessed 5 April 2019].

√Cevenini, C., Contissa, G. and Laukyte, M. (2007) '*Agent-based contracting in virtual enterprises*', in Camarinba-Matos, L., Afsarmanesb, H., Novais, P. and Analide, C. (eds) Establishing the foundation of collaborative networks. IFIP International Federation for Information Processing, vol.243/2007. Boston: Springer, pp. 225–232.

Chansey, M.E. (1999) 'Meta-Tags and Hypertext Deep Linking: How the Essential Components of Web-Authoring and Internet Guidance are Strengthening Intellectual Property Rights on the World Wide Web'. *Stetson L. Rev.* 29, p. 230.

√Chavez, A. and Maes, P. (1996) 'Kasbah: an agent marketplace for buying and selling goods' in *Proceedings of the First international conference on the practical application of intelligent agents and multi-agent technology*. Blackpool: Practical Application Co. Ltd, pp. 75–90, CiteSeerX [Online]. Available at: http://citeseerx.ist.psu.edu/viewdoc/summary?doi=10.1.1.21.1129 [Accessed: 13 May 2019].

√Chiu, K.W.D., Wang, C., Leung, H.-F., Kafeza, I. and Kafeza, I. (2005) '*Supporting the legal identities of contracting agents with an agent authorization platform*' in Li, Q and Liang, T.-P (eds) ICEC'05: proceedings of the 7th international conference on electronic commerce: Xi'an, China, August 15–17, 2005. ACM International Conference Proceeding Series,113. New York: Association for Computing Machinery, pp. 721–728, Chinese University of Hong Kong. Department of Computer Science and Engineering [Online]. Available at: https://www.researchgate.net/publication/221550472_Supporting_the_legal_identities_of_contracting_agents_with_an_agent_authorization_platform [Accessed: 10 April 2019].

√Chopra, S. and White, L. (2009) 'Artificial agents and the contracting problem: a solution via an agency analysis', University of Illinois *Journal of Law Technology & Policy*, 2, pp. 363–403, SSRN [Online]. Available at: http://papers.ssrn.com/sol3/papers.cfm?abstract_id=1589564 [Accessed: 20 June 2019].

√Choudhuri, R. (2017) '*The Impact of AI/Machine Learning on the Indian E-commerce and Price Comparison Startup Space*'. [Online] EDITIONS. Available at: https://yourstory.com/read/4ccba9fa6d-the-impact-of-ai-machine-learning-on-the-indian-e-commerce-and-price-comparison-startup-space [Accessed: 12 March 2019].

√Chung, M. and Honavar, V. (2000) 'A negotiation model in agent-mediated electronic commerce' in *Proceedings of International Symposium on Multimedia Software Engineering: Taipei*, Taiwan, 11–13 December 2000. Los Alamitos: IEEE Computer Society, pp. 403–410, IEEE Explore [Online]. Available at: http://ieeexplore.ieee.org/xpl/freeabs_all.jsp?arnumber=897242 [Accessed: 29 April 2019].

√Cobb M., (2011) '*Best practices for audit, log review for IT security investigations: Device logs can be one of the most helpful tools infosec pros have, or they can be a huge waste of space*'. computerweekly.com [Online]. Available at: https://www.computerweekly.com/tip/Best-practices-for-audit-log-review-for-IT-security-investigations [Accessed: 3 April 2018].

√Civic Consulting, (2011) '*Consumer market study on the functioning of e-commerce and Internet marketing and selling techniques in the retail of goods*', Executive Agency for Health and Consumers, Final Report Part 1: Synthesis Report [pdf]. Available at: http://www.civic-consulting.de/reports/study_ecommerce_goods_en.pdf [Accessed: 3 April 2018].

√CIRSFID: Interdepartmental Research Centre in History of Law, Philosophy of Law, Computer Science and Law; NRCCL: Norwegian Research Center for Computers and Law and FIDAL: FIDAL Law Firm (2006) *Report on legal issues of software agents*. Document no.14, LEGAL-IST Project European Commission IST-2–004252-SSA. CiteseerX [Online]. Available at: http://citeseerx.ist.psu.edu/viewdoc/summary?doi=10.1.1.87.8059 [Accessed: 20 March 2017].

√Clark, J. (2016) '*IBM Watson Trend: An app to outthink holiday shopping stress*'. [Blog] IBM. Available at: https://www.ibm.com/blogs/internet-of-things/watson-trend/ [Accessed: 12 March 2019].

√Clarke R. (1996) 'Identification, anonymity and pseudonymity in consumer transactions: a vital systems design and public policy issue' in *Smart cards: the issues conference*. Sydney 18 October. Roger Clarke website [Online]. Available at: http://www.rogerclarke.com/DV/AnonPsPol.html [29 April 2019].

√Collins, H. (2005) 'The Unfair Commercial Practices Directive', *European Review of Contract Law*, 4, pp. 417–441.

Collins, J., Jamison, S., Mobasher, B. and Gini, M. (1997) '*A market architecture for multi-agent contracting*', University of Minnesota. Department of Computer Science, 18 April [Online]. Available at: http://www-users.cs.umn.edu/~gini/papers/tr97-15.pdf [Accessed: 4 May 2019].

√Collins, J., Tsvetovatty, M., Mobasher, B. and Gini, M. (1998) '*MAGNET: a multi-agent contracting system for plan execution*', in Interrante, D.L. and Luger, F.G. (eds) Proceedings: artificial intelligence and manufacturing workshop: state of the art and state of practice. Menlo Park: AAAI Press, pp. 63–68. [Online]. Available at: http://www.aaai.org/Papers/SIGMAN/1998/SIGMAN98-009.pdf [Accessed: 4 May 2019].

√Coteanu, C. (2017) *Cyber consumer law: state of the art and perspectives*. Bucharest: Humanitas.

√Couldry, N. and Turow, J. (2014) 'Advertising, big data and the clearance of the public realm: Marketers' new approaches to the content subsidy'. *International Journal of Communication, 8*, pp.1710–1726.

√Cox, A. (2014) '*EU Network and Information Security Directive: Is it possible to legislate for cyber security?*' [Online]. Available at: http://www.mondaq.com/ireland/x/349932/data+protection/EU+Network+And+Information+Security+Directive+Is+It+Possible+To+Legislate+For+Cyber+Security [Accessed: 5 October 2018].

√Cranor, L.F. (2014) '*Privacy engineering, privacy by design, privacy impact assessments, and privacy governance*'. Cy Lab Usable Privacy & Security Laboratory [pdf]. Available at: https://cups.cs.cmu.edu/courses/pplt-fa14/slides/141111privacyengineering.pdf [Accessed 5 April 2019].

√Craig, P. (2004) '*The Hierarchy of Norms and the inter-institutional balance of power within the EU*', p.80, Trimidas T., Nebbia P. (eds). European Union Law for the Twenty-first Century: Constitutional and Public Law External Relations, (W.G. Hart Workshop), Hart Publishing Oxford and Portland Oregon.

√Craig P. and de Búrca G. (2011) '*EU Law: Text, Cases, and Materials*' 5th edition, Oxford University Press.

Cranor, B.J. and Leenes, R.E., (2014) 'Privacy Regulation Cannot Be Hardcoded. A Critical Comment on the 'Privacy by Design' Provision in Data-Protection Law', *International Review of Law*, Computers & Technology 28(2), pp. 159–171. Available at: https://papers.ssrn.com/sol3/papers.cfm?abstract_id=2564791 [Accessed 5 April 2019].

Crawford, K. and Schultz, J. (2014) 'Big data and due process: Toward a framework to redress predictive privacy harms', *BCL Rev.*, 55, pp. 93–128.

√Cross, S. (2007) '*Consumer protection compliance in agent negotiated business to consumer transactions*' in Galves, F. (ed.) Law and technology: September 24 – 26, 2007, Berkeley, California, USA. Anaheim: ACTA Press, pp. 24–33.

√Cruquenaire, A. (2001) 'Electronic agents as search engines: copyright related aspects', *International Journal of Law and Information Technology*, 9(3), pp. 327–343. [Online] DOI: 10.1093/ijlit/9.3.327 [Accessed: 10 May 2009].

Cumbley, R. and Church, P. (2013) Is "big data" creepy? *Computer Law & Security Review, 29*(5), pp. 601–609.

√Dahiyat, E.A.R. (2006) 'Intelligent agents and intentionality: should we begin to think outside the box?', *Computer Law & Security Report*, 22(6), pp. 472–480. [Online] DOI: 10.1016/j.clsr.2006.09.001.

Daniel, J. (2004) 'Electronic Contracting Under the 2003 Revisions to Article 2 of the Uniform Commercial Code: Clarification or Chaos?', *Santa Clara High Tech. L.J.* (20) 2, pp.319–346. Available at: https://digitalcommons.law.scu.edu/chtlj/vol20/iss2/3 [Accessed: 21 June 2019].

Deakin, F.S., Johnston, A. and Markesinis, B. (2013) '*Markesinis and Deakin's Tort Law*', 7th edition, Oxford University Press.

√De Andrade, N. N. G. Chen-Wilson L., Argles D., Wills G., Di Zenise S.M. (2014) '*Electronic Identity*', Springer.

√De Azevedo Cunha and Mario Viola (2013) '*Data Protection Systems in the European Union: The Italian Experience.*', Market Integration Through Data Protection, pp. 143–183. Springer Netherlands.

√De Kare-Silver, M. (2011) '*E-shock 2020: How the Digital Technology Revolution Is Changing Business and All Our Lives*' Palgrave Macmillan.

De Rocquigny, M. (2001) '*Court condemns unlawful use of advertisements on an internet site offering job advertisements*', IRIS Legal Observations of the European Audiovisual Observatory, 10(12) [Online]. Available at: http://merlin.obs.coe.int/iris/2001/10/article28.en.html [Accessed: 5 March 2019].

√Dekker M. (2013) '*Network and Information Security Legislation in the EU*', ENISA [pdf]. Available at: http://www.rsaconference.com/writable/presentations/file_upload/sper-r07-network-and-in formation-security-legislation-in-the-eu.pdf [Accessed 5 April 2019].

√Dekker, M., Karsberg, C. and Moulinos, K. (2013) '*Security framework for Article 4 and 13a, Proposal for one security framework for Article 4 and 13a*', Version 1.0, ENISA [Online]. Available at: https://www.enisa.europa.eu/publications/proposal-for-one-security-framework-for-articles-4-and-13a/at_download/fullReport [Accessed: 3 April 2019].

Diepens, C.W.A. (Sanne) (2017) '*Information Overload: The Impact on a Consumer's Product Choice Online*' Bachelor Thesis Psychology Tilburg University, [pdf]. Available at: http://arno.uvt.nl/show.cgi?fid=143280 [Accessed: 3 April 2019].

DLA Piper Rudnick Gray Cary UK LLP Belgium (2006) *Legal study on unfair commercial practices within B2B e-markets: final report*. European Commission Study ENTR/04/069. EDZ ArchiDok [Online]. Available at: https://ec.europa.eu/growth/content/legal-study-unfair-commercial-pra ctices-b2b-e-markets-0_en [Accessed: 10 February 2019].

√DLA Piper (2009) 'Liability of online intermediaries' in EU study on the New rules for a new age? Legal analysis of a Single Market for the Information Society, November 2009, [Online].Available at: http://ec.europa.eu/information_society/newsroom/cf/document.cfm?doc_id=835 [Acces-sed: 3 April 2019].

√Donnelly, M. (2016) 'Payments in the digital market: Evaluating the contribution of Payment Ser-vices Directive II', *Computer Law & Security Report* 32(6), August 2016 [Online]. Available at: https://www.researchgate.net/publication/305886276_Payments_in_the_digital_market_Evalua ting_the_contribution_of_Payment_Services_Directive_II [Accessed: 5 April 2019].

√Dumortier, J. (1999) '*The European Directive 1999/93/EC on a Community framework for Electro-nic signatures*', K.U. Leuven – ICRI, in Lodder, A.R., Kaspersen, H.W.K. (eds) eDirectives: Guide to European law on E-Commerce. Commentary on the Directives on Distance Selling, Electronic Signatures, Electronic Commerce, Copyright in the Information Society, and Data protection. Law and Electronic Commerce Series, Vol 14, Kluwer law International, pp.33–65. Available at: http s://www.law.kuleuven.be/citip/en/archive/copy_of_publications/58the-european-directi ve-19992f90.pdf [Accessed: 5 April 2019].

√Ebers, M. (2008) '*C. Unfair Contract Terms Directive (93/13)*', in Schulte-Nölke, H., Twigg-Fles-ner, C. and Ebers, M. (eds) Consumer law compendium: comparative analysis, pp. 341–437. Eur-opean Commission Service Contract No. 17.020100 / 04 / 389299. European Commission [Online]. Available at: http://citeseerx.ist.psu.edu/viewdoc/download?doi=10.1.1.183.3328&rep=rep1&type=pdf [Accessed: 10 June 2019].

√Edwards, L. (2003) 'Consumer Privacy, On-Line Business and the Internet: Looking for Privacy in all the Wrong Places', *International Journal of Law and Information Technology*, 11(3),

AUTUMN, Pages 226–250 [Online]. Available at: https://doi.org/10.1093/ijlit/11.3.226 [Accessed: 5 April 2019].

Edwards, L. and Hatcher, J. (2009) '*Consumer privacy law 2: data collection, profiling and targeting*' [Pre-print], in Edwards, L. and Waelde, C. (eds) Law and the internet: regulating cyberspace. 3rd edition. Oxford: Hart Publishing, SSRN [Online]. Available at: http://papers.ssrn.com/sol3/papers.cfm?abstract_id=1435105 [Accessed: 5 September 2018].

√Egertz, A. (2015) '*PSD2 Narrows Exclusions from Payment Institution Licence – How Commercial Agents and Limited Networks are Regulated under the New Regime*', Linkedin [Online]. Available at: https://www.linkedin.com/pulse/psd2-narrows-exclusions-from-payment-institution-licence-egertz?forceNoSplash=true [Accessed 5 April 2019].

√Ellison, C. (no date) '*Non-repudiation*'. Available at: http://world.std.com/~cme/non-repudiation.htm [Accessed 5 April 2019].

√Erdos D. (2016) '*European Data Protection Regulation and the New Media Internet: Mind the Implementation Gaps*' Gaps (September 1, 2015). A revised version of this paper is in the Journal of Law and Society (Winter 2016 Forthcoming); University of Cambridge Faculty of Law Research Paper No. 30/2015 [Online]. Available at: https://papers.ssrn.com/sol3/papers.cfm?abstract_id=2611583 [Accessed 5 April 2019].

√Erlanger, L. (no date) 'Online privacy seals lack significance: what do online "privacy seals" really mean?', *ABC News*, 4 February [Online]. Available at: http://abcnews.go.com/Technology/ZDM/story?id=97377&page=1 [Accessed: 6 May 2019].

√European Group of Tort Law (2005) *Principles of European tort law* [Online]. Available at: http://www.egtl.org/ [Accessed: 10 September 2019].

European Research Group on Existing EC Private Law: Dannemann, G., Rochfeld, J., Schulte-Nölke, H., Schulze, R., Terryn, E., Twigg-Flesner, C. and Zoll, F. (2009) '*Position paper on the Proposal for a Directive on Consumer Rights*', Oxford University Comparative Law Forum, 3 [Online]. Available at: http://ouclf.iuscomp.org/articles/acquis_group.shtml [Accessed: 12 February 2019].

√Expert Group on B2B Internet Trading Platforms (2003) *Report of the Expert Group on B2B Internet Trading Platforms: final report* (30 April 2003). European Commission. [Online]. Available at: http://www.e-thematic.org/download/B2B%20Internet%20trading%20platforms,%20July%202003.pdf [Accessed: 2 May 2019].

√Fallows, D. (2005) *Search engine users: internet searchers are confident, satisfied and trusting – but they are also unaware and naïve.* [Online]. Available at: https://www.pewinternet.org/wp-content/uploads/sites/9/media/Files/Reports/2005/PIP_Searchengine_users.pdf.pdf [Accessed: 26 March 2019].

√Fasli, M. (2006) 'Shopbots: a syntactic present, a semantic future', *IEEE Internet Computing*, 10(6), pp. 69–75, IEEE Explorer [Online]. Available at: https://ieeexplore.ieee.org/document/4012599 [Accessed: 20 July 2018].

√Fasli, M. (2007) 'On agent technology for e-commerce: trust, security and legal issues', *Knowledge Engineering Review*, 22(1), pp. 3–35. [Online] DOI: 10.1017/S0269888907001014.

√Fasli, M. (2009) '*The next generation of shopbots: semantic interoperability and personalization*', in Wan, Y. (ed.) Comparison Shopping Services and Agent Designs. Hershey and London: Idea Publishing Group, pp. 19–36.

√Faure, M. (2016) 'Attribution of Liability: An Economic Analysis of Various Cases', *CHI.-KENT L. REV.* 91 (603). Available at: https://scholarship.kentlaw.iit.edu/cgi/viewcontent.cgi?article=4121&context=cklawreview [Accessed: 5 April 2019].

√Feliu, S. (2001) 'Intelligent agents and consumer protection', *International Journal of Law and Information Technology*, 9(3), pp. 235–248. [Online] DOI: 10.1093/ijlit/9.3.235.

çFernández-Díez I.G. (2014) '*Comparative Analysis on National Approaches to the Liability of Internet Intermediaries for Infringement of Copyright and Related Rights*', [pdf]. Available at: http://www.wipo.int/export/sites/www/copyright/en/doc/liability_of_internet_intermediaries_garrote.pdf [Accessed: 3 April 2019].

√Fleming, J. (2015) '*Cyber security directive held up in face of 'Wild West' Internet*', EURACTIV.com [Online]. Available at: http://www.euractiv.com/sections/infosociety/cyber-security-directive-held-face-wild-west-internet-313431

√Frazer, M. and Stiehler, B.E. (2014) 'Omnichannel retailing: The merging of the online and off-line environment'. *Global Conference on Business & Finance Proceedings*, 9(1), p. 655.

√Froomkin, M.A. (2000) 'The death of privacy?' *Stanford Law Review*, 52(5), pp. 1461–1543, University of Miami. School of Law [Online]. Available at: http://osaka.law.miami.edu/~froomkin/articles/privacy-deathof.pdf [Accessed: 12 July 2018].

√Furst, S. (2006) *Recent important decisions and their practical application.* [Seminar]. 20 October. [Online]. Available at: http://www.mondaq.com/uk/x/44148/Market+Commentaries/Recent+Important+Decisions+And+Their+Practical+Application [Accessed: 17 February 2018].

√Gandomi, A. and Haider, ☒. (2015) 'Beyond the hype: Big data concepts, methods, and analytics. *International Journal of Information Management*, [Online] ScienceDirect (ELSEVIER), 35(2), pp. 137–144. Available at: https://ac.els-cdn.com/S0268401214001066/1-s2.0-S0268401214001066-main.pdf?_tid=53a6d610-f09a-11e7-ab1d-00000aab0f6b&acdnat=1514993308_573f4fbff64bc10f44e6cf9cabe9343a [Accessed: 12 March 2019].

√Gautrais, V. (2003–2004) 'The colour of e-consent', *University of Ottawa Law and Technology Journal*, 1(1–2), pp. 189–212. [Online]. Available at: https://papers.ssrn.com/sol3/papers.cfm?abstract_id=764744 [Accessed: 15 May 2019].

√Gellert, R. (2015) 'Data protection: a risk regulation? Between the risk management of everything and the precautionary alternative'. *International Data Privacy Law*, 5 (1) [Online]. Available at: https://academic.oup.com/idpl/article-abstract/5/1/3/622981?redirectedFrom=fulltext

√Giesen, I. (2009) '*The burden of proof and other procedural devices in tort law*' in Koziol, H., Steininger B.C (eds.) European Tort Law 2008, pp.49–67, Springer [Online]. Available at : https://www.researchgate.net/publication/226728355_The_Burden_of_Proof_and_other_Procedural_Devices_in_Tort_Law [Accessed: 5 April 2019].

Gomez, F. (2002) '*The European Directive on Consumer Sales: An Economic perspective*' in Grundman S. and Bianca C.M. (eds) EU Sales Directive Commentary, Intersentia, (Antwerp-Oxford-New York) 2002, pp.53–78.

√Graham-Rowe, D. (2001) '*Robots beat human commodity traders*', New Scientist, 9 August [Online]. Available at: http://www.newscientist.com/article.ns?id=dn1131 [Accessed: 30 April 2019].

√Greenwald, A. and Stone, P. (2001) 'Autonomous bidding agents in the Trading Agent Competition', *IEEE Internet Computing*: Special Issue on Virtual Markets, 5(2), March/April, pp. 52–60, The University of Texas at Austin. Department of Computer Science [Online]. Available at: http://www.cs.utexas.edu/~pstone/Papers/bib2html-links/TAC00.pdf [Accessed: 29 April 2019].

√Gritzalis, A.D., (2004). 'Embedding privacy in IT applications development', *Information Management & Computer Security*, 12(1), pp.8–26, [Online]. Available at: https://doi.org/10.1108/09685220410518801 [Accessed 5 April 2019].

√Groebner, B. (2004). 'Oops! The Legal Consequences of and Solutions to Online Pricing Errors', *Shidler J. L. Com. & Tech.* 2. [Online]. Available at: https://digital.law.washington.edu/dspace-law/bitstream/handle/1773.1/354/vol1_no1_art2.pdf?sequence=1

√Groom, J. (2004) 'Are 'agent' exclusion clauses a legitimate application of the EU Database Directive?', SCRIPT-ed: A Journal of Law, *Technology & Society*, 1(1), pp. 83–118. [Online]. Available at: https://papers.ssrn.com/sol3/papers.cfm?abstract_id=1137542 [Accessed: 2 April 2018].

√Gutmann, (2005) '*Digital Signature Legislation*' [pdf]. Available at: http://dgaby.free.fr/FTP/Archive%20M1%202004–2005/Structures%20R%E9seaux/Pdf/part2a.pdf [Accessed 5 April 2019].

√Gulli, A. (2005) 'The anatomy of a news search engine', in *Special interest tracks and posters of the 14th international conference on world wide web.* New York: Association of Computing Machinery, pp. 880–881. [Online]. Available at: http://www.ra.ethz.ch/cdstore/www2005/docs/p880.pdf [Accessed: 8 April 2019].

√Guttman, H.R., Moukas, G.A. and Maes, P. (1998) 'Agent-mediated electronic commerce: a survey', *Knowledge Engineering Review*, 13(2), pp. 147–159. [Online] DOI: 10.1017/S0269888998002082 [Accessed: 15 June 2018].

Haataja, L.-M. (2015) '*Payment Services Directive II Effects on Business Models and Strategies*', Master's Thesis Espoo, May 21, 2015, Aalto University School of Science. Available at: https://pdfs.semanticscholar.org/4e48/c5cbf2196bc3af7b1ea20e71a707f5dde7c1.pdf [Accessed: 21 June 2019].

√Harris D., Campbell D., Halson R. (2005) '*Remedies in Contract and Tort*' 2nd edition, Cambridge University Press.

√Heckman, C. and Wobbrock, O.J. (1999) '*Liability for autonomous agent design*', Autonomous Agents and Multi-Agent Systems, 2(1), pp. 87–103, SpringerLink [Online]. Available at: http://www.springerlink.com/content/rt41626157760556/ [Accessed: 10 April 2019].

√Hes, R. and Borking, J. (2000) '*Privacy-enhancing Technologies: the path to anonymity*', The Hague, 2000, Revised edition of Rossum, H. van, e.a. (1995). Privacy-enhancing Technologies: the path to anonymity. Den Haag: Registratiekamer. Available at: https://www.researchgate.net/publication/243777645_Privacy-Enhancing_Technologies_The_Path_to_Anonymity [Accessed: 5 April 2019].

√Hillman, R. A. and Rachlinski, J. J., (2002) '*Standard-Form Contracting in the Electronic Age*', Cornell Law Faculty Publications, 1062. Available at: https://scholarship.law.cornell.edu/facpub/1062 [Accessed: 3 April 2019].

√Hillman R. (2006) '*Online Boilerplate: Would Mandatory Website Disclosure of E-Standard Terms Backfire?*', Cornell Law Faculty Publications. Paper 542, [pdf]. Available at: http://scholarship.law.cornell.edu/cgi/viewcontent.cgi?article=1658&context=facpub [Accessed: 3 April 2019].

√Hirsch, D. (2013) In Search of the Holy Grail: Achieving Global Privacy Rules Through Sector-Based Codes of Conduct (December 1, 2013). *Ohio State Law Journal*, 74(6). Available at: https://papers.ssrn.com/sol3/papers.cfm?abstract_id=2393757 [Accessed: 3 April 2019].

Hon, W. K., Kosta, E., Millard, C., & Stefanatou, D. (2014) '*Cloud accountability: The likely impact of the proposed EU Data Protection Regulation*', Queen Mary School of Law Legal Studies Research Paper No. 172/2014, Tilburg Law School Research Paper No. 07/2014. Available at: https://ssrn.com/abstract=2405971 [Accessed: 3 June 2019].

Hou, C. (2004) '*Predicting agents tactics in automated negotiations*', in IAT '04: Proceedings of the IEEE/WIC/ACM International conference on intelligent agent technology. Los Alamitos: IEEE Computer Society Press, pp. 127–133, IEEE Explorer [Online]. DOI: 10.1109/IAT.2004.1342934. [Accessed: 19 July 2018].

√Howells, G. (2004) '*Co-regulation's role in the development of European fair trading laws*', in Collins, H. (ed.) The forthcoming EC Directive on unfair commercial practices: contract, consumer and competition law implications. The Hague: Kluwer Law International, pp. 119–12.

√Howells, G. (2005) 'The potential and limits of consumer empowerment by information', *Journal of Law and Society*, 32(3), pp. 349–370.

√Howells, G., Twigg-Flesner C. and Willett, C. (2017) '*Product Liability and Digital Products*' in Synodinou, T.E., Jougleux, P., Markou, C., Prastitou T., EU Internet Law: Regulation and Enforcement, pp.183–195, Springer International Publishing.

√Huang, C.C., Liang, W.Y., Lai, Y.H. and Lin, Y.C., (2010) '*The agent-based negotiation process for B2C e-commerce*'. Expert Systems with Applications, 37(1), pp.348–359.

√Inacio, C. (1998) '*Software fault tolerance*', Carnegie Mellon University. Electrical and Computer Engineering Department. Dependable Embedded Systems [Pre-editing]. Available at: http://www.ece.cmu.edu/~koopman/des_s99/sw_fault_tolerance/ [Accessed: 10 April 2018].

International Standards Organization. Information Technology – Open Systems Interconnection—Security Frameworks for Open Systems – Part 4: Non-repudiation. International Standard ISO/IEC 10181–4, (1996).

√Irion, K. (2012) '*The Governance of Network and Information Security in the European Union: The European Public-Private Partnership for Resilience (EP3R)*' Gaycken, Krueger, Nickolay (eds.). The Secure Information Society. Berlin: Springer Publishing. Available at: http://papers.ssrn.com/sol3/papers.cfm?abstract_id=2075916 [Accessed 20 June 2019].

√Iyer, G. and Pazgal, A. (2003) 'Internet shopping agents: virtual co-location and competition', *Marketing Science*, 22(1), pp. 85–106, JSTOR [Online]. Available at: http://www.jstor.org/pss/4129725 [Accessed: 28 July 2017].

√Jonkheer, K. (1999) '*Intelligent agents, markets and competition: consumers' interests and functionality of destination sites*', First Monday, 4(6) [Online]. Available at: https://firstmonday.org/ojs/index.php/fm/article/view/675/585 [Accessed: 13 July 2018].

√Julià-Barceló, R. (1999) '*Liability for online intermediaries: a European perspective*', EU Commission ESPRIT Project 27028: Electronic Commerce Legal Issues Platform, Deliverable 2.1.4. ECLIP [Online]. Available at: https://researchportal.unamur.be/en/publications/liability-for-on-line-intermediaries-a-european-perspective [Accessed: 23 March 2018].

√Julià-Barceló, R. and Koelman, J.K. (2000) 'Intermediary liability in the e-Commerce Directive: so far so good, but it's not enough', *Computer Law & Security Report*, 16(4), pp. 231–239. [Online] DOI: 10.1016/S0267-3649(00)89129-3 [Accessed: 10 December 2018].

√Jurewicz, M.A. (2005) '*Contracts concluded by electronic agents: comparative analysis of American and Polish legal systems*' [working paper]. Bepress Legal Series, Paper 714, Bepress Legal Repository [Online]. Available at: http://law.bepress.com/expresso/eps/714 [Accessed: 10 December 2018].

√Kamara, I. (2017) 'Co-regulation in EU personal data protection: the case of technical standards and the privacy by design standardisation 'mandate'', *European Journal of Law and Technology*, 8(1). Available at: http://ejlt.org/article/view/545/723 [Accessed 5 April 2019].

√Karnow, E.A.C. (1996) 'Liability for distributed artificial intelligences', *Berkeley Technology Law Journal*, 11, pp. 147–183. [Online]. Available at: https://heinonline.org/HOL/LandingPage?handle=hein.journals/berktech11&div=8&id=&page= [Accessed: 8 October 2018].

Kelleher, K. (2017) '*How Artificial Intelligence Is Quietly Changing How You Shop Online*', March 1, TIME (Online). Available at: https://time.com/4685420/artificial-intelligence-online-shopping-retail-ai/ [Accessed: 21 June 2019].

√Kelly, V. (2012) '*Better Than Human: Why Robots Will – And Must – Take Our Jobs*'. Wired [Online]. Available at: https://www.wired.com/2012/12/ff-robots-will-take-our-jobs/ [Accessed: 12 March 2019].

√Kennedy E. and Millard C. (2015) '*Data Security and Multi-Factor Authentication: Analysis of Requirements Under EU Law and in Selected EU Member States*'. Queen Mary School of Law Legal Studies Research Paper No. 194/2015. Available at: https://papers.ssrn.com/sol3/papers.cfm?abstract_id=2600795 [Accessed: 12 March 2019].

√Kephart, J.O. (2002) '*Software agents and the route to information economy*', Proceedings of the National Academy of Sciences, 99(3), pp. 7207–7213. [Online]. Available at: http://www.pnas.org/content/99/suppl.3/7207.full [Accessed: 1 May 2019].

√Kerr, I. (1999) 'Spirits in the material world: intelligent agents as intermediaries in electronic commerce'. *Dalhousie Law Journal*, 22, pp. 189–249, SSRN [Online]. Available at: http://ssrn.com/abstract=703242 [Accessed: 10 March 2018].

√Kerr, I. (2001) 'Ensuring the success of contract formation in agent-mediated electronic commerce', *Electronic Commerce Research Journal*, 1, pp. 183–202, SSRN [Online]. Available at: http://ssrn.com/abstract=728366 [Accessed: 10 June 2018].

√Kerr, I. (2004) 'Bots, babes and the californication of commerce', *University of Ottawa Law and Technology Journal*, 1, pp. 285–324, SSRN [Online]. Available at: https://papers.ssrn.com/sol3/papers.cfm?abstrac_id=705002 [Accessed: 15 October 2018].

√Kersten G., Noronha S. and Teich J. (2000) 'Are all e-commerce negotiations auctions?' in *4th International conference on the design of cooperative systems.* Sophia-Antipolis 23–26 May. InterNeg Research Centre [Online]. Available at: http://interneg.concordia.ca/interneg/research/papers/1999/08.pdf [Accessed: 29 April 2019].

√Keuleers, E. and Dinant, J.-M. (2005) 'Data protection and multi-application smart cards: the use of intelligent servers to ensure interoperability and data flow requirements', *Computer Law & Security Report*, 21(2), pp. 146–152. [Online] DOI: 10.1016/j.clsr.2005.02.001.

√Kirsner, S. (1999) '*Shopping bots are back*', CNN.com, 14 May [Online]. Available at: http://edition.cnn.com/TECH/computing/9905/14/bots.ent.idg/index.html [Accessed: 23 March 2009].

√Kis, S. (2004) '*Contracts and electronic agents*,' LLM thesis. University of Georgia, Georgia. [Online]. Available at: https://digitalcommons.law.uga.edu/stu/llm_25/ [Accessed: 16 April 2019].

√Kitchin R. (2014) '*The Data Revolution: Big Data, Open Data, Data Infrastructures and Their Consequences*' SAGE Publications Ltd.

√Ko, A.J. and Myers, B.A., (2005) 'A framework and methodology for studying the causes of software errors in programming systems. *Journal of Visual Languages & Computing*, 16(1), pp.41–84.

√Koops, B.J., Lips, M., Nouwt, S., Prins C. and Schellekens, M. (2006) '*Should Self-Regulation be the Starting Point?*' in Koops B.J. et al (eds) Starting Points for ICT Regulation, ITeR, The Hague and the authors. Available at: https://www.researchgate.net/profile/Miriam_Lips/publication/254806605_Should_Self-Regulation_Be_the_Starting_Point/links/53f5c0470cf2fceacc6f63fc.pdf [Accessed: 5 April 2019].

√Koops, B.J. (2014) '*The trouble with European data protection law*', International Data Privacy Law, Available at: https://m.isaca.org/Groups/Professional-English/privacy-data-protection/GroupDocuments/2014-08-24%20%20The%20Trouble%20with%20European%20Data%20Protection%20Law.pdf [Accessed 5 April 2019].

Koops, B.J. and Leenes, R. E. (2014) "Privacy Regulation Cannot Be Hardcoded. A Critical Comment on the 'Privacy by Design' Provision in Data-Protection Law" (March 15, 2014), *International Review of Law, Computers & Technology* 28 (2), pp. 159–171, 2014. Available at: https://ssrn.com/abstract=2564791 [Accessed 21 June 2019].

√Kuner, C. (2012) 'The European Commission's Proposed Data Protection Regulation: A Copernican Revolution in European Data Protection Law', *Bloomberg BNA Privacy and Security Law Report*, pp. 1–15. Available at: https://papers.ssrn.com/sol3/papers.cfm?abstract_id=2162781. [Accessed 5 April 2019].

Kuner, C., Cate, F. H., Millard, C., and Svantesson, D. J. B. (2012) 'The challenge of 'big data' for data protection', *International Data Privacy Law*, 2(2), pp.47–49. Available at: https://doi.org/10.1093/idpl/ips003 [Accessed 5 April 2019].

√Kopytoff, V. (2010) '*eBay Sends Shoppers to Offline Stores*'. [Blog] Bits. Available at: https://bits.blogs.nytimes.com/2010/12/21/ebay-sends-shoppers-to-offline-stores/ [Accessed: 12 March 2019].

√Korff, D. (2002) *EC study on the implementation of the Data Protection Directive: report on the findings of the study.* EC contract ETD/2001/B5-3001/A/49. SSRN [Online]. Available at http://papers.ssrn.com/sol3/papers.cfm?abstract_id=1287667 [Accessed: 12 May 2018].

√Korff D. (2014) '*Warning: the Eu Council is trying to undermine Privacy Seals (and through this, the General Data Protection Regulation)*', EU Law Analysis [blog]. Available at: http://eulawanalysis.blogspot.com.cy/2014/10/warning-eu-council-is-trying-to.html [Accessed: 3 April 2019].

√Kosta, E., Vanfleteren, M., Cuijpers, C. and Koops, B.J. (2006) '*Legal aspects*', in Hildebrandt, M. and Meints, M. (eds) RFID, profiling, and AmI, FIDIS Deliverable 7.7, Version 1.0, pp. 28–48. [Online]. Available at: http://www.fidis.net/fileadmin/fidis/deliverables/fidis-wp7del7.7.RFID_Profiling_AMI.pdf [Accessed: 10 December 2018].

Kosta, E. and Stuurman, K. (2015) '*Technical Standards and the Draft General Data Protection Regulation*' in P. Delimatsis (ed), The Law, Economics and Politics of International Standardization, (Cambridge University Press, 2016), pp.434–459. Available at: https://ssrn.com/abstract=2642331 or http://dx.doi.org/10.2139/ssrn.2642331 [Accessed: 21 June 2019].

√Kulk, S. (2011) '*Search Engines Searching for Trouble? Comparing Search Engine Operator Responsibility for Competitive Keyword Advertising Under EU and US Trademark Law*', LLM Thesis, Amsterdam, University of Amsterdam, pp.10–11.

√Laffey, D.J. (2008) '*Value configurations in e-commerce: evidence from comparison websites*', in Golden, W., Acton, T., Conboy, K., van der Heijden, H. and Tuunainen, V. (eds) 16th European conference on information systems, pp. 61–72. LSE Information Systems and Innovation Group [Online]. Available at: https://aisel.aisnet.org/cgi/viewcontent.cgi?article=1265&context=ecis2008 [Accessed: 30 July 2017].

√Laffey, D.J. and Gandy, A. (2009) 'Comparison websites in UK retail financial services', *Journal of Financial Services Marketing*, 14(2), pp. 173–186, Business Source Premier, EBSCOhost [Online]. Available at: https://link.springer.com/article/10.1057%2Ffsm.2009.15 [Accessed: 30 July 2018].

Laine J. (2012) '*Finland report in Digital content services for consumers Comparative analysis of the applicable legal frameworks and suggestions for the contours of a model system of consumer protection in relation to digital content services*', Helberger, N. (editor) University of Amsterdam, Centre for the Study of European Contract Law (CSECL) Institute for Information Law (IViR), REPORT 1: Country Reports With an executive summary of the main points [Online]. Available at: https://www.ivir.nl/publicaties/download/Digital_content_services_for_consumers_1.pdf [Accessed: 3 April 2019]

√Lando, O. and Beale H. (2000) '*Principles of European Contract Law: Parts I and II*'. Kluwer law International.

√Lazaris, C. and Vrechopoulos, A. (2014) 'From multi-channel to "omnichannel" retailing: review of the literature and calls for research' in the *2nd International Conference on Contemporary Marketing Issues* (ICCMI).

√Lentner G. M. and Parycek P. (2016) 'Electronic identity (eID) and electronic signature (eSig) for eGovernment services – a comparative legal study', *Transforming Government: People, Process and Policy,* 10 (1), pp. 8 – 25. Available at: http://www.emeraldinsight.com/doi/full/10.1108/TG-11–2013-0047 [Accessed 5 April 2019].

√Lerouge, J. (1999) 'The use of electronic agents questioned under contractual law', *John Marshall Journal of Computer and Information Law*, 18, pp. 403–433, WestLaw UK [Online]. Available at: http://uk.westlaw.com [Accessed: 10 May 2018].

√Leroux, I. and Lagache, O. (2008) '*The Business chameleon*', AIPPI e-News, 1, April [Online]. Available at: https://www.aippi.org/enews/2008/edition01/business_chameleon.html [Accessed: 1 April 2018].

√Lewis, R. (2005) '*Insurance and the Tort System*' (September 22, 2005). (2005) 25 (1) Legal Studies 85 – 116, [Online]. Available at: https://papers.ssrn.com/sol3/papers.cfm?abstract_id=2499466 [Accessed: 3 April 2019].

√Liew, C.-C., Ng, W.-K., Lim, E.-P., Tan, B.-S. and Ong, K.-L. (1999) '*Non-repudiation in an agent based electronic commerce system*', in Tjoa, M.A., Cammelli, A. and Wagner, R.R. (eds) Tenth International workshop on database and expert systems applications: 1–3 September, 1999: Florence, Italy. Los Alamitos: IEEE Computer Society, pp. 864–868, IEEE Explorer [Online]. Available at: http://ieeexplore.ieee.org/xpl/freeabs_all.jsp?arnumber=795295 [Accessed: 19 July 2017].

√Liikanen, E. (2000) '*Co-Regulation: a modern approach to regulation*' SPEECH/00/162 in Meeting of Association of the European Mechanical, Electrical, Electronic and Metalworking Industries (Orgalime) Council. Available at: europa.eu/rapid/press-release_SPEECH-00–162_en.doc [Accessed 5 April 2019].

√Linskey, O. (2014) '*Deconstructing data protection: the 'added-value' of a right to data protection in the EU legal order*', LSE Research [Online]. Available at: http://eprints.lse.ac.uk/57713/1/__lse.ac.uk_storage_LIBRARY_Secondary_libfile_shared_repository_Content_Lynskey%2C%20O_Lynskey_Deconstructing_data_protection_2014_Lynskey_Deconstructing_data_protection_2014.pdf [Accessed: 10 January 2017].

√Lloyd, J.I. (2000) '*Information technology law*'. 3rd edition. London: Butterworths.

Lloyd, J.I. (2014) '*Information Technology Law*' .7th edition, Oxford University Press.

√Lodder, R.A. and Voulon, B.M. (2002) 'Intelligent agents and the information requirements of the Directives on distance selling and e-commerce', *International Review of Law Computers & Technology,* 16(3), pp. 277–287, Informaworld [Online]. Available at: https://www.tandfonline.com/doi/abs/10.1080/136008602760586732 [Accessed: 23 May 2018].

Lodder, R.A. (2017) '*Directive 2000/31/EC on certain legal aspects of information society services, in particular electronic commerce, in the internal market*', in Lodder, R.A. and Murray, A.D. (eds) EU Regulation of E-Commerce: A Commentary, Edward Elgar Publishing, pp.15–58.

√Loos, M. B. M., & Mak, C. (2012) '*Remedies for buyers in case of contracts for the supply of digital content*' UvA-DARE (Digital Academic Repository), University of Amsterdam [pdf]. Available at: http://dare.uva.nl/document/513426 [Accessed: 3 April 2019].

√Loos M. B. M., Helberger N., Guibault L., Mak C., Pessers L., (2012) 'Digital content contracts for consumers', *Journal of Consumer Policy,* 37–57 (1) [Online]. Available at: https://www.ivir.nl/publicaties/download/Journal_of_Consumer_policy_2012.pdf [Accessed: 3 April 2019]

√Madnick, E.S. and Siegel, M. (2002) '*Seizing the opportunity: exploiting web aggregation*', MIS Quarterly Executive, 1(1), pp. 35–46. [Online]. Available at: https://papers.ssrn.com/sol3/papers.cfm?abstract_id=303827 [Accessed: 2 August 2017].

√Maes, P. and Guttman, H.R. (1998) '*Cooperative vs competitive multi-agent negotiation in retail electronic commerce*', in Klusch, M. and Weiß, G. (eds) Cooperative information agents II: learning, mobility and electronic commerce for information discovery on the internet: second international workshop, CIA '98: Paris, France, July 4–7, 1998: proceedings. Lecture Notes in Artificial Intelligence, vol. 1435. Berlin: Springer, pp. 135–147.

√Mackenzie, T. (2012) *App store fees, percentages, and payouts: What developers need to know.* TechRepublic [Online]. Available at: https://www.techrepublic.com/blog/software-engineer/app-store-fees-percentages-and-payouts-what-developers-need-to-know/ [Accessed 5 April 2019].

√Mann, J.R. and Belzley, R.S. (2005) 'The promise of internet intermediary liability'. *William and Mary Law Review*, 47(1), pp. 239–307. [Online]. Available at: https://scholarship.law.wm.edu/wmlr/vol47/iss1/5/ [Accessed: 9 April 2019].

√Markou C. (2011) '*Consumer software agents in the online buying process: risks, issues and the EU legal response*', EThOS (BRITISH LIBRARY) [Online]. Available at: http://ethos.bl.uk/OrderDetails.do?uin=uk.bl.ethos.619275 [Accessed: 12 March 2019].

√Markou, C. (2014) 'Online penny auctions and the protection of the consumer under EU law.' *Computer Law & Security Review* 30.5 (2014): 540–559.

Markou, C. (2016) '*Behavioural Advertising and the New 'EU Cookie Law' as a Victim of Business Resistance and a Lack of Official Determination.*' Data Protection on the Move. Springer Netherlands, 2016, pp. 213–247.

Markou, C. (2017a) 'The Consumer Rights Directive' in Lodder, R.A. and Murray, A.D. (eds) *EU Regulation of E-Commerce: A Commentary*, Edward Elgar Publishing, pp.177–229.

√Markou, C. (2017b) 'Advanced automated contracting and the problem with the pre-contractual information duty of the Consumer Rights Directive', *Journal of Internet Law,* 20.8 (2017): 3–23.

√Mason, S. (2006) 'Electronic Signatures in Practice', *J. High Tech L.* 148. Available at: https://cpb-us-e1.wpmucdn.com/sites.suffolk.edu/dist/5/1153/files/2018/02/Mason-1hnn1dr.pdf [Accessed: 5 April 2019].

√McCullagh A. and Caelli W. (2000) 'Non-Repudiation in the Digital Environment', *First Monday,* 5 (8 – 7). Available at: http://firstmonday.org/ojs/index.php/fm/article/view/778/687 [Accessed: 5 April 2019].

McGregor, H. (2009) '*McGregor on Damages 18th ed*', Sweet & Maxwell Ltd.

Micklitz, Hans -W. (2010) '*Unfair commercial practices and European private law*' in Twigg-Flesner, C., The Cambridge Companion to European Union Private Law, Cambridge University Press, 2010, pp 229–242.

Millett, C. (2006a) 'OGC to trial radical project-wide cover', *Contract Journal*, 16 August [Online]. Available at: https://library.laredo.edu/eds/detail?db=b9h&an=22154082&isbn=00107859 [Accessed: 10 January 2019].

Millett, C. (2006b) 'Project insurance: spread the risk (news analysis)', *Contract Journal,* 23 August [Online]. Available at: http://www.contractjournal.com/Articles/2006/08/23/51962/project-insurance spread-the-risk-news-analysis.html [No longer available].

√Minalto A., (2017) *"BEST eBay Sniper?", BEST eBay Snipers REVIEWED*! Andrew Minalto [blog]. Available at: https://andrewminalto.com/best-ebay-snipers/ [Accessed: 3 April 2018].

√Miskevich D., (2012) '*Comparative Analysis of Online Intermediary Liability Regimes in US and EU*'. Central European University March 29. [Online]. Available at: http://www.etd.ceu.edu/2012/miskevich_dzmitry.pdf [Accessed: 3 April 2018].

√Mont, C.M. and Yearworth, M. (2001) '*Negotiated revealing of trader credentials in e-marketplaces mediated by trusted and privacy-aware admittance controllers*', Hewlett-Packard White Paper. [Online]. Available at: https://pdfs.semanticscholar.org/38df/e740ef8b590c43a1a0265ecbc1b03de2570c.pdf [Accessed: 4 May 2019].

√Murray, B.K. and Häubl, G. (2001) 'Recommending or persuading?: the impact of a shopping agent's algorithm on user behaviour', in *EC '01 proceedings of the 3rd ACM conference on electronic commerce.* New York: Association for Computing Machinery, pp. 163–170. ACM Portal [Online]. Available at: http://portal.acm.org/citation.cfm?doid=501158.501176 [Accessed: 20 July 2018].

[No Author], 'Consequences Arising from Mistake in Transmission of a Telegraphic Offer for the Sale of Goods'. *The Yale Law Journal*, 27(7) (1918), pp. 932–35. doi:10.2307/786058.

√Nordhausen, A. (2006) *Information requirements in the digital environment.* Briefing note to the European Parliament, IP/A/IMCO/FWC/2006–168/C3/SC1. European Parliament. [Online]. Available at: http://www.europarl.europa.eu/comparl/imco/studies/0701_digitalenv_en.pdf [Accessed: 20 November 2018].

√Ockenfels, A. and Roth, E.A. (2002) 'The timing of bids in internet auctions: market design, bidder behaviour and artificial agents', *AI Magazine*, 23(3), pp. 79–87. [Online]. Available at: https://doi.org/10.1609/aimag.v23i3.1658 [Accessed: 29 April 2019].

√O'Dell, E. (2017) 'Compensation for Breach of the General Data Protection Regulation' in 40(1) *Dublin University Law Journal* (ns) 97–164. Available at: https://papers.ssrn.com/sol3/papers.cfm?abstract_id=2992351 [Accessed: 10 December 2018].

√Oliphant K. (2011) '*England and Wales*', Winiger B., Koziol H., Koch BA., Zimmermann R. (eds), Digest of European Tort Law, 2, Essential Cases on Damage, Walter de Gruyter GmbH & Co K. G., Berlin/Boston.

√OnlineShoppingRights (no date) *Security and price comparison websites.* Available at: http://www.onlineshoppingrights.co.uk/security-price-comparison-websites.html [Accessed: 4 September 2018].

√Parsons, S., Sierra, C. and Jennings, N. R. (1998) 'Agents that reason and negotiate by arguing', *Journal of Logic and Computation*, 8(3), pp. 261–292, ECS EPrints [Online]. Available at: http://eprints.ecs.soton.ac.uk/2113/1/jlc-arg.pdf [Accessed: 29 April 2019].

Pearson, S. and Charlesworth A. (2009) 'Accountability as a way forward for privacy protection in the cloud.', *Cloud computing*, pp. 131–144. Springer-Verlag Berlin Heidelberg. Available at: http://barbie.uta.edu/~hdfeng/CloudComputing/cc/cc13.pdf [Accessed 5 April 2019].

√Peguera, M. (2009) 'The DMCA safe harbors and their European counterparts: a comparative analysis of some common problems', *Columbia Journal of Law & the Arts,* 32(4), pp. 481–512, SSRN [Online]. Available at: http://papers.ssrn.com/sol3/papers.cfm?abstract_id=1468433 [Accessed: 26 June 2018].

√Pereira, R. (2001) 'Influence of query-based decision aids on consumer decision-making in electronic commerce', *Information Resources Management Journal*, 14(1), pp. 31–48, ABI/INFORM Global [Online]. DOI: 10.4018/irmj.2001010104 [Accessed: 30 July 2010].

√Perogianni, M. (2003) '*B2B Internet trading platforms: opportunities and barriers: a first assessment*', European Commission Enterprise Papers No. 13. Luxembourg: Office for Official Publications of the European Communities. [Online]. Available at: https://ec.europa.eu/growth/content/b2b-internet-trading-platforms-opportunities-and-barriers-smes-first-assessment-1_en [Accessed: 21 February 2018].

√Pertet, S. and Narasimhan, P. (2005) '*Causes of Failure in Web Applications*' (CMU-PDL-05–109). figshare. Paper. Available at: https://doi.org/10.1184/R1/6619463.v1 [Accessed: 5 April 2019].

√Pinsent Masons LLP (2007) '*Government refuses to extend legal protections for search engines*', OutLaw.com, 18 January [Online]. Available at: https://www.pinsentmasons.com/out-law/news/government-refuses-to-extend-legal-protections-for-search-engines [Accessed: 8 April 2019].

√Piotrowicz W. and Richard Cuthbertson R. (2014) 'Introduction to the Special Issue Information Technology in Retail: Toward Omnichannel Retailing', *International Journal of Electronic Commerce,* 18:4, 5–16. [Online] Available at: https://courses.helsinki.fi/sites/default/files/course-material/4482600/17.3_JEC1086-4415180400.pdf [Accessed: 15 April 2017].

√Pornin T. (2011) '*What is the difference between authenticity and non-repudiation?*' Information Security, Stack Exchange [Online]. Available at: https://security.stackexchange.com/questions/6730/what-is-the-difference-between-authenticity-and-non-repudiation [Accessed: 3 April 2018].

√Potoska, I. (2018) '*How to Develop a Shopping Assistant App Using Data Intelligence and Human Consultants*'. Yalantis [Online]. Available at https://yalantis.com/blog/developing-a-personal-shopping-assistant-app-what-you-need-to-know/ [Accessed: 12 March 2019].

√Poullet Y. (2001) "*'Adequate' protection or how a state authority can impose its values in a flexible manner on a third country in the global information society*" in Walden, I., Hörnle, J (eds), E-commerce Law and Practice in Europe, pp.21–22, Woodhead Publishing Limited.

√Press, G. (2014) '*12 Big Data Definitions: What's Yours?*' [Online]. Available at: https://www.forbes.com/sites/gilpress/2014/09/03/12-big-data-definitions-whats-yours/#5747ff8613ae [Accessed: 3 April 2019]

√Princeton Survey Research Associates (2002) *A matter of trust: what users want from websites: results of a national survey of internet users for Consumer WebWatch*. [Online]. Available at: https://advocacy.consumerreports.org/wp-content/uploads/2013/05/a-matter-of-trust.pdf [Accessed: 26 March 2018].

√Provos, N. et al. (2007) '*The Ghost in the Browser Analysis of Web-based Malware*', [pdf]. Available at: https://www.usenix.org/legacy/events/hotbots07/tech/full_papers/provos/provos.pdf?48,07,03,02,04,2008 [Accessed: 3 April 2019]

√Prouteau, V. (2008) '*What liability for providers of sponsored links?*' Cabinet Regimbeau [Online]. Available at: http://www.regimbeau.eu/download.aspx?folderurl=Ressources%2F2008+05+vp+responsabilite+fournisseurs+liens+juillet+2008.pdf [No longer available].

√Punj, N.G. and Rapp, A. (2003) 'Influence of electronic decision aids on consumer shopping in online stores', *International conference on the networked home and the home of the future* (H.O.I.T. 2003). Irvine, California 6–8 April. University of California Irvine. Center for Research on Information Technology and Organizations. Available at: https://www.researchgate.net/profile/Girish_Punj_publication/228610029_Influence_of_Electronic_Decision_Aids_on_Consumer_Shopping_in_Online_Stores/links/0deec532b6d6e51be8000000.pdf [Accessed: 30 July 2018].

√Raj, R. (2015) '*This startup uses artificial intelligence to help you buy a phone*'. Techinasia [Online]. Available at: https://www.techinasia.com/startup-artificial-intelligence-buy-phone [Accessed: 12 March 2019].

√Rahwan, I., Ramchurn, S. D. Jennings, N. R., McBurney P., Parsons, S. and Sonenberg L. (2003) 'Argumentation-based negotiation', *Knowledge Engineering Review*, 18(4), pp. 343–375. [Online] DOI: 10.1017/S0269888904000098.

√Rao, L. (2011) '*eBay Bets on Online to Offline Shopping, Adds Milo's Local Product Availability to Search*'. techcrunch [Online]. Available at: https://techcrunch.com/2011/03/31/ebay-bets-on-online-to-offline-shopping-adds-milos-local-product-availability-to-search/ [Accessed: 12 March 2019].

√Rasmusson, L., Rasmusson, A. and Janson, S. (1997) 'Using agents to secure the Internet marketplace: reactive security and social control', in *2nd International Conference on the Practical Applications of Agents and Multi-Agent Systems*. Blackpool: The Practical Application Company Ltd, Swedish Institute of Computer Science [Online]. Available at: http://www.sics.se/~sverker/public/papers/paam97.pdf [Accessed: 2 December 2018].

Rayna, T. (2008) 'Understanding the Challenges of the Digital Economy: The Nature of Digital Goods' (September 1, 2008), *Communications & Strategies*, 71, 3rd quarter 2008, pp. 13–36. Available at: https://ssrn.com/abstract=1353583 [Accessed: 21 June 2019].

Reed Business International Ltd (2006) 'Insurance revolution', *AGS News*, 53, January 2007, p.3 [Online]. Available at: http://www.ags.org.uk/site/newsletters/Issue53.pdf [No longer available].

√Rees, J. (1988) "Self Regulation: an effective alternative to direct regulation by Osha?", *Policy Studies Journal*, 1988 [Online]. Available at: https://doi.org/10.1111/j.1541–0072.1988.tb01871.x [Accessed: 5 April 2019].

√Reijers, J. (2016) '*Payment Service Directive 2 Dutch supervision on the security and data protection of third party access*', Radboud University Nijmegen Faculty of Science, Master's thesis Information Sciences (1 June 2016) [pdf]. Available at: http://www.ru.nl/publish/pages/769526/z_jos_reijers.pdf

√Resolution Foundation (2007) *Resolution Foundation seminar: launch of comparison websites research report to stakeholders.* [Online]. 11 October. Available at: https://www.resolutionfoundation.org/events/seminar-launch-of-comparison-websites-research-report-to-stakeholders/ [Accessed: 29 July 2018].

Riefa, C. (2008) 'eBay case: liability of third parties for sale of goods', *E-commerce Law and Policy*, June, pp. 13–15.

√Riefa C. (2015) '*Consumer Protection and Online Auction Platforms: Towards a Safer Legal Framework*', Routledge 1st Edition.

√Riefa, C. and Markou, C., (2015) '*Online Marketing: Advertisers Know You are a Dog on the Internet!*', Savin, Trzaskowski (Eds) Research Handbook on EU Internet Law (Edward Elgar 2014), pp. 383–410. Available at: https://papers.ssrn.com/sol3/papers.cfm?abstract_id=2668968 [Accessed 5 April 2019].

√Riemer, K. and Lehrke, C. (2009) 'Biased listing in electronic marketplaces: exploring its implications in on-line hotel distribution', *International Journal of Electronic Commerce*, 14(1), pp. 55–78, Business Source Primer, EBSCOhost [Online]. DOI: 10.2753/JEC1086-4415140102 [Accessed: 17 September 2017].

√Rietjens, B. (2006) 'Trust and reputation on eBay: Towards a legal framework for feedback intermediaries', *Information & Communications Technology Law*, 15 (1), pp. 55–78 [Online]. Available at: https://www.tandfonline.com/doi/abs/10.1080/13600830600557935 [Accessed 5 April 2019].

√Ritter, G. (2017) '*AI can take over our mundane tasks. Here's how human workers can learn new, more stimulating skills-The "coaching cloud" will create the first Facebook-scale enterprise business.*', recode [Online]. Available at: https://www.recode.net/2017/10/18/16492156/coaching-cloud-future-work-jobs-artificial-intelligence-ai-enterprise-employee-training [Accessed: 12 March 2019].

√Robertson, R.J. Jr (1998) 'Electronic Commerce on the Internet and the Statute of Frauds', *South Carolina Law Review* 49 (1998), pp. 787–846.

√Robertson, S. (2010) '*Europe should adopt US behavioural advertising icon and quick*', Out-law.com, 4 February [Online]. Available at: http://www.out-law.com/page-10730 [Accessed: 10 March 2018].

Robertson S. (2010) '*Viewing a website is a 'transactional decision', says OFT's behavioural ad study*' Topics, Commercial, Out-Law.com [Online]. Available at: http://www.out-law.com/page-11066 [Accessed: 3 April 2018].

√Roe, M. (2010) '*Cryptography and evidence*', Technical Report Number 780, University of Cambridge, Computer Laboratory, (UCAM-CL-TR-780 ISSN 1476–2986), May 2010, Available at: https://www.cl.cam.ac.uk/techreports/UCAM-CL-TR-780.pdf [Accessed: 15 April 2016].

Roetzel, P.G. (2018) 'Information overload in the information age: a review of the literature from business administration, business psychology, and related disciplines with a bibliometric approach and framework development', *Business Research*, Springer International Publishing. pp. 1–44. Available at: https://doi.org/10.1007/s40685-018-0069-z [Accessed: 5 April 2019].

√Romanosky, S. and Acquisti, A. (2009) 'Privacy Costs and Personal Data Protection: Economic and Legal Perspectives', *Berkeley Technology Law Journal*, 24(3), [Online]. Available at: http://scholarship.law.berkeley.edu/cgi/viewcontent.cgi?article=1802&context=btlj [Accessed 14 April 2017].

√Rosaci, D. and Sarnè, G.M., (2014) 'Multi-agent technology and ontologies to support personalization in B2C E-Commerce'. *Electronic Commerce Research and Applications*, 13(1), pp.13–23.

√Rossi, L. (2014) '*Proposal for the Reform of the Regulation of Digital Services*'. [Online]. Available at: http://dx.doi.org/10.2139/ssrn.2541593 [Accessed: 5 April 2019].

√Rothman, W. (2007) 'The search engines of commerce', *Money Magazine*, 36(4), p.130, EBSCO [Online]. Available at: http://eds.b.ebscohost.com/eds/detail/detail?vid=4&sid=763546de-cc69-49e3-874d-2e9a5c25e967%40sessionmgr103&&bdata=JnNpdGU9ZWRzLWxpdmU%3d" \l "AN=edsbig.A160867282&db=edsbig [Accessed: 27 July 2017].

Rubinstein, I. S. (2009), '*Privacy and Regulatory Innovation: Moving Beyond Voluntary Codes*', NYU School of Law, [pdf]. Available at: https://www.ftc.gov/sites/default/files/documents/public_comments/privacy-roundtables-comment-project-no.p095416-544506–00103/544506–00103.pdf [Accessed: 21 June 2019].

√Rubinstein I. S. (2011) '*Privacy and Regulatory Innovation: Moving Beyond Voluntary Codes*', 6 ISJLP 355, 357–58.

Rubinstein, I. S. (2013) 'Big Data: The End of Privacy or a New Beginning?' *International Data Privacy Law*, 3 (2), May 2013, pp. 74–87. Available at: https://doi.org/10.1093/idpl/ips036 [Accessed: 21 June 2019].

√Ryder N., Griffiths M. and Singh L. (2008) '*Commercial Law: Principles and Policy*' Cambridge University Press.

√Sandholm, T. (2002) 'eMediator: a next generation electronic commerce server', *Computational Intelligence, Special Issue on Agent Technology for Electronic Commerce*, 18(4), pp. 656–676, Carnegie Mellon University: School of Computer Science [Online]. Available at: http://www.cs.cmu.edu/~sandholm/eMediator.ci.pdf [Accessed: 29 April 2019].

√Sandholm, T. and Huai Q. (2000) 'Nomad: mobile agent system for an Internet based auction house', *IEEE Internet Computing*, 4(2), March/April 2000, pp. 80–86, Brabdeis University. Computer Science Department [Online]. Available at: http://www.cs.brandeis.edu/~jcastano/w2080.pdf [Accessed: 29 April 2019].

√Sartor, G. (2002) '*Agents in cyberlaw*', in Sartor, G. (ed.) The Law of Electronic Agents: Selected Revised Papers. Proceedings of the Workshop on the Law of Electronic Agents (LEA 2002). Bologna: CIRSFID, Universita di Bologna.

√Sartor, G. (2009) 'Cognitive automata and the law: electronic contracting and the intentionality of software agents', *Artificial Intelligence and Law*, 17(4), pp. 253–290, SpringerLink [Online]. Available at: https://link.springer.com/article/10.1007/s10506-009-9081-0 [Accessed: 17 January 2019].

√Schreurs, W. and Hildebrandt, M. (2005) '*Legal issues*', in Schreurs, W., Hildebrandt, M., Gasson, M. and Warwick, K. (eds) Report on actual and possible profiling techniques in the field of ambient intelligence, FIDIS Deliverable 7.3, Version 1.0, pp. 36–58. [Online]. Available at: http://www.fidis.net/fileadmin/fidis/deliverables/fidis-wp7-del7.3.ami_profiling.pdf [Accessed: 15 February 2017].

√Seng, D.K.B. (2014) '*Data Intermediaries and Data Breaches*', in Simon Chesterman (ed.), Data Protection Law in Singapore: Privacy and Sovereignty in an Interconnected World. Academy Publishing, Contributors and Singapore Academy of Law.

√Sentient (2015) '*AI goes shopping Canadian shoe site uses artificial intelligence to power visual search*'. [pdf] 2016 Contagious. Available at: http://www.sentient.ai/wp-content/uploads/2016/03/contagious-ai-visual-search-goes-shopping.pdf [Accessed: 12 March 2019].

√Siems, M.M. (2002) 'The EU Directive on Electronic Signatures – a World Wide Model or a Fruitless Attempt to Regulate the Future?', *International Review of Law, Computers & Technology*, 16, pp. 7–22, 2002 (updated in 2007). Available at: https://papers.ssrn.com/sol3/papers.cfm?abstract_id=853884 [Accessed:5 April 2019].

Signorini, A., Gulli, A. and Segre, M.A. (2008) 'Distributed marketplaces using P2P networks and public-key cryptography' in *3rd international ICST conference on scalable information systems.* Vico Equense, Italy 4–6 June. Institute for Computer Sciences, Social-Informatics and Telecommunications Engineering, ACM Portal [Online]. Available at: http://portal.acm.org/citation.cfm?id=1459736 [Accessed: 20 June 2017].

Singh, D. (2009) '*Software Failure, Fault and Error*' [Online]. Available at: http://softwaretestingqc.blogspot.com/2009/05/software-failure-fault-and-error.html [Accessed: 19 July 2018].

√Skylogiannis, T. (2005) *Automated negotiation and semantic brokering with intelligent agents using defeasible logic*, MSc thesis. University of Crete, Heraklio [Online]. Available at: http://www.ics.forth.gr/isl/publications/paperlink/Skylogiannhs.pdf [Accessed: 29 April 2019].

√Smith, D.M. (2002) 'The impact of shopbots on electronic markets', *Journal of the Academy of Marketing Science, 30*(4), pp. 446–454, SAGE Journals Online [Online]. Available at: http://jam.sagepub.com/content/30/4/446.abstract [Accessed: 28 July 2018].

√Smith, J.H.G. (2007a) *Internet law and regulation.* 4th edition. London: Sweet and Maxwell.

√Smith, W.R. (2007b) '*BGH: eBay can be forced to block listings deemed harmful to young people*', The H, 13 July [Online]. Available at: http://www.heise.de/english/newsticker/news/92658 [No longer available].

√Smith, M. and Brynjolfsson, E. (2001) 'Customer decision-making at an internet shopbot: brand matters', *Journal of Industrial Economics*, 49(4), pp. 541–558, Ingentaconnect [Online]. Available at: http://www.ingentaconnect.com/content/bpl/joie/2001/00000049/00000004/art00009 [Accessed: 27 March 2019].

√Snyder, B. (2014) '*Surprise! TRUSTe Can't Always be Trusted, FTC Says*', Consumer Electronics, CIO [Online]. Available at: http://www.cio.com/article/2849556/consumer-technology/surprise-TRUSTe-cant-always-be-TRUSTed-ftc-says.html [Accessed 5 April 2019].

√Solum, B.L. (1992) 'Legal personhood for artificial intelligences', *North Carolina Law Review*, 70, pp.1231–1287, SSRN [Online]. Available at: http://ssrn.com/abstract=1108671 [Accessed: 1 May 2017].

√Song, R. and Korba, L. (2001) *Anonymous internet infrastructure based on PISA agents.* National Research Council Canada. NRC Publications Archive [Online]. Available at: https://pdfs.semanticscholar.org/f19d/bd1c83e6c8104983deb36683a68d6d1d5dd5.pdf [Accessed: 20 June 2017].

√Spindler, G., Riccio, G.M. and der Perre, A.V. (2007) *Study on the liability of internet intermediaries.* European Commission study Markt/2006/09/E – Service contract ETD/2006/IM/E2/69. European Commission [Online]. Available at: https://ec.europa.eu/commission/index_en [Accessed: 8 September 2018].

√Spindler, G. (2017) '*Responsibility and Liability of Internet Intermediaries: Status Quo in the EU and Potential Reforms*' in Synodinou, T.-E., Jougleux, P., Markou, C., Prastitou, T. (Eds.) 'EU Internet Law: Regulation and Enforcement', Springer, pp. 289–314.

√Spitz, B. (2007) '*Google video held liable for not doing all it could to stop the broadcasting of a film*', Copyright and Media in France Blog, 29 November. Available at: http://copyrightfrance.blogspot.com/2007/11/google-video-held-liable-for-not-doing.html [Accessed: 6 April 2018].

√Spyrelli, C. (2002) 'Electronic Signatures: A Transatlantic Bridge? An EU and US Legal Approach Towards Electronic Authentication', *The Journal of Information, Law and Technology* (JILT) 2002(2). Available at: https://warwick.ac.uk/fac/soc/law/elj/jilt/2002_2/spyrelli/ [Accessed: 5 April 2019].

√Stokes, S. (2015) '*Update on the network and information security directive*', Blake Morgan [Online]. Available at: https://www.blakemorgan.co.uk/update-on-the-network-and-information-security-directive/. [Accessed: 20 October 2017].

√Study Group on a European Civil Code and the Acquis Group: Research Group on EC Private Law (2009) *Principles, definitions and model rules of European private law: Draft Common Frame of Reference (DCFR),* Outline edition by von Bar, C., Clive, E., Schulte-Nölke, H., Beale, H., Herre, J., Huet, J., Storme, M., Swann, S., Varul, P., Veneziano, A. and Zoll, F. (eds). Sellier European Publishers. [Online]. Available at: https://www.law.kuleuven.be/personal/mstorme/2009_02_DCFR_OutlineEdition.pdf [Accessed: 20 June 2018].

√Su, B. (2007) 'Consumer e-tailer choice strategies at on-line shopping comparison sites', *International Journal of Electronic Commerce*, 11(3), pp. 135–159, Business Source Premier, EBSCOhost [Online]. Available at: https://www.tandfonline.com/doi/abs/10.2753/JEC1086-4415110305 [Accessed: 30 July 2018].

√Subirana, B. and Bain, M. (2005) *Legal Programming: Designing Legally Compliant RFID and Software Agent Architectures for Retail Processes and Beyond.* New York: Springer Science and Business Media Inc.

√Sukthankar G. and Rodriguez-Aguilar J.A., (2017) '*Autonomous Agents and Multiagent Systems: AAMAS 2017 Workshops, Best Papers, São Paulo, Brazil, May 8–12, 2017, Revised Selected Papers*'. Available at: https://books.google.com.cy/books?id=jkRADwAAQBAJ&dq=multi-agent+marketplaces+2017&source=gbs_navlinks_s [Accessed: 3 April 2019].

Tene, O. and Polonetsky, J. (2011) 'Privacy in the age of big data: a time for big decisions', *Stan. L. Rev.* (64) Online, pp.63–69.

Tene, O. and Polonetsky, J. (2012) 'Big data for all: Privacy and user control in the age of analytics', *Nw. J. Tech. & Intell. Prop.*, 11(5), pp.239–274.

√Teubner, G. (2006) 'Rights of non-humans? Electronic agents and animals as new actors in politics and law', *Journal of Law & Society*, 33(4), pp. 497–521.

√Tsvetovatty, M., Gini, M., Mobasher, B. and Wieckowski, Z. (1997) 'MAGMA: an agent-based virtual market for e-commerce', *Applied Artificial Intelligence*, 11(6), pp. 501–523, Ingentaconnect [Online]. Available at: http://www.ingentaconnect.com/content/tandf/uaai/1997/00000011/00000006/art00003 [Accessed: 29 April 2017].

√Twigg-Flesner, C., Parry, D., Howells, G. and Wilhelmsson, T. (2005) *An analysis of the application and scope of the Unfair Commercial Practices Directive: a report for the Department of Trade and Industry.* [Online]. Available at: https://webarchive.nationalarchives.gov.uk/20110318165513/http://www.dti.gov.uk/files/file32095.pdf [Accessed: 10 October 2017].

√Valcke P., Vandezande N., and De Velde N. (2015) '*The Evolution of Third Party Payment Providers and Cryptocurrencies under the EU's Upcoming Psd2 And Amld4*', Swift Institute Working Paper No. 2015–001 (23 September 2015), SWIFT INSTITUTE [pdf]. Available at: https://www.swiftinstitute.org/wp-content/uploads/2015/09/SIWP-No-2015-001-AML-Risks-of-the-Third-Party-Payment-Providers_FINAL.pdf [Accessed 5 April 2019].

√Van Haentjens, O. (2002) '*Shopping agents and their legal implications regarding Austria Law*', LEA 2002 workshop on the law of electronic agents. Bologna 13 July. University of Bologna. Interdepartmental Research Centre in History of Law, Philosophy of Law, Computer Science and Law [Online]. Available at: http://citeseerx.ist.psu.edu/viewdoc/download?doi=10.1.1.201.9341&rep=rep1&type=pdf [Accessed: 12 May 2018].

√Vate, M. and Dror, D.M., (2002) '*To Insure or Not to Insure? Reflections on the Limits of Insurability* 'in Dror D.M., Preker A.S., eds., SOCIAL REINSURANCE: A NEW APPROACH TO SUSTAINABLE COMMUNITY HEALTH FINANCING, pp. 125–152, World Bank & ILO, 2002, [Online]. Available at: https://www.researchgate.net/publication/255996871_To_Insure_or_Not_to_Insure_Reflections_on_the_Limits_of_Insurability [Accessed: 3 April 2019].

√Vatis, A.M. and Retchless, D. (2008) 'User-generated content: website liability', *E-commerce Law and Policy*, July, pp. 6–7.

√Verhagen, T., Meents, S. and Tan, Y.-H. (2006) 'Perceived risk and trust associated with purchasing at electronic marketplaces', *European Journal of Information Systems*, 15, pp. 542–555, Palgrave Macmillan [Online]. Available at: https://www.researchgate.net/publication/221409104_Perceived_risk_and_trust_associated_with_purchasing_at_electronic_marketplaces [Accessed: 2 May 2019].

√Viefhues, M. and Schumacher, J. (2009) 'Germany', *World Trademark Review*, February/March, pp. 62–63. [Online]. Available at: http://www.worldtrademarkreview.com/issues/Article.ashx?g=eeb7d9a1c36e-4455-989f-b99ad8d149a6 [No longer available].

√Vytelingum, P., Dash, K.R., He, M. and Jennings, R.N. (2005) '*A framework for designing strategies for trading agents*', IJCAI-05 workshop on trading agent design and analysis. Edinburgh 1 August. Swedish Institute of Computer Science. Available at: https://www.researchgate.net/publication/313347672_A_Framework_for_Designing_Strategies_for_Trading_Agents [Accessed: 10 November 2018].

√Wagner, G. (2005) '*Tort Law and Liability Insurance*' Paperback – 1 Oct 2005.

√Wan, Y. and Liu, Y. (2008) 'The impact of legal challenges on the evolution of web-based intelligent agents', *Journal of International Commercial Law and Technology*, 3(2), pp. 112–119. [Online]. Available at: https://www.researchgate.net/publication/26503560_The_Impact_of_Legal_Challenges_on_the_Evolution_of_Web-based_Intelligent_Agents [Accessed: 13 May 2019].

Wan, Y., Menon, S. and Ramaprasad, A. (2003) 'A classification of product comparison agents', in *ICEC '03 Proceedings of the 5th international conference on Electronic commerce.* ACM International Conference Proceeding Series, 50. New York: Association for Computing Machinery, pp. 498–504, ACM Portal [Online]. Available at: http://portal.acm.org/citation.cfm?id=948069 [Accessed: 2 August 2018].

√Wan, Y., Menon, S. and Ramaprasad, A. (2009) 'The paradoxical nature of electronic decision aids on comparison-shopping: the experiments and analysis', *Journal of Theoretical and Applied*

Electronic Commerce Research, 4(3), pp. 80–96. [Online]. Available at: http://www.jtaer.com/ [Accessed: 31 July 2018].

√Watnick, V. (2004) 'The electronic formation of contracts and the Common Law "mailbox rule"', *Baylor Law Review*, 56, pp. 175–203, HeinOnline [Online]. Available at: https://heinonline.org/HOL/LandingPage?handle=hein.journals/baylr56&div=11&id=&page= [Accessed: 10 May 2009].

√Wearden, G. (2005) '*Argos in the clear over 49p TV e-commerce error*', ZDNet UK, 2 September [Online]. Available at: https://www.zdnet.com/article/argos-in-the-clear-over-49p-tv-e-commerce-error/,1000000097,39216130,00.htm [Accessed: 7 February 2019].

Weitzenböck, M.E. (2001) 'Electronic agents and the formation of contracts', *International Journal of Law and Information Technology*, 9(3), pp. 204–234. [Online]. Available at: https://doi.org/10.1093/ijlit/9.3.204 [Accessed: 10 February 2018].

√Weitzner, D.J., Abelson H., Berners-Lee T., Hanson C., Hendler J., Kagal L., McGuinness D.L., Sussman G.J., Krasnow Waterman K. (2006). '*Transparent Accountable Data Mining: New Strategies for Privacy Protection*', Computer Science and Artificial Intelligence Laboratory, Technical Report (MIT CSAIL Technical Report-2006–007) [Online]. Available at: http://www.w3.org/2006/01/tami-privacy-strategies-aaai.pdf [Accessed 5 April 2019].

√Wein, E.L. (1992) 'The responsibility of intelligent artifacts: toward an automation jurisprudence', *Harvard Journal of Law and Technology*, 6, pp. 103–154. [Online]. Available at: http://jolt.law.harvard.edu/articles/pdf/v06/06HarvJLTech103.pdf [Accessed: 1 May 2019].

√Wellman, M.P., Wurman, P.R., O'Malley, K., Bangera, R., Lin, S., Reeves, D. and Walsh, W.E. (2001) 'Designing the market game for a trading agent competition', *IEEE Internet Computing: Special Issue on Virtual Markets*, 5(2), March/April, pp. 43–51, University of Michigan. Electronic Engineering and Computer Science Department [Online]. Available at: http://wewalsh.com/papers/tacic-final.pdf [Accessed: 29 April 2019].

Wettig, S. and Zehendner, E. (2003) '*The Electronic Agent: A Legal Personality under German Law?*', Department of Computer Science, Friedrich Schiller University Jena, Germany [pdf]. Available at: http://www.wettig.info/biometrie_uni_jena-s/el_agent-legal_personality_under_german_law20030624.pdf [Accessed: 21 June 2019].

√Wildstrom, H.S. (1998) '"*Bots" don't make great shoppers: intelligent agents that search the Net often miss out on the best bargains*', Business Week, 7 December [Online]. Available at: https://www.bloomberg.com/news/articles/1998-12-06/bots-dont-make-great-shoppers [Accessed: 13 June 2018].

√Wilhelmsson, T. (2006) '*Scope of the Directive*', in Howells, G., Micklitz, H-W. and Wilhelmsson, T. (eds) European fair trading law: The Unfair Commercial Practices Directive. Aldershot and Burlington: Ashgate Publishing Ltd, pp. 49–82.

Wilken and Villiers (2003) '*The Law of Waiver, Variation and Estoppel*', 2nd ed, Oxford University Press.

Willett, C.C. (2008) General Clauses on Fairness and the Promotion of Values Important in Services of General Interest. *Yearbook of Consumer Law 2008*, October, pp. 67–106.

√Winn, J. K. and Haubold, J. (2002) 'Electronic promises: contract law reform and e-commerce in a comparative perspective', *European Law Review*, 2002, 27(5), October, pp. 567–588. Available at: https://www.worldcat.org/title/electronic-promises-contract-law-reform-and-e-commerce-in-a-comparative-perspective/oclc/847260326 [Accessed: 5 April 2019].

Wood, C. (2007) *Compare and contrast: how the UK comparison website market is serving financial consumers.* Resolution Foundation. [Online]. Available at: https://www.bl.uk/britishlibrary/~/media/bl/global/social-welfare/pdfs/non-secure/c/o/m/compare-and-contrast-how-the-uk-comparison-website-market-is-serving-financial-consumers.pdf [Accessed: 29 July 2017].

√Woods L. (2017) '*When is Facebook liable for illegal content under the E-commerce Directive? CG v. Facebook in the Northern Ireland courts*', EU Law Analysis [Online]. Available at: http://eulawanalysis.blogspot.com.cy/2017/01/when-is-facebook-liable-for-illegal.html [Accessed: 3 April 2018]

√Wouters, J.J. (2004) *Searching for disclosure: how search engines alert consumers to the presence of advertising in search results.* Consumer Reports WebWatch. [Online]. Available at: https://advocacy.consumerreports.org/press_release/searching-for-disclosure-how-search-engines-alert-consumers-to-the-presence-of-advertising-in-search-results/ [Accessed: 26 March 2019].

√Wouters, J.J. (2005) *Still in search for disclosure: re-evaluating how search engines explain the presence of advertising in search results.* Consumer Reports WebWatch. [Online]. Available at: https://advocacy.consumerreports.org/wp-content/uploads/2013/05/search-engine-disclosure.pdf [Accessed: 26 March 2019].

√Wurman, P. R., Wellman, M.P. and Walsh, W. E. (1998) 'The Michigan internet auctionbot: configurable auction server for human and software agents', in *AGENTS '98: proceedings of the second international conference on Autonomous agents.* New York: Association for Computing Machinery, pp. 301–308, University of Michigan. Electronic Engineering and Computer Science Department [Online]. Available at: http://citeseerx.ist.psu.edu/viewdoc/download?doi=10.1.1.73.151&rep=rep1&type=pdf [Accessed: 29 April 2019].

√Youll, J. (2001) 'Agent-based electronic commerce: opportunities and challenges', in *Fifth international symposium on autonomous decentralized systems.* Los Alamitos: IEEE Computer Society, pp. 146–148, IEEE Explorer [Online]. Available at: http://ieeexplore.ieee.org/xpl/freeabs_all.jsp?arnumber=917407 [Accessed: 19 July 2018].

√Zacharia, G., Moukas, A. and Maes, P. (1999) 'Collaborative reputation mechanisms in electronic marketplaces', in *Thirty-second annual Hawaii international conference on system sciences.* Los Alamitos: IEEE Computer Society, IEEE Explorer [Online]. Available at: http://ieeexplore.ieee.org/search/freesrchabstract.jsp?tp=&arnumber=773057&queryText%3DCollaborative+reputation+mechanisms+in+electronic+marketplaces%26openedRefinements%3D*%26searchField%3DSearch+All [Accessed: 19 July 2018].

√Zarei, S., Malayeri, A.D. and Mastorakis, N.E., (2012) 'Intelligent model in B2C e-commerce using fuzzy approaches' in *Proceedings of the 11th WSEAS international conference on Applied Computer and Applied Computational Science*, pp. 238–242, World Scientific and Engineering Academy and Society (WSEAS).

Index

For Product Safety Concerns and Information please contact our EU
representative GPSR@taylorandfrancis.com
Taylor & Francis Verlag GmbH, Kaufingerstraße 24, 80331 München, Germany

www.ingramcontent.com/pod-product-compliance
Ingram Content Group UK Ltd.
Pitfield, Milton Keynes, MK11 3LW, UK
UKHW050051200926
475702UK00019B/2771
9780367726737